C000151179

Worldwide Praise from Critics and Fans for the Erotica of John Patrick!

"I am a fan of John Patrick's...His writing is clear and straight-forward and should be better known in the gay community."
- *Ian Young, Torso Magazine*

"John Patrick is a prolific and prize-winning novelist whose ability to crank out wide-ranging homoerotica is as deft and sure as that of a dairy maid churning butter. In 'Angel' there is enough graphic sex of just about every description to perk up even the most jaded imaginations. Patrick knows how to mix 'n' match spicy combinations and his enormous cast of characters includes porno stars, sleazy producers, cute young studs with insatiable appetites (there's a bathhouse scene that takes some beating) with sadism, degradation and - improbably - love and affection. This writing is what being brave is all about. It brings up the kinds of things that are usually kept so private that you think you're the only one who experiences them."
– *The Gay Times*, London

"Tantalizing tales of porn stars, hustlers, and other lost boys...John Patrick set the pace!"
- *The Weekly News, Miami*

"...Some readers may find some of the scenes too explicit; others will enjoy the sudden, graphic sensations each page brings. Each of these romans á clef is written with sustained intensity. 'Angel' offers a strange, often poetic vision of sexual obsession. I recommend it to you."
- *Nouveau Midwest*

"Self-absorbed, sexually-addicted bombshell Stacy flounced onto the scene in 'Angel' and here he is again, engaged in further, distinctly 'non-literary' adventures...lots of action!"
- *Prinz Eisenherz Book Review, Germany*

"Patrick's 'Superstars' is a fast read...
if you'd like a nice round of fireworks before the Fourth of July, read these essays aloud at your next church picnic..."
- *Welcomat, Philadelphia*

Legends

World's Sexiest Young Guys
Third Enlarged, Updated Edition

Edited By
JOHN PATRICK

STARbooks Press
Sarasota, FL

Books by John Patrick

Non-Fiction

A Charmed Life: Vince Cobretti
Lowe Down: Tim Lowe
The Best of the Superstars 1990
The Best of the Superstars 1991
The Best of the Superstars 1992
The Best of the Superstars 1993
The Best of the Superstars 1994
The Best of the Superstars 1995
The Best of the Superstars 1996
What Went Wrong?
When Boys Are Bad
& Sex Goes Wrong
Legends: The World's Sexiest
Men, Vols. 1 & 2
Legends: 3rd Ed.
Tarnished Angels (Ed.)

Fiction

Billy & David: A Deadly Minuet
The Bigger They Are...
The Younger They Are...
The Harder They Are...
Angel: The Complete Trilogy
Angel II: Stacy's Story
Angel: The Complete Quintet
Angel: The Complete Quintet
(Expanded International Ed.)
A Natural Beauty (Editor)
The Kid (with Joe Leslie)
HUGE (Editor)
Strip: He Danced Alone
The Boys of Spring
Big Boys/Little Lies (Editor)
Boy Toy
Seduced (Editor)
Insatiable/Unforgettable (Editor)
Heartthrobs
Runaways/Kid Stuff (Editor)
Dangerous Boys/Rent Boys
(Editor)
Barely Legal (Editor)
Country Boys/City Boys (Editor)
My Three Boys (Editor)
Mad About the Boys (Editor)
Lover Boys (Editor)
In the BOY Zone (Editor)

Library of Congress Card Catalogue No. 91-065823-R
ISBN No. 1-877978-74-4

INTRODUCTION

For a male sex symbol to become a legend in his own time, everything he shows us must always look mysteriously new, so full of exciting possibilities that he always encourages us to linger, investigate, and, finally, have our way with him in our dreams.

A true legend always gives us a few more glittery things to hoard in our imagination and fondle in our memories when life gets a little dull. Their greater profusion, even in a vehicle unworthy of their miraculous talents, only creates a stronger desire, as if we are somehow moved to defend them.

They promise endless stimulation, inexhaustible sensations. They seduce us with sensual images, promising a larger, richer world and unbounded freedom to roam in it. Yet they always elude our attempts to grasp them and keep them in their place, as if to tell us, with a twinkle in their eyes, "Hey, you're never gonna see everything!"

Sometimes, usually after the legend has passed on, a clearer picture of them emerges. For instance, the actor Nick Adams, pal of James Dean and legendary in his minor own way, is described by noted gay historian Leigh Rutledge: "Although married and divorced with two children, he had a reputation for being aggressively bisexual. Some people have suggested he was simply one of Hollywood's restless mercenaries and didn't care who he slept with as long as there was something in it for him."

Supposedly hugely endowed and uncut, Nick hitchhiked to Hollywood in 1951 and quickly became popular among the johns who cruised Santa Monica Boulevard and the Sunset Strip. Then he met Dean and the two became good friends, leading to speculation about the true nature of their relationship. After Dean's death, Adams used his friendship with Natalie Wood (with whom Dean had made "Rebel Without a Cause," also starring the gay actor Sal Mineo), to ingratiate himself with her lover at the time, Elvis Presley. In his book, *Elvis*, Albert Goldman sees Adams performing the same functions for the king of rock 'n' roll that he did for Dean, calling him the "only man Elvis would befriend in the movie colony." Adams was to die of an overdose in 1968 at the age of 37. Boyd McDonald calls him "one of Hollywood's most interesting lays." In Alanna Nash's book, *Elvis Aaron Presley: Revelations from the Memphis Mafia*, Marty Lacker says, "The gay rumors first got going when Elvis started hanging out with Nick Adams. And you can see why gay men would be attracted to Elvis. His cousin Gene Smith was looking at him one time, and he said, in that funny way he talks, 'Elvis, you know I ain't no damn queer, but you're the prettiest thing I've ever seen.' And it was true."

Rutledge's take on Nick's sexuality succinctly sums up how we like to view all the stars we lust after. We want to be able to say "maybe," because we know that once a young man has been exposed to the fast track of Hollywood, "he didn't care who he slept with" is more often true than false.

Despite the freedoms gays have won over the years, things never really change in Hollywood, where image is everything. So many stars are forced to be elusive when it comes to their private lives, so circumspect that you have to love 'em. In fact, they beg you to understand; they beg you to love them. And who are we to refuse?

Star Quality

A note before we commence: It's been said that reporters hold up mirrors to the communities they serve, giving their readers as accurate and complete a view of the world around them as they can. Reporters don't set out to offend anyone but it would be impossible to publish a book that would please everyone. Besides, it'd be boring to read. So, as the great Bette Davis once said, "Fasten your seat belts, it's gonna be a bumpy ride."

For generations, we have become fascinated by Hollywood dreamboats who possess the curious mystery and magic that are the wellsprings of their power. But now it seems stars are being subjected more and more to the vagaries of over exposure and too much public contact.

"Not that I have anything against Socrates," Ellen Goodman,

wrote in *The Boston Globe*. "I agree with the wise Greek who said that the unexamined life is not worth living. But he came up with the one-liner before the invention of film and videotape, all the paraphernalia of electronic recording.

"But now I wonder if it's the overexamined life that isn't worth living. Or the inner life that is suffering from overexposure.

"In the era of high-tech, we have entered the world of personality. Personality becomes our most important product.

"It spills over the edges of everything else. In 'Truth or Dare,' the director makes a visual line between person and performer. He uses black-and-white film for backstage, color for onstage. But Madonna crosses that line in performing her role, play acting real life.

"In the strikingly narrow world that she rules as a superstar, the projection of her personality is her greatest artistic achievement."

"It is no longer enough to create art," Marcel Duchamp once said with tongue in cheek. "One must now be art."

What is this curious magic that creates real star quality? We know it is more than the obvious technical gifts of the artist or even physical appearance. Some blessed karma shows through and envelopes them in a distinctive atmosphere, surrounding them in luminous radiation. It's been called personality, charisma, and presence. I think it's a sixth sense.

Whatever it is, can it be learned? I doubt it. One can perfect the techniques of one's performing trade. Learn good grooming. Develop taste and style. Practice a disciplined health routine. One can be born with super good looks and even sleep with the right producer, but none of that guarantees success or the ownership of that special magic. We say that audiences make the stars and they do. But that's because, over and above everything else, it's the audience that finds and recognizes that unique and rare individuality.

In the now defunct magazine *After Dark*, William Como said: "This dynamic exchange of feeling definitely concerns itself with quality and, happily, sensitivity. Good looks have never been enough. In the end, chalk it up to grace and soul. And the freedom to really be."

Being is what it is all about. As Joan Crawford said, "I love being a celebrity. I never go out on the street unless I expect and anticipate and hope and pray I'll be recognized. That someone will ask for my autograph. When they do, I'm prepared and ready and as well-dressed as I can possibly be. And when someone cries out, 'There's Joan Crawford!' I say, 'It damn sure is!'"

Noted Hollywood manager Jay Bernstein says: "I'm interested in stars, not actors. They're different businesses. The first thing I look for is not talent but that quality. Talent is something that can be developed. Quality can't."

"The more enduring stars know how to build, then bank, a fire," the author Gerri Hershey says. "Staying hot is as effortless as breathing. Unlike ordinary people, stars integrate their sexuality into their lives and work. And they never, ever worry about how it will play.

"Sex has been around for some 3 billion years, ever since randy protocells first jumped one another in the primordial ooze. Yet never has so much time, thought, effort and ad revenue been spent on sexual prescriptives. What a treat it is to pick up the *New York Times* and read this cold shower of a headline: 'IS SEX NECESSARY? EVOLUTIONISTS ARE PERPLEXED.'

"Marilyn Monroe didn't know from safe sex. There is the same kind of set-the-shrubbery-afire crackling over the memories of others we've canonized. Theirs are lives of sainted sinners; they may not have done everything right, but they did it with feeling."

Marilyn set the standard for passion. Richard Schickel says, "Think of all the girls who have played bits and posed with their breasts bulging out of their bathing suits and given blow jobs to the boss and then think how few have gone on not just to stardom but beyond it into 'legend.'"

No, real passion doesn't need a publicist. It telegraphs across miles, across time.

Interestingly, the passionate always burn brighter as binary stars. Ever since David and Bathsheba, there have been couples who haven't been able to keep a lid on it, even in public. And in that helplessness lies their power. The thrum of libido charges their slightest activity. Tension hangs over them at state dinners and photo opportunities. Four star hotels grid for their arrival, paparazzi take out dental insurance.

Sex has always sold and it still sells. It is the key ingredient in what makes a person, place or thing, hot. Sex still gets attention. The problem now is shelf life. Diluted sexuality fades faster. Many of today's stars are perfectly suited to flashcard sex, quickies like Erik Estrada and in porn, wooden Indian Lex Baldwin. Hot today, fodder for quiz shows or, in the case of gay porn, 900 line advertisements tomorrow.

More than anything else, sex is in the eyes, ears and viewing demographics of the beholder. There are so many voices telling us what's hot and what's not that it's become positively clinical.

"The famous keep alive the romance of individualism," according to the best-selling biographer John Lahr. "Fame is democracy's vindictive triumph over equality: the name illuminated, the name rewarded, the name tyrannical. Fame glorifies the omnipotence of the invented self and diminishes the authentic one. It is literally self-destructive."

For Andy Warhol, the image reigned supreme. He said: "I thought if they took my picture, I would become the picture."

The whole "fame thing," as former president George Bush would say, is terribly seductive. The publicity business is booming. The fantasy is that a publicist will help create you, then protect you and make certain that you remain forever in the tabloids, the "I don't care what they say about me as long as they spell my name right," philosophy.

Actor Spalding Gray: "It dawned on me that I was torn between two conflicting realizations: first, that I myself was responsible for conditioning, even manipulating the audience to desire me more, which made me feel a little sleazy and, second, that I was on the verge of burning out if I didn't retreat just a little and try to be more private, which made me feel healthy."

The downside of being so terribly hot is the inevitable fall from grace, when the fickle public moves on to a newer model. The attention span of the public is notoriously short. Comebacks are few and far between, and then usually with a shocking, often surreal return from the dead quality.

When it comes to beauty, notwithstanding the vagaries of individual taste, occasionally guys come along who were meant, like the bands on a coral snake or the face of the Matterhorn, to showcase what Mother Nature really intended. And nobody responds more than gays, who embrace these present and future icons, finding in them the eternal hope of possibility. The sex stars become safe harbor on a stormy night and, in our fantasies, we can make them do anything we want.

Because variety is the spice of life, you are often stunned with the multiplicity of choices. I must confess that I want to go to bed with everybody in this book. As the actress Sandra Bernhard succinctly puts it, "One man, however splendid, simply cannot meet all your needs. That is why the search continues, but never in vain. They all give me a gift that has enriched my soul, changing me forever."

The stars featured in this book have all enriched my soul with their performances, their mere presence in the world. Their beauty transcends the moment, their fame built on our passionate desire to possess them. And you know how it is, we are conditioned to want something and when we can't get close to it, we want it even more.

The Star Fuck

We who pursue perfection in ourselves or others, Pete Townshend says, are searching for God: "A perfect father or mother, brother or sister, dreamed of in a 'psychotherapeutic placebo,' often embodied in the image of a chosen star."

Some people have been in intimate contact with a well-known individual for years. Some, only for a short time. Donald Rawley, for instance, remembers Tennessee Williams and his telling him, "Just wait till you're old and gray."

"It was six in the morning," Donald says, "and we were in his suite at the St. James hotel in London. The year was 1977. He was drunk and upset. I was drunk and 19, a student at a drama academy and a serious habitue of nightclubs full of rich men and gorgeous young things, all ready to strike.

"Tennessee was upset because I was more interested in his bodyguard, Craig Dudley, than I was in him. We had started out the evening on Kensington High Street, at a discotheque called El Sombrero. Earth, Wind and Fire was big. I was dancing with a girl-about-town known only as Jordan and Derek Jarman, the film director.

"Tennessee collapsed into my booth, smiled at me, and waved. I was a tough cookie. I waved back, and continued to dance. As in many nights with Tennessee, there was a bottle of red wine for him – he drank it like soda pop – and a bottle of champagne for me. I was a stickler at that young age for Cordon Rouge. It was either Cordon Rouge, very cold, or I didn't sit down.

"Tennessee was determined to get me in bed, and I was equally determined not to be gotten. We talked and laughed. It was our fourth 'date.' I didn't just go 'out' with men. It had to be a date; that way they paid. Tennessee told me I had a forehead like Merle Oberon. I thanked him and blushed. I always liked Merle.

"We moved on to the next club, Maunkberry's on Jermyn Street. By this time, Tennessee was on his third bottle and had taken two or three Seconals to relax. David Hockney walked in, looking perplexed, and then walked out. Divine was in a corner, eating six different plates of food. I found that sad, because Maunkberry's at that time served what I can only call 'cocaine dishes' – elaborate plates with tiny bits of food on them, ideal for anyone with powder in their nose and gums. I think Divine really wanted something filling. Fish and chips with vinegar and salt, rolled on a copy of the *Daily Mail* that would have done the trick.

"The dance floor was in the back, behind the overpriced restaurant. Rudolf Nureyev was dancing with a very muscular black man. Mia Farrow, tiny veins popping in her cheeks, was sitting very much alone, her hands in her lap. Elton John came in with his manager, John Reid. Rod Stewart came in with a blonde with an American accent.

"It was two A.M. and Tennessee and I moved on to a party at a Moroccan-style apartment in Knightsbridge. This, of course, meant only one thing: black hashish. It was on this night I remember he laid his head on my lap and told me he loved me. Being a tough cookie in London in 1977, I answered, quite simply, 'Good for you.'

"At dawn, we were back at the St. James hotel. Tennessee pretended to be drunk. In fact, he could walk a straight line even when he was so loaded he could barely breathe. But the doorman winked and said, 'Of course, Mr. Williams, of course your friend can help you up to your suite.'

"Craig Dudley was asleep in the room next door. I visited him for what seemed to be a relatively short amount of time – Craig had the ability to *seize the moment* – and then went back to Tennessee. He was lying on his bed wearing a satin robe and, of all things, a dark green-and-yellow paisley cravat.

"'It's July,' I said. 'That cravat is a bit much, I think.' I was no longer stoned, just drunk. At that point in my life, my alcohol and drug intake veered up and down. It was one of the lovely things about being 19.

"Tennessee pulled off the cravat and flung it at me. 'Then take it,' he snapped. 'I'm old and rotten. You could make me happy, you know. I knew an angel once. He was an angel, beautiful, beautiful, but they took him away and they locked him up.' Tennessee was going to cry. I'd seen it happen before, same story, and I wasn't going to buy it.

"'I've got to get some rest, darling. How about tomorrow night?' I asked with a soothing voice.

"He began to grow belligerent. 'Remember what I said,' he hissed at me. Just wait till you're old and gray.'

"Los Angeles has a way of taking the big shots from New York, the beauties from London and Paris, and turning them into just another rice cake. I was driving a truck for a living, delivering paintings for an art gallery, when I heard on the radio that Tennessee had died. I had to pull over to the side of the road.

"Soon I shall be 38, and yes, Tennessee, I am learning what it is like to be old and gray, suddenly an anachronism. All my friends from the seventies and eighties are dead, and we are stuck with the untalented, the not-so-beautiful, those who lack imagination.

"I remember seeing Tennessee in Key West, then in New York, briefly, and then never again. Sometimes I take out his cravat and show it to some drama types, 21 or 22, tops. They say, 'Who?' And look at each other, exchanging sarcastic glances. And I realize they are now the tough cookies of Los Angeles."

(Tennessee would be amused that he now has a U.S. postage stamp issued in his honor. "It's a wonderful thing that the old queen finally got someone licking up to him," quipped Robert

Bray.)

Brandon Judell tells of his brief encounter with a celebrity: "...I was lying on one of those filthy cots in the old Everard bathhouse when who should come swishing in but Paul Lynde. He said in as butch a voice as he could muster, 'Baby, you're beautiful, and I'm going to make you feel good.' He was wearing a towel and a gold chain with some oversized medallion hanging from it, and there was a pack of cigarettes stuffed between the towel and his waist.

"I thought to myself, Well, he is a celebrity and maybe I could use this sometime in the future. Then I thought, Well, I'll probably be too embarrassed to tell anyone I *sehtupped* with Mr. Lynde. But it was too late. He had closed the door and had thrown his towel to the ground. His locker key was around his right ankle.

"Mr. Lynde's stomach was more than a little fleshy and his legs were calveless, but he surprisingly had some tits. Also his cock looked to be close to eight inches and was thickish. He also had big balls that hung low. (I usually don't remember these details, unless they're about a celebrity or the sex is exquisite.)

"Anyway, I'm lying there and he starts licking me from my balls to my chin. Then he sticks his thick tongue down my throat. I remember wishing he hadn't worn so much cologne. Anyway, I close my eyes and I imagine myself lying on the desk of the center square of *Hollywood Squares* as Paul Lynde rims me in front of an appreciatively applauding audience. Suddenly, I open my eyes to Paul and reality, and I see the 'Bye Bye Birdie' star lifting my legs over his shoulders, spitting on my asshole and on his cock. 'Oh no! Now I can't tell anyone this story. It would be all right to fuck Mr. Lynde, but to be fucked by the queen of queens? Shit!'

"So I close my eyes again, but he slaps my face and says, 'When you get fucked by Lynde, baby, you keep your eyes open.' And, truthfully, it was a *great* fuck. Lasting for over twenty minutes or so. I was moaning and screaming. It felt like he was hitting my prostate with every stroke. Sadly, the medallion kept hitting my nose, but I didn't care.

"'Chew my nipples,' he ordered. I did.

"Then he screamed, 'I'm coming, baby. I'm coming.' But

instead of coming inside of me, he shot all over my face...drop after drop after drop. Then he licked the cum splatter all up. 'I love how I taste, baby. Now turn over.'

"I did. Suddenly I felt him writing on my ass. He must have had a pen or tiny marker or something in that cigarette case. He then turned me over and kissed me good-bye.

"Ten minutes later, I ran to the bathroom and checked out what he wrote. It said on my firm left ass cheek: FUCKED BY PAUL LYNDE."

In memorable encounters such as these, a companion's secrets, hopes, and dreams have not exactly been shared with the star, but he is somehow bound up in them. "They all know me but I don't know them," the star often says. The idolater begins to forget that he is totally unknown to the star and he resents that fact. With an undercurrent of anger, a chip grows on his shoulder. Through experience, the star learns to maintain a distance. Esther Williams put it best: "Walk fast, don't stop and shake hands. You touch them, they don't touch you." But regal graciousness is not what a fan wants from an old friend. He wants to be able to tell them what they mean, what they have meant to them, how they have inspired them. Like any lover, to put reality behind the dream.

Such a reality, even culminating in an act of intimacy, has been around as long as there have been stars – "stars" for this purpose being, according to taste, anybody from princes to poets to basketball players – but it was with the rise of the rock industry in the '60s, with all those gigs and tours and festivals, that stars became ubiquitous, and numerous, and, above all, available. The status of the Star Fuck as a lopsided modern romance ascended yet higher in the celebrity-fixed '70s and '80s and soon sexual urges began to fuse with action. After all, what was John Hinckley but a lovelorn swain with a gun? Lennon's tragic death illustrates how tragically the love story can end.

But violence is the province of psychopaths, carrying what we're talking about here to the extreme, a lunatic's last attempt at getting the love object to acknowledge his fantasy of intimacy as a reality.

The advent of television permitted the barriers to fall that formerly existed between the well-known and the unknown. In films, the characterizations stars offer as they move through a fictionalized story constantly remind us that these are shadows and not necessarily what they seem to be, however real their performances. With TV, the need to remind ourselves we are only watching a well-rehearsed "program" is ever greater.

But, still, whatever the medium, we feel we know our favorite stars so well. We feel we are privy to their secret thoughts and emotions, revealed through their unconscious gestures. We feel we can read them at a glance. The star has a secret, many certainly, like all of us. And we know it. It makes him all the more attractive because gaymales hang on every hint that he might be "one of us." Higher gossip heightens our sense of false intimacy with them, further blurring the line between fantasy and reality.

We can become auteurs, self-creating our own scenarios of what the celebrity might be like. Their films become not as ends in themselves, discrete creations, but as incidents in a larger and more compelling drama – the drama of the star's life and career, the shaping and reshaping of the image of him we hold dear in our minds.

Dr. Andrew Stanway, author of *The Art of Sensual Loving*, explains: "They are seen on stage or screen larger than life, often with sexual or romantic overtones. No wonder, then, that they become the dream subjects of so many. Fantasies of having sex with a famous person are simply an extension of this process. In such fantasies, the dreamer identifies with them and their lifestyle and, for a while, becomes the sort of person the star might fancy enough to have sex with, given the chance.

"Of course, few people know what sort of lover Tom Cruise might be in real life. Yet for fantasies it hardly matters. Fans are influenced by what the publicity machine sells, and accept unquestioningly that the object of their adulation would make a wonderful lover. And in a world full of harsh realities and unfulfilled dreams, who can blame them?

"As with so many other fantasies, the key here is safety. There is no chance of being rejected by a famous rock star, if only because you wouldn't have the opportunity to get into his bed anyway. How much more satisfying then, to have an affair in the mind with the star so that you can make everything just how you want it."

Star Dick

More than anything it seems, we're everlastingly curious about Star Dick. What does the star's cock look like? How big is it? Is it cut or uncut? If a star is rumored to have a big dick, other factors melt away. Take, for instance, actor John Ireland, a minor player at best in often Grade B product. Once it became known he had one of the longest wands in Tinseltown, he developed a gay following. Gary Griffin, author of *Penis Enlargement Methods*, says that Ireland, along with Milton Berle, Forrest Tucker and Freddy Frank, made up the "original Alaska Pipeline! Early in his career, Ireland participated in 'aqua shows' and his enormous endowment was impossible to conceal even under modest bathing suits. Casting agents and talent scouts quickly 'discovered' him. When he and his wife Joanne Dru did summer stock together, he was known to put his hand in his trouser pocket and pull the fabric closer to his body to reveal the outline of his horsecock. The first six rows of those audiences were known to be occupied by gay 'size queens' who came to drool over their phallic idol."

Other "phallic idols" of note include cute Robby Benson, of "Ode to Billy Joe" fame. He is reported to sport a cock in the nine inch range, according to Griffin's industry spies. And the sexy, blond "Dukes of Hazard" (and now country music) star John Schneider has "a beautiful and pendulous 8 1/2 inch plus" cock. Handsome Christopher "Superman" Reeve, it is said, had a hard time fitting into those skimpy tights. Film censors in England who were examining early footage of the first film in the series noted that the huge member was hanging on one side of his costume and then mysteriously shifting to the opposite side in subsequent scenes. The solution was to fit the star with a cup to help conceal the enormous bulge. The late actor Michael Landon, so cute as "Little Joe" on "Bonanza," also had a thick tool that was about eight inches soft. (Hardly "little!" More like a "bonanza!")

The one-time Tarzan, Ron Ely, has a dick that also measures a hefty nine when soft. Indeed, some of Hollywood's hunkiest actors have cocks to go a long with their admirable physiques. Clint Walker of "Cheyenne" fame, reportedly worked out at Vince's Gym and spies there say the "tall, handsome actor with the sensuous basso profundo voice " brandishes a thick, uncut, veiny cock that matches his "barrel-chested build."

Aldo Ray became involved in porn after his legit career died in the late '60s and Griffin says he has a photo of the "Battle Cry" actor which displays his impressive flaccid member hanging at nearly eight inches.

"Hercules" star Steve Reeves had a cock that "swung back and forth like the trunk of an elephant" when he walked. Jim Brown, the football player who starred in action flicks such as "100 Rifles," keeps the myth alive that blacks are bigger with an astounding cock that measures 9 1/2 inches long by 8 inches in circumference. (Eddie Murphy and his buddy Arsenio Hall are also said to keep the myth alive.)

And recently a photo surfaced (which was subsequently published in *SPY* magazine) showing the world's biggest box-office attraction, Arnold Schwarzenegger, has marvelously big muscles everywhere.

Rock Hudson and Jim Nabors, who were married in a mock ceremony, would seem to have been a match made in heaven, if it hadn't all been in jest. Nabors' penis "has been seen by many individuals who all concur that he is hung like a mule, measuring between nine and ten inches in erect length (and nearly as long when flaccid)," Griffin says. Hudson's cock sported a slight curve and measured 8 1/2 - inches when he was aroused. Hudson's buddy, Roddy McDowall, has one of the biggest dicks in Hollywood. Griffin has a photo of the star as a youth and the cock is "wrist-thick and veiny."

Legendary stars Humphrey Bogart, Errol Flynn, and Cary Grant are also rumored to have impressed with their equipment.

Of the legends spotlighted in this book, Warren Beatty is said to be hung like a donkey but Griffin says that he has a photo which shows Warren's cock is only "normal." Sean Connery, according to writer Jim Boyd, is "splendidly hung," as was Gary Cooper.

Aaron Travis, famous for his *Hollywood Hunks in the Raw* series, describes David Bowie's meat: "(His) enormous uncut dick and lemon-sized balls swing between his legs during the sex scene only in the 138 minute version (of 'The Man Who Fell From Earth') distributed by Thorn EMI."

In her memoirs, Pamela Des Barres (*I'm With the Band*) talked about her torrid affair with Don Johnson, who was supremely gorgeous at 22: 'I'm trying hard not to let my imagination run away with me, but it appears that we're both madly infatuated. It would be quite nice, for here are his attributes: 1. Really into acting; in love with it, secure in it. 2. Getting very into music; writing it, learning guitar. 3. On THE path. 4. HUGE cock. I'm getting off like I haven't in ages. We do 'get it on' perfectly and last night was heavy wildness. I kept seeing myself in his eyes so beautifully, and forever it seemed, we were either fucking or laughing." Johnson's equipment was also "noted" by his friend David Cassidy, who was introduced to the "Miami Vice" star by a mutual friend, Sal Mineo. David, telling a German newspaper he was bisexual, said he and Johnson "go back a looooong time."

Of course, David himself was endowed with a penis that is reputed to be extremely long, thin, and quite beautiful. Gina Lollobrigida even called it "the Monster." The Cassidy brothers, David and Shaun, through a wonderful stroke of fate (they both had the same father) are marvelously endowed. Shaun, who just married for the second time, possesses a cock that is said to be astoundingly thick. Griffin reports that one of his spies met Cassidy in the Embers in Portland and eventually went to bed with him. The spy says that he's never seen a cock so thick, and he's seen many. He could not encircle it with his hand, and he has large hands: "A good approximation of his size is 8 inches in circumference and 9 to 9 1/2 inches in length."

Other than the last first-hand report, all of these "sightings" are inconclusive. It is only in the field of porn that we are able to actually know for sure what we're getting and, even then, according to Griffin, porn stars are the most celebrated examples of phallic hyperbole. To achieve outlandish measurements, Griffin says, they measure their cocks underneath, pressing the ruler back until the balls are firmly against the anus. Griffin suggests that John Holmes' publicity spinners were particularly guilty of inflating his dimensions. John himself always joked, "It's bigger than a Cadillac." He knew it was only ten, but it was 8 1/2 inches soft and incredibly thick, an astonishing "Mighty Python" of dick. John's big advantage was that he knew what to do with it. Most porn stars, in person, are not particularly tall. John was a six footer, so the length of it in repose was not overwhelming as it is in the case of the diminutive Tom Steele, who appears to be, when nude, all cock, which is wonderful because it is by far the most beautiful one I have ever had the pleasure of sampling.

Other super-hung porn stars in this book, Roger, Jeff Stryker, and Rick Donovan, are like Holmes in that they know what to do with the blessing between their legs.

One fan and inveterate penis-watcher wrote that he laments the fact that the teen fanzines have become more chaste than they were in the late '60s and '70s. "In those days," he writes, "you could tell from the photos how well-hung the boys were and even if they were cut or uncut. Then we went into the Reagan era and everybody went to sleep."

Indeed, in the '70s, the teen dream magazines were like pre-pubescent *Playgirls,* with semi-nude shots of the boys on the beach, in the bathroom or, best of all, lying seductively on their beds. The editor of *16* at the time said that she tried to downplay the flesh but a sample issue from those days shows at least a dozen guys shirtless or less over a six-page "Adonis" photo spread. "We once ran a shot of John Travolta by the pool," former editor Danny Fields recalls, "and you could see every vein of his cock outlined in his briefs but nobody complained."

"Leif Garrett," a collector writes, "was perhaps the only teen star I know of who was seemingly quite happy to show off everything he had. Invariably dressed in tight jeans or shorts or silk pants that revealed the outlines of his dick which, even at the age of 14 or 15 was very impressive, at least five inches soft or more, by my calculations. He even proudly posed, at 16, in very revealing red bikini briefs for 'Rock Stars in Their Underpants,' a book I bought in London." Garrett was also the most undressed of the American teen fanzine favorites of that era. He was usually pictured semi-nude.

This avid collector grieves for the loss of some of his treasured photos of those days, such as the shot of the cute little blond of TV's "Dennis the Menace" fame, Jay North, at 14, riding with Sajit Khan on the back of an elephant in "Maya." It was in this film that Jay exposed his buns, drying himself after a swim.

Through the wonders of the VCR and the Nickelodeon channel, this collector has been able to save nearly all of the "Flipper" shows, which featured Luke Halpin and Tommy Norden. "This surely was my Arcadia!" the collector gushes. "Two cute boys in tight cut-offs revealing bulging baskets (Tommy even had a more impressive showing than Luke!) and cavorting topless with their super-tolerant and loving father in the idyllic setting of the Florida Keys. Pure homoerotic bliss! Among the new crop of teen stars, this fan likes Christian Bale, who evidenced a nice bulge in "Newsies" and Wil Wheaton of "Toy Soldiers." (The collector says to watch the scene just before Wil's character gets killed in slow motion to "see Wil's willy.")

And gaymales aren't the only ones obsessed with the penis, Star Dick or just regular. "Over and over again the penis makes its way into discussions I've had with many men," Susan Evershed says, "and if these males happened to be fourteen years old I could understand the fascination, because at that age the body part, which tends to grow hard and point, is something that's still fairly new. But I am not referring to teenagers. I am talking about grown men who have been accustomed - or should be - to their genitalia for some time."

Theirs surely, but the other guy's is what fascinates.

"Gay America's fascination with monumental genital endowment was for many years its most open secret," Doug Richards says. "To say that size was not important, that it was the individual that mattered, that what a man did with his dick was more significant than its dimension was both politically correct and psychologically mature - but we have always suspected that there was less honesty in these platitudes than in the old joke, 'There are two things I hate - size queens and small dicks.'"

Richards says that in 1982, size fixation came out of the closet. The occasion which prompted this sexual glasnost was the release of Falcon Studios' "Huge," directed by Matt Sterling and starring Lee Ryder and seven other men of enviable proportions. So successful was "Huge" that it spawned a sequel and dozens of imitators. Richards says that Holmes ceased to be a anomaly, and became "merely a phenomenon.

'Show Hard!' was no longer the most popular graffiti to be found on tearoom walls – now it was: 'Show Big!'"

Indeed, an entire magazine has been devoted to this subject, the popular *Inches*. Typical of the readers' obsession with this subject is this letter a man in Ohio: "The 'Reader's Meat' feature in your magazine each month really sets you apart from all the others. It's fascinating, unique verification that not all the big meat in the world hangs between the legs of professional models. 'Biker Rick' and our anonymous friend from Denver in the July 1993 issue define the term 'well hung.' Biker Rick is surely one of the biggest uncut specimens ever. "

In his book *Man to Man*, Dr. Silverstein says: "In the gay world of today...the penis is revered. The big cock is the prize, adorned and adored, the possessor enormously attractive to the hungry hunter who wants to engulf it or to be overpowered by it, with minimal regard for other physical characteristics, and none whatsoever for social or emotional ones. It is worshipped as a symbol of masculine sexual abilities: the bigger the cock, the more masculine."

For a couple of years, Cody James was the biggest thing in porn. Our favorite scene has Billy Houston adoring Cody's huge dick in "The Private Invitation of Billy Houston," from Avalon Video. Billy is entertaining a little friend and at one point he switches on the VCR to show him what he terms "the biggest dick in the world." What follows is a reverential scene of Cody just lying back enjoying what Billy and the other boy do to him. Billy's mouth nearly proves inadequate to the job and, sad to say, we are not treated to the spectacle that would have ensued had Billy allowed the spear to invade his ass, at least on camera. James is one of the few BIG boys we have encountered who never seems to have trouble getting it up and keeping it up. His scene in "Carnival" is a perfect example of his prowess. He takes on two guys and does each of them with great finesse before shooting one of his patented gushing loads.

Now the BIG name is Kevin Dean, who starred for John Travis in "Rawhide" and was immediately inked to do several more films on an exclusive contract. Travis says that Dean has gotten more mail than any other porn performer in recent memory.

A distinct advantage a porn performer has over a fan is that not only does he get paid to have sex with hot men but he can also, on occasion, pick his co-stars. Damien made only two videos and then dropped out of the performing end of the business, but Chi Chi LaRue lured him back to do an oral scene in "Bad Break" because he had always wanted to work with Tom Chandler: "He's incredible," Damien says. "He's 6'4" with dark hair. He's straight, and he has a twelve-inch dick. I mean this thing was frightening! I've never seen anything like it! We let him come in my mouth on my tongue, which I don't think they do often. The only reason I did it was that he and I had become buddies and had started talking for a couple of weeks before. I watched the scene and it's amazing."

"Size fixation," Richards reminds us, "is certainly not without historical precedence. Phallic worship has existed since the Stone Age, and continued unabated through the Neolithic Era and the Bronze Age. The Christian tradition de-emphasized the cock by not exaggerating in art. It was not until this century that the philosophy of 'Bigger Is Better' came to the fore."

"Bigger the Better" has always been part of The American Way, Richards says, and "certainly this philosophy has not been limited to homosexual males, or to all males, for that matter .

"Most men," observes Handman and Brennan in *Sex Handbook*, " unless they're born with cocks that hang down to their knees, worry about whether their penis is big enough. The size of the cock, contrary to popular myths, has nothing to do with sexual potency...and there's absolutely no relation between cock size and the power of your own orgasm."

We would have to agree to that. I think the most orgasms I have managed over a single piece of tape had nothing to do with the size of the wand. The possessor of the celebrity cock that turned us on more than any other is that of Rob Lowe. Having had wet dreams about this most beautiful of actors for many years, the delight we experienced in seeing him going at it as if there were no tomorrow was beyond comprehension. As you will read later in this book, the pirated tape of his escapade in Paris is a treasured possession of mine because, as fuzzy as it is, it's still distinct enough to permit me the satisfaction I have always sought: to see my idol erect and in action. Having the boys of the closed circuit TV program "Midnight Blue" rap on and on about Rob's remarkable prowess (aided, we are certain, by some drugs) only added to the my enjoyment. Seen in profile, Rob's dick is no slouch and he, quite obviously, knows how to use it. Plus, he has another guy in that hotel room in Paris who was participating in the action! To me, such a winning combination enshrines him forever as not only one of the most beautiful of men but, more importantly, one of the most potent of the legendary lovers of the silver screen.

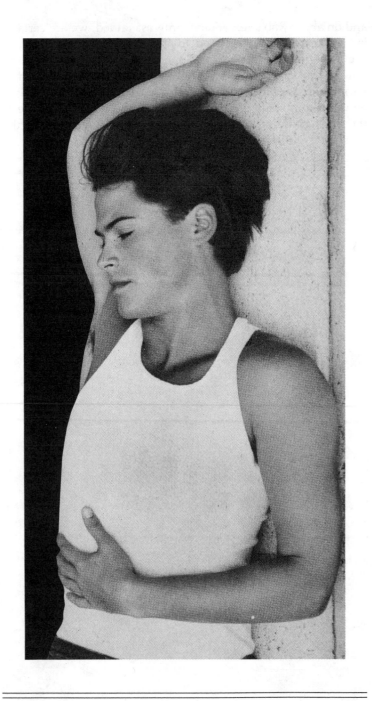

BOOK I.

LEGENDARY MOVIE
AND MUSIC STARS

Movie concepts may come and go but steamy scenes, racy dialogue, and lusty characters have always had a place on the silver screen. And when it comes to the actors who bring them to vivid life, gay men have long memories and great loyalty. The movie actors we idolize are sometimes cast aside by the general public before we're done with them, their power lying in the cultivation of our special sensibilities and fantasies.

Many of the stars in this book are still on top of the international heap. As William Goldman reminds us, "Foreign box office now is often more than U.S. box office. And overseas, they're much more star-happy than we are. Stars die a decade later over there."

In the early '90s, *Premiere* magazine rated the stars and automatically bankable were Mel Gibson and Tom Cruise. (The most bankable star in the world being, of course, Arnold Schwarzenegger.) "A" list stars whose presence did not guarantee an automatic foreign presale but made one a good bet included Warren Beatty, Richard Gere, Marlon Brando (early icon); On the "B" list, meaning the star's name doesn't have much to do with it (script, director count more) but doesn't hurt, were John Travolta, Don Johnson and Matt Dillon. Rob Lowe was nowhere to be found, so unbankable these days that his movies seem to go straight to video, where gay men enjoy the star's images the most anyhow.

In another gauge of popularity, *People* magazine annually picks the sexiest men alive. A recent choice, Patrick Swayze, joins an august company that includes the legendary Tom Cruise, John F. Kennedy Jr. and Mel Gibson, as well as such dubious choices as Mark Harmon and Harry Hamlin. They named Sean Connery far too late in life for the distinction to do him any good, but they restored our faith in their aptitude when in January 1995 the editors named Brad Pitt the "sexiest man alive."

In a more humorous vein, *Playgirl* annually names their "sexiest men in America" and most of the time its list has a decidedly tongue-in-cheek quality, especially when they include Boy George and John Candy.

Not to be outdone, *US* magazine polls its readers on an annual basis and it found the sexiest actors in films are: Patrick Swayze, Kevin Costner, Mel Gibson, Tom Cruise and Richard Gere. The memory of Swayze dancing dirty with Jennifer Grey and the pottery lesson he gave Demi Moore, to say nothing of the scene in "Road House" where he bares all, have endeared the former ballet dancer to the ladies and many gay men as well. Midwesterners, the magazine noted, voted solidly for Cruise. Ladies over 45 went for Gere in a big way, meaning that perhaps the gray hair in "Pretty Woman" was a good career move for the man gays remember as the greatest gigolo of all time.

Indeed, even as Gere gets married, lets his hair grow gray, and stops doing nude scenes, he remains a gay icon. In his book of poetry, *Sex with God*, Ty Wilson writes:

"The bathhouses, the bookstores, the bon hommie
might just be a rendezvous with sexual satisfaction,
but we accept it, and safely so,
because it's all we've got.
That and the hope that Richard Gere
might be gay and call someday."

So it might be said of all the stars in this book, not just the indestructible Richard, are still the sexiest men in the world, young or not-so-young, dead or alive.

EARLY ICONS

Rudolph Valentino
from the Everett Collection

Gary Cooper on vacation, photographed by his wife,
and on location for "The Westerner" in 1940.

In A Class By Themselves:
Rudolph Valentino
&
Gary Cooper

"Rudolph Valentino was not just another movie star," notes historian Richard Koszarski of the American Museum of the Moving Image. "He was a one-man cultural phenomenon who shattered his audience's long accepted notions of male sexuality." Before Valentino, the popular male stars were Douglas Fairbanks, Harold Lockwood and Wallace Reid, handsome but hardly sexy; the kind of guys girls would be proud to bring home to meet Mom. Valentino was something else entirely. He was an openly sexual icon designed to feed the most hidden fantasies of the cinema's largely female audience, to say nothing of the gaymale. Traditional values were trashed when he appeared on screen, hinting of violent sexuality and miscegenation.

Years ago, Miriam Hansen challenged the prevailing assumptions of feminist film scholarship by arguing that Valentino's vehicles were the first movies to recognize female spectatorship as a mass phenomenon. The fact that women were fascinated by Valentino despite the widespread contempt of male authorities (who regarded him as perverse or worse) prompts Hansen to conclude that Valentino's films articulate a desire outside motherhood or the family. Valentino was attacked as unmanly (variously rumored to be homosexual, impotent, masochistic, dominated by lesbians) because he posed a threat, not a threat merely of sexual difference but, as Hansen puts it, of a "different kind of sexuality."

Boze Hadleigh, the author of *The Lavender Screen*, has researched in depth the sexuality of film stars and says that Valentino married two lesbians, first wife Jean Hacker, and second wife Natasha Rambova, who was really Winnifred Shaughnessy of Salt Lake City, also the protegee of Alla Nazimova, a lesbian actress-producer. Both marriages were sexless and Rambova dominated her husband completely, so interfering with the filming of her husband's movies that she was barred from the set. "Studio hands gossiped about the way Valentino palled around with the fey young actors," Hadleigh says, "but most of his friends were youthful and handsome like himself. Years earlier, while working in New York tango parlors as a professional dance partner and sometime gigolo, he'd formed deep attachments to various young men. One former tea-dancer reportedly tried peddling the *real* Valentino story but nobody would publish it and tarnish the Latin lover's legend, which was bolstered by beautiful, ostensibly heterosexual actresses who publicly admitted to non-existent love affairs with the late star. Whether he was a confirmed homosexual or merely had drifted into bisexuality may never be known. There is enough proof to proclaim him bisexual, and no less a source than Ramon Novarro, the Mexican silent screen star who boasted about his loving relationship with his fellow Latin."

Indeed, Rudy even played a part in Novarro's grisly end. The black lead art deco dildo Valentino gave the star of "Ben Hur" was shoved down his throat by a pair of hustlers.

"Today, the star's unrestrained mannerisms – eyes bugging lust, his nostrils all aquiver – are simply outrageous," says Ted Elliott, Jr., "but he was a repressed audience's projection of passion. We're used to frankness now." But consider, when he died in 1926 of a perforated ulcer, women rioted in the streets, some even committed suicide. "After all," Elliott says, "in films like 'The Sheik' and 'Blood and Sand,' Rudy's melancholy Latin smolder shook up an entire gender." To say nothing of the gaymales in the audience.

"The biggest thing Valentino did," said co-star Alice Terry, "was to die." His exit prepared the way for future death cult figures – Monroe, Dean, Morrison, Presley, Clift. Thus becoming what Elliott calls "the prototype of our most beloved star - the doomed."

Besides being doomed, Valentino was incredibly sexy and he opened the door for a pantheon of other male actors and each year new ones emerge, some to flicker only briefly, others to begin building substantial careers, beguiling gaymales as they grow older and some, even sexier, before our eyes.

One who was sexy throughout his career and continues to intrigue us today is Gary Cooper. According to Hadleigh's research, a man like Cooper went unsuspected of bisexuality, for his public image precluded such speculation, even among much of Hollywood. In real life Coop was much more eloquent, elegant and urbane. He was also a reported bisexual, although his most publicized affair was with Patricia Neal.

A now-retired character actor living in Santa Barbara, Hadleigh says, was once a friend of Cooper's: "I knew him from early on, when he was a rising young star. I sensed he was lonely and we latched on to each other and discovered we had plenty in common. We talked mostly about dames. Nothing ever came up about fairies. Not during the making of 'Morocco,' but a year later we bumped into each other at a party thrown by two gay actresses who were lovers but lived apart.

"A little after midnight, Coop got really loaded. He wasn't a legendary drinker and the only time his inhibitions really melted away was at parties in the presence of a friend or two. He whispered in my ear to accompany him upstairs to the bathroom. After he took a leak he sort of flashed his dong so I could see it well. I couldn't tell if he was showing off because it was bigger than most, or if it was an invitation. I was sort of shocked myself, so I just grabbed for it. But he pushed it back in and, smiling from ear to ear, called me a 'naughty boy.'

"We never did anything, then or ever, but it was the first time we realized how it was. Neither of us were faithful bisexuals, but there's a time and a place for everything. No one's straight all the way, all the time. After he finished we sat down in a loveseat in the bedroom and talked for a while about our teenage experiences with other boys. Coop never came right out and admitted he liked having a man every once and a while, but that was the gist of it. He was very curious to find out whether I myself had done anything in the past few years with another man. We drifted apart over the years but whenever we chanced to meet he was friendly."

The actor says that if anybody had proof about Coop they would never have used it against him because he was a very kind man.

Cooper came from Montana, where he punched cows until his English mother sent him abroad at the age of nine to have the rough spots smoothed over at his father's alma mater,

Dunstable School in England. When he returned to the ranch at the age of sixteen he must have cut a charming figure in his well-cut black suit and a little Eton collar.

The designer Bill Blass says, "There have been many remarkable men in American fashion but none could match Cooper. He was unique in America the way the Duke of Windsor was unique in England. Both ventured beyond dark suits, white shirts, and dark ties, and both managed to look as if they didn't care what they were wearing, as if their clothes were chosen at random, when in fact every arrangement was calculated. His wife Rocky says that he never had a valet, he handled everything himself. He was absolutely mad for clothes, buying up Mexican fabric in shocking pinks and greens, washing it and fading it in the sun, then having it made into things he'd wear in Southampton and the South of France. He did the same thing with his jeans, washing them again and again, bleaching them on a rock. He said they felt better in the saddle. I've seen beautiful clothes hanging from a lot of tall and beautiful men, but nowhere have I seen Cooper's standard matched. He was a man of perfect proportions."

Well, almost perfect. As penis researcher Gary Griffin says, "He sported a long and thin jack-hammer which was clearly visible under his slacks, as he preferred wearing boxer shorts. Knowledge of his exceptional endowment helped establish his reputation as one of Hollywood's most prodigious lovers."

"Coop was hotter than anyone for a helluva long time," Bill Blass says. "He was even known as the 'It' boy for a while. For him, clothes were an exquisite, final detail, a weapon he used brilliantly, but scarcely needed."

It was Tallulah Bankhead, of all people, who in the early '30s, spoke for us all when she was asked why she had come to Hollywood. "Darling," she replied, "they offered me all that money, and I thought I'd go to Hollywood and fuck that divine Gary Cooper."

Marlon Brando in "A Streetcar Named Desire"

Marlon Brando

"Marlon's T-shirt disclosed the heavily muscled torso of a truck driver, he mumbled like a moron, he scratched his asshole, digging in deep to get at the itching and, to show that he had a perpetual hard-on, he wore tight jeans to outline the bulge of his genitals."
— *Brando's friend Carlo Fiore*

In 1956, when Elvis Presley shut his eyes, whacked his guitar and cried, "Awopbopaloobop, alopbamboom!" and his pelvis went crazy, everybody got the message. Paving the way for Elvis was Marlon Brando, one of the most brilliant and charismatic talents of the 20th century.

As a fan wrote *Manshots* magazine: "I grew up in the fifties, and as a budding gay I identified with Marilyn, but as I went through puberty, it was the young Brando with his sweaty muscles bursting out of his torn T-shirts that taught me lust." Indeed, Brando had in his youth a supreme sexual persona; he became an icon who entered our dreams and transformed the way we saw the world. Even in his worst, most eccentric and self-parodic performances, he never fails to fascinate.

Contemporary actors owe a great debt to Brando because, lacking access to hardening experiences of factories, or freighters or battlefields, they search for masculinity by aping him.

Brando's portrayal as Stanley Kowalski in Tennessee Williams' "A Streetcar Named Desire" in 1947 (and the screen version in 1951) was, in the words of critic Camille Paglia, "one of the most spectacular and explosive moments in modern art." Critic Gary Carey: "Brando created a style and he was - is - an original. In the sweepstakes for the title of the greatest American actor of our time, he is the only contender."

Actors act parts and singers sing lyrics that suit their voices, or, if they have no voice, their appearance. Arrogant and manipulative, seething with raw sensitivities and burning rage, alternately harsh and kind, selfish and generous, the character of Stanley was closer to the real Brando than even he cared to admit at the time.

People who saw the actor the night "Streetcar" opened on Broadway cannot forget the sense that they were seeing the beginning of something for which there was no precedent. And the performance was preserved, even enhanced on film, especially in the newly released original cut, playing in Los Angeles and other venues.

The historian Richard Schickel writes: "The performance's greatness was born out of detestation. He detested the character he was playing. In those days he was an utterly beautiful young man: his chunky body was sculpted almost like a weight lifter's, there was a dark and enigmatic depth in his eyes, something noble about his brow and nose. The contrast between this handsomeness and the literally cocksure qualities of the character he was playing made us understand how the genteel Stella fell under his sexual thrall: he may have been a brute but he was a beautiful one. More than that, one sensed in his characterization unspoken dimensions, dimensions that were no more than shadows in the writing."

From such a spectacular performance, Marlon realized his goal: "to be important enough for my word to mean something." He was courted by columnists, though none wanted to talk about politics or world affairs or starving children like Marlon thought they should.

Instead they asked him about his likes and dislikes: what he ate (peanut butter), read (Spinoza), hobbies (drums), sports (boxing, swimming in the nude), his pet peeves (giving interviews) and his love life, about which he offered no response whatsoever.

The evading of questions about his romances fueled rumors of, if not homosexuality, at least bisexuality. The whispers about the star began during his early days in New York and was centered on the fact that his boyhood friend, the actor Wally Cox, who was later to gain fame as "Mr. Peepers" on TV, was his roommate. Years later, it was revealed that Wally often slept on a mattress in the living room while Marlon entertained girls in the bedroom. Whatever their love life may have been, their living quarters on Fifty Seventh Street were chaotic. They shared the two-room flat with a raccoon named Russell and room had to be made for Marlon's drums and

42

Wally's electric train set.

Their relationship matured during this period and they remained the best of friends until the comedian's untimely death in February 1973.

Schickel remembers, "There was a certain strange and wild humor in Brando, an element of put-on in all this. But as always there was a seepage between his public persona and his screen roles and, in time, one began to detect on screen glimpses of the star profession's essence - its insecurities, its endless, quiet-bubbling contempt for the people they work for and, above all the nagging, peculiarly American fear that acting may not be suitable work for a grown-up heterosexual male."

By 1954 and his Oscar win for "On the Waterfront," Brando had been accepted by almost everybody, his word really "meant something" in Hollywood.

Moreover, he had done it his way: He had worn blue jeans in Beverly Hills long before they were fashionable, he had insulted Louella O. Parsons, he had picked his nose in public, and he had said nasty things about terrible people in the industry. He was truly the star as anti-star, emerging as a monumental personality of profound complexities and contradictions. Years later he even went so far as to admit in the European press that he'd "done things" with men but he was discreet, naming no names.

One man it seems he didn't sleep with was the "Streetcar" playwright Williams. Tennessee wrote in his memoirs that, although he thought Marlon "about the best looking man I had ever seen, with one or two exceptions, (his lover Frank Merlo and Montgomery Clift, the actor)" he had never played around with actors. "It's a point of morality with me. And anyhow Brando was not the type to get a part that way." Brando made a trip to Cape Cod to visit the playwright to read for the part of Stanley and Tennessee recalled: "Then, before he was famous, Brando was a gentle, lovely guy. He was very natural and helpful. He repaired the plumbing that had gone on the whack and he repaired the lights that had gone off. He did it without our asking him to help."

When the actor left the house, Williams gave him a $20 tip. And he got the part, of course. "There was no point in discovering him, it was so obvious. I never saw such raw talent in an individual. I knew at once he was Stanley."

In 1972, at the age of 47, Brando made the X-rated "Last Tango in Paris." Originally, the film had a scene in which his genitals were shown but it was later excised from the finished product "for structural reasons, to shorten the film," according to the director, Bernardo Bertolucci. The scene in which his naked buttocks are revealed remained.

No romance developed between Marlon and his co-star Maria Schneider. She said the star was just a "daddy" to her: "I never felt any sexual attraction for him, though all my friends told me I should. But he's almost fifty and he's only beautiful below the waist."

It took a year for the film to open in New York, unwinding at a little East Side showcase on a reserved seat basis at $5 a clip, the tariff that was being charged at that time for the hit porn flicks "Deep Throat" and "Boys in the Sand." Norman Mailer said of the film: "The crowd's joy is that a national celebrity is being obscene on screen. To measure the media magnetism of such an act, ask yourself how many hundreds of miles you might travel to hear the President of the U.S. speak a line like: 'We're just taking a flying fuck at a rolling doughnut,' or 'I went to the University of the Congo; studied whale fucking.'"

In his biography of Brando, Richard Schickel writes that if the star had died young and beautiful like his imitator James Dean, his legacy could be instantly grasped and the ionic force of his work multiplied many times.

But he lives. And his memory is failing. Recently, he began his autobiography, which should be a best-seller, and when he got to the part about his life in Rome 33 years ago, details failed him. He called Ursula Andress, hoping she could provide some answers. He forgot the time change, waking the actress in the middle of the night in Rome. He said, "Hello, Ursula, this is Marlon. I'm writing my memoirs and I can't remember, did we ever have an affair?"

Ursula, thinking it was a crank, hung up.

Days later, after checking it out, Ursula realized it really was Marlon, so she called him back. The two stars talked for 45 minutes until Ursula began worrying about her phone bill. "I have to go," she told Marlon.

"But wait, just one more question." And they continued to talk for another two hours. Before Ursula finally was able to hang up, she told Brando how worried she was about the phone bill. He told her he'd take care of it. Sure enough, eight days later, a check arrived for $400. Ursula made money on the deal – Brando has his memories, and we'll have to wait for the book to find out just what went on between them.

And that book may be quite some time in coming. The man who orchestrated the book contract (reportedly a $5 million deal) and was set to help Brando write it, George Englund, a movie producer and longtime friend of the star, has left the project after an argument over the division of fees and decided to write his own book. "Marlon's book has had an *extended* gestation period," Englund says. "I also realized that I had a different view of the life we shared, so I decided to write my own book. I will be able to write about things now that I could never have mentioned had we been working together."

"Exasperated yet somehow content," Schickel writes in an open letter to the subject of *his* biography of Brando, "I am stuck with you, just as you are stuck, more exasperated and less content, with that partially false self we unconsciously conspired to create for you some forty years ago." The "we" here is the pre-World War II "Silent Generation," the last ones to have no distinct youth culture of their own and the ones who exhibited the most furtive worship of Brando and his early, smoldering image. Schickel admits his book is as much about audiences as about an actor, as is this one.

Schickel concludes that if a star wants to be immortal, it's best to die young. In dying young, the star seems to say, Look what I've done to myself living my life for you! Here, at last is the intimacy their fans always wanted. They could do more than that, becoming permanent icons of confused values, kept alive in memory by the untimeliness of their departures. James Dean, Montgomery Clift, Marilyn Monroe, Elvis Presley and Jim Morrison followed this procedure to great effect.

Poor Brando simply died at the box-office.

As Pete Townshend said, "It is quite sobering to realize that someone who writes about you as though you are the most important person in the world doesn't need you to be alive in order to eulogize you."

Montgomery Clift, from the Kobal Collection

Montgomery Clift

*"I knew right away he was addicted to little boys. It shocked me
and I told him so, and I said it would weaken him artistically.
His father was furious. 'How can a son of mine stoop to this?'
he asked. He said I was entirely too gentle about the matter."*
- Sunny Clift, mother of Montgomery Clift

In 1929, at the age of ten, Montgomery Clift was already so
extraordinarily handsome people would stare at him on the
street. His features were perfect, as if carved, and his manners
were described as "like those of a little prince."

In 1933, the family moved to New York and in the afternoons
Monty's mother Sunny would take him to Broadway to
audition.

After a few months, someone told Sunny to register Monty
with the John Robert Powers Model Agency. Powers was
enthusiastic about Monty's "supreme good looks and poise"
and got him jobs modeling for advertisements. Monty found
modeling boring and he hated it with a passion, but it did bring
in money that the family sorely needed.

Eventually Monty's parents separated and he moved to
Connecticut with his mother. There he appeared on stage in a
comedy called "Fly Away Home." People who remember the
show say Monty was the most poised thirteen-year-old they
had ever encountered. Nothing fazed him. The play moved to
Broadway and ran seven months. Monty never missed a
performance and the theater exerted an irresistible attraction for
him. Monty's brother Brooks recalled, "He had this charisma
about him, he carried his own spotlight, as the saying goes. He
was only thirteen, but he seemed in total control on that stage.
And I could tell he was enjoying himself in that fantasy
situation. His physical presence and intensity were hypnotic.
You couldn't stop looking at him."

As he appeared in more plays, Monty began to develop a
following, especially among young girls who would remark
about his compelling gaze. "He'd look at you with those

gorgeous eyes of his and you'd feel faint," one fan remembers.

Monty was to have the same effect on girls when he began appearing in films. His biographer Patricia Bosworth notes: "Watching Monty on the screen, especially in the love scenes, one sees in him the potential of a grand romantic hero - full of erotic promise and seductiveness and charm. But his sex appeal is subtle and indirect - his sexuality has a poignancy and a vulnerability, a 'please don't hurt me' quality. He seems to be projecting his own value judgment on the act of love. Behind his beauty is a striving, a determination that keeps him from succumbing completely to narcissism. The inner tension makes Monty fascinating to watch. Sex isn't everything, he seems to say with his eyes, it's just a beginning."

But Monty disliked Hollywood with a passion. "I'm not an actor out there," he would complain, " I'm a hot property. And a property is only good if it makes money. A property is lousy if it loses money at the box office."

"Right off he was labeled as an outsider," a press agent said. "The minute you refuse to play the game in Hollywood exactly as they want it, and that means totally giving up your body and your soul and your guts to becoming a STAR, you become an outsider. The minute you have integrity, which is what Monty had, you are an outsider. The minute you refuse to sell yourself as a commodity, a product, the agent and producers and directors who literally feed off talent call you an outsider, and it is much harder to survive. Hollywood couldn't have cared less that Monty preferred to live in New York and disapproved of the pap about him in fan magazines. To survive being a star in Hollywood with Bogart or Cooper, you have to be sensitive and ruthless, humble and arrogant. Monty was sensitive, period."

Monty was a pathological idealist, actor Bill LeMassena feels. "He would wonder why do people do the right things for the wrong reasons or the wrong things for the right reasons. He would ramble on into the night questioning why some of the bums or dishwashers or soldiers he consorted with had more quality in their suffering than his Park Avenue pals."

When Monty was making "Red River" with John Wayne, director Howard Hawks tried to draw him into their circle but he wouldn't go along. Monty said, "The machismo thing repelled me because it seemed so forced and unnecessary."

On March 26, 1948, "The Search" opened to wide acclaim and Clift was suddenly famous. "He became," Joe Morella and Edward Epstein say in the book *The Rebel Hero in Films*, "a new hero to postwar audiences - a man with a conscience whose vulnerability and disillusionment with the world he wasn't the least bit embarrassed at revealing."

"In close-up, Monty was absolutely riveting," Bosworth notes. "One was practically absorbed into his eyes, which are clearly formidable and perhaps his best asset as an actor. Large, grey, infinitely expressive in his beautiful but rather deadpan face, they could register yearning, intelligence and despair in quick succession."

Clift was the first actor audiences could identify with instead of look up to, actor Bill Gunn said. "Yet at the same time he became a fantasy figure and romantic visual icon for moviegoers. And he had an individual attitude about himself. He wasn't bland, or all grins. He wasn't even that nice. He just was."

The New York Times' Caryl Rivers wrote: "All the girls in the eighth grade fell in love with Montgomery Clift in 'Red River.' His face had the perfection of a fragile porcelain vase. His beauty was so sensual and at the same time so vulnerable it was almost blinding...his dark eyes like the deep water of a cavern pool holding the promise of worlds of tenderness; the straight perfect blade of a nose that could have been the work of a sculptor the equal of Michelangelo."

Look magazine raved that Clift was now the hottest actor since Valentino.

Without being aware of it, audiences were witnessing a new kind of eroticism on film, one that sprang from the contradictions in Clift's personality, he was open, he was hidden, he was gay, he was straight; in essence, he seemed to represent a new kind of man, a man who refused to make judgments on sexual preference. "He was so ambiguous sexually it was a relief," said press agent Mike Mazlansky.

"For Monty, however," Bosworth says, "his sexual ambiguity was a private torture. He lived in New York between pictures so he could conduct his private life without too much publicity." And he avoided being seen with known gays.

Tennessee Williams said: "Monty disliked me because I was so open about being gay and he wasn't."

Bill LeMassena said being a public figure tore Monty up. "He hated, loathed and despised deception, and he was having to hide. In the theater he could have swung both ways and it wouldn't have mattered. But as a Hollywood star, he had to be the all-American male one hundred percent or else."

Monty said: "You have to be so completely self-centered and believe in yourself so totally or people will think you're nuts. Success out here has nothing to do with accomplishment. Some of the biggest successes here are the grandest slobs."

LeMassena says that Monty was extremely generous with most people: "He allowed people to come in to his life that had no business his life - the lowlifes, the degenerates, eccentric losers from New York and California. He allowed them in and he gave to them as deeply and fully as he did his friends. Yet he treated the man he was living 'like shit.' And this guy took it because he loved Monty and thought he was an inspired human being. Monty would get him to do everything for a party and then just before the guests would arrive, he would dismiss him. He knew better than to come back before the party was over."

He spoke of what he called "unisex" being "the wave of the future and he dreamed of getting married. He was sick of the pick-ups and the one night stands. He was even tired of his most recent lover, a young actor who borrowed money from him and seemed to be using him to further his career. So Monty would drink. And then he would wind up in bed with someone. Still he was lonely. Herb Machiz, a director, said: "The tragedy in most homosexual lives and for a person as sensitive as Monty was having to accept the tremendous disappointment of never finding a man worthy of him."

Elizabeth Taylor said Monty showed up one night at her house with a mincing chorus boy and the next with a very proper young lady, as if he was saying, "Look Ma, I can - and I must - do both." LeMassena said, "He'd pick up guys and bring them to the duplex. He'd sleep with them and that would be that. He'd get bored. Once he said to me, 'I don't understand it. I love men in bed, but I really love women."

But Taylor was not, as near as anyone has ever been able to

determine, one of Clift's female conquests. They remained close and, after refusing all scripts offered to him in 1955, he began "Raintree County" with Elizabeth in 1956. Then, on the night of May 12, after a party at Elizabeth's, driving down the mountaintop she lived on with Michael Wilding, the actor crashed his car. "He survived," Patricia Bosworth says in her biography of the actor, "and lived ten more years. But his real death occurred as he lay bleeding and half-conscious in Elizabeth Taylor's arms. Nothing would ever be the same for him after that."

"Before the accident," Basworth reported, "Clift had drifted into countless affairs with men and women. It suited his personality to have sex with a variety of partners. It was also a way of meeting different kinds of people, exploring different worlds, searching, always searching for the right person with whom he could develop a lasting relationship."

After the accident, Monty needed someone to take care of him and Giles, whom Monty met after making "The Young Lions," was willing to make himself useful. Giles was a charming Frenchman, 26, slightly built, with dark curly hair. "He was high strung and cried a lot," Bosworth says, "but he could make people laugh when he told jokes in his pronounced French accent." Giles had wanted a career in fashion and had been kept by a dress manufacturer for several years. After the accident, he moved into Clift's brownstone in New York in 1958. While making "Lonelyhearts" in Hollywood, Monty stashed Giles away at the Bel Air hotel and didn't allow him to leave.

He became addicted to Giles' scene of drugs and kept men, young Europeans who slept with both men and women for money. Giles organized parties at Monty's where chorus boys, male models, and hustlers wandered through. But, despite the ugliness, Monty remained "pure, untouched." "It was if the sordid-goings on passed through him and then disappeared into the air," Joshua Logan remembered.

Monty had a powerful relationship with his psychiatrist, Dr. Billy Silverberg. He saw him every day when he wasn't working, spoke of his great wisdom and kindness. Silverberg had set an impossible goal for Monty: to accept his homosexuality and live with it. But he hated being gay. "There is a deep-seated prejudice against homosexuality," Clift would say. "While there may be tolerance for it privately, it will never be accepted even in the most liberated circles."

Monty's brother Brooks maintains his brother was "bisexual." "I met two girls he got pregnant. He was never exclusively one thing or the other; he swung back and forth. Because we'd been raised in Europe where homosexuality was more or less accepted, he never felt ashamed - until much later when he grew up. Monty disliked effeminacy, and he used to talk wonderingly about how some heterosexual men are so effete and some gay men so masculine."

After the accident, Monty's drug addiction became more serious and sex less important. Cocaine began to have an attraction. He said there was a golden glow of self confidence, and it kills the pain of being yourself.

He remained unflinchingly loyal to his old friends Taylor and the jazz singer Libby Holman. He would cruise Forty-second Street in New York. And, after a split-up with Giles, few knew of the beatings he suffered at the hands of male hustlers, or the robberies that occurred because he was too drunk to stop them.

By the time he made "Freud," the four-time Academy Award nominee was uninsurable.

In comparing himself to his contemporary rival, Marlon Brando, Clift was the first to admit that the chemistry was lacking. "It's a chemical thing. Marlon connects more immediately with an audience than I do. Working harder doesn't seem to matter."

Brando himself said: "Monty was *the* actor. He was the one you measured yourself against."

Fellow actor Mike Kellin remembers: "When he acted a scene it was sculpted forever. There was a solidness about the work - a rock-like quality. There was nothing casual about his acting. If he had a genius it was that he revealed himself so totally as an actor - he stripped himself naked. He hid his real life - nobody was as mysterious or remote as Monty. But in his acting he revealed himself as powerfully as a scream."

Actor Don Keffer said, "He was in no way intellectual. His gift was emotional and intuitive. He has extraordinary imagination as well as extraordinary empathy for the characters he worked on. So much so that he could give each of them a shape and you could almost imagine what they were feeling and seeing."

In 1966, Monty was looking forward to working with Elizabeth Taylor again in "Reflections in a Golden Eye." He had stopped drinking to get into shape for the movie. Near midnight on the 22nd of July, his friend Lorenzo James asked Monty if he wanted to watch one of his movies, "The Misfits," which was on TV. He said no and went to bed. In the morning, he was found by James "lying face up in bed, glasses on, no clothes on. Right arm flexed. Both fists clenched. No evidence of trauma." The results of the autopsy indicated their was no evidence of foul play or suicide. "Mr. Clift died of occlusive coronary artery disease."

Clift's last film opened on November 16, 1966; it was titled "The Defector."

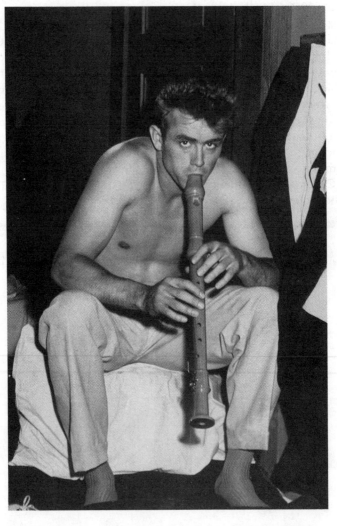

James Dean blows a mean recorder in "East of Eden"

James Dean

"He's a punk and a helluva talent.
He likes racing cars, waitresses - and waiters."
- Film Director Elia Kazan

James Dean idolized Montgomery Clift. "He was affected by Brando but he was more moved by Monty," actor Bill Gunn, a friend of both stars, said. "Jimmy dug Monty's fractured personality, his dislocated quality. Brando was too obvious. Monty had more class."

It is certainly possible that Jimmy empathized with Clift's sexual ambiguity, recognizing how the conflicts within affected his behavior. But unlike Clift, who had a privileged childhood and a doting mother, Jimmy's mother died when he was nine and he went to live with relatives until his father was able to take care of him. He never forgave his father for sending him away and carried that resentment with him all of his life.

Jimmy was sturdily built but small for a boy his age, with a handsome, almost beautiful face. He wore eyeglasses because he was extremely nearsighted.

During his high school years in a small town in Indiana, Jimmy discovered he had a real talent for acting and he was introduced to an experience that was to start him on the road to the sexual ambivalence that would enable him to swing whichever way he needed to reach the top of his chosen profession. He had a schoolboy infatuation with Dr. James DeWeerd, a stocky, handsome pastor with a jovial laugh. Although a war hero, DeWeerd was considered "prissy" by the townspeople, some of whom called him "Dr. Weird." It was no secret he liked to take young boys to the YMCA gym and swim in the nude with them. After one such outing, Jimmy began to visit DeWeerd in the home the older man shared with his mother and their adventures began. DeWeerd introduced each new adventure by saying, "The more things you know how to do, and the more things you experience, the better off you will be." Jimmy and DeWeerd shared many personal intimacies which the pastor warned Jimmy never to reveal.

Jimmy was extremely busy during his senior year. When he wasn't acting or having little "adventures" with Dr. DeWeerd, he was starring on the basketball court. He also began a relationship with a woman who was teaching physical education at his high school. By this time, Jimmy believed he could have sex with either a man or a woman, and with ease. But his Quaker upbringing made him feel gay sex was wrong, thus he was never able to let anyone, male or female, get truly close to him.

Dean biographer Joe Hymans said that depending on which of his ex-lovers he interviewed Dean was either heterosexual, asexual, bisexual, or homosexual. Friends described him as generous and mean- spirited, moody and a party animal, macho and feminine, wise for his years and supremely adolescent. But everyone agrees he was a fascinating person and tremendously gifted actor who was able to tap into something deep inside of himself that resonates within all of us.

During his early days in Hollywood, Jimmy parked cars at a restaurant and one day he met Rogers Brackett, a 35-year-old advertising executive who had many contacts in the film capitol. When Brackett asked Jimmy to move in the young man did so immediately. Brackett got him parts on radio shows and bit parts in movies. He dated starlets but went to exclusive parties often given by and attended by gays.

Eventually, when he was twenty-one, Jimmy went to New York to pursue his acting career, working as a dishwasher and attending mass auditions known as cattle calls. Brackett followed him to New York and they lived there together but, Hymans maintains, Jimmy's feelings for gay men alternated between resentment and friendliness: "Although he disliked the role he had to play with them, they were a potential source of employment."

One of Dean's early affairs was with another actor, Jonathan Gilmore. One night, Jimmy asked Jonathan, "Can you be fucked?"

"Jesus, I don't think so," Jonathan said.

"I want to try to fuck you," Jimmy said.

They kissed and tried to make love.

"Jimmy," Jonathan says now, "was neither homosexual or

bisexual. I think he was multisexual. He once said that he didn't think there was any such thing as being bisexual. He felt that if someone really needed emotional support from a man he would probably be homosexual, but if he needed emotional support from a woman he would be more heterosexual." Jimmy himself once said, "I'm certainly not going through life with one hand tied behind my back."

After months of near starvation, he began working regularly on TV but, interestingly enough, it was his appearance on Broadway as a homosexual Arab houseboy that made audiences and critics notice him. His role in Gide's "The Immoralist" won him both a Tony and Daniel Blum Award, which brought him to the attention of Hollywood.

When Jimmy was becoming successful in Hollywood, Brackett lost his job and wanted to borrow some money from Jimmy, Dean refused, claiming that he now had a business manager and such a loan would have to be done in a businesslike manner. When Brackett protested, reminding Jimmy of the times he had helped him out without a written promise of repayment let alone a demand for collateral, Jimmy retorted that he had outgrown Brackett and his "fairy friends."

In the spring of 1954, Elia Kazan cast Dean as the bad brother Cal in the Cain-and-Abel-type story "East of Eden," based on the John Steinbeck best-seller. His screen test, with handsome Dick Davalos playing the good brother, set in Cal's bedroom, had homosexual overtones and in the final version of the film the scene had to be cut entirely.

Dean was four months and nine days shy of his 25th birthday when he died in a grinding head-on crash on California's Route 46. On Friday, September 30, 1955, he was driving to a sports car race in Salinas when his Porsche Spyder thundered into a Ford sedan driven by college student Donald Turnupseed at about 85 mph in the crossroads hamlet of Chalome, 25 miles east of Paso Robles.

Dean died instantly. His body was battered, his neck broken.

Shortly after the accident, friend Nick Adams said that when he told Dean he didn't care for the car, that he "felt funny" about it, the star laughed and said his death in a speeding car was ordained

And after the accident, the car itself continued to follow a deadly script. Researchers Richard Winer and Nancy Osborn of *Old Cars* magazine have traced the history of the Porsche.

After the accident, the original owner, custom-car builder George Barris, bought it for $2,500, even though it had given him an "eerie" feeling every time he got near it even before Dean bought it from him. "I bought it for the parts," Barris says. "Now I wish I'd sent it to the junk yard to be shredded."

What Barris did was sell the engine to one doctor and the drive train to another. Both doctors, amateur race car drivers, were to die later at the wheels of their cars.

After two of the fans who tried to steal pieces of the wreck were seriously cut, Barris decided to lock the thing away, but shortly after he did, the California Highway Patrol called him wanting to use the car in a traveling highway safety exhibit. Barris welded pieces of the car together so that it would not fall apart. It was shown without incident at two exhibits, then stored in a patrol garage in Fresno overnight, to be shown the following day. That night, the place caught fire and every car in the garage was totally destroyed – except the Porsche, which suffered only minor damage to its paint.

The car was taken to Sacramento, where it slipped off its exhibition stand and broke the hip of a teenaged bystander.

Several weeks later, when the car was being transported to an exhibit in Salinas, the driver lost control of the truck and was thrown from the cab. The Porsche tore loose from its moorings and crashed down on the driver, killing him instantly.

Two years later, en route to Oakland on a truck, the Porsche broke in two and dropped onto a freeway, causing a non-fatal accident. Barris said that the way it was welded together, it was virtually impossible that such a thing could have happened.

In 1960, the car was trucked to Florida where the state highway patrol used it in a safety exhibit in Miami. After the show, the car was crated and put on a truck for the return trip to Los Angeles. But somewhere between the two cities, in an ironic touch that would have delighted Edgar Allan Poe, the truck, its driver, and the Dean death-car vanished and haven't been seen since.

To add to the weirdness, Dean's tombstone disappeared on

the night of April 12, 1983 and was replaced by a crudely fashioned wooden cross. Two weeks later, the tombstone reappeared, only to disappear again in August of that same year. A new stone, bolted with steel rods and attached to the base with space-age glue, now appears to be intact. Pieces from the tombstone have been chipped and chiseled away by fans who have come from all over the world to visit the gravesite in Fairmont, Indiana. They smother the stone with lipstick kisses; make rubbings with paper and charcoal; and place red jackets with the color upturned and packs of Chesterfield cigarettes on the grave. The police do have their limits, however, and have hauled away people lying on the grave in sleeping bags, holding seances over the headstone, and, of course, couples fucking at the gravesite and even gays ejaculating on it.

For Dean's funeral, Dr. James DeWeerd, then a pastor in Cincinnati, flew by private plane from Ohio following his noon telecast there to deliver the eulogy, "James Dean: A Play in Three Acts." Jimmy's pallbearers were high school friends and members of his basketball squad.

At the time of his death, neither "Rebel Without a Cause" or "Giant," the film based on the Edna Ferber best-seller which he made with Elizabeth Taylor and Rock Hudson in Texas, had been released. Only "East of Eden" had been shown.   When "Rebel" was released soon after his death, fans were delighted to see him as the prince of teenage torment, sometimes flying at his father in a rage, sometimes curled up in a fetal crouch. Director Nick Ray used Jimmy's bisexuality to good purpose and his scenes with Sal Mineo are the best part of the film for gaymales. (Sal denied he and Dean had been lovers but said they could have, "just like that.")

On the day after Jimmy died, the autumn air all across America was filled with the high-pitched wail of teenagers in mourning. "Teen grief," *People* magazine said, "got its first poster boy." After his death, Dean's fans grew to legendary proportions. Many of them refused to accept his death and a worldwide cult developed. "For young fans in the '50s," *People* said, "an era that valued conformity, Dean's scowl, his motorcycle and his back-off manner personified their own dream of breaking free – of parents, authority and the world's expectations. He called himself 'a serious-minded and intense little devil,' and he meant it. His injured manner made him irresistible to young fans. But they misunderstood him too. In life, their hero wasn't a rebel so much as a riddle. Always starved for affection, Dean became a boy toy for both sexes. Yet he also had a loner's petulance that could make him a brat without a pack who indulged dark moods that drove off friends and lovers."

Joe Hyams says, "Often called a cult figure or an international cultural icon, Dean has lost none of his appeal and stands as a personification not just of the restless youth of the '50s but of some larger notion, something that embraces all the tragedy and hope of youth, particularly American youth. No one before or since has ever looked better in jeans and a leather jacket. Jimmy doesn't look like anyone else but generations have sought to look like him."

"If he had lived," *People* reminds us, "he would now be over sixty. Because he died, he will always be 24."

By 1991, more than 250 companies had registered items from the James Dean Foundation, including a life-sized mannequin made in Japan, jogging suits, T-shirts, posters, pillow cases and sunglasses. Mark Roesler, president of the Foundation said, "In a homogenous society like Japan, they admire rebels. In England, his appeal is from nostalgia. And the French think he is sexy."

On the last weekend in September every year in Fairmont, fans meet to imitate and otherwise eulogize the late actor.

As reported by Paul Alexander, who is working on a biography of Dean, the fans wear blue jeans, a white T-shirt, and a red windbreaker, the outfit the actor wore in "Rebel Without A Cause." They all "do" Dean, tucking in the chin and tilting down the head ever so slightly, squinting the eyes just so, hunching the shoulders. They also have a look-alike contest that is the highlight of the festival.

One attendee told Alexander, "I really loved that guy." Another showed up with the crucifixion pose from "Giant" tattooed on his back. It cost him $1,200 and enormous pain. Another reported he had a dream: "I could hear him saying that my body was perfect for his soul and that he wanted to enter my body. I felt him coming into me." He pointed to his heart: " I actually feel Jimmy right now, right here."

"His early death was a sordid crack-up, not the glorious immolation that every adolescent secretly holds in his or her heart," Ty Burr says, "but the reason his cult holds is that Dean let us know he saw it coming. Pinned in the headlights of self-annihilation, he raged for us all."

In 1992, the Foundation earned almost $6 million for the relatives of James Dean; not bad when you consider his salary for making "Rebel Without a Cause" was $10,000.

Perhaps it was another legendary actor, Humphrey Bogart, who summed the Dean phenomenon up best: "He left behind a legend. If he had lived, he never would have been able to live up to the publicity."

Tyrone Power

Cary Grant

Rock Hudson

Anthony Perkins

After They've Gone:
Ty, Cary, Rock and Tony

Tyrone Power

"I did consider marrying Tyrone Power. But I decided he was too fond of the boys for it to work out."
— Alice Faye

Of Judy Garland's numerous affairs, David Shipman writes in his biography of the songbird, "An involvement that was undoubtedly serious – one also complicated by sexual ambiguity – was with actor Tyrone Power, upon whom Garland had developed a crush after her marriage to bandleader David Rose fell apart. Power was in fact homosexual – and if Garland wasn't aware of this, she was the only person in Hollywood who wasn't."

Coming from a multi-generational theatrical family, Tyrone Power was born in Cincinnati in 1913. His father was a noted stage actor, his grandfather was a celebrated pianist, and his great-grandfather was a famous comedian in his native Ireland. There was never much doubt as to what career young Ty would choose. When Power was seven, after living in both Ohio and New York, his family moved to California because of the youth's ill health. After graduating high school, Power attended a Shakespearean drama school, and his first professional role was on the Chicago stage in a production of "The Merchant of Venice."

Power moved to New York in 1935, making his Broadway debut in 1936. It was his numerous stage appearances which led to a contract with 20th Century Fox, and in 1936, Power moved to Hollywood to begin his film career (though he had appeared in one other film in 1932, "Tom Brown of Culver," while visiting Los Angeles as a teenager). The exceptionally handsome Power became a star with his third Fox film, "Lloyds of London," and for fifteen years afterward, was one of the studio's biggest box-office draws, except for the years (1942 through 1945) he served as a Marine pilot in World War II.

Though Power is most often referred to as a film star, he did in fact return to the Broadway stage and other theatrical venues for most of his life.

"While living in New York in the years prior to his budding film career," Raymond Murray, editor of *Images in the Dark*, says, "Power was lovers with Robin Thomas, the stepson of John Barrymore. Their relationship lasted for several years, and was ended by Power when he moved to Hollywood."

He soon married actress Annabella, which ended in divorce, and married twice thereafter. Rock Hudson was godfather to Power's son, Tyrone III. Hector Arce's *The Secret Life of Tyrone Power* delves into Power's relationships with both men and women, citing brief affairs with Errol Flynn and Lorenz Hart, among others. He was supposedly a lover of an unnamed actor and co-star who was one of Fox's biggest stars of the 1940s.

At 45, Power died of a heart attack while working on "Solomon and Sheba."

Cary Grant

Paul Rudnick, writing as Libby Gelman-Waxner, says Cary Grant is her Ultimate Dream Date: "My dream date would be a good actor, but talent isn't necessary; mostly, he must seem like someone who, if he met me or any of my friends, would sweep us off our feet; take us out for an intimate dinner; look terrific, but not too perfect; reveal that he's both sexy and sensitive but not a wimp; make us feel sexy, thin, and appreciated; and generally behave like the exact opposite of the guys we're married to or currently seeing ('seeing' means the man is too phobic even to use the words 'dating' or 'going out with'). Cary Grant, as my colleague Pauline Kael has pointed out, is the ultimate Dream Date; and while I love Sly Stallone, Arnold Schwarzenegger, and even Danny DeVito, they will never be Dream Dates, except maybe for each other.

"Dennis Quaid is so sexy that he almost goes beyond Dream Date-dom and into the Dangerous Zone; this is the category for guys who might say, Let's have sex in a car going off a cliff, and you'd say, Let me just leave a note for the sitter. Bruce Willis, like Richard Gere, is his own Dream Date."

In 1980, comic actor Chevy Chase appeared on a talk show

and, while commending Cary Grant for his acting genius, suddenly limped his wrist and lisped, "I understand he was a homo. What a gal!" Grant, still very much alive, slapped Chase with a $10 million lawsuit which eventually was dropped. Indeed, Cary was not about to air his dirty laundry in public.

"The most successful of Hollywood's romantic light-comedy actors - suave, sophisticated, with a dashing boulevardier smile and oh-so sexy cleft chin which drove both sexes to distraction - Cary Grant endured a personal life far removed from his screen image," says David Bret in *Quintessentially Queer*.

Born Archibald Alec Leach, the actor began showing an interest in the theatre at the age of six and his father signed the consent paper for him to join a troupe of travelling acrobats, The Penders, declaring him to be the then legal working age of ten.

"Archie stilt-walked all over England with The Penders, and in the summer of 1920 sailed with them for an engagement in New York aged sixteen and well aware of his sexuality," Bret insists. "His first love affair took place on ship, with an Australian music-hall star ten years his senior, Charlie Spangles, who later wowed Broadway audiences with his 'Joseph and Josephine' routine, for which he dressed one half of his body as a bearded sailor, the other as a beautiful woman.

"Whilst working the Hippodrome with The Penders, Archie met the female impersonator Francis Renault, who became his lover whilst the youth was familiarizing himself with New York. This relationship ended abruptly when be was introduced to the Australian painter-designer Jack Kelly. Archie moved into Kelly's Greenwich Village apartment, where they were soon joined by Charlie Spangles, and he augmented his meager income by taking a job as a sandwich-board man on stilts, advertising theatre productions in Times Square. He also appeared in a number of forgettable revues until 1925, when his enormous comedy potential was recognized by the famous producer, Jean Dalrymple, who cast him opposite Jeanette MacDonald in *Boom-Boom!*

"By now there was an additional lover, Phil Charig, a hunky young composer who had worked in England with musical comedy star Jack Buchanan. Hinting at his fondness for Australians, Charig nicknamed Archie 'Kangaroo', and took him under his wing, though the rivalry between Charig and Jack Kelly for Archie's affections was thwarted by Archie's rapidly developing promiscuity. As more and more lovers appeared nightly at their apartment, Cary devised a 'code' wherein neither Charig nor Kelly was allowed into the place if classical music could be heard playing in the bedroom - this meant that Archie was 'entertaining' any one of the dozen young men who formed his 'kangaroo circle.'

In Hollywood, Cary and Charig moved into an apartment on North Sweetzer Avenue, making no pretensions about how close they were. Any would-be scandal was covered up by having Cary pose for beach photographs with pretty girls. Then, just as this ploy seemed to be working, he met Randolph Scott. Scott, whom Bret describes as a "tall, 195-pound beef-packed blond athlete from Virginia" had already had an affair with Howard Hughes and with Cary, "it was absolute passion from the word go."

The lovebirds set up housekeeping in Santa Monica and engaged a gay secretary and threw wild parties. *Modern Screen* magazine reported, tongue-in-cheek, that "'Cary and Randy are really opposite types. Cary is the gay, impetuous one, Randy is calm and quiet." *Photoplay* spent a "typical" day with the couple, who were snapped cooking each other breakfast, enjoying a singsong at the piano, and frollicking by the pool in skimpy shorts.

In his book *From Rags to Bitches*, Mr. Blackwell says he had an affair with Tyrone Power and was a frequent guest at the home of Grant and Scott. But "the details aren't important. This isn't a porno book! I was pleased that I became part of unions, part of relationships that gave me confidence, that made me feel wanted. I gave them, those people – and there were many more – the same feeling of joy, of confidence, of need. Cary and Randy were just two terrific people who took me in. What those two did for me, at that time of my life, I would have no idea how to repay them."

As Cary's fame increased, Paramount warned him to "straighten" himself out and he began dating actress Virginia Cherrill.

"But," Bret says, "this had a detrimental effect on his personality. He grew moody, depressed and unpredictable, compelled as he was to reject his sexuality by presenting an image which was for him unnatural and hypocritical."

Early in 1934, Cary and Virginia visited his family in England. They travelled on different ships. "Meanwhile," Bret reveals, "Cary and Randy gave their fellow passengers plenty to gossip about by sharing a cabin and engaging in a menage-a-trois with the actor David Manners. Within days of arriving in London, Cary was rushed to a hospital suffering from severe anal bleeding. Doctors diagnosed a precancerous condition of the rectum and a torn sphincter muscle. For obvious reasons every attempt was made to prevent such a story from hitting the press, though Tallulah Bankhead did find out and quipped, 'I always said Randy Scott was a pain the ass, darling!' Although he could not stop such remarks, Cary hoped that by marrying Virginia he would no longer be thought of as gay."

But, according to Bret, the marriage was a disaster. "When the newlyweds moved into the Santa Monica beachhouse, Randy stayed put. Cary became more promiscuous than ever, and began bashing his wife. On two reported occasions Virginia had to have stitches in her face after he had hit her, though Cary pleaded amnesia the next day. Eventually she filed for divorce on grounds of cruelty, as did his next three wives: Woolworth heiress Barbara Hutton, actress Betsy Drake, and sctress and now filmmkaer Dyan Cannon, who bore him his only child, Jennifer, in 1966."

Cannon told the French gay magazine *Hommes*, "Being married to him was hell. He saw things only from his point of view. He was egotistical, and when high on LSD and booze would fly into the most terrible rages and thrash me for no reason at all."

It was rumored that Cary's first three marriages were not consummated, with his wives being compelled to turn a blind eye to his indiscretions and the almost constant presence of a regular male lover - supplementing the everready Randolph Scott.

Bret reveals that in 1942 Cary was arrested after an "encounter" with a young man in a department store lavatory. When the police announced that someone would have to be prosecuted, Cary was dropped off between the store and the police precinct with a ticking-off, and another well-known gay actor arrested in his place after a huge amount of money had exchanged hands. The man was later released on grounds of insufficient evidence.

Cary appeared in drag in "I Was A Male War Bride" and his most famous line is found in "Bringing Up Baby:" after Katharine Hepburn removes his clothes while he is taking a shower and he is forced to answer the door wearing her dressing gown, he tells the caller, "I just went gay all of a sudden!" The most classic set of innuendos, however, occurs in "My Favorite Wife," in which Cary stars with Irene Dunne and Randolph Scott. Cary plays a lawyer who has remarried, believing his first wife to have drowned in a shipwreck. She has in fact spent several years on a desert island with fitness-freak Randy - "a clean-living, 100 percent American" - but returns to eventually break up the new marriage and reclaim her husband. The denouement scene occurs at a hotel poolside where Randy thrills the patrons with Tarzan-like displays on the trapeze-rings. Instead of getting angry, Cary's eyes almost pop out of his head when his adversary strips off to take a dip. "Is that Johnny Weissmuller?" a woman asks, to which he quips, as Randy flexes his pecs and careens into the water, "I wish it were!" Later the pair meet for lunch, and Cary asks him, "Does turkey appeal to you, or do you confine yourself to raw meat?" And when Dunne falls into the water and the rivals rush to her home to collect a change of clothes, Cary is caught in one of her hats and holding a dress up in front of him. "It's for a friend of mine. He's waiting downstairs," he feebly explains.

Rock Hudson

"(His) image may be synthetic but the man is real. There is an inner core of warmth and decency there that can't be counterfeited – and it plays on the screen."
– George Stevens, director of "Giant"

"The life and career of Rock Hudson was riddled with contradictions, half-truths, misquotes, movie magazine pap, and lies," Garfield Williams says. "He was not (as reported) discovered lounging against his truck in front of Universal Studios."

People wanted to believe it was that easy, but it was just another Tinseltown myth. "Rock Hudson worked hard to capture their millions of audience members. Becoming a star entailed much more than just being at the right place at the right time. One had to have that special 'something.' It should be mentioned that in the Hollywood of the 1950s actors were put under studio contracts and showcased. The competition was ruthless for the box office dollars. Few succeeded... The fatality rate was staggering. The air at the top was very thin indeed.

"Another myth about the Hudson persona was where he lived, and how. As his fame grew, so did the exaggerations. The gay undercurrent of gossip maintained that his home was a cornucopia of pornographic toys, teens, and temperament. Although the tales were a bit exaggerated, Hudson actually did have a rather ostentatiously gay home, especially by the standards of the day. There were five-foot-high, wrought iron statues of nude boys which stood in his flower beds. There was also a huge headboard at the top of the bed carved with male nudes draped in garlands. Furthermore, there was no mistaking the fact that Rock liked his male skin-flicks. He had a 'flower child' in a 'head shop' on Wilshire Boulevard send him the newest triple-X reels as soon as they got in his back room. It is true he hid where he lived like a national secret, and photographs were never taken of the house or grounds, in order to maintain the one luxury that fame steals away: privacy.

"There was some truth to the gossip mumbled around the bars, though, for Hudson had a high sex drive. (Very normal for a healthy, homosexual male.) It is ironic that he told close friends that once someone he became interested in realized there was going to be sex – with Rock Hudson – they became intimidated by the fame, and impotency was often the result. An embarrassing limp lay from usually rock-hard Romeos. The normally aggressive, muscular hunks seemed to wither into fumbling schoolboys, intimidated by the star myth. Rock said that at times he wished his name was John Smith, just an anonymous guy out for a good time. Fame could be an ordeal when cruising, he said. Indeed, his fame was immense. Time would prove that no male star of the era rose higher or stayed longer, and no name sparked the public's imagination more, than that of Rock Hudson.

"Of course, Rock Hudson was not his real name. Although the star's real name is often listed as Roy Fitzgerald, this is inaccurate. Rock Hudson was born Roy Harold Scherer, Jr. in Winnetka, Illinois, on November 17, 1925. The six thousand citizens of Winnetka were situated fifteen miles north of the windy city of Chicago; it was a suburb of middle-class working people. His mother, Kay, and his father, Roy, Sr., were poor by 1920s standards. She was no jazzy flapper, just a pretty dark-haired housewife. He was a brooding, often unemployed auto mechanic. There were no stage aspirations in the Scherer household. The thought of anyone in the family pursuing a livelihood in the theater would have been laughable. Timid Kay had been to the vaudeville houses in Chicago's Loop. She had seen the stars in the 'flickers' too, and she was shocked. This was a well brought up young lady who thought the entertainment world was 'fast.' (She was right!)

"As the 20s ended, the Scherers separated and finally divorced. Roy, Sr. left to seek employment in Oregon, then California. He never returned; he moved out of Kay's life forever. The divorcee with an infant son to support now had to face the Depression of the 1930s. The bread lines with their grim-faced, unemployed workers were everywhere. She was lucky, finding work as a telephone operator. At this job she met a lineman named Wally whom she married in 1931. His full name was Wallace Fitzgerald and he adopted Kay's son, who then became Roy Fitzgerald – the name he used until Hollywood made other plans for him.

"His childhood was normal, but times were hard and money was short. Roy/Rock said he never realized he came from a poor family until he saw how they lived in Hollywood.

"The future star did not set the world on fire with his studies. He got poor grades and was known as a shy boy who slouched to minimized his towering frame. He was the tallest student in school, and practically all of his former classmates said he was 'nice,' but nothing exceptional. The opinion seemed to be that he was handsome, but not too bright. After gradutaing from high school, Roy enlisted in the Navy, becoming a mechanic on cruiser planes. With this sudden exposure to a navy of strapping young men, it was not long before Roy realized what he liked sexually. His fleeting sexual experiences with bunk mates were secretive and fraught with the risk of court-martial or physical violence.

"Luckily," Williams says, "no one suspected that the masculine, gangly six-foot-four giant was homosexual. He served until the end of the war and was honorably discharged in California, but he did not return to Illinois. The thriving gay subculture of Long Beach was well-known to Roy by the time of his discharge. He had cruised the beaches and slept in the sea 'shacks,' but Hollywood was where he wanted to be. He believed the fan magazines and despite the million to one odds, he moved closer to Hollywood to get into the movies.

"Soon, he was settled in a tiny flat in West Hollywood, and had gotten a job driving a truck for 'Budget Pack.' With his weekly salary and discharge pay, he was doing fine, just fine, but he knew this was not nearly fine enough. He had portrait pictures taken and sent them to every studio and agent's office in town. He did not get a single response for a month, and was beginning to grow depressed. Then the day came when David O. Selznick's talent office called and set up an appointment with the head of an agency, Henry Willson. Roy had never heard of Willson, but he would soon be an important entity in the newcomer's career, and personal life as well.

"Henry Willson was a powerful name in the movie industry. He was also the most well-known homosexual in the industry at the time and made few pretensions about his sexuality.

During a period when most men felt they had to hide it in the closet, Henry Willson said 'to hell with that.' A short, middle-aged man, with a receding hairline, a fleshy body, a big nose, a soft chinline, Willson had an insatiable sex appetite. He knew he was not attractive, but this mattered little; there was an army of movie-crazy young men who would do anything for a chance at stardom. Willson was well aware of this and took full advantage, exploiting their bodies while dangling the bait of Hollywood fame. He nightclubbed with his harem of fawning boyfriends. The starmaker once discovered a handsome, blond nineteen-year-old named Art Gelien, and changed his name to Tab Hunter. He negotiated an exclusive contract at Warner Brothers for him, and launched his million-dollar "heart throb" career. Willson magic was repeated with an even blonder hunk soon to be called Troy Donahue. However, when Roy Fitzgerald was ushered into Willson's office, the rules of the fawning game were instantly changed. The agent thought he had seen it all before, but he was wrong. He was bowled over by the chiseled features and winning smile; this was the handsomest man he had ever seen! From that moment on, he left his other clients to the horrors of the unemployment lines and studio intrigues. Presto! The romance of the powerful agent and the would-be star began. Willson now devoted all his energies to the personal and professional fortunes of Rock Hudson.

"Universal Studios was a movie factory, but it was also a training ground. It not only put its new contractees into small bit parts, it gave them larger parts when they showed promise. It held drama classes, and it was mandatory for all new players to attend. They stressed diction, poise, publicity and had a full gym on the back lot for working out. Almost immediately, people on the lot could sense Rock had something special. He was the most photogenic of all his contemporaries. He had no bad side. He was cooperative to the extreme, and took his acting lessons seriously. Little by little he started working up a credit list of many long forgotten 'quickies.' During the filming of one of Rock Hudson's earliest pictures, 'Seminole,' Tyrone Power walked across the lot to the sound stage. On this particular day, the youthful Rock was nearnaked in his loincloth, Native American body makeup, and moccasins. Needless to say, Rock's rock-hard muscles were spectacular to see. The sight was not lost on Power. His suave charms and the smiling shyness of Hudson blended immediately: they adjourned to the commissary and over coffee made a date for dinner that evening. This chance meeting fostered the blazing affair of the fading 1940s movie idol and the burgeoning 1950s future star.

"One of Hollywood's most forgotten and underrated directors was London-born Edmund Goulding. He directed some of movietown's most famous stars in their greatest roles and pulled a star performance out of Ty Power in his return-from-the-service picture, 'The Razor's Edge' in 1946. This assignment is where the 'meeting of the minds' occurred; the dignified fifty-year-old director with the perfectly cut gray hair, Saville Row suits, and quiet manner was the most respected homosexual in the picture business. The gossips knew that 'ladies' director' George Cukor was homosexual, but he low-profiled it. Everyone knew about Goulding, but there was never any talk about it. No one would dare to approach this dignified artist with personal questions – much less hint that he slept with men! He was not 'mysterious.' He socialized with the heterosexual hierarchy as their equal. He had a very social wife who came with designer gowns, glib conversation, and a cool manner. They were accepted in the finest parlors, but the sophisticated Englishman had a cleverly hidden secret life. Only the true insiders knew that Edmund Goulding had a midnight tandem marriage, and a list of 'play for pay' players who used his Beverly Hills mansion to rendezvous with the rest of his gay friends. By the time Goulding was assigned to Fox's Tyrone Power drama, 'Nightmare Alley' Ty had been to the director's home often for parties – very private orgies indeed. With the cream of the goodlooking male hookers from the Sunset Strip, plenty of liquor and marijuana, and high walls to keep out unwanted eyes, the gay movie crowd relaxed.

"At one such party Power was startled to run into ladies' man Errol Flynn. The 'opium outed' swordsman was bleary eyed, but frank. He liked sex both ways and loved fellatio. At another party, Ty reacquainted himself with billionaire Howard Hughes and bedded the bisexual Howard once again. (The promiscuous Mr. Hughes had no shame! He loved the sex intrigues of the sordid jungle called Hollywood. On one of Ty's biggest successes, 'Blood and Sand,' Hughes bedded all the stars: Ty, Rita Hayworth, Linda Darnell, and the scenic designer, cameraman, and most of the male grips.)

"A star as big as Tyrone Power and a fast-rising newcomer like Hudson realized they had to be careful. They could be seen smiling at premieres, pictured dining in exclusive restaurants, sipping at Ciro's night club on the Strip, but little else. There were no designated gay bars in the 1950s. There were a few underground clubs that catered to 'that type,' but they were dangerous to patronize. The police raided them often (if they didn't pay off) and the name of everyone in attendance was published in the morning tabloids.

"There were few places for famous gay men to gather but Power said he knew the perfect place, and he suggested to Rock that they go there for a party. This was, of course, Goulding's secluded hide-a-way. The first evening opened up a new world for Rock Hudson: a world of soft lights, hard muscles, and available men. There was nude swimming in the lighted pool, fellatio in the lounge chairs, dancing on Italian marble, groping in the bedrooms, and a casual fantasy atmosphere that was a shock to the uptight newcomer who was constantly on guard to be macho. At one party, he met Goulding's boyfriend, a handsome blond contract actor at Paramount. At another gathering, has-been cowboy star 'Red' Barry made a pass at him. (The westerner was more infamous than famous; he once bedded Susan Hayward, and his screaming boyfriend threw a hairbrush at the exiting siren. The tabloids got wind of it and played it up big in headlines, but they changed the gender to 'girlfriend.' At both of these parties, the fledgling actor and the ol' cowpoke were both naked and drunk.) Yes, this world was a far cry from Winnetka.

"For the next couple of years Ty and Rock met at Goulding's or at a secluded beach house Ty leased in Malibu for trysting. Sometimes it was one-on-one, sometimes in groups, but as it so often happens, gradually it 'petered' out."

By 1954, by the time of the release of "Magnificent Obsession," Rock was getting 3,000 letters a week. He became the biggest star on the Universal lot, and would eventually become their biggest attraction ever. Thus, it became a serious matter when the scandal rag *Confidential* was planning to expose him. They supposed had the inside scoop on who he did "it" with, when, where and how often. "The studio powers went into a panic," Williams asserts. "A plan had to be worked out! Their devious natures saved the day. A sly tradeoff was agreed upon. 'Don't use anything on Rock and we'll give you Rory.' Rory? Yes, the next issue showed semi-star Rory Calhoun's ugly police pictures and told about his youthful criminal record. Insiders breathed a sigh of relief. The high-charged Hudson's career was saved, and eventually the sleazy monthly tabloid was bankrupted with lawsuits by other stars.

"Shortly after this near-miss with the tabloids, there were headlines about Rock: A marriage announcement! On November 2, 1955, he eloped to Santa Barbara with Phyllis Gates. They then sped to Florida and on to Jamaica for a flower-bedecked honeymoon. The pretty brunette with the perfect teeth and curvy figure just happened to be agent Henry Willson's secretary. The columnists said Miss Gates was a 'career girl' and soft-pedaled where she worked. Secretaries across the nation visualized themselves in her glass slippers. The American dream could come true. The girl behind the typewriter marries the hunky motion picture star and rides off on dreams of sex and sequins. The marriage lasted two turbulent years, until Phyllis sued for divorce as the flashbulbs popped on April 10,1958, citing 'extreme mental cruelty' (Rock said nothing), and she got their honeymoon house on Warbler Place as her permanent residence. She also got $35,000 in stocks and $250 a week for ten years."

Many years later she would write a book, denying that the marriage was arranged to stop the gay talk that was swirling around the Hudson persona.

By now, Hudson was at his most popular, being Oscar-nominated for his role in "Giant." The charms of co-star James Dean were definitely not for him – but, Williams insists, he did warm up to newcomer Sal Mineo. They went out a few times. Hudson confided to friends after filming was over that it was nothing serious, just a few dates. Years later, given some booze to free his tongue, Sal would say the encounters were more than just dates, he said they were very sexual indeed.

"The gay culture at L.A.'s Manhattan Beach was strong,"

Williams says. "They entertained often and were even popular with straight locals (the rich, influential and fun crowd.) It was a very progressive gay community for the early 1970s. One year, a group of gay men celebrated Dietrich's birthday and set out campy invitations. At the party, the drag queens in the crowd worked hard to be glamorous and as 'Marlene' as they could be. The next year, someone suggested sending out invitations to a marriage between Rock Hudson and Jim Nabors. Everyone laughed, but that was just what they did. The mock ceremony was a hoot, complete with blue tuxedos, wide lapels, and middle-aged 'flower girls.'

"This seemingly harmless joke had some startling repercussions. A gossip columnist accidentally got hold of one of the invitations, and believed the flower child foolishness was real. He broadcast the news as gospel and every stand-up comic from coast to coast lampooned the ceremony as part of their act. The entire nation was tittering at the thought of Gomer Pyle and the hunky Hudson in wedded bliss.

"The truth of the matter was that Rock had appeared on Nabor's TV variety show, and they had become casual friends. There was never a sexual union. Ironically, of all the Rock affairs that could have been whispered about and been true, this one never happened. The two liked each other. They both liked the bubbly and sang drunken barroom ditties together. Now suddenly they could not socialize or even be pictured together. Pictures would add proof to the rumors. When Jim moved permanently to Hawaii, Rock called to wish him well, but was reluctant to visit. Unfortunately, these friends of many years never saw each other again because of false rumors."

At 57, with his movie role offers few and far between, Rock went on the road, touring in "Camelot." He acquired a companion, a 29-year-old tall, good looking blond with clear blue eyes, mustache, a pumped up body, and a pleasant likable manner. His name was Marc Christian and although there would be later problems, at the beginning the relationship was happy.

Then Rock noticed a sore on his neck, and he had started losing weight. At first the loss was welcomed, for middle age had thickened him around the waist. He needed to exercise vigorously to keep his weight down. Suddenly the pounds started to melt off, but the sore never healed. Finally, he went to his doctor, and after extensive testing, the dreaded AIDS diagnosis was confirmed.

"This was June 1984," Williams recalls. "For the next few months he told friends that he was fine. (He said he was dieting to tighten up his physique and because he seemed in such general good health no one questioned the logic.) Those around him (except, it seems, Marc Christian) finally became alarmed. The press started asking blunt questions about his suddenly skeletal appearance. He tried to be casual, but the pose was getting harder by the day. The reporters were accustomed to a beefy, laughing Hudson, but now he seemed tired and bony. After his appearance in December on the 'Dynasty' TV series, even fans suspected something was wrong. He looked terrible, a shadow of his former self.

"As a favor to former co-star Doris Day, he had promised to appear on Monday, July 15, 1985 for a press conference to launch her TV show about animals. Since her retirement, Doris had lost contact with most of her show business friends. She lived in Carmel as a recluse and busied herself with animal rights causes. She had not seen Rock in over two years, although they had remained close by phone. She had no idea he had been ill, but once she saw him she tried to stop him from facing the press. He could not be discouraged; he had promised. His appearance was so shocking and his mumbled responses so incoherent that no one asked any personal questions. Rock Hudson had always been well liked by the press. Now, he stunned the assembly into a sad silence. Soon the entire world would know the real reason for his appearance."

There were hundreds of reporters outside the American Hospital in Paris on the gray morning of July 25, 1985. A spokesman arrived and read a formal statement: "Mr. Rock Hudson has Acquired Immune Deficiency Syndrome which was diagnosed in the United States. He came to Paris to consult with a specialist in this disease." He ended the statement by reading, "He doesn't have any idea how he contracted AIDS."

The public started to think, "if Rock Hudson could be infected, a person who laughed with Doris Day, co-starred with John Wayne, and socialized with President Reagan, it could happen to anyone." It was suddenly an illness that could afflict the most respected members of society. The fanatics, who said the "gay plague" was a sign from above, were suddenly being silenced. The cards, letters of cheer, and well-wishers arrived by the thousands.

Rock Hudson died on October 2, 1985, at the age of 59. He had been given the last rites by a Roman Catholic priest and received communion. A Pentecostal prayer group led by singer Pat Boone and his wife Shirley visited, and his friends were there. Ironically, on the very day of his death, the United States House of Representatives appropriated $190 million toward finding a cure for AIDS. "If Rock had known," Williams says, "he would have roared with laughter. You just know he would have said, 'Well, it's about time.'"

Film historian Raymond Murray sums it up: "He was one of the most popular box-office stars of the 1950s and early '60s, appearing in a series of successful melodramas and sophisticated sex comedies. He was voted more than once the world's most favorite actor. He was nominated for an Oscar. And he was the star of one of the most popular TV shows of the 1970s ('McMillan and Wife'). But, sadly, it is not impressive acting credentials for which actor Rock Hudson is most remembered: for Hudson was the first well-known personality to die of AIDS, and to an entire nation he put 'a face' to an 'anonymous' disease." Writer Vito Russo had commented: "This is a watershed in shattering the myth of what gay people are. He really is gentle and macho and strong and soft-spoken...and gay. It shatters that old limp-wristed stereotype." And author Armistead Maupin said, "His visibility as a gay person would mean a lot toward cleaning up misconceptions the American public has about homosexuality.

Rock himself said it best, "I am not happy I have AIDS, but if that is helping others, I can, at least, know that my own misfortune has had some positive worth."

Anthony Perkins

In the mid-1950s, I found a role model of a sort in Tony Perkins, the tall, sensitive young man who invariably fell into bed with an understanding older woman. I thought there was hope for me yet!

The son of Osgood Perkins, a noted actor of the early 20th century, Anthony was born in New York in 1932. He started acting as a teenager in summer stock, which led to his film debut in 1953's "The Actress." Afterward, he appeared on TV, and on Broadway in "Tea and Sympathy," taking over for John Kerr. In 1955, he auditioned for "East of Eden," losing out to James Dean. A year later, he appeared opposite Gary Cooper in "Friendly Persuasion," and his performance was so good he was nominated for an Oscar and his career took off.

"Perkins was painfully shy," Raymond Murray reveals, "and not coincidentally many of his early roles shared this characteristic. It is in these parts in which Perkins excelled; his best performances ('Friendly Persuasion,' 'Fear Strikes Out,' 'The Matchmaker' among them) are founded in the sensitive young man mold. After the tremendous success in 1960 of 'Psycho,' Perkins landed few good parts, due in large part to his identification as Norman Bates. In the 1970s, a more mature Perkins fared much better appearing in a series of character parts either in lead or secondary roles. He also co-wrote with Stephen Sondheim the thriller 'The Last of Sheila.'"

In an 1983 interview with *People* magazine, Perkins admitted he had numerous gay affairs, but called them "unsatisfying."

Perkins said these unsatisfying relationships drove him to drugs. And he had his share of scrapes with the law because of this, Michael Munn reported in the book *Hollywood Bad*. "He fell foul of the law in Great Britain. Nobody would have known that he was planning to puff on home-grown cannabis in Wales if it hadn't been for the ironic coincidence that another Mr. Perkins had mistakenly opened a package addressed to the actor.

"Perkins had grown his own cannabis back home in Los Angeles and had thought to avoid being busted by customs by posting it to the hotel in Wales where he was due to stay in

June 1989. But in a severe case of mistiming, or just under-estimating the efficiency of the postal service, the package arrived five days before he did.

"Opened by another Mr. Perkins who was staying at the same hotel, the package was passed to police who were ready and waiting for the actor when he arrived at the hotel in Cardiff. He was fined £200 by Cardiff magistrates for smuggling in 1.32 grams of cannabis. The court heard how he intended to use the drug to help him relax while filming for HTV in South Wales. The cannabis was worth only £4.50 and would have made no more than six cigarettes. 'He uses cannabis very infrequently and always discreetly,' said his solicitor.

"But this wasn't the first time Perkins had been charged with drug possession in Britain. Five years earlier he had been fined £100 by magistrates at Uxbridge for trying to smuggle cannabis and LSD through customs at Heathrow Airport."

Eventually, Tony married the model Berrie Berenson and the couple had two children.

In the late 1980s, Perkins was told he had tested positive for the AIDS virus, and like other actors, kept his status private in order to keep working. However, the *National Enquirer* got wind of it and revealed that he was HIV-positive. Before his death in 1992 at the age of 60, Perkins commented, "There are many who believe that this disease is God's vengeance, but I don't. I believe it was sent to teach people how to live and understand and have compassion for each other."

In the recent biography *Anthony Perkins: A Haunted Life* by Ronald Bergan, Perkins is painted as a loner, living under the shadow of "Psycho" and ambivalent about his sexuality. One reviewer called the book "excellent – sniffing around like a cat after a terrified mouse."

However, book critic John Naughton was revolted by the book, calling it "dishonest: On its back cover (a picture of Perkins standing in front of the Bates Motel) it quotes the late actor bemoaning the fact that his career had telescoped into the man with the overripe mum: "I couldn't believe that all the other films I had done previously had been forgotten and that I was being narrowed into this one image that other people had of me.'

"So what does the book do? Posthumously narrows Perkins

into that one image by drawing the crudest psychological links between him and Bates. Both their fathers died when the boys were only five years old, both had domineering mothers, both were sort of homosexual, one was a psycho, the other got psychotic at being forever compared to Norman Bates by dunderhead film critics.

"Perkins' life seems to have been unhappy enough not to need this kind of attention. Following Osgood's death, Perkins' mother made a point of mentioning him on a daily basis while converting their New York apartment into a shrine littered with pictures of the late thespian. Small wonder, then, that Perkins chose to follow in his father's footsteps, a decision which meant his homosexuality would always remain covert. The irony, of course, is that in roles that are now for the most part forgotten Perkins proved himself the most able of actors, and one who might have prospered without the fatal stereotyping that later befell him.

"Not that Bergan bothers himself unduly with such niceties. With lurid chapter headings such as 'A Boy's Best Friend Is His Mother,' 'I Am Norman Bates,' 'Psycho Therapy' and 'The Bates Motel Revisited,' Bergan leaves no one in any doubt what he's getting at. The manner in which he gets there, however, leaves a lot to be desired – you can't help thinking Perkins deserved better."

THE CONTEMPORARIES

Christopher Atkins at 17 in a publicity still for
"The Blue Lagoon," his first movie.

Christopher Atkins

"He was the most beautiful chicken I ever saw. It was in the days before the age of video so I had to go back to the theater time after time to see him but I never tired of it. It seemed as if I got to know him, know him very well. I knew he was supposed to be acting but I also knew that he'd never had an acting lesson in his life; he must have been playing himself. I was watching the most beautiful chicken in the world playing himself in a lush multimillion-dollar movie. It was heaven! The only thing that could have made it better was if Tom Selleck had been shipwrecked on that island with him instead of Brooke. Talk about Robinson Crusoe! Talk about Friday! I would leave the theater and rush home to relieve my torment, the torment of having him only for the length of the movie. I wanted him in every way possible, to have him with me, to have him in me, to have me in him, to kiss and suck every miraculous inch of his splendid body. I prayed he'd make it in Hollywood, that there would be more opportunities to see him naked. God, he didn't even mind appearing completely, blessedly nude! What a fabulous kid!"
— The author, remembering 1980.

The nice thing about obsessive compulsives is that it's so easy to strike up a conversation with them. You meet Gustav von Aschenbach and you ask him about Tadzio. You run into me and you ask me about Christopher Atkins.

On that subject, I can never say enough.

Ah, Christopher.

In 1979, the very week he shot his first and only commercial for a line of designer jeans, 19-year-old Ford agency model Atkins tested for a movie role. "I was freaking out," the star recalls. "The commercial was the big one for me. The idea of a movie was unbelievable. I did the screen test on Wednesday, standing up against some file cabinets in an office with house plants on the floor, filmed the commercial on Thursday, Friday the producers told me I had the part, Saturday I flew to California, Sunday I did a screen test in a bathing suit, Monday and Tuesday were filled with passports and doctors, and Wednesday we were in Fiji. Thursday, the cameras rolled."

Retired talent agent Zan Benham was with the J. Michael Bloom agency when a friend of hers recommended Chris, then 17, for the part of Richard in "The Blue Lagoon." "I'll never forget when he came in for the interview," she recalls. "He was just so cute he was totally disarming." She remembers that casting directors on both coasts had interviewed thousands of boys for the part opposite Brooke Shields but had come up dry. "They had trouble finding someone who was, first, tall enough to be with her, and second had the right combination of innocence and handsomeness that the part called for. They found it in Chris. But he was put before the cameras prematurely. When I saw the film, I thought the scenes where he had to play anger were poor. He just didn't know that anger has to come from the body, not the mind. He had talent, but it was raw at that time. In later years he grew more in touch with adult feelings."

Critic Brian Hirsch says, "When one looks at this movie today, it's hard to say why he was chosen, aside from his pronounced resemblance to another filet then in favor, Mark Hamill. Perhaps director Randal Kleiser guessed correctly that Atkins, with a kisser every bit as blank as Brooke Shields', would not get in the way of teens filling in the spaces with their own adolescent daydreams about coming of age on that ravishing island. That theory at least helps to explain how a movie this mindless could have turned out to be the runaway hit of the year, turning Atkins into a movie star."

"The Blue Lagoon" went on to gross over $100 million worldwide, thanks in good measure to the effect the gorgeous blond had on gaymale and female members of the audience alike.

It didn't hurt a bit that the star bravely appeared nude in two underwater swimming scenes and a brief full frontal view on a waterslide. It didn't hurt that he also did his own stunts, including high dives from craggy island peaks. And it didn't hurt that he fielded questions about his sexual responses to Brooke Shields in a gentlemanly manner: "You think I got aroused? Really it was no big deal. Brooke is such a young girl. She was 14 when she made the movie and still had a little girl's body, so it wasn't that exciting – not yet. She had the face and the legs. Gorgeous legs. The rest of her had to catch up. We became very close, went scuba diving and walked up and down the beach collecting shells."

One critic summed up the finished product: "When Lolita meets Tadzio in 'The Blue Lagoon,' a Disneysque sex manual of picturesquely innocent sensual discovery, an audience has to wonder for whom the film is intended. With its strictly juvenile mentality and it's absolutely adult realization, its R rating which will keep the kids away and its everything else that will keep the adults away, it is a bizarre, fascinating experiment in commercial moviemaking.

"A two hour show-and-tell session about the birth of erotic consciousness as two teenagers go through microcosms of experience against lush Fiji backdrops of breathtaking beauty. Nestor Almendros has photographed so many purpled sunsets, beige beachscapes, spidery jungles, etc., that the film has a gorgeous travelogy look. And endless inserts of parrots and the island's other flashy fauna interrupt the action senselessly. Atkins' adolescent intensity will certainly sustain the attention of any Gustav von Aschenbachs in the audience."

And so it did. For a decade now, we Gustavs have been wild about that boy's "adolescent intensity." To this day, every time I hear Noel Coward's "Mad About the Boy" I think of Christopher. It seemed he was simply too good to be true. We even considered it a tremendous plus that he, born on February 21, 1961, in Rye, New York, is a Pisces. God, everybody loves a Pisces. They're quiet, slow to anger, and often work non-stop days and overtime nights. Especially those nights!

Oh, and it didn't hurt that we thought Chris was just one sweet guy, a humble guy that couldn't believe his good fortune. "Why me?" he asked. "I still feel guilty that I was put into the picture. To think people go to acting school and wait for years for that big break. I know it's not fair." Fair or not, he didn't complain. And neither did we.

Oh, we did mind one thing: Hollywood, in it's infinite wisdom, saw fit to sequel even "Blue Lagoon." The 1991 horror, "Return to the Blue Lagoon" was universally panned and closed in a week. Caryn James in *The New York Times*: "The 1980 hit 'Blue Lagoon' was nothing more than a teen-age titillation movie but it had a sweet, dopey simplicity. The 19th century orphans learned about sex the way Adam and Eve must have (if they had been very discreetly photographed) and still had trouble figuring out where the baby came from.

"Well, that baby is back, and he is the unluckiest child on earth. Trapped in 'Return to the Blue Lagoon,' he is destined to replay a more complicated and even lamer version of his parents' coming of age. The Fijian background looks pretty but there's no escaping the fact that the tropical flowers and trees are smarter and more appealing than the people."

Nothing against earnest young Brian Krause but, after all, we couldn't help it: we hated the sequel.

We also disliked the rip-off of "Blue Lagoon," "Paradise," starring TV idol Willie Ames, who appeared nude, but then said he didn't when he found the movie was a big dud at the box-office. We Gustavs won't settle for second-best. We want the real thing. And, in true legendary fashion, Christopher forced us to pay good money to see him regardless of how awful the movie was. And God were they dreadful! "The Child Bride of Short Creek" and "The Pirate Movie," an arch mixture of "Beach Party" and "The Pirates of Penzance," were about the worst Hollywood had to offer. Hirsch says, "Nobody blamed Atkins; in fact, he is so blatantly unable to act, there's no one to blame for anything in his career except the idiots who cast him. 'Idiots' is not too strong a term for the people who gave him top billing in 'A Night in Heaven.' This is the so-bad-you've-gotta-see-it-to-believe-it story of a shy schoolmarm's adulterous affair with a much-younger pupil, who is stripping his way through college. Here, Atkins really is a slab of meat on display: bumping it, grinding it, and - for the big finish - baring it all."

Yes, our loyalty was finally being rewarded, in spades, with the 1983 release of "A Night in Heaven." Being what the studio called "a contemporary story of sexual obsession," this movie was right down our alley. And the actor not only stripped with gay abandon but allowed us a glimpse of his lovely cock in a steamy love scene with Lesley Ann Warren.

To further enshrine this blond god in Gustav heaven, he also seemed to delight in his nude posing for *Playgirl* magazine. Would wonders ever cease?

But movie moguls were unwilling to accept that he was something more than simply decorative. As Hirsch remarked, "His career came to a screeching halt." Not taken seriously, he ended up doing a stint as host of "Rock 'n' Roll Summer Action" in 1985, appeared in another stinker called "Beaks, the Movie," in 1987 and coasted through a season on "Dallas" as perennially overwrought Linda Gray's young love interest. But for about 20 weeks Friday nights weren't the same. We were able to get a fresh fix of Chris every week! And since he played a swimming coach, most of the time he appeared in a bikini. Talk about nights in heaven! Hirsch commented, "He certainly looked fit in the Speedos he wore in almost every scene."

But by the late '80s, Speedos or no Speedos, the bloom was definitely off the rose. Christopher had married his high school sweetheart Cindy Gibbs, had children, and occasionally appeared on the celebrity tennis circuit. He turned up in a slasher called "Mortuary Academy" and in 1989 he played a featured role in "Listen to Me," an obnoxious Kirk Cameron movie. His thesping was so poor that he won a Golden Raspberry as "worst supporting actor," joining the ranks of other recipients such as Pia Zadora and Bo Derek.

Late in 1990, celeb columnist Liz Smith reported: "For a hot minute he seemed on the brink of a big movie career...and now a more mature Christopher, married with children, will have a spate of new movies in the coming year. Two are already in the can, 'Shakma' and 'Fatal Charm' and 'Fire, Ice and My Wife,' an offbeat look at relationships in the '90s." We have no idea what happened to "Fire, Ice and My Wife" but "Fatal Charm" ended up as a Showtime movie, then was released on video. In it, Chris plays a charmer who gets sent to prison for raping and murdering six women. During his trial, a guileless teenager becomes enamored with him. Says she, "Why would anyone that gorgeous have to rape anyone?" That's exactly what we asked. Indeed, critic Ken Tucker said, "Atkins, all angry glares, isn't believable for a second." The girl starts writing to Chris in prison. Before long, the correspondence gets so hot and heavy that Chris breaks out of prison to visit her. Bear in mind, he's had to fight off all those cons who want a piece of his ass. In fact, we get a scene wherein a man actually goes so far as to kiss Chris before he is rebuffed. "The rest of the movie," wrote

Tucker, "is an overweight tease, endlessly postponing the girl's inevitable meeting."

"Shakma" finally began playing on Cinemax in 1993. The story, about students trapped with a testy baboon while playing a fantasy game in a research building, is an embarrassment for all concerned, not just Chris.

Chris' turn at playing a vampire in "Dracula Rising" also went directly to video and he failed to make much of an impression.

During the summer of 1993, Chris starred in two Grade B films that also went directly to video, by-passing theatrical release. In "Die Watching," Chris plays a video director who auditions some of Hollywood's most promising actresses and makes them subjects in his own private fantasy of desire and murder.

Also released in 1993 was "Wet and Wild Summer," an Australian film, known there as "Exchange Lifeguards." In this turkey, Chris plays the son of a resort developer (Elliot Gould, of all people!) who wants to turn Mullet Beach in Australia into a resort for rich folks. Chris is sent Down Under to negotiate the deal and, because of the sensitive environmental nature of the project, he goes incognito as a lifeguard. This enables us to have several wonderful shots of Chris in tight blue Spandex. Plus, because the beach is nudity optional, we get a superabundant view of Atkins' buns. The good news is that Chris still looks wonderful.

Christopher Atkins may have been a flavor of the month in Hollywood but we Gustavs have long memories and great loyalties to those who have been kind to us. By giving us his all, literally, right from the start, we revere the golden boy as arguably the most delicious flavor of a generation and who, now in his 30's and hardly chicken, remains as tasty as ever.

Warren Beatty in a publicity still
for "Splendor in the Grass."

Warren Beatty

"I have never known such pleasure.
He could handle women as smoothly as operating an elevator."
– Britt Ekland in her 1981 autobiography, "True Britt"

It was upon seeing Jose Quintero's filmization of Tennessee Williams' novella, "The Roman Spring of Mrs. Stone," that I fell in love with Warren Beatty. I had been enamored by his strikingly beautiful presence alongside Natalie Wood in 1961's "Splendor in the Grass," his first film, but it took this moody, seldom-seen masterpiece, released later that same year, to make me forever a Beatty fanatic.

In the film, an imperious, declining celebrity, the actress Karen Stone, played by Vivien Leigh, goes to Rome and is attracted to, and challenged by, a princely male hustler, Paolo (Beatty). In his novella, Williams described the gigolo: "While he was being shaved and massaged, Paolo, who was quite tall for a Southern Italian, sat far down in the chair with his legs dropping wide apart and with one hand laid on the center of his being, which was his groin. That hand laid there was like an electric wire plugged into a socket for the purpose of giving power and light to the invariable subject of discussion which was the sexual experience by which, and for, the young Paolo existed."

While Karen occasionally has an aggressive bearing, Paolo frequently seems effeminate, as when he preens himself and grows petulant at her neglect of him. He, as she has done, will sell his beauty for a living. In contrast to Paolo is the nameless boy who follows Karen throughout the film and ends up with her, a grisly parody of the faithful fan.

For the most part, the film visualizes what the novel describes. The sensuality that Williams inferred from the physical setting is conveyed in the many shots of the people of Rome buying sexual favors: old men and women buying handsome or available young boys, the decadent courting the poor with religious earnestness. While the novel employed a narrator, the film does not, but it first assumes the perspective of Karen and this adds to the sensuality of scene when she, and, by extension, the audience, first meets Paolo. We do not see his face for some time; instead, we see him slouching deep in his chair, with his legs provocatively spread (the novel refers to his "odalisque poses"). For Karen not to note his face for so long suggests that her interest in him is crudely sexual.

As in all of Williams' work, sex is seen as both quick and impersonal, as a promiscuous release and as a religious ecstasy which violates community convention. Of all of the films of Williams' works, this was said to be his favorite. With Beatty as his star, no other film depicts the playwright's celebration of physical beauty and sexual prowess as masterfully as this one. Williams always looked at the peacock male with both awe and disapproval and was often prone to punish his sexual stars, but didn't do this in "Roman Spring," unless your idea of being punished is having to go off at the end with a bimbo, portrayed by Jill St. John. It is to the screenwriter Gavin Lambert's credit that the character is never softened. The male prostitute is never compromised, or deepened, by feeling love for the forlorn Mrs. Stone.

Originally, the Warner Brothers studio executives were going to film the picture in Rome with a young Italian playing Paolo. But before production started, they changed their mind, deciding they needed some box-office insurance and were shopping for a young name actor to cast opposite Leigh.

Meanwhile, William Inge, the gay playwright, had become fascinated by Warren and in 1959 chose him for the lead on Broadway in his play "A Loss of Roses." Then Beatty went to Hollywood to star in Inge's "Splendor in the Grass" at Warners. The film was a big hit and Inge recommended his hot young protege and made sure Beatty got a copy of the script. The object was to convince Williams. Encouraged by the story of Marlon Brando's tactic of meeting and impressing the playwright, Warren dressed in an Italian suit, wore olive make-up and went out in pursuit of Williams. Beatty says: "I found him in a gambling casino in Puerto Rico and began to talk to him in an Italian accent. In fact, I brought him a glass of milk on a tray because I had been told he had ulcers from the reviews of 'Sweet Bird of Youth.'" Warren proposed himself for the part of Paolo and Williams was charmed. Later that night,

Warren went to Williams' hotel room wearing only a bathrobe. Williams is said to have sighed and said, "Go home to bed, Warren. I said you had the part."

Most reviews of the film were unfavorable but Paul V. Beckley noted in his *New York Herald Tribune* appraisal that "Beatty plays the gigolo with an obvious appetite. He wheedles and poses and purrs and occasionally exposes the character's ugly interior in sharp, horrible insults."

William Inge figured prominently in Warren's career again when the actor appeared in "All Fall Down" in 1962. Inge wrote the script based on James Leo Herlihy's novel. Warren again captivated his audience with his earnest portrayal of a young stud who brought heartache to an older woman, this time played by Eva Marie Saint. His image seemed to be nourished by his playing of the part of the selfish, cruel young man who used women only to cast them off when they outlived their usefulness. This film was even more poignant than "Roman Spring" because Brandon de Wilde, whom I had idolized in "Blue Denim," was cast as Warren's younger brother in a delicious juxtapositioning of good and evil.

After these three films, Beatty became an "adamant enigma" and we saw him most clearly, but never too well, with Joan Collins, Natalie Wood, Leslie Caron, Michelle Phillips, Julie Christie, Diane Keaton, Isabelle Adjani and, most lately with Annette Bening, with whom he had a child at the ripe old age of 54. In announcing the event, *US* magazine headlined: "Warren Gets Pregnant!" *Entertainment Weekly* joked: "Sleeping with Beatty is like visiting the Farmer's Market: It's something you have to do when you're in L.A." Indeed, the tony British catalog of celebrity sex partners called "Who's Had Who," begins its long section on Beatty by saying: "Fasten your seat belts and hold your hats, this is the big one!"

Woody Allen once said he wanted to be reincarnated as Warren's finger tips. Coming from a man who dated Diane Keaton when Warren was done with her, he might have the inside track on what makes Beatty such a great lover.

Mamie Van Doren has the unusual distinction of making headlines by *not* sleeping with Warren, but she did confess he'd romanced her and that he was a "wet kisser."

In her autobiography Joan Collins says, "He was insatiable.

Three, four, five times a day, every day, was not unusual. And he was able to make phone calls at the same time."

As was the case with his older sister, Shirley MacLaine, it was recognized early on that Beatty would be successful. The yearbook of the class of '55 at Washington-Lee High School, Arlington, Virginia, notes that the then Warren Beaty (he added the extra "t" later) was Class President, Variety Show Emcee, and played football. He was also voted "Best All-Around Boy."

"Best all-around" definitely included sex, something that Warren loves, but it's more than that. He says, "It is very lonely for me to live without a woman, without relating life with or to another person. Somehow, when you are with someone, it is like seeing life through four eyes rather than through two. It's a big cliche, I know, but it is also a big truth: Life means so much more when it's shared."

Warren shared his life with Madonna during the filming of "Dick Tracy" and she called him "old man." He called her "Buzz Bomb." About Warren's equipment, Madonna would only say, "I haven't measured it, but it's a perfectly wonderful size." For his part, Warren said she was "more fun than a barrel of monkeys." When she said, "If you have to give Warren Beatty safe sex lessons, what's the world coming to?" we could sympathize with the legendary lothario because we've learned just how damningly difficult it is getting into the habit of slipping on a condom , especially when you're over 30.

But we never thought Warren and Madonna were anything more than hype for each others' movies anyway. As Ellen Goodman pointed out in her column in *The Boston Globe:* "In 'Truth or Dare,' the camera that had been tracking Madonna day and night through her tour, plumbing her depths and shallows, now accompanied her to the throat doctor and filmed everything but her larynx.

"Until then, the audience had seen Madonna at her best with all her in-your-face outrageousness. They'd seen her at her worst with all her 'I have to protect my artistic integrity' banality. But suddenly the voice of reason and sanity passed to none other than Warren Beatty. The older star gasped at the younger's exhibitionism in its most literal form. In the line that's been snatched and repeated most from this movie, he offered a footnote of bewilderment: 'She doesn't want to live off-camera, much less talk. She seems to be saying, Why would you bother to say something off camera?'"

National Review's Joseph Sobran sniffed: "Imagine a film in which it's left to Warren Beatty to sound the only note of common sense!' Imagine indeed. It could be that Goodman knows that Madonna finds herself drawn only to "emotional cripples" and that prompted many to wisely conclude that poor Warren was simply dating himself during his brief fling with the material girl. 'There he was, tagged forever as a member of a generation that actually draws a line, however often violated, however egotistically crossed, between life and art, between the private and the public self." As John Simon so succinctly concluded, "It is the privilege of celebrity, at least as conceived nowadays, to be its own morality: hype makes right. Impudence passes for candor; exhibitionism, for honesty."

From the old school, Warren is a maverick in the true sense of the word, a man who has never stopped believing in his own values and principles, a man who doesn't buckle to public pressure where life or work is concerned. Suzanne Munshower, in her book, "Warren Beatty," concludes that Warren "is one of those rare human beings whose life, no matter how spontaneous it might appear on the surface, has never been a tale of impetuosity." In other words, he's planned it all. "Beatty's success with the opposite sex long ago passed from the stage of gossip to the pinnacle of legend," she says. "What makes a man so single-minded in the pursuit of success, success on his own terms, as Warren Beatty?" Her answer: "The same balance of personal attributes that combine to make him so devastating to women and so acceptable to men."

Rona Barrett, who has known Warren since his lean days in New York, says: "I see him now and then and it's always warm and friendly. I love Warren, but I think he's a whore. He's very spoiled and selfish. He only does what he wants when he wants to do it. He was that way when he was poor and he's that way now."

What endeared us to Warren is that we knew he was a whore but a whore who was paranoid about all this sex talk. He became an occluded Hollywood god, one who shuts up and off and imagines himself invisible. Afraid of being misunderstood, he says nothing and is more misunderstood, and he likes it that way. But unlike Brando's silence, Beatty is showy in his silence.

Barbara Walters called him "the most difficult interview I ever did." Rex Reed once was commissioned by *Esquire* to do a piece on the star and he said that getting him to answer a question was akin to "asking a hemophiliac for a pint of blood.". After being driven around Hollywood for hours by Warren's press agent, continually being told how hard Warren was to see, the writer did manage to interview the star for an hour. The result was published under the headline, "Will the Real Warren Beatty Please Shut Up." After doing a round-up of rumors about the star, Reed came down to it: "Nobody knows very much at all about Warren, including Beatty himself."

Years later, the star himself said: "I don't know what to say about a person like that. You would have to address yourself to the symptoms of American journalism and what allows that kind of sickness to sustain itself. This guy said he thought I was the best actor of my generation and that he'd seen these films of mine over and over again. He tried to get me to pose for a picture with thirty girls. I thought it was insane. Why would I do that? He ended up involving me with women I'd never met in incidents that never took place. I would say the whole thing may come out of some homosexual anxiety. He sat there for an hour and the only word I can think of to describe Reed is 'dewy-eyed.' I remember having a feeling of sympathy for him and trying very hard to answer seriously the questions he asked. I think the man is contemptible, dishonest and a very hostile creature."

Not only will Warren not discuss himself, it is his belief that if he has to explain a character in one his films, he hasn't played the role well enough. He will frequently snap, "You tell me" at a reporter's inquiry about his character's motivation.

In 1975, Warren was to expose himself a little bit. In the hit film "Shampoo," when he is in the bathroom with Julie Christie, he lowers his pants so that the upper half of his buns are revealed. Later, when he is fucking Christie and Goldie Hawn walks in on them, his buns are shown in a long shot.

For years afterward, before the film "Dick Tracy," Warren was so mum he all but evaporated. But posturing does have its limitations, and with the film's release, suddenly, he was on every talk show, speaking softly, editing every syllable, slicing off personal color, steering away from introspection. It is said he works at rendering himself a blank. But it is a blank that is charming, puckish and smooth, a man it is said who seduces anything that is not mineral. As the actor Robert Downey Jr., once seen in "Less Than Zero" getting his cock blown, said: "Warren is really knowledgeable in a lot of areas, especially fucking."

You have to admire Warren for withholding so much of himself and his Romantic calculation that there is more energy likely to be stirred by his absence than his presence. After his first three movies set the tone, I must confess I have spent a wonderful thirty years wondering just how good that much-used, "perfectly wonderful"-sized cock of Warren's would feel as he entered me. (Any orifice, Warren, any one at all.)

Sean Connery on the set of "Dr. No."

Sean Connery

*"He has been at the top of the A-list for nearly 30 years.
At the age of 60, People magazine named him 'The Sexiest Man
Alive.' With typical aplomb, his reply was,
'It's all downhill from here.'"*
- Critic Richard Ashton

In 1962, the filmmaking team of producers Harry Saltzman and Albert R. Broccoli and director Terence Young approached the debut of Ian Fleming's James Bond hero boldly and cheekily, as if it was the middle of the 007 series. No small part in this success was due to the actor hired to play the secret agent, Sean Connery, who strode through his first big-screen adventure with seasoned confidence. As the *New Yorker* noted, "Connery was in the first flower of his hunkdom," and draws out his introduction with blase machismo: it's both funny and thrilling to hear him tell tart, glamorous Sylvia Trench (Eunice Grayson) that his name is "Bond...James Bond."

In 1962, I wanted him to play "Daddy" to my little boy and I still do. What has always attracted me to Connery is the physical authority he presents on-screen as well as off. "It's a mysterious thing really," said Philip Kaufman, director of Connery's "Rising Sun," released in the summer of 1993. "Steve McQueen had it. Cagney had it. If an actor has it, it means that he can be taking stuff out of a supermarket freezer and there's something special about it. There's a sense in which people go to films to learn how to behave; the fact is people are very attracted to the way Sean behaves. They have an empathy with him - or they would like to have empathy. They would like to feel that they have his qualities, his grace under pressure."

This, writer Zoe Heller suggests, is because Sean stands six foot two in his socks, "and he's Jack Sprat lean." He was a bodybuilder as a young man and his vast torso still forms a pleasing, equilateral triangle. Director Sidney Lumet says, "Whatever the width of the doorway, Sean seems to fill it."

"Apart from his build," Holler says, "there is the way he

moves." She revealed that the Bond team hadn't really made up their mind until they spotted him on the street below, striding like a panther. Broccoli said later that the difference between Sean and the other actors they auditioned for the part was like comparing "a still photograph with a film."

Connery gets his animal grace from the years he spent dancing prior to making movies. He says, "The dance is all important to me. The place where you stand, how you use your space, is the number-one priority. How you stand in relation to other people in scenes, how you dance with them – that's what it's all about."

Looking back now, Connery can scarcely believe he's come this far from the Edinburgh tenement in which he grew up. "If I ever stop to think how far I'd come," he says, "how much fame one's had, how much money one's made, how much traveling one's done, one would think, well, it's just not possible, considering where I've come from."

"When he was a baby," Holler reports, "his crib was a bottom drawer. He began delivering milk at the age of nine to help supplement his father's income. After he left school, he tried his hand at a variety of jobs - bricklayer, cinema usher, coal man."

No matter what job Sean had, he never neglected his soccer playing and fitness training. As Andrew Yule notes in his biography of the actor, *From 007 to Hollywood Icon*, during fitness class one day, his instructor, Arthur Brennan, a former Mr. Scotland, took special note of Sean's "impressively developing musculature" and suggested he supplement his income by modeling at the Edinburgh School of Art. "He did this for a spell," Yule reveals, "stripped down to a G-string pouch that created no end of interest, whether he was tossing a discus or reclining on a lounger."

"It's murder staying in one pose all that time," Sean complained, adding bashfully, "The girls always want to sketch me up close. It's *embarrassing*."

Yes, if you can imagine it, Sean was very shy, "introverted and unsure," as a young man, he says now, and while competing in a "Mr. Universe" contest, he heard the touring company of "South Pacific" was looking for chorus boys. Again imagine, a rough-looking bricklayer with tattoos and a gold tooth - perfect for dancing to "There's Nothing Like a Dame." Suddenly he found himself in the company of people who read Ibsen. "I was so impressed by actors and how articulate they were, how much they seemed to know about everything. I was impressed by most people I met. I was impressed by people that could express themselves. I had no confidence in terms of intellect at all because I'd had no exposure to it."

Speaking of exposure, Yule says: "From the beginning of 'South Pacific's' tour, Connery had been in his element with the newfound freedom derived from living the life of a 'traveling player,' darting from town to town on his humble motorbike. The backstage camaraderie had been marred just a little by one of the actors with whom he shared a dressing room. This particular character hogged the mirror, constantly struck poses, and came over to Connery as a monumental pain-in-the-neck 'theatrical.' Glad to see the back of him when he left, Sean sat, nonchalantly naked, as his replacement arrived. Clad in a fur coat and clutching a teddy bear, the versatile entertainer Victor Spinetti initially looked every bit as bad as his predecessor. The newcomer beheld the resplendent Connery physique, eyes traveling down the torso, appreciatively taking in every inch. 'A pigeon sitting on two eggs?' Connery suggested when he saw where Spinetti's eyes were riveted. 'Not a pigeon,' Spanned admiringly replied, 'more like an eagle!'"

Given great encouragement by one of the theater company's managers, Connery embarked on a course of self-education. And he decided to pursue an acting career. Now he says that when a person chooses to be an actor he's already made some moves to express the feminine side of himself. "You really have to free yourself to be an actor. You have to be willing to make an arse of yourself."

Connery has now become the senior statesman of the movies, but years on the screen have not softened him. Holler says that it is impossible not to end up liking Connery's frankness and his refusal to schmooze. "He doesn't flash an ingratiating orange-peel smile and beg you to like him. In the best tradition of male heatthrobs, he doesn't give a damn." He can afford it. A Scot, he has invested carefully, and maintains homes in Monte Carlo, on Lyford Cay in the Bahamas, and in

Marbella, Spain. And, when he drives, he drives a Toyota.

In reviewing Connery's "Rising Sun," the *New Yorker* said: "The most defensible and honest reason to watch expensive, handsomely mounted studio movies is the fun of seeing stars like Connery at play. He hasn't looked so elegant since the Bond movies and he uses his daunting air of assurance to tremendous effect." Just the kind of man you'd want as a Daddy, right?

Tom Cruise, as photographed by the famed Herb Ritts

Tom Cruise

*"The greasers, with their sleek muscles and androgynous faces,
display a leonine athleticism as they move through dusty lots or do a
graceful two-handed vault over a chain link fence.*
*"Their camaraderie is familial, embracing, unselfconsciously
homoerotic. Left to their better selves, they can easily go all moony
over sunsets, quote great swatches of Robert Frost verse, or fall
innocently asleep in each other's arms.*
*Their ideal world is both a womb and a locker room; no women need
apply to this dreamy brotherhood. With its soft, silvery lighting, its
slow fades and dissolves and a lush score, it means to create the
greasers' dream world even as it describes the real world in which
they live and die."*
– Time magazine critic Richard Corliss
describing "The Outsiders."

I'll admit it: I went crazy when I saw Tom Cruise dancing
around the living room in just his briefs in "Risky Business"
and I went absolutely nuts when he stripped to the buff in "All
the Right Moves." And I'm not alone; Cruise is arguably the
only movie star under forty who is what Hollywood moguls call
bankable, meaning, if he's the star, you're going to make a
profit.

But for a period in the early '90s, Cruise's films weren't the
big profit makers their backers had hoped.

All that changed with "A Few Good Men" and "The Firm,"
where he got back doing what he does best, playing the
ultimate jock. "Good-looking, athletic Cruise," writes critic
George Mayer about "The Firm": is playing the sort of role he
should play – very American, confident, and with not a little
innocence and idealism. In other words, every gaymale's
fantasy of the perfect lover. Handsome but not too handsome,
sexy but not too sexy, and very dependable. In other words,
bankable. And sincerely so. As film critic Roger Ebert says,
"One look at Cruise and we feel comfortable, because he
embodies sincerity. He is also, as in many of his roles, just a
little slow to catch on; his characters seem to trust people too

easily, so it's convincing when he swallows the firm's pitches."

"Damned if Tom Cruise doesn't once again discover his integrity," says critic David Denby. "He discovers, you know, the law, and begins making speeches as if he were still playing his part in 'A Few Good Men.' One would think Cruise was too old to still be clinging to his moral virginity, but that's the way everyone wants to see him." Especially us gay guys.

As Tom's fans will recall, in 1992's big release, Rob Reiner's production of "A Few Good Men," Tom shone brightly beside an over-acting Jack Nicholson in a military-run-amok tale. Tom was so good, he received his second Oscar nomination.

"As he did in 'Rain Man' and 'The Color of Money,'" Georgia Brown observed, "Cruise plays a hotshot, a shallow young man whose depths are hidden even from him. In the movie's trajectory, Cruise's character grows in stature...his noisily eating an apple can make a whole scene."

"It helps if, like me," Owen Gleiberman writes in *Entertainment Weekly*, "you're ashamed to admit you enjoy Tom Cruise's gliding-on-air bravado. At this point, there probably isn't much he can do to win over his detractors but in 'The Firm' he has just the quality that's called for: the sneaky-minded agility of a true conspiracy-buster."

"Cruise embodies the smooth, insinuating conformism of the '80s," critic Dave Kehr said, "using a low-key, low-intensity sitcom charm to work his way into the affections of his audience and win them over. His youth and relative immaturity turn out to serve the secret undercurrents of the film extremely well." Mayer agrees: "Under these bleak conditions (which require delivering some excruciatingly cliched lines) Cruise gives a performance of surprising conviction. He also appears to be quite unaware how bad a movie he's in, which seems to have helped." It also helped that Tom was getting $12 million for being convincing.

All this adulation over his performance in "Men" was heartwarming to Tom whose summer release of 1991, "Days of Thunder," barely broke even and his big summer romance of 1992, "Far and Away," also fizzled at the box-office. "Far and Away" cost $54 million to make, including the star's salary, plus $26 million in prints and promotion, so the total cost was over $80 million. The film grossed only $50 million in the U.S.

during its release, which means that the studio got back $25 million. The worldwide box-office could go to $130 million, meaning $65 million for the studio. With cassette sales, cable-TV sales, foreign cassettes, and airplane showings, it could earn another $20 million. So you spend 80 and you get 85 back. Hardly an investors' dream but then, when all is said and done, it didn't lose money either.

"Far and Away" was notable for Cruise fans only because he spent so much of the film's interminable running time with his shirt off, and lots of shots of Tom's beautiful butt in the Boston sequence, even a scene in the buff with only a chamber pot covering the family jewels. His co-star, his wife, the Australian actress Nicole Kidman, gets the big laugh in the movie when she walks into the room and finds Tom sleeping so she lifts the pot. Then, visibly impressed, turns back for a second look. *New York* magazine likened the film to one of those old Burton/Taylor vehicles "retooled for teenyboppers." Denby remarked, "Tom is in great shape and the camera feasts on his smoothly muscular flesh." And Denby felt that Nicole brought out an engagingly unspoiled side in Cruise: "Kidman is extremely entertaining. Her acting is rudimentary, but she has great instincts. The scene of her staring at Cruise's member is so funny because of the amazed yet eager look that comes over her face. She knows how to make fun of herself."

Denby and other critics noted Tom's voice sounded thin and high in the movie. But it wasn't supposed to be that way. Upon the film's release, *SPY* magazine revealed that what really bothers Tom is his adolescent voice: "Cruise belongs to the Church of Scientology, the cult that believes all of life's difficulties can be overcome by hooking yourself up to a quack electronic gadget. So when he shared his squeaky-voice obsession with some Scientologist friends, they convinced him that the solution, at least as far as his movie voice was concerned, was a special high-tech recording system. Luckily for Tom, the Church owns a professional sound studio and his pals there developed a system just for him. The price: well over $100,000. Now, the better the system, the more faithfully it captures sounds - a squeaky adolescent voice will only sound more exquisitely squeaky and adolescent. But Cruise seems to believe this gizmo can give him a new, improved voice. When

Ron Howard hired him for 'Far and Away,' he was obliged to lease this special, allegedly squeak- suppressing system."

One wag said that it wasn't Tom's voice that bothered him, it was his dopey Irish accent, which "has him sounding eerily close to the cartoon leprechaun on the Lucky Charms cereal commercials." "Libby Gelman-Waxner," columnist for *Premiere* magazine, thought Tom's accent was "on loan from an Irish Spring commercial." She went further: "At most movies, I suspend disbelief, and at least for a while, I agree to accept Tom Cruise as a race-car driver or a pool hustler or a person. 'Far and Away' is very strange – it's like watching Tom in a $60 million school play, where you never really forget that he's really the star quarterback and the class president." As expected, celeb columnist Liz Smith raved: "Cruise is spectacular. He is as appealing, photogenic and charismatic as ever. Yes, he is a good actor but he can't escape his looks and charm and, at 29, shouldn't even try."

William Goldman agrees: "We want Tom Cruise when he makes us comfortable: playing a contemporary kid in a pickle. Not an Irish immigrant."

But Liz Smith said that when she attended a premiere of "The Firm" in New York, the scene in which Tom confessed his infidelity to his wife drew laughter from the young people in the audience. Perhaps they expected if they were married to Tom, he'd be unfaithful? Said Liz: "Tom and Jeanne Tripplehorn are fine - if not inspiring...her emotional reaction to Tom's one-night stand caused considerable giggling. Brrrrr! We're a cold, callous bunch these days."

Liz should know. Earlier in the year, she was told by Tom's publicist that her item regarding the potentially hot love scenes between Tom and Jeanne Tripplehorn in "The Firm" had gotten her into trouble. "So, don't be surprised," she joked in print, "if the real-life Mrs. Cruise shows up on the set with Tom's lunch." "Tom was hurt by the item," the publicist said. "He may find it hard to do an interview with you."

"Here's a guy," Liz countered, "I've praised to the skies – his looks, his talent, his obvious adoration of his wife. Never have I heard a word from Mr. Cruise! As with most of the big stars I cover, it's like writing into a vacuum, all very noblesse oblige. I guess I should expect that. I should be grateful to be able to print their names. And I expect that. I suppose I should be used to this irrational super-sensitivity as well. But it's always a surprise."

Another one who's surprised by Tom is Madonna's ex-husband Sean Penn, Tom's co-star in "Taps." He recalled: "Tom surprised me a lot. Not so much that he became a very big star – because I think he's done some very good work - and not because I didn't think he was gifted; but he seemed so naive at the time that I worried if he was going to get lost on his way home." Tom sees Sean occasionally, and some of his old "Brat Pack" crowd, including Emilio Estevez, but mostly he pals around with his wife. "We're together twenty-four hours a day, seven days a week. She's become my best friend." At least he won't get lost on his way home.

When it comes to women, you might call Tom a "robolover." Although he has dismissed his first marriage to Mimi Rogers as "not even something I think about," his comments about his two wives are strikingly familiar. For instance, in 1990, Tom told *Rolling Stone*: "We live a lot of life together...Since I've been with her, it's opened me up a lot." Then, two years later, he told the same reporter he and Nicole "do a lot of stuff together" and that with his marriage to Nicole "a whole new life had opened up."

We're glad of that, after what Mimi told *Playboy* that their marriage ended because Cruise was mulling a career change from a hunk to a monk and she thought he had to be "celibate to maintain the purity of his instrument." Perhaps he was using his "instrument" elsewhere?

US magazine summed up Tom's appeal: "At his best, Tom Cruise isn't a bad actor, yet when he's really cooking on screen, in say 'The Color of Money,' it's not his skill as a performer that we're responding to. It's his free-gliding confidence as a star, the easy delight he takes in his own charisma. That big, toothy grin is actually his least streamlined feature; what's so winning about it is the spontaneity with which he lets it rip. When he smiles, he seems to be acknowledging – to the other characters and to every female in the audience, that his sexiness is something he can't control. It just comes beaming out of him.

"He's like a high school girl's dream of a brash-but-sensitive jock, and as long as he's playing hustlers or top guns, or the selfish smoothie of 'Rain Man,' he's great fun to watch."

"Now when he puts on the breaks," writer Trish Deitch Rohrer says about interviewing the star, "I feel caught in the act of caring. This is Cruise's power as well as his talent: to always make you care, whether on screen or in person, about the complicated young man, coming from a painful nowhere, who uses everything he has - looks, charm, wits, maniacal ambition, and superhuman energy - to succeed."

"I just surrounded myself with people who wanted to see me succeed," the star told Rohrer. "You're only as good as the people that you surround yourself with. And you better be careful about that.

"I look at certain people that aren't doing well and say, 'Well, who's around him? Do they want to see this person do well?' And often I might find one person that really doesn't want to see this guy succeed. And I've been very careful - and lucky - in avoiding that. Because sometimes you can waste your life dealing with problems that you're not even making yourself. You know? There's a lot of fat in life that you don't want to have to deal with."

Rohrer was ushered out of the interview and then Tom suddenly appeared at the door again saying, "Hey, again, thank you for everything. It was a real pleasure." And then he flashes his eyes at her, a signal from the guy inside the movie star, wishing his interviewer, a friend of a friend, a genuine goodbye. "I come away not knowing whether Cruise is someone who just doesn't talk about his darker side, or whether he's a soldier of a pseudoscience that asks him to repress his more chaotic feelings. I wonder whether he ever wakes up in the middle of the night, suddenly aware that his life is more complicated than he'd like it to be, or less satisfying...I wonder whether he'll be able to play deeper and more complex characters without first confronting his own depth and complexity."

Speaking of confrontations, gays in England certainly would like to confront Tom; the star took the "Hunk of the Year" honors in Capital Gays annual readers' poll in 1992. And speaking of awards, "If points were awarded for style, grace and poise," says the writer Michael Angelli, "Tom would get the silver boner award. Fault him for schmoozing it up on

'Barbara Walters,' but as an actor required to make love at will, here's your top gun. Watch him during that train ride with Rebecca DeMornay in 'Risky Business' and you'll see a young man with impeccable manners in matters of the sexual cha-cha, an actor who articulates ecstasy and pain without the bathos, a guy who brings something mystical to the dance of the seven veils and a guy with nice teeth."

Tom didn't make many friends as a teen, let alone do the sexual cha-cha. By the time he was 17, he had attended three high schools and studied for a year at a Franciscan seminary. "I never really seemed to fit in anywhere," he says. But we bet he was the cutest novice in history!

But Tom did develop some important survival mechanisms. "In every different place, I became another person. You've got to create your own world when you move like that. That was just my way of dealing with things. When you have to cope with a lot of problems, you are either going to sink or you are going to swim. You're either going to take the challenge and rise to the occasion or it's just going to devour you. You just make that choice. Am I going to survive? Or am I going to get eaten alive? And I was trying to survive the best I could."

In his senior year of high school, a knee injury kept Tom off the school wrestling team and he was miserable. Then he auditioned for a part in a school production of "Guys and Dolls" and got the part. From then on, he knew acting was what he wanted to do.

As legend has it, when the distinguished gay director Franco Zeffirelli heard Tom read for a role in his film "Endless Love," he uttered only: "Bellissimo!" and hired him on the spot.

Following "Love," Tom played a part in "Taps," then came "The Outsiders," one of the star's most treasured memories. It didn't bother him that some of his already-limited scenes ended up on the cutting-room floor: "I didn't look at it in terms of the size of the role or anything other than a chance to work with Francis Ford Coppola and all those guys." *Those guys* included Patrick Swayze, Rob Lowe, Ralph Macchio, Leif Garrett, and C. Thomas Howell. The lead actor, Matt Dillon, was already a star when the film, about troubled teens in Oklahoma in the sixties, was made. While the other so-called Brat Packers are a stylized, moody group, producer Brian

Grazer recalls Tom being "clean, straight-ahead, with the sort of positive energy force field that transcends all the posturing."

"I became more confident," recalls Tom about the filming. "Francis takes chances and I have a lot of respect for him. That's what I want to do with my career, take chances."

And in 1983, taking a chance was what "Risky Business" was all about. Director Paul Brickman says: "When he read for the part, he stopped himself halfway through and said, 'Wait, I think I can go in this direction,' and started over again. That was a courageous thing for a 19-year-old to do, but Tom is a courageous guy." Courageous and gorgeous, and as soon as he stripped to his underwear and tore into Bob Seger's "Old Time Rock 'n' Roll," Tom became full-fledged star. "Dancing with your pants off, that's total freedom," he recalls about the filming.

"At first Tom was vibrant local color," Richard Corliss wrote in Time, "one of the beautiful faces, a hunk for hire. Fast-forward through an early Cruise movie and you will find him in the corner of the frame, a winsome thing in love with his body, exuding the jock wholesomeness of a baby Christopher Reeve. Superboy. Dozens of such sleek stud puppies pass through Hollywood every year, usually boy toys that come and go without attracting much more than vagrant pubescent lust. There is little job security in being this week's pinup on the bedroom wall of American girlhood."

Not content on being merely a pin-up, Tom followed the huge success of "Risky Business" with an endearing performance as a blue collar worker's son in "All the Right Moves." He recalls, "I think the love scene was really sweet. She (Lea Thompson) had never done a love scene before and it was my second one. Love scenes are always really hard to do. You're taking your clothes off with this other person that you know from working with, but to bring the tenderness and the intimacy to that is very tough. I just try to relax and be supportive of the actress." Lea recalls that Tom was very supportive in not making it an exploitative scene. "He was really protective and really open and really great about it." When originally scripted, only the girl was to be nude but Tom decided to take all of his clothes off as well. "We wanted to make it as real as possible," Lea says, "that's why we had the long underwear. They waited until the last day to shoot it so I had to worry about it for three months; it's part of you that you aren't used to showing to other people, much less millions of them on cable. Once you get into it, it's not so bad: you worry about your dad, and that's about it."

Tom next made the film "Legend" and he appeared to be stranded amid all the special effects. "I can't predict what is going to be box-office and what is not. I think anyone who says, 'This is going to be a hit,' before the thing is made really doesn't know. Nobody knows. So you'd better do something you believe in and you love because if it's not financially successful, you'll still walk away with something."

The film "Top Gun" turned things around dramatically for Cruise, becoming the biggest grosser of the year. Cruise followed that smash with "The Color of Money," "Cocktail," "Rain Man," and "Born on the Fourth of July." Of "Cocktail," he says, "I really thought we were doing something special. But I never believed it was New York. It just wasn't the night scene in New York. When we saw it on the screen, we went, 'What is that? What the hell is that?'" For "July," Tom received an Academy Award nomination as best actor, but lost out to Daniel Day-Lewis, who won for his marvelous performance in "My Left Foot."

"I know where my faults are," Tom admits. "Somewhere I guess you want to find out, how far can I fall? How deep is the well? When am I going to hit? I want to feel that; I want to know that. How far can I take this? When it's all said and done, I want to be able to look back and say I've pushed it as far as I could. I've made some damn big mistakes and I look like an asshole a lot of the time but I did some good stuff, too."

Rumors that Tom might be "bi" got an amusing spin when the irreverent SPY magazine talked to some renowned Hollywood psychics. With an 8 x 10 glossy in hand, they asked, "Look at this movie star and tell me about his previous life." Psychic James Van Praagh said: "People assume things about him, but he keeps fooling everybody." Psychic Mary said: "He is a young soul. This is his first time in the world. I feel he's happy, but not really happy. People think he's a womanizer, but he is not. Some people have accused him of being gay. I feel a woman in his life but I don't see a connection between them." Psychic Helen: "He is a good athlete. He was an athlete before he was an actor. Maybe he should have stayed an athlete. I don't see a woman in his life right now. I feel he's hiding."

But there is a woman in his life, Kidman, the daughter of an Australian psychiatrist. She played the role of the doctor who patches up his race car driving character. After Tom divorced Rogers, he wed Nicole on Christmas Eve in 1990 in Telluride, Colorado. "Tom and I never have bodyguards," his bride says. "Honestly, I've never noticed any dangerous situation. And I'm not going to let it get to the point where I'm afraid to go to the supermarket. We go out and people will kind of wave when they see us. There's a great deal of interest in him wherever he goes but it's not a sort of mobby-type thing of ripping off his clothes. It's more like guys saying, 'Hey man, loved that movie.' And with girls it's more like 'Tee-hee' and gazing sort of lustfully at him. Seeing the way he gets treated took a few months to get used to but also one of the first things I thought when I met him was, he's a nice guy. Sure he has a nice car and he seems to have a lot of money and a beautiful smile, but when it comes down to what he's really like in his heart, his whole approach is just like anybody else."

Although Tom lost the Oscar twice now, Michael Caine has high praise for his talents, saying, "He'll have to wait until he's my age and ugly since only the pros can see how good he is."

Late in 1993, it was announced that the 1976 novel "Interview With the Vampire" would finally be brought to the screen with Tom and Brad Pitt co-starring. This immediately set gay hearts throbbing all over the world. But Anne Rice, author of the "Vampire Chronicles," said she was in a state of shock. "I'm speechless," she said. "Those actors are like Huck Finn and Tom Sawyer. They are not 18th-century vampires. This casting is so bizarre, the movie could be one of the biggest disasters of all time."

Could be. But not. "It's night, and you're flying," Anne Stockwell said in her *Advocate* review of "Interview With the Vampire." "The darkness is distinctly sexy as you float above the shadows of the Golden Gate Bridge. Then you bank and swoop in over the lights of San Francisco – a city with a pulse. That's how 'Interview With the Vampire' begins.

"It may not be politically correct, but the legend Of the vampire speaks in special ways to gay people. Like those other creatures of the right, we've been hounded and despised. We've primped to the fangs and hunted flesh after midnight And on countless mornings we've returned to the silence of our own coffin – the closet.

"Whether or not we claim that nightlife as our own, we understand its pull. And in her wildly popular Vampire Chronicles, novelist Anne Rice has put our feelings into words.

"...'Interview' is stunning. As the book's fans know, the vampire of the title is Louis (Brad Pitt). His tale begins in the Creole New Orleans of two centuries ago; a young plantation owner mourning his dead wife, Louis accepts the 'dark gift' – the chance to become a vampire – from a seductive French stranger named Lestat (Cruise, in a shocking and superb performance). But once the deed is done, Louis bitterly regrets it.

"Stuck with a dreary mate, Lestat decides that what the relationship needs is a baby. And with the entrance of the child vampire, Claudia (played by the remarkable Kirsten Dunst), Rice's tale really takes off. In this little family of killers who can't be killed, domestic violence takes on a whole new meaning. What's surprising is that their blood feuds are also deliciously funny.

"Every department of this movie pumps full throttle... Director of photography Philippe Rousselot triumphs over darkness, producing image after image of a night teeming with color and detail. Special-effects veteran Stan Winston uses the boldest strategy of all – restraint. His vampires' condition is betrayed only by little valicose veins – as if they used moisturizer with a blue-cheese base.

"...Suffice it to say that Rice's homoerotic undertones definitely make it to the screen."

Daniel Mangin in the *Bay Area Reporter* agreed: "Who said they took the homoeroticism out of 'Interview With the Vampire?' No way – this is one of the queerest pics of the year. Tom Cruise munching on Brad Pitt (so to speak), a half-minute two shot of Brad Pitt and Antonio Banderas on the verge of a smooch for the ages, Tom and Brad as gay fathers. Loved it!"

For her part, Anne Rice said, "When I saw Tom walking past

the mosquito netting around the bed, and I heard his voice, and I saw that he *was* Lestat. I knew it instantly. He had gotten it. And I do credit him. That actor, for some reason, really made contact with that character, and he produced a fabulous version of him. He made Lestat his own without taking my Lesat from me, and I feel tremendous love for Tom as a result. And in my conversations with him, I found him to be just a completely loving person. I really don't know Brad Pitt at all. I'm not connected with him. I know the readers loved him."

"This is no conventional horror flick told from the point of view of mere mortals thwarting forces of supernatural evil with pointed sticks," raved Andrew Collins in *Empire*. "Rather, it is a morbidly fascinating insight into the lifestyle of the undead that kicks in at minute eight, when aristocratic, fun-having, blond Lestat (Cruise erasing 'Top Gun' from your mind forever) gets his teeth into Louis.

"(It is) deliciously laced with pan-sexual innuendo (a pair of twin boys are offered to Lestat as a sweetener; women are drained without lust; Dunst's orphan Claudia treats Louis as her mother; male vampires are considered 'beautiful')."

One of the most persistent rumors in Hollywood is that Cruise is actually gay and the marriage was an elaborate publicity cover-up. Kidman won't talk about her husband's Scientology interests, but she certainly isn't shy about discussing his other proclivities.

"Honestly, wholeheartedly, looking you straight in the eye – it's *not* true," she says, getting a bit worked up. "It's utterly ridiculous, a total rumor. I suppose because I'm married to somebody very famous, our love life is under great speculation by many, *many* people at their dinner tables every night. But it gets invasive. Both of us are private people. We don't feel comfortable discussing what we do in bed at midnight – even though it *is* pretty damn good." She catches her breath and calms down. "Look, Tom and I are heterosexual, we're together, we're in love. It's weird even to have to answer that question."

From the outside looking in, at least, the two do seem almost bizarrely compatible. *Entertainment Weekly* suggested, "Both Cruise and Kidman prefer to live on the road, with homes in L.A. and Australia. Both enjoy jumping out of airplanes ('We love to sky-dive,' Kidman reports. 'It's a great rush'). And both possess famously ingratiating personalities."

Gay journalist Frank Sanello has been itching to write the definitive Cruise bio, but after a year of interviews, "I never met anyone who sucked Tom Cruise's cock." Michael Szymanski interviewed Tom and reported that it was, in his words, "quite pleasant." He did say, however, that "throughout our chat the *gaydar* wasn't even registering! I must agree with Tom's ex, Mimi Rogers, who confided (while we sat on her hotel room bed), 'I've known plenty of gay men in my life – dated some – but in four and a half years I never saw any indication that Tom was gay.'"

And speaking of magical duos, in January of 1991, at a gathering of movie industry pros, Tom was given the American Distinguished Achievement Award. When he accepted the honor from presenter Sean Connery, Tom told the audience that he was disappointed Nicole wasn't able to attend. At that point, Sean jokingly put his arm lovingly around Cruise, as if to say, will I do? Tom laughed, "I'm sorry. I like 'em a little younger." Shucks.

Alain Delon

Alain Delon

"I reacted to him the way I did years later to Rob Lowe and then Brad Pitt. Such outrageous handsomeness was somehow perverse, obscene. And the smile! The smile was beyond compare. Then when I read in a gay magazine that, when he was a teen, he was the most beautiful peddler of ass in all of Paris, I couldn't get enough of him. I searched for the proper French phrase to summarize him but none was adequate enough. Perhaps he was simply my reason d'etre for going to the movies in the '60s."
– The author, remembering 1965

During the sixties, America had Beatty, France had Delon. And there were striking similarities between these two gorgeous men. Alain was born in 1935, two years before Warren, and, like Warren, was catapulted to stardom by gay men. In Beatty's case it was the playwrights William Inge ("Splendor in the Grass") and Tennessee Williams ("The Roman Spring of Mrs. Stone"). For Delon, it was the notorious director Luchino Visconti and his lover and protege Franco Zeffirelli.

Like Beatty, Alain was top-billed at the beginning of his career. But, unlike his American counterpart, the French actor's origins were humble and he had little acting training. A rebellious youth, Delon was the product of a broken home and was expelled from numerous Catholic schools before enlisting in the French Navy at the age of 17 and serving as a parachutist in Indochina. (This experience served him well in 1965 when he made "The Lost Command" starring with Anthony Quinn, based on the novel "The Centurions" by Jean Larteguy.)

When he was 22, the handsome man was discovered at the Cannes Film Festival and was soon appearing before the cameras in Visconti's 1960 Italian film, "Rocco and His Brothers," starring as the saintly Rocco. The film was named the best of the year at the Venice Film festival and became an international hit. The film, with stunning photography by Giuseppe Rotunno, was restored to its original length of 180 minutes in 1991 and that is the version available on video today.

In 1962, in Michelangelo Antonioni's "Eclipse," opposite Monica Vitti, Rene Clement's adaptation of Patricia Highsmith's "The Amazing Mr. Ripley," the amazing Alain was Tom Ripley, a stockbroker of questionable morals (surely a man ahead of his time). The fascinating film, seeing Rome and its men through the filter of Vitti's character, had abundant scenes of Delon's lean, bare torso in swim trunks, and was released the same year that Beatty was also playing a ladykiller in "All Fall Down."

In 1963, a gangster film, "Any Number Can Win" with Jean Gabin, featured plenty of footage of the star in bathing attire on the French Riviera. That same year, Delon appeared for Visconti again in "The Leopard," with Burt Lancaster, and the film was the winner of the Golden Palm as Best Picture of the Year at the Cannes Film Festival. Originally released in America in 1965 in a badly dubbed, 165-minute version, it has been finally restored to its original 205-minute length, and Leonard Maltin says the concluding hour long banquet is "one of the greatest set pieces in motion picture history." Maltin also rates the coupling of Delon and his co-star Claudia Cardinale as "close to final word in romantic pairings."

The following year, Delon's fans were treated to a demonstration of his charming, French-style lovemaking techniques in Rene Clement's "Joy House," based on the novel by Dany Keene. He played a playboy on the run who seeks refuge in an old mansion run by two American women, Lola Albright and Jane Fonda.

A year later, Alain appeared as an ambitious photographer in a segment of Anthony Asquith's all-star "The Yellow Rolls Royce" for MGM, attempting to lure Shirley MacLaine, playing a dim-witted moll, from the clutches of mobster George C. Scott, under the understanding, watchful eyes of *aide de camp* Art Carney. Besides being a delightful romp, it was a chance to glimpse the star at the peak of his beauty in the bathing attire of pre-World War II days. That same year, he also appeared in Rene Clement's all star "Is Paris Burning?" Even in this depressing tale of Paris being occupied by the Nazis, filmed in black and white, Delon's beauty ignites the screen.

It was during this period that Hollywood discovered Alain.

In 1965 he was imported to Tinseltown to star in "Once a Thief" with Ann Margret and Van Heflin and, of all things, a western called "Texas Across the River," with Dean Martin, but the show was stolen by Joey Bishop as a deadpan Indian.

His Hollywood films did not fare well at the box-office and were poorly received by critics. Michael Winner, the director of 1973's "Scorpio," again with Burt Lancaster and one of Alain's few good American movies, recalls: "His English was so poor I asked him to speak slower and he stormed off the set. 'On all my other American pictures, they told me to speak fast so it would look like I understood what I was saying!' he fumed. 'Well,' I said, 'all of your other American pictures were total disasters!'" "Scorpio," it turned out, was also a box-office failure because it was ahead of its time, showing, before it was fashionable, the CIA doing naughty things.

During the late '60 and early '70s, Delon continued to be wildly popular in his native land, appearing, as usual, with a succession of top international beauties including Marianne Faithfull ("Girl on a Motorcycle" for Jack Cardiff), Joanna Shimkus ("The Last Adventure"), again with Fonda, in her period with Roger Vadim and Brigitte Bardot ("Spirits of the Dead") and Romy Schneider ("The Swimming Pool"), but it was in gangster films that the public adored him most. In 1970, he scored in "The Sicilian Clan," again with Jean Gabin, and "Borsalino," with Jean-Paul Belmondo, in which the star wore the same period bathing suit he did in "The Yellow Rolls Royce."

In 1975, the year Beatty had his greatest success with "Shampoo," exposing tantalizing glimpses of his flesh, Delon was shedding all his clothes in "Shock," (re-titled "Shock Treatment" in some venues). The scenes when Alain goes skin-dipping with some friends gave his fans a decent full frontal.

Following Beatty's lead, Delon began producing his own films but sadly without his American counterpart's success. Still, he continued to appear with the top female stars of the day, all anxious to work with the durably sexy star. He made "Mr. Klein" with Jeanne Moreau and "Dirty Money" with Catherine Deneuve.

In 1984, a biographer alleged that Alain had been intimately involved with the Marseilles underworld and also was a bisexual. Delon got a court injunction to stop the book from being distributed but its first printing was sold out in a matter of weeks.

Burned by his Hollywood experience, Alain in recent years has seldom ventured across the Atlantic. But in 1990 he was persuaded to visit Florida to add some showbiz glamour to the French Film festival in Sarasota. Originally, festival planners had wanted Alain to preside at the opening ceremonies and actress Catherine Deneuve was scheduled to receive a special tribute the following day. But Deneuve, who doesn't get along with Alain and was not about to be upstaged by him, demanded that she be the first one in the spotlight. Her appearance was rescheduled for Friday afternoon.

The official opening-night selection was Alain's "Dancing Machine," which was panned by critics and audience members alike. At a critics' panel, an *Esquire* magazine reviewer called it "such a bizarre disaster that I found it rather enjoyable." Local critic George Mayer wrote, "It's not enjoyable to see Delon in the tacky 'Dancing Machine.' The plot involves some claptrap mystery about why people keep dying with Delon in the vicinity. Seems he's run a dance company since a motorcycle crash ended his days on stage and his devotees want his approval so much they pay him lots of money and then dance themselves literally to death.

"Well, if you buy that you may also buy Claude Brasseur as a cop whose intuition points a finger at Delon. Complications and visual cliches pile up as often as corpses. Finally, a stunningly stupid rooftop chase resolves everything."

At the opening night ceremonies, with Delon in attendance, Artistic Director Molly Haskell, who later admitted she was not a trained diplomat, said that Gerard Depardieu and Daniel Auteuil were "the two finest actors in French cinema today."

While he might not be highly regarded as a thespian, Delon has been an international star for thirty years and, like Warren Beatty, still gets raves as a male sex symbol. As Mayer said, "Showing some distinguished gray and a Don Johnson stubble, he looks just fine."

Johnny Depp

*"Brando adores him. He loves Johnny's genuineness and modesty
and that he is who he is. You're not a great actor
like Brando for nothing, you know.
He knows how to recognize a sham in any shape."*
– Co-star Faye Dunaway

One of the pleasanter aspects of being a published editor
dealing in the perverse is that you get wonderful letters from
guys all over the world who wish to share with you their latest
"finds." For instance, in the spring of 1995, Neil in California
wrote, "For a hard-on that lasts two full hours, see Johnny
Depp in 'Don Juan DeMarco.'"

Well, hard or no hard, it was good to see Depp the Delicious
in a glamorous part for a change. Writing in the *New Yorker*,
Anthony Lane agreed, "The part wasn't written for him but
makes perfect sense as a extended riff on the fact that at least
half the human race already finds Johnny Depp completely
adorable. Once his hand has slipped into Juan's glove, he's
snug in the role, and too smart to try and squeeze us for extra
sympathy."

Bob Satuloff, in the *New York Native*, found Johnny was
snug in his pants as well: "...(It) bears all the earmarks of a
desperate, Band-Aid job, and roles for Marlon Brando and Faye
Dunaway that give them scant opportunity to display the
thespic fireworks that made their legendary reputations, it is
nevertheless worth seeing, if not at the eight-bucks-a-pop going
rate, at least on video – for the charismatic, technically dazzling
performance of Johnny Depp, who is without a doubt the best
young actor in American movies.

"Depp breathes life, humor, sensuality, and enormous depth
of feeling into a role that's really an unplayable literary conceit.
The character claims to be the descendant of the world's
greatest lover. Dressed in a low-cut, blousy shirt, poured-into
pants, boots, and a mask, he makes a most convincing case for
himself in the film's opening scene as he strides into a New
York hotel dining room, sits down, uninvited, at a small table
opposite a beautiful woman (Marita Geraghty), and proceeds to
seduce her, first with his poetic words, then physically, in an

upstairs room."

Owen Gleiberman in *US* agreed: "Writer-director Jeremy Leven's coup was to cast Johnny Depp as Don Juan, Marlon Brando as his shrink, and Faye Dunaway as the doctor's wife – and to let whimsy rip... Depp, in a soft, seductive accent, makes a serious, tender Don. The role falls smack in the middle of Depp territory – a misfit with a romantic heart – but there's more appealing manliness in this performance than could be tweezed out (of any of his others.)"

Johnny's "appealing manliness" was best described by Holly Millea, senior editor of *Premiere*, when she wrote, "Depp's face possesses a beauty usually reserved for apostles and saints and silent-movie stars. Draped over perfect bone structure, his impossibly pale skin is without a line or a crease – this despite 31 years, too many cigarettes, other interesting substances, and frequent extreme acts of human expression. It is a countenance one would not hide, but in 'Don Juan DeMarco,' Depp is a masked man."

Masked or unmasked, Johnny is simply irresistible, but there's more to him than a pretty face. His "What's Eating Gilbert Grape" co-star Leonardo DiCaprio says, "There's an element of Johnny that's extremely nice and extremely cool, but at the same time, he's hard to figure out. But that's what makes him interesting." Interesting to almost everybody, it seems. "Teenage girls swoon over horses and ballet dancers and rebels," writer Johanna Schneller says. "Depp is somehow all those things. He wears work boots and befriends fringe people and gives money to sick children. He thinks deep thoughts and pulls stupid pranks with his friends. He is a stoner – he is the philosopher-king of the stoners."

"The first day on 'Benny and Joon,' my husband and I had just split up, and I was in that hysterical funk you get in when you're trying to be pulled-together," says Mary Stuart Masterson, Depp's co-star in the film. "But when Johnny walked in, the energy in the room changed. There's something really amazing about him, his generosity of spirit."

Depp's wardrobe guy Ken Smiley has helped him transform his trailer from beige Americana to Oriental opium den, draping walls, ceiling and furniture with gold-embossed Indian fabrics. One end of the living area has been converted into a shrine: a copy of William Saroyan's *The Trouble With Tigers*, a purple lava lamp and a pewter heart-framed portrait of Depp and his girlfriend, the model Kate Moss, flicker in the light of a dozen votive candles. Burning incense and Ravi Shankar sitar music complete the effect. "Johnny is so totally different from most actors," says Smiley. "He really likes who he is and he's really secure in that. He treats other people the way he wants to be treated. That's why we stay with him."

But *Saint* Johnny is not without his demons: insomnia, a fear of crowds, chain smoking, a natural antagonism toward authority figures and an "erratic" personality that makes him a little tough to live with. "I'm 30 different people sometimes," he says. "One day you wake up and you're somebody else, nowhere near who you were when you went to sleep."

Previous to the infamous incident when he broke up the furniture at the Mark hotel in New York, Depp had been arrested three times, for getting into a fight in Vancouver, speeding in Arizona, and once in Beverly Hills, for jaywalking. "The cop was one of those guys who puts on a uniform and suddenly he feels his penis begin to grow," Depp says. "He's all bent out of shape and hard as nails, a real idiot." As he was writing out the jaywalking ticket, the cop ordered Depp to put out his cigarette. Depp refused, so the cop twisted his wrist until the cigarette fell from his hand. He lit another. "Next thing I knew, him and his partner handcuffed me and put me in a cell for a few hours. I'm not scared by those people, they just make me angry. You get the feeling there's nothing you can do, but there is something you can do. Don't take shit from them."

If there was one thing he learned from these incidents and his four-year on-again, off-again relationship with Winona Ryder, it's that no matter how many details you feed the media, or as he likes to call it "the sick pig machine," it's never satisfied. Says the star, "You'll never see one of those tabloids say, 'God, what a nice guy Johnny Depp is because people just aren't interested.

"Initially, I tried to be open," he says of his early days in Hollywood. "[I thought] I'll just say what I'm feeling right now, let them swallow that and then they'll leave me alone. [But] that creates even more of a monster. You're walking around, you eat a piece of pizza, go visit the Colosseum, next thing you know there's a guy with a lens about as long as your leg taking pictures. Whether Kate and I are together or not is not going to save anybody's life. It's nobody's fucking business but mine or hers. I'd rather come out in the press and say I'm fucking dogs or goats or rats than attempt to [rely on them to] write anything real about my relationship."

"There is venom in his choice of words," his interviewer for *Esquire* reported, "but they are spoken matter-of-factly, with an almost eerie absence of malice in the tone. Depp is uncomfortable in the role of the angry man, he'd much rather play the clown. He has an appreciation for the more absurd characters and circumstances of life. He derives fiendish pleasure, for example, from checking into hotels under naughty pseudonyms, forcing friend and stranger alike to participate in the joke."

One of Depp's favorite jokes is to check into a hotel as Mr. Donkey Penis. He says, "It's funny to get a wake-up call at some ludicrous hour, like 5:30 am, and the guy has to say, 'Good morning Mr. Donkey Penis. You have to get up now.'

"Unfortunately, I feel more comfortable in front of the camera now than I do in life," he admits. "On the set, you feel close to the people; you're working together. When you're in a restaurant in real life, you're having dinner with the girl, drinking wine, you're looking around and there are all these people looking at you. It's a little weird."

Weird too was his trip to the Oscar ceremony. "There I was. Jesus, I still don't know why. I figured, 'Well, fuck it, maybe I'll just see what it's like, you know?' It was Fellini on intense psilocybin, the company picnic gone absolutely screwy. Everybody pretends to know each other. You've never met each other and it's, you know, 'Hey, howya doin'?' It was so much like a circus that I was howling. I was really nervous. I actually met Tom Cruise at the Academy Awards. He came up and said, 'Hi Johnny, how are you?' I said, 'Hi Tom, how are you doing?' He said, 'This is my wife, Nicole,' and I said, 'How do you do, Nicole? Nice to meet you.' And everybody went about their business, I wiped off my shoe and he wiped off his jacket *[laughing]*. No, he was actually sweet. Then I'm backstage, pacing around, *desperate* to smoke a cigarette in this politically correct climate. I just wanted to fill my lungs with smoke. Then I met Al Pacino back there and he was really cool, telling me, 'This is awful, isn't it?' It made me feel better because I *love* Al Pacino. But when I was gonna walk out and do the thing, I didn't know if I was gonna drop, pass out completely, just spontaneously combust, or projectile vomit into the audience. Apparently, I got the words out fairly clearly, went outside, smoked, got into the car and split. I was real freaked out."

America first heard his impossibly perfect showbiz name in 1987, when it tripped off the lips of every American teenage girl. The son of John and Betty Sue Depp, now divorced, had dropped out of high school eight years before and had spent most of his youth tearing up his hometown of Miramar, Florida, outside Miami, where his dad was a public-works official. It was no small irony that Depp would shoot to fame at age twenty-four as an undercover high school narc on *21 Jump Street*.

"As a kid I was very bored until I discovered the guitar, which is my first love," he explains. "For all that confusing period of puberty, you don't know what's going on. I locked myself in my room and played guitar. Guitar, guitar every day. That was my obsession. I was pretty much a normal kid. I was just a little too bored and maybe a little too curious."

His first experiences of sex were not a success he claims. He took his first real date to see "Star Wars" at a drive-in. "I was all excited but it turned into a total disaster because we both ended up getting bitten everywhere by mosquitoes," says Johnny. "It was so bad that I had to get some insect repellant. It sounds funny now but it wasn't at the time, believe me."

He was committed enough to rock 'n' roll to pack up his guitar, his wife (Lori Allison, whom he married and split from within a year), and his band (the Kids) and move to Los Angeles, where he subsisted by selling pens over the phone ("My first acting job") until his wife's ex-boyfriend Nicolas Cage helped him get his first real acting job, in "A Nightmare on Elm Street." Depp remembers making $1,200 a week for six weeks of work. ("Never had I seen anything like that.") Next came "Private Resort," which didn't make him famous but did give us the only view so far of his naked butt. A small part in "Platoon" followed, but it was didn't make him famous, it did show his naked butt. *Street* introduced Depp to bigtime celebrity and led to a peak of ten thousand letters a week from lovesick fans.

Controversy has dogged him ever since he broke into acting. He received numerous death threats including one from a man who had been stalking him for several months. The man was convinced he was the real Johnny Depp and he vowed to prove it by assassinating the actor.

"There are two kinds of fans," Depp observes. "There's the kind who just wants your autograph or to say something nice. That's fine. But there are these guys who are too cool for autographs. People try to piss you off. They want to get your attention, including some who want to take away my life. When you start to think about the reality of that, it makes you stop and say, 'What the hell do I do?' Why does a stranger suddenly want to stop me from breathing, stop me from experiencing life? I'm sure this kind of thing happens to a lot of people but it's something I'll never get used to.

"I carry a gun now because of the death threats. Some people seem to attract a certain amount of weirdness and I'm one of them."

One interviewer suggested that after looking in vain for something wrong with Depp's perfect features, you start getting picky. His blue work shirt, white T-shirt, and gray jeans do a nice job of not distracting you from his face: "At the moment, he sits in a black vinyl booth at his black-walled Hollywood hangout, the Viper Room, demonstrating his perfect ability to be cool without trying. He's almost annoyingly good at it. Without waiting for an answer, Depp gets up to pour himself another cup of black coffee from behind the bar. The guy drinks an enormous amount of coffee. After hanging out with Depp for a while, you start to realize how he came to be awake in his hotel suite at five in the morning and maybe a little jittery. He returns to the booth, and within seconds another cigarette comes out of the open pack of Camel Specials at his right elbow. That pack sits on top of an unopened one. He picks up a gun and pulls the trigger. A flame comes out. 'It doesn't always work,' Depp says, glaring at the lighter contemptuously."

About the Mark incident, "Let's just say that my stay there

wasn't particularly comfortable," Depp says. This may strike those who stay in Marriotts as a relative term. But for a man who has spent the better part of three decades in jeans and T-shirts, comfort is a top priority. Indeed, *Movieline* devoted several pages to photos of Johnny's various "fashion statements" through the years: "Long leather jacket and shades for that Jim Morrison look, the white T-shirts, the ever-growing hair, unwashed and not just hanging in, but literally draping his face , and the work boots and bowling shirt. What's he rebelling against? Those fabulous cheekbones? Depp's too pretty to be too bad, and he knows it: it doesn't matter what he shows up wearing they'll still go gaga. So he tries the sleazy lounge-lizard look, hair slicked back, and adds the pen in his pocket for perhaps no better reason than that it's nerdy, fashion nihilism. A lot of the time when you see Depp out on the town these days, he's well over the edge into disheveled. An out-of-towner might think gee, why doesn't this guy pay some attention to his appearance, look in the mirror once in a while? Friends, he does. This look is the work of an expert."

He also fancies himself as somewhat of an expert in the sack and he couldn't pay for sex. "That's not my thing, paying for sex. Even if I did, I wouldn't talk about it. You're in a certain position, you gotta be careful, you gotta be smart, you gotta think a little bit. And the first thing is: don't say a word to nobody about nothing anytime ever. This is a rumor-fueled society.

"And it's a weird time to do anything. Not only do you have to worry about screwing and wearing condoms and shit like that, you have to worry about kissing, about being sneezed on, and your fucking flesh rotting off. It's violence and shit everywhere."

In Depp's view, the source of his discomfort at the Mark was Jim Keegan. As the hotel's midnight-to-eight security guard, Keegan saw Depp frequently coming in and out of the Mark's quiet, austere lobby. Depp, an insomniac, had been out several nights on the town in New York, and his peak partying hours coincided with Keegan's watch.

"It seemed like this guy couldn't stand Johnny," says Jonathan Shaw, a close friend since the early 1980s, when Depp was a Los Angeles rock 'n' roller in the slow lane and Shaw a local tattoo artist. "Johnny dressed in leather and jeans and not all fancy like everybody else in the joint." Shaw remembers this from his own visits to the hotel to see Depp, who confirms the description. 'The guy was a little froggy,' Depp says. "He decided that he was going to 'Let me get in the famous guy's face.' I don't really take too well to that."

"That guy had probably one too many cups of coffee that night," Depp reflects, and he is in a position to know. "He was particularly feisty. He decided to call the shots in a way that I didn't think was particularly necessary. If I walk into an antique shop and I bend down to look at something over here and I accidentally knock a pot off the rack, of course I'd pay for it. If I bust a piece of glass, I smash a mirror or whatever, I'll pay for it. I can probably handle the bill. That's that."

Keegan told Depp he'd have to leave the hotel or he would call the police. Depp offered to pay for the damages but argued that he shouldn't have to check out. So Keegan called the police, and Johnny left in the company of three officers from the Nineteenth Precinct. (By the time of his release the next afternoon, Depp had occupied three cells: at the precinct, at Central Booking, and in the Tombs behind New York City police headquarters. Women officers mobbed him at all three.)

The night after the hotel incident, Depp went with Jonathan Shaw and some other pals to a downtown bar called Babyland. By the next day, he'd become another headline across Page Six in the *Post*: DEPP PALS IN EAST VILLAGE BRAWL. It didn't take long for Johnny Depp-lorable *to* show his wild side again following his hotel hijinks the other night," Page Six read, saying Depp "allegedly sparked a fight." The item quoted one man's version that Depp "slammed into me" and said, "Fuck you."

Depp tells it differently: "This guy walked past me in the bar. He pulled out what resembled a penis – but I have a sneaking suspicion it might have been a thimble, this goofy fucking guy – and said something like, 'Suck my dick.' I'd *just* gotten out of jail. They'd said, 'You're to stay out of trouble for six months.' Meanwhile, it's less than six hours later. My first instinct was to . . . we all have that animal instinct inside of us . . . your instinct is, Go for the throat."

Most gays would reach a little lower if they got Johnny in

front of them. *The Advocate* said what is of interest to Depp's gay fans is when he will play a gay character. "Of course I'd play a homosexual in a movie," he says without hesitation. The subject gets a little stickier, though, when the question of whether the actor would play a gay love scene arises. "Sure," he insists, "but actual penetration would pose a slight problem."

Then how about an on-screen kiss? Says Depp with just the right amount of shy sex appeal: "Yeah, that'd be all right."

In fact, Johnny's had dreams of being ravaged by one of the most famous queers of all time: "I've stayed at this little hotel in Paris, in the room where Oscar Wilde died," says Depp. In homage to the wit, the furniture is kept in the style that it was at the moment of his passing. "I slept in the room that Oscar Wilde died in, and I thought that quite possibly, if I fell asleep too deeply, somewhere about 5 A.M. I might be abused in some obtuse way. Get taken advantage of. At least he had a good sense of humor.

"Then some tabloid said that I was a huge homophobe. Figure this out. One of my best friends is John Waters. We went for a drink in a gay bar that John has gone to in New York City. A guy comes up and says, 'Hey John, I'm a big fan of your films,' and, 'Oh, Johnny, I've liked your movies.' A real nice guy. He began to tell us about himself and said, 'I'm HIV-positive.' And what do you say to that kind of thing? At the end, when we were saying good-bye, he said, 'John, do you mind if I give you a kiss on the cheek?' John said no and the guy kissed him on the cheek. And he said, 'Johnny, do you mind?' and I said, 'No, go ahead,' and he gave me a kiss on the cheek too. We finished our drinks and split, went to some other bar or something. The next day, one of those tabloid shitheads said I was standing at the bar with John Waters and some guy came up and kissed me and I ran out of the place freaked out, all fucking weirded out by the whole scenario. If I was homophobic, why would I be in the bar and why would one of my best friends be John Waters? [But] they can say what they want because I don't read it."

Another of Johnny's gay pals is the poet Allen Ginsberg. His conversation with the poet was published in *Interview*. Johnny recalled they had talked about hemp when last they were together. "Yeah, because they used to make everything, rope and paper, out of hemp."

"That would certainly change the war on drugs a bit [laughs] Well, shall we continue this talk another time?"

"Yeah, I would love to. Anytime. I'm around."

"O.K. I love you."

"Hey, thank you, man. I love you, too."

"Bye."

George Wayne reported that ever since the last California earthquake when his house was destroyed, Depp began shuttling all over the world from one chic hotel to the next. He and Kate could be found holed up at fashionable inns in Port Antonio, Miami Beach, London and New York, where, of course, he was busted. "In South Beach, the duo took over a suite at the Raleigh, and their strange behavior had all those nosy queens who infest the hotel in a tizzy. Stories of Johnny and Kate rarely leaving their messy suite, ordering room service and barely touching it – their recent SoBe sojourn had those queens smacking out all kinds of rumors. If I were them, I would stay anywhere else *but* the Raleigh."

Depp feels he attracts of lot of this "weirdness" because of his Los Angeles nightclub, The Viper Room. It was outside the club that River Phoenix died from a drug overdose.

"It was devastating. It was a very tragic loss," says Johnny. "I respected River tremendously. He was a good person and a good soul. And he had a great heart and a great brain and a very, very promising future. It's a sad and unfortunate loss. I really feel for his family and friends.

"The tragedy was that a very sweet guy made big, big mistakes, fatal mistakes. The rest of it has the press writing and speculating horrible things that were hurtful to River's family, friends, fans and the people close to him in his life. They turned tragedy, the unfortunate passing of River Phoenix, into a circus."

And made life hell for Johnny for awhile. "In Hollywood they are not comfortable if they can't label you. If they can't call you something, they don't know what to do," Depp says. "I don't want to be called anything other than just a guy who acts now and again.

"They may think of me as an actor who does unusual roles,

like 'Ed Wood,' but it certainly isn't the same as being called a heart-throb. And it's not the same as being called a teen idol. If they're calling me an oddball or a guy who does unusual stuff, at least that's closer to home."

Besides his success as Don Juan, Johnny was terrific as Ed Wood. *Rolling Stone* said, "The usually recessive Depp breaks form to express Wood's wide-eyed optimism. Depp is terrific in a hilarious heartfelt performance, but his fast-talking, arm-flailing hustle throws you at first. Selling himself to Grade Z mogul George Weiss (Mike Start) or starletgirlftiend Dolores Fuller (Sarah Jessica Parket in a wicked sendup of Fuller's stiff emoting), Wood sounds like Jon Lovitz's MasterThespian ('Acting!' 'Get to know me!'). There is little delicacy, just delicious fun."

His completed movie "Dead Man" is a black-and-white western by independent filmmaker Jim Jarmusch. which he's following with perhaps his most commercial project yet, a thriller, "Nick of Time," trusting himself to director John Badham ("Saturday Night Fever" and "WarGames"). "I mean," Johnny said, "if Keanu can go to a gym – "

But despite his low-budget returns, Depp has managed to keep the industry believing he is a star – a title sometimes defined by an actor's talent for keeping his name in the papers. Still, the "hotel thing" hasn't hurt his career. Says John Waters. "He looked good under arrest. I loved the handcuffs – they always work. Criminal movie star is a really good look for Johnny."

Matt Dillon as he appeared during
the filming of "The Outsiders."

Matt Dillon

*"He's easy on the eyes. There's the perfectly tousled coif, the
flawless skin and the puppylike gaze, full of longing. His
curvy lips were built to pout but generally stay parted, as if to say
'Whaa - ?' You can see why his face works so well on film.
When he smiles, he almost looks backlit: The cheekbones flare and
the chin squares off, just as a rakish grin starts to spread. His
only less-than-classical features are a small, shy nose and the soft
angle of the skin beneath his chin, a soupcon of baby fat."*
– Writer Lucy Kaylin

Matt Dillon is an anomaly. He's the only actor of his
generation to continue to make movies while never having had
a real blockbuster hit. An icon on the dark side, he's so
handsome that he becomes almost stylized looking, which in
movies goes a long way. It is the kind of handsomeness that
hypnotizes the camera, lures it to follow him even if it might
not want to go. And the camera loves him so much that it's
nearly impossible to remember the names of his female co -
stars.

In 1979, casting director Vic Ramos plucked the blossoming
14-year-old fuck-up out of his class at Larchmont's Hommocks
School and put him in "Over the Edge." Dillon was in the
picture for only half of its running time but he dominates it.
Ramos, in casting for 20 years, took Dillon seriously from the
start. He wrote on a note card: "Should be a movie star." "It
took me maybe thirty seconds to realize that Matt had
everything. Fourteen years old, five foot five, 125 pounds, and
yet he had it all.

"I knew what was going to happen with the cheekbones and
the body, that he was going to grow taller and more handsome,
but it was his instincts that impressed me. He knew we were
looking for a tough kid and he came in as the toughest. He had
the wit, the savvy to whip that act together and become that
character." Ramos has been his manager ever since.

In his next film, "My Bodyguard," Matt seemed to be
genuinely turned on by his capacity to bully the wimp pacifist

he chose to pick on. "Little Darlings" cemented his heartthrob status, largely because he played a long scene in nothing but his jockey shorts. He became less fleshy, more angelic and beautiful during this period in a way that most pin-ups don't.

In 1983, with roles in both of Francis Ford Coppola's adaptations of S. E. Hinton's novels, "The Outsiders" and "Rumble Fish," Dillon became not only a star but an icon, THE teen idol of the early eighties. Each month for years Dillon related contests, fan club news, recycled interviews and photos clogged the pages of tacky teen fan magazines. During the filming of "Tex," smitten girls surrounded his dressing room and just stood there screaming. Matt recalls: "Having girls flip out over you was appealing at first, but it was never what I was in it for, ever. Ever, ever."

While "The Outsiders" was the most well received of the Coppola films, "Rumble Fish" remains Dillon's favorite of all of his films.

But the star will tell you he wasn't those characters: "I'd read the scripts and say, 'Okay, I can relate to that,' then jerk 'em, fool 'em into thinking I'm that." Director Coppola: "Matt is such a regular kid, a very sweet natured, unaffected kid. You almost don't want to say any more about him because it might destroy it."

When you see him in person, you can't ignore the fact that he doesn't look like other people. He's tall (six-foot-one) and slim and his facial bone structure is exquisitely chiselled; his hair thick and impeccably coiffed. Reflecting on his own beauty, the star says: "I really don't think I'm handsome. I don't see myself that way. When I look at myself, I see someone who is OK-looking, but I definitely don't get it when I'm called handsome. Oh, I have pretty decent features and even if I am handsome in the eyes of others, well, it's not a bad thing. It's been more of an asset than anything else. But it can also be a barrier of sorts. There were certain roles I couldn't get because people thought I was, I don't know, too pretty or whatever, but there's nothing I can do about that.

"I felt like the teen idol thing just missed the point of who I was. I dislike the terms idol and heartthrob and beefcake. I am an actor and I would like to be considered an actor, not an idol."

On screen, to be heroic, to be loved, to save people, to be redeemed, didn't seem to be in the cards for Dillon. In fact, in five of his movies, he's been shot. But he was at his cagiest in "Flamingo Kid," Garry Marshall's unassuming little comedy that has probably made the most profit of any Dillon picture. His worst experience was making "Rebel" in Australia. "A nightmare. The worst movie I've ever done. I don't even want to talk about it." Not far behind was Arthur Penn's "Target" with Gene Hackman. "I just couldn't get hold of that character. I was too old for it, they should have cast somebody younger."

About his critically acclaimed role in "Drugstore Cowboy," Matt says it was exciting working with novelist William S. Burroughs, who played a junkie priest. "That's the real deal you're looking at there, the granddaddy of the beat generation."

In "A Kiss Before Dying," a film noir remake of an old Robert Wagner vehicle, Dillon exposed his naked buttocks for the first time. Wrote a columnist in a gay newspaper: "Check out Matt Dillon's hot male buns in a scene...it's worth dying for!" Another gay critic said: "Dillon is convincingly evil, but gets little opportunity to display his character's charm that's supposed to make him so irresistible. (Speaking of his irresistibility, he shows quite a bit of his body in some medium-hot love scenes.)" Another critic had high praise for Dillon but not his co-star: "With Dillon's career on its way up, his acting ability sharpening along the way, a casting with a mediocre actress like Sean Young is a sad mistake."

Although he often bemoans the fact that some of the best roles go to Tom Cruise (or Costner or Rourke) instead of him, Dillon admires his one-time co-star: "Tom works hard. I wouldn't have done some of the movies he chose to do and I couldn't have done 'Top Gun' but everyone has to go their own way." He's turned down roles he wished he'd taken but says, "I can't cry over spilled milk. It's just not my way. At the end of the day, it's only a movie."

In "Singles," released in August, 1992, Matt got good reviews playing wanna-be rock star Cliff Poncier, leader of a band called Citizen Dick, a hunky trash guitarist: "...a wonderfully droll, dopey Dillon..." one critic said. Owen Gleiberman raved: "Dillon looks terrific in his Valkyrie locks and is the movie's ace scene stealer. He strikes an endearing balance between glamour and stoned goofiness."

In late 1993, Matt appeared on screen in the aptly titled "Mr. Wonderful," in which he tries to find a husband for his ex-wife so he can quit paying alimony. "The film teaches us there is a Mr. Wonderful – it's just not the person that anybody imagines it's going to be," says director Anthony Minghella. And Matt co-starred with Danny Glover in "The Saint of Fort Washington," about a homeless Vietnam vet who takes an abandoned schizophrenic under his wing.

Also in 1993, Matt was busy directing Dinosaur Jr.'s video, "Get Me," and realizing a dream by doing background vocals for the Flying Burrito Brothers' "Hot Burrito #2," which was available only in the U.K.

In 1995, Matt appeared oposite Nicole Kidman (Mrs. Tom Cruise) in "To Die For." Based on Joyce Maynard's novel (turned into a drippingly satirical screenplay by Buck Henry), the pitch-black comedy has Kidman playing a rapacious small-town TV personality who'll do anything to get ahead – including persuading her teenage lover (Joaquin Phoenix – River's brother) to kill her husband (Matt). It may well be the box-office hit that has always eluded Dillon.

Matt rarely drinks, quit smoking, and has no more "wild periods" when he went "looking for trouble" like he did in the '80s. "Everybody goes through a period like that," he shrugs, but doesn't define "period" or "trouble." To keep himself straight, he stays away from Hollywood. "Every time you turn around in L.A.," Matt says, "it's show biz. That town'll break you, no matter how tough a bronco you are when you ride in." In New York, where he lives, sometimes in an apartment, sometimes in a hotel, he is able to satisfy his taste for jazz, blues, and other things that predate him. Writer Lucy Kaylin: "He's stuck on the city's air of edgy sophistication and values things and people tested by time, with a grittiness to prove it."

If he could live anywhere in the world, though, he'd take Florence. "I love beautiful things and I'm interested in painting myself. My father bought me some oils for Christmas. He's a portrait painter. I do a lot of drawing and stuff, but this is a whole other thing. I've gotta take some classes. I like the lifestyle in Italy. I like a siesta. I like the way that living your life becomes an art itself. In America you can lose track of that; everything's based on the values of success."

To see what the star is really like, you have to go to New York, to spend some time with him, this living youth symbol with the world weary voice, who always arrives late despite his famous early start. You find that, in person, he's tinged with the pubescence of a teen idol. The novelist Bret Easton Ellis (*American Psycho*) tells of the day he had lunch with Dillon at Umberto's in New York: "His driver for the day, Irving, waits patiently for him, smoking a cigarette on the curb, the street almost comically lined with limousines of all colors and lengths, some double-parked. Dillon has a loose, easy-going rapport with Irving and when Irving hears Dillon lament the demise of vinyl and how difficult it is to find 45s, he tells him that his son has a collection of old jazz 45s he's trying to sell. Dillon writes down Irving's number, promising to call over the weekend. Talk of music prompts Dillon to ask Irving to stop at Tower Records, where he wants to pick up the new Replacements tape. As much as Dillon genuinely seems to want to be treated like the rest of us, to demonstrate his every-guyness, it just doesn't work. Tower Records on a crowded Friday afternoon conspires against him, as does the black stretch limo and driver.

"Teenage girls literally swoon as he strides past the store's CD racks. He's moving too fast through the crowd, instantly locating the stairs that lead to the cassettes, for the girls to regain their composure and get up the nerve to ask for autographs.

"He quickly browses through the new releases and finds the tape he wants. The girl ringing up the sale does the inevitable double-take and, though she obviously recognizes the star, she still meekly asks, 'Do I know you? You look really familiar.' Dillon can't help it, he playfully lowers his sunglasses and says, 'Yeah?' What else can he do? The girl says, 'You're Matt Dillon!' He nods while opening his wallet, then, accepting the change, gives a huge, piercing, movie-star grin that causes her to blush, gratified.

"Back in the car, as 'Merry Go Round,' the first single on the cassette, comes on, Matt Dillon bops up and down and stares out the tinted window of the limo, smiling contentedly."

Richard Gere

Richard Gere

"As a pinup, he's a knockout.
You don't have to know who he is, have any information about him
or bring any associations to get a charge out of looking at him.
Gere's torso is a thing of beauty in its own right, not a torso with
numbers on it like Schwarzenegger's, or a fighting machine like
Stallone's. It's not athletically wiry like Travolta's or massive like
Nolte's. There's nothing hulking or worked over about it; it's
smooth as silk, almost feminine. It's a bedroom body, the way people
were once said to have 'bedroom eyes.' It says Sex for Sale.
He'd be the perfect date for an orgy; you'd slide in and out among
the couplings and triplings without embarrassment or guilt. One
night stands with no tomorrow, the zipless fuck, the no-name affair!
Sexually, he's without conscience or principles - he'll do it with
anyone as long as he doesn't have to hustle.
Although he's never played a bisexual, he suggests
someone who'd rather switch than fight."
— Celebrity Reporter Molly Haskell

In 1979, a female reporter from *The Ladies Home Journal* asked Richard Gere, "How does it feel to be a sex symbol?"

Getting no response, she probed further, "Are you gay or what?"

At that, the star dropped his pants.

"The answer, apparently," a columnist wrote later, "is that life as a semi-bankable sex symbol is an entirely flaccid experience."

Later, Richard said: "It's basically a psychoanalytical problem that America has. America's got this dick problem.

"It's nobody's business but mine who I'm fucking or who I'm not fucking," he went on to say. "The rack sheets, the press blurbs, the gossip pages, it's all crap. You can't possibly understand my deepest emotions."

What we *could* understand was one of the first lines he uttered on-screen, in "Looking for Mr. Goodbar:" "How would you like the best lay of your life?"

We could also appreciate what his character in his most

perfect role from a gaymale perspective, in "American Gigolo," says as he explains his mission in life: "The other night I was with a woman who hadn't had an orgasm in maybe 10 years. It took me three hours to get her off. For a while I didn't think I was going to do it. When it was over, I felt like I'd done something, something really worthwhile."

In the movie, his utterly smooth, sinuous body was beautifully lit and photographed. And, as part of the ambiance, mind you, he even went so far as to give his fans a memorable glimpse of cock.

Before "Gigolo," in 1978, Richard gave an impressive performance in the seldom-seen film "Bloodbrothers," as a boy-man in hard-hat country, a sensitive youth caught between a desire to be free of his crude but loving father and uncle and an even stronger desire to stay. In the Richard Price novel, the boy stays but in the movie, he goes away with his girlfriend. The original ending would have made a far more memorable film.

Soon after completing "Bloodbrothers," Gere appeared on Broadway in "Bent," the story of Nazi persecution, cast as a decadent gay who is forced to acknowledge love in a concentration camp. His performance was praised but, as one critic put it, "all I can remember is the barbed-wire setting and beefcake beautiful Gere stripped to the waist."

In his film roles following "Gigolo," including "Yanks" (1979), "An Officer and a Gentlemen" (1982) and "Beyond the Limit" (1983), he exhibits a soft quality that must be eradicated before he can go on to martial bliss. Not blissful was his pairing with Debra Winger in "Gentlemen." Debra says their love scenes were extremely painful. "On screen, pain looks like pleasure," she says.

Although she called Richard "a complete professional," she admitted that she "never felt less for a co-star than I did for Gere."

Perhaps because of that experience Gere decided to seek out his own female co-stars and, with shades of the later antics of superstud Rob Lowe, for "Breathless," he reportedly spent three days, mostly naked, in a Paris hotel room, testing a French actress on videotape. But, as it turned out, Valerie Kaprisky got the part in the film, what Steven Scheuer calls "an empty-headed remake" of Jean-Luc Godard's 1959 French classic. The saving grace of this film was that it afforded several views of the naked Gere.

By 1984, *Playgirl* was asking, "Has there ever been a movie in which he didn't appear naked?" They called him the Ultimate Bad Boy, the one who wrote the rules for the rest. "I had no qualms about showing my body," he once said. "I thought it was adventurous, adventurous of me personally and adventurous for any man to do it. But, yeah, I was driving it."

A string of losers, including "King David," "Days of Heaven" and "The Cotton Club" ground his career to a halt but it was "Pretty Woman" that brought him back, at the age of 41, gray hair and all, still touching our hearts with his undeniably seductive, cool sensuality.

Still seeing himself as "an actor with an Off-Broadway mentality," Richard feels he can "walk away from the whole thing." He was in analysis once. "I'm still screwed up," he says, "but who isn't?"

Author Gary Indiana tells of seeing Gere, before his marriage, with a woman named Susan who played one of his wives in "Internal Affairs" in New York: "I told him about the Gotti trial. He didn't know who John Gotti is, but she did. He'd just come back from Russia. Richard now fancies himself a real expert on Russia.

"There's something lovable about Richard and of course something monstrous, but then, he's a movie star. He asked me if I wanted to go for a walk so we all went to Barney's to look at jewelry."

Richard and his bride, the supermodel Cindy Crawford, were spotted by the Mad Monks (Jim and Mike) of *Monk* magazine on their visit to L.A. at the time of the Academy Awards ceremonies. Here is their report:

It's 5:15 and Mike is now standing a foot away from Gregory Peck, feeling the pulse of stardom. Mike's flying high looking through his viewfinder and finds Jim across the way looking through HIS viewfinder at Mike. They connect like two buzzards caught in mid-flight before plunging to the bottom of the canyon to scarf up another piece of fresh kill.

"Shoot 'em! Shoot 'em!" Mike yells.

"My god, the boobs! It's the land of the boob, silicone valley, miles

beyond perky. These are nightmarish boobs, rock hard with killer nipples that slug you in the face like a cold slap from the sea." Mike's whispering.

"Richard! Richard! Over here Richard!" Jim yells.

The Spanish and Italian journalists desperately try to capture Richard's attention, holding up a sign that reads, "What's the name of your date?"

Her name is Cindy Crawford and she towers above the crowd.

"She's GORGEOUS!" gasps one of the paparazzi, as he snaps away at the Charly girl and the American Gigolo. Now a whole colony of paparazzi descend on the pretty pair, shouting directives at Mr. Gere.

"Please," he says with a smile, "You're making me nervous."

The press is overanxious – big money's on the line if they don't come home with the goodies.

Mr. and Mrs. Gere move on through the hysterical crowd, as a large booming voice from the third bleacher above the runway cuts through the din: "Hey Richard, is samsara nirvana?"

The perfectly coiffed and modulated devotee of the Dalai Lama turns and looks the questioner right in the eyes. "Yes, it's all the same," he says with a knowing smile, as Cindy whispers in his ear, turning back to gaze at the stranger. It's Jim the Mad Monk, and Mr. and Mrs. Gere have just been MONKED.

But it seems Richard really is a MONK and, alas, Mr. and Mrs. Gere, at least Cindy and Richard, were not to be.

Despite Cindy's presence at Gere's forty fifth-birthday party and at the British premiere of "Mr. Jones," and despite Gere's gal pal Laura Bailey calling reports of their romance "complete rubbish," rumors of an impending break-up flourished.

Indeed, the rumors grew more squirrelly by the day. When model Gail Elliott briefly moved into Cindy's apartment in New York after the failure of her own marriage in September, speculation began that *she* and Crawford were an item. In October, Gere took the stage at a fundraising event for a gay-and-lesbian lobbying group in London and said, "You've all heard some rumors about me over the years. *I* guess this is the moment to do it. My name is Richard Gere...and I am a lesbian." That same month, several tabloids noted that Cindy was no longer wearing her wedding ring. The Gere's Bel-Air house quietly went on the market.

Friends close to Gere suggested that the marriage amounted to a career move for Crawford and now she had signed to appear in her first film and really didn't need him anymore.

Meanwhile, Gere's rented house in London was under siege. Laura Bailey was photographed leaving on several consecutive mornings in November. The British tabloids had a field day with that. Bailey's father, an Oxford don, grumbled that when his daughter gave up academics for modeling, it was "the saddest day of my life."

On the set of his new film "First Knight," Gere kept his cool. "He's a guy who has volatility and anger inside him, which is part of what makes him a great screen presence," director Jerry Zucker says. "But he moderates it, he sublimates." Becoming a character – especially Lancelot – was a great escape; Gere's turmoil reflected the central theme of Zucker's movie, the tug-of-war between obligations and emotions.

"'First Knight' is a Richard Gere vehicle," Georgia Brown said in the *Village Voice* when the film opened in July. "I'm not amongst those who hold the silky Gere in contempt, though I do believe his milieu, his psychic period, to be the contemporary – his best films being hip urban dramas like 'American Gigolo,' McBride's 'Breathless,' the slimy 'Internal Affairs.' Sommersby's Civil War period was a time stretch. Gere's is the Armani era.

"Set somewhat further back in time, 'First Knight' opens up at a peasant fair where Gere's sword-wielding Lancelot takes on all comers. Writer William Nicholson takes off from the myth of Lancelot the invincible, Lancelot the unhappy itinerant swordsman, who wishes to die but is foiled by God. This scene is painful because Gere smirks and prances before a circle of spectators and behaves in a smug, unbecoming I'm-Richard-Gere-and-You're-Not way. Not even an I'm-Lancelot-and-You're-Not way. When Lancclot meets Guinevere (Julia Ormond) he's full of himself: 'I can tell when a woman wants me,' says he in his Richard Gere way."

Straight or bent, Richard's offscreen comments are often obscure: "Whatever I tell you today will be obsolete tomorrow."

But he is forthcoming about his line of work: "The first time I was ever paid to act was at the Provincetown Playhouse one summer when I was 19. I was ill-equipped to play any of the roles but for some reason they allowed me to play them. We wore plastic masks through which we spoke our lines in normal, prosaic ways, and then we'd take the masks off and speak our innermost feelings.

"I don't know if one ever shows their true face. Maybe when you die, that's about it. I think the gig is either to have no mask at all or else to have an infinite number of them and keep shuffling them. It's probably more fun to have an infinite number of them." One is reminded of the Oscar Wilde dictum that if you want someone to reveal themselves, you give them a mask. The reverse corollary being: their true face is far less expressive.

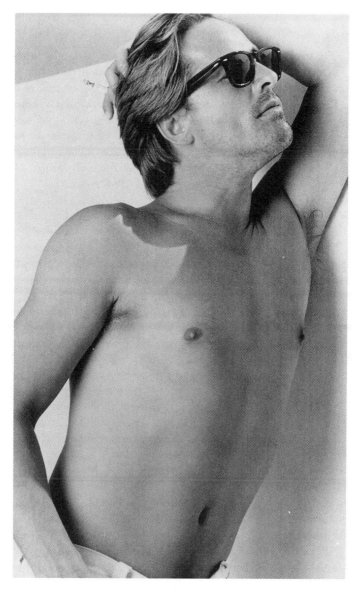

Don Johnson

Don Johnson

*"I'm trying hard not to let my imagination run away with me,
but it appears that we're both madly infatuated. It would be quite
nice, for here are his attributes: 1. Really into acting; in love with
it, secure in it. 2. Getting very into music; writing it, learning
guitar. 3. On THE path. 4. HUGE cock. I'm getting off like I
haven't in ages. We do 'get it on' perfectly and last night was
heavy wildness. I kept seeing myself in his eyes so beautifully, and
forever it seemed, we were either fucking or laughing."*
*– Pamela Des Barres ("I'm With the Band")
on her torrid affair with Donnie, then 22.*

Born in Galena, Missouri, son of a farmer, Don Johnson was
studying at the prestigious American Conservatory Theater in
San Francisco in 1969 when Sal Mineo came up from
Hollywood to have him read for a part in his Los Angeles
production of the acclaimed prison drama, "Fortune and Men's
Eyes." Mineo hired him on the spot. And Don got good
reviews for his performance in the play, which contains a
harrowing scene in which Mineo "rapes" him. "Word of
Johnson's youthful beauty and full nudity spread and kept the
show running for over a year," remembers gay historian
Marvin Jones. "More than any other actor, Don Johnson's
career was the result of a conscious appeal to the gay audience.
He gave interviews to gay magazines and even posed nude for
centerfolds in gay publications."

It is said that his relationship with Mineo led to his
friendship with David Cassidy, who was also a friend of Sal's.
When quizzed about Johnson, David cooed, "We go back a
looooong time." David later confessed his bisexuality to the
German press.

Although Don and his sister lived with Sal for a time, the star
has always denied he and the late actor had ever been intimate.
"Oh, he was gay, openly so," Don says, "and he was
fascinated with me and my persona. He was obsessed with me
to a point. But he was also a gentleman and he respected me.

There was no future in it as far as I was concerned. But don't get me wrong. I don't differentiate between any of it – it's all love to me. I feel you can get just as real a love from a guy as you can from a chick. I mean, if there were nothing but old whores and nasty old hard women around, I'd be looking for some young, sweet little 15-year-old boy. But instead, I've got a sweet little girl and that's enough for me now."

The sweet young thing he was speaking of is Melanie Griffith, the daughter of actress Tippi Hedren, one of Don's co-stars in "The Harrad Experiment." The movie was a pretentious piece of claptrap based on a best-seller about co-ed college dorms and is notable today only because it gave us a lovely full frontal of Don at his cheekiest. But for Don, its filming will always be a treasured memory for it was during that time that he met Melanie, only 14 years-old. It was lust at first sight; Don jokes, "Her extreme maturity and my lack of maturity probably worked out pretty well." It must have; they married, divorced, and eventually re-married, unable to live without each other.

None of Don's early films, including "The Magic Garden of Stanley Sweetheart," "Zachariah," the first and only rock 'n' roll western, and "Return to Macon County" with Nick Nolte, made money.

"Far more successful was Don's career with women," Hollywood insider Nancy Collins reports. An early conquest, when he was only 22, was Pamela Des Barres. In her memoir, *I'm With the Band*, she talks about her torrid affair with Donnie: "Standing in front of me was Donnie Wayne Johnson. The big screen hadn't done him justice and I wondered where this absurdly beautiful specimen of manhood had been all my life. He ushered me into his Hollywood bachelor pad where many a burgeoning actress had been successfully seduced. It reeked of male conquest and female acquiescence. I was reduced to a lump of blushing flesh. The guy was a hunk of burning love. A sex god. A good time. A very good time. At least that's what I was hoping as I sipped a glass of red wine and listened to him play his Gibson and singing in a pure sweet voice that defied description. I was enthralled. I accepted his offer of gnarled ginseng root and chewed it while I danced all over the living room. I could dance anytime, anywhere. I made a valiant effort to be witty and droll despite the trembles because I wanted to be invited back.

"...I couldn't take my eyes off him for more than a few seconds at a time, sometimes stopping in mid-sentence, flagrantly dumbfounded by his face. He loved to laugh and I could send him reeling. That first week of blissful prelove, precommitment was one big too-good-to-be-true party.

"...He escorted me gallantly to his bedroom, picked me up at the door and carried me to his bed. I was vibrating with desire run amok and could hardly wait to peel his Jockey shorts down. "(Later, I wrote in my diary:) 'I'm trying hard not to let my imagination run away with me, but it appears that we're both madly infatuated. It would be quite nice, for here are his attributes: 1. Really into acting; in love with it, secure in it. 2. Getting very into music; writing it, learning guitar. 3. On THE path. 4. HUGE cock. I'm getting off like I haven't in ages. We do 'get it on' perfectly and last night was heavy wildness. I kept seeing myself in his eyes so beautifully, and forever it seemed, we were either fucking or laughing.

"...We went back to his house and fucked by the firelight for hours. I gazed in wonder at his Adam in Eden nakedness, his aquiline Elvis nose, and sweet red lips. I cradled him to my bosom and my love for him transcended space and time.

"...We went 'out there' on love, made love all night and the air was heavy and sweet. Everything was sticky and wet and hot. We were so high. Heavy business. Sometimes I love Don so much I can't see straight."

One of his mistresses, Patti D'Arbanville, the mother of his son Jesse, is credited by Don with helping save him from self destruction with drugs and alcohol. "That life," Don recalls, "ended on September 11, 1983." That was the day he, a self-proclaimed "major party animal," ended a decade of abuse by going cold turkey. "It's known now but nobody really ever knew because nobody gave a shit in Hollywood. They don't tell you to stop. I was miserable. I knew my life was not working, knew a long time before I quit that if I didn't get a grip on things, I'd have no career, no future.

"Ultimately I realized not to feed an insecurity by going along with the masses. Looking for acceptance by doing what everybody else was doing - no matter how destructive - was not intelligent. It took me eighteen months to shake down from that way of life.

"There are no victims, no accidents, only opportunities. That's my philosophy in a nutshell."

David Cassidy recalls, "When I first met Don, who's about a year older than I am, I was still in high school; Don was just out. He was very charming and self-centered. I liked him because he had a sense of humor and was interesting. We were contemporaries with the same goal – to make it as actors. Don was always gushingly friendly toward me, although I sometimes sensed under that friendliness a certain degree of competitiveness toward me. Perhaps everyone did with him.

"I'm sure Don believed Sal could help his career, which may have been one reason Don was with Sal. I viewed Don as an opportunist. He struck me as having something of a hustler spirit about him. I had an idea that he was going to survive in Hollywood – which can be pretty rough, especially for a newcomer – no matter what it took. I've seen that syndrome a lot in Hollywood over the years. You'd be surprised at the various lengths, figuratively or literally, that people will go to be famous or successful in show business.

"But Don was already a very talented actor when I first met him. I remember going to see him in one play that Sal directed, a production of 'Fortune and Men's Eyes,' around 1969; he was very good in it. I had every confidence he'd make it. He had the talent."

Donny was dried out by 1983, but he was, in his own words, "vegetating," waiting for the phone to ring. Universal was toying with a TV project called, at that time, "Dade County Fast Lane." One of the leads was a Southern good ol' boy and Don thought he'd be perfect for it. When he found the script, he said, "God this is it. This guy's been following me around. This is my life. " As Sonny Crockett, the actor became a sex symbol.

"People always ask me what it's like being a sex symbol. My answer is that it is not something I aspired to be. I never intended to go out and be a teen idol. I fought against that. To be picky, I have these hoods over my eyes that are not particularly attractive and I have dirty-dishwater blond hair and dark eyebrows. Most people think I've bleached my hair or dyed my eyebrows which annoys me because I'm a purist when it comes to that. I don't believe in tucks, pinches and lifts.

"And, shit, I'm humble! I think the most humbling experience was my fifteen years in Hollywood. That's the most humbling experience anybody can have. Let's put it this way: I didn't take the town by storm. I think you can safely say I was less than the hurricane I intended to be. And fifteen years waiting for it to blow can really humble the shit out of you."

As an instance of how humble things can get around dandy Don, when he was with his son Jesse, a woman asked him for his autograph and the star says that he gave it to her "real quick because I don't like to do that stuff in front of the kids. I don't want 'em to get a distorted sense of importance about that stuff. Well, I needn't have worried! Eight-year old Jesse looked me over and said, 'Can you believe they want your autograph?' I laughed, 'No, I still can't believe it!'"

These days Don tries to stay humble by saving all the terrible reviews he's gotten in his career. Perhaps he has plans for revenge against those critics? "Yes," he jokes, "I have some Haitians making little dolls."

"I want to live life to the hilt," the star says. "Whatever power there is in the universe that creates, sustains, life meant for us human beings to be almost hedonistic about it. I mean, get down and wallow in it, enjoy life and be happy. And for me to be happy, I want to pack this life full. I want it all."

Don still has it all, even at nearly forty. In Dennis Hopper's "Hot Spot," we see Don with a bit of thickness about the middle but the admirable bulge in his swimsuit will never change. In one scene, we are treated to long look at his bare ass. In 1991, good ol' boy Don emerged again in "Harley Davidson and the Marlboro Man," a vehicle with Mickey Rourke, a chowderheaded biker movie full of what one reviewer called, "guns, grease, gangsters, bourbon, and other wry-eyed homoeroticism for unshaven adolescents of all ages," which is, after all, as it should be. A little homoeroticism never hurt anybody, least of all good ol' boy Donnie Wayne.

Don and Melanie appeared together in 1991 in "Paradise." While not a success, the film gave Paul Rudnick, writing as Libby Gelman-Waner, a golden opportunity to joke about the stellar pair and their little film: "In the movie, Melanie and Don are estranged because they lost their little daughter three years earlier, and Melanie feels guilty because she was sewing when the child choked on a piece of candy. Since the child's death, Melanie has been unable to have sex, but if you ask me, she could just knock off the sewing. A little boy comes to stay with Don and Melanie and heals their emotional wounds, like Dr. Ruth in a polo shirt; this is the kind of movie that alternates between tearful hugs and nature-study close-ups of swamp grass and whippoorwills, and after the first five minutes, you know that the climax will involve getting the little boy into physical danger – if 'Paradise' were more fun, Lassie would rescue him.

"Even though they're supposed to be working-class, Don and Melanie always seem as if they're on their way to Swifty Lazar's Oscar party at Spago; their all-cotton, country-casual outfits look as if they came from the local Emporio Armani, the one between the K Mart and the Piggly Wiggly. Don and Melanie are wonderful actors, but they're too pampered to play small-town folks; when Melanie washes dishes or hangs laundry, she looks like Marie Antoinette discovering Clorox, and when Don's out on the shrimp boat, you wait for the other fishermen to gush over his new blond highlights. Josh and I decided that Don and Melanie should play us in our home movies, unless we can get Patrick Swayze and Demi Moore; they all can be counted on to wear the latest $900 Melrose Avenue prescription sunglasses while playing housewives and mechanics. They all have luscious skin and great haircuts and look as if they're carried around very gently by teams of masseurs, colorists, and astrologers; they're the kind of actors who stay in touch with reality by having a chartered jet fly them to their Montana ranch so they can sit around in old clothes and play charades with Jack Nicholson."

Don and Melanie's story reads like a Harlequin romance. Their relationship has survived drugs, booze and his romances with actress Patti D'Arbanville (with whom he as a son, Jesse), and Barbra Striesand, her marriage to actor Steven Bauer (which whom she has a son, Alexander).

After a separation of almost 12 years, hot off her success in "Working Girl," Melanie stopped drinking, and got back together with Don, who also detoxed back in 1983.

In June of 1994, Don checked into the Betty Ford Center in Rancho Mirage, Calif., for treatment of alcohol and prescription drug abuse. At first, Melanie appeared ready to stand by her man. Then, in 1995, the off-again/on-again marriage of Johnson and Griffith appeared to have hit it's biggest obstacle yet, in the person of Antonio Banderas. Banderas told Stephen Rebello of *Movieline* why he really can't talk about his love affair with Melanie Griffith – an affair which began on the set of "Two Much" and that broke up both of their marriages. (Antonio was married to Spanish actress Ana Leza for nine years.)

"People right now may not understand my love and what I have done for it. But I repeat the truth: I am in *love*. The one thing I can tell you, the one thing I want people to understand is that a person fell in love with another person. I fell in love with Melanie. I feel loved by her... Melanie has kids and that means a lot to her. We're trying to move things on the right track, hurting people as little as possible. I am trying to stabilize my life. I cannot say more to you about this, *please*.

"I accept everything – everything – she brings with her. I am not trying to change her. I want to help her. I want to make her happy. I want to give her all the love I can. She's very alluring and sexy and she understands her own charm. Men find her a tough one to resist."

Just like her estranged husband, Donnie Wayne!

Rob Lowe

Rob Lowe

"He emerged from the shower, a towel barely covering his body, and I fell in love. I had never seen such perfection: the blue eyes, the lithe body (5'-11", 160 pounds), the dark brown hair and, especially the face, the handsomest face I had ever seen. He was, to borrow from Cole Porter, 'de-lightful, de-licious, de-lovely."
– The author upon seeing Rob Lowe appearing as
"Sodapop Curtis" in "The Outsiders" in 1983.

On July 22, 1991, in L.A., Rob Lowe married Sheryl Berkoff, a 30-year-old makeup artist he met during the making of the 1989 film "Bad Influence," and the media speculated the move would effectively put an end to his battles with his reported addictions to cocaine, alcohol, Ecstasy and sex. Once Rob said, "When I decide to get married, it will be because I want to give myself completely. I will get married, but most likely late in life. That's the one that will last forever, the absolute, whole hearted commitment. I just don't ever want a divorce. I guess that's why a child has to be the last step. Divorce is bad enough, but when there's a kid..."

His own childhood, he admits, was "pretty confusing." (He was born on March 17, St. Patrick's Day, in 1964.) "I was pretty much a loner type kid. I went to quite a few schools because we moved around a lot. I was born in Charlottesville when my dad was going to University of Virginia law school. Then my mom met somebody else and we moved to Dayton, then Colorado, then Malibu. I ended up with one dad and two stepdads."

At thirteen, Rob decided to pursue an acting career, commuting to Hollywood from Malibu, riding the bus for 45 minutes to go on interviews. "Believe me," he recalls, "I cared enough to go out and get work. I didn't wait for it to come to me. If I'd stayed in Ohio, I might be dead now. Of my three best friends there, two are dead and one is in prison. Acting gave me an interest that took me away from stealing cars and gangs. But it sure makes going back strange. I guess I don't quite fit in there anymore."

And speaking of fitting in, the image of Rob Lowe at thirteen, loose in Hollywood, is enough to give any boylover fantasies for days.

Rob played small roles on TV shows, then got his big break in "The Outsiders." Soon, the outrageously handsome star became known less for his performances than the teasing glimpses of his flesh which were, in the true nature of legends, the only reason to watch his films.

In "Class," for instance, besides several scenes of the bare-chested star, we were also rewarded with the sight of him in semi-drag. In 1986's "About Last Night..." we saw his buns and close to a full frontal. In the same year, "Youngblood" was released, permitting us a long view of the 5' 11", 160 lb. body in a tight jockstrap, followed by a sensational shot of his buns in retreat. To show you just how irresistibel Rob is, *Playgirl* reported that sometimes the line between art and life is indeed fine. "One of our Hollywood sources tells this savory story about the 1986 hockey movie 'Youngblood:' While co-stars Rob Lowe and Cynthia Gibb were shooting a sex scene, he allegedly got so caught up in the moment that he tried to insert his penis in her and she actually *let* him."

The following year, Rob gave the sexiest performance ever recorded in a mainstream film in director Bob Swaim's American debut, "Masquerade," which featured sizzling segments of Rob with Kim Cattrall and Meg Tilly which provided abundant footage of his slim, sexy torso and his glorious buns. Critic Hal Rubinstein said: "Swaim cast angel-puss Rob Lowe as a sailor whose charm is his anchor, a wilier Nick Carraway at play in the fields of the bored." Swaim likes to cast adolescents as grownups: "I find kids playing adults appealing, sexy, and disturbing, because the audience feels they are almost too young to have minds capable of doing such things." Although Rob was hardly an adolescent when he made "Masquerade," he was perfect casting and the film remains a personal favorite.

Rob often chooses his films on the basis of the talented people he would be working with, often with disastrous results. Peter Bogdanovich, for example, directed Rob in the film "Illegally Yours," released directly to video. The film was "unwatchable," in the words of one critic, "except for the perverse spectacle of Rob Lowe (in Bogdanovich-like glasses) imitating John Ritter imitating Ryan O'Neal imitating Cary Grant."

In 1987's "Square Dance," Rob worked with great actors Jason Robards and Jane Alexander and he earned a Golden Globe nomination for his performance as a mentally retarded young man. It was, according to the *New York Times*, Rob's "most arresting" performance. In this film, Rob tried to expand his range by playing a retarded fiddle player with a pronounced Southern accent who cuts off his own dick after the character played by Winona Ryder discovers him boning an oversexed hairdresser. Joe Queenan says, "Particularly memorable is the scene where Lowe beseeches Winona, 'Read me a story, one about them bears, and they're eatin' their cereal.' Even less forgettable is the scene where Jane Alexander, playing Ryder's long-suffering hairdresser mother, tells her daughter that she must clear out quickly, lest the police implicate her in the tragic demise of Lowe's penis. 'I got to get you outta here,' rasps Alexander, 'I gotta take you somewheres...Aggie (Alexander's fellow *coiffeuse*) take me in there and I just about got sick. Her hanging there like shoddy plumbing, and him laying here bleeding, and my haircutting scissors on the floor next to your Bible. Baby, you're in big trouble.'"

And speaking of Big Trouble, Rob's greatest challenge in life came with the scandal that would make him a legend in his own time for gaymales everywhere. All hell broke loose on July 17, 1989, when the star was in Atlanta for the Democratic convention. After a party for Ted Turner, Rob went to Club Rio with some friends and they were given a table in a private room. Eventually, Rob invited Jan Parsons, 16, in the club with a fake ID, and an apprentice at a Marietta, Georgia, salon called Superhair, to sit at the table. "I met a lot of girls that night, but I very specifically remember meeting Jan because she was very pretty and she seemed very nice and she kept walking back and forth past me. You know, by the seventh pass you notice somebody."

After lots more booze and Ecstasy, Rob ended up taking Jan and her girlfriend, a 22-year-old admitted lesbian, back to his $650 a night suite, No. 2844, at the Atlanta Hilton. He showed them some videos he'd taken with himself and starlets, then encouraged the girls to undress and get into the king-sized bed together. He got nude and then videotaped them in the throes of lesbos lust, occasionally stepping into the picture to give them directions. Rob said later, "It was one of those quirky, sort of naughty, sort of wild, sort of drunken things that people will do from time to time. It was just one of those things." While Rob was in the bathroom the two girls disappeared, along with some cash and the videotape. But it was when the footage from Paris on the same tape (Rob is notoriously cheap) featuring the star, Justin M. (a male production assistant on "Masquerade") and a girl identified only as "Jennifer," surfaced that gave gay men such a thrill and became an underground classic. Portions of it ended up on the adult cable TV show, "Midnight Blue," revealing footage that was amateurish in the extreme but showing Rob's cock, very hard, a cock so glorious it prompted the "Midnight Blue" host to comment, "Rob's got a big dick! He could work in porn films...that may be the only work he'll get from now on!" Rob, high on drugs, just couldn't get enough of the whore's pussy. He'd take a break and let Justin in the saddle, then go back for more. ("No wonder girls follow him around!" the "Midnight Blue" host raved about the star's drug-induced inexhaustibility.)

The tape is surreal but, as Norman Mailer observes, "surrealism has become the objective correlative of our time. A private glimpse of the great becomes the alchemy of the media, the fool's gold of the century of communication. In the age of television we know everything about the great but how they fart - the ass wind is, ergo, our trade wind." Lowe, through no design of his own, gave us a glimpse of his kinks and his kinks offer sympathetic vibration to our kinks.

Lena Arlene Wilson, the mother of Jan, filed a personal injury suit accusing Lowe of using "his celebrity status as an inducement to females to engage in sexual intercourse, sodomy and multiple-partner sexual activity for his immediate sexual gratification, and for the purposes of making pornographic films of these activities."

To avoid doing jailtime, Lowe agreed to do two years of community service.

Later, there were rumors that the girls were part of a shadowy club group that included several bisexuals. The tabloids screamed that Rob was now worrying he had contracted AIDS during the encounter in Georgia.

A woman in Atlanta who's part of the club scene said: "We make love to each other, and anyone else, whenever we feel like it. And why wouldn't Jan want to fuck Rob Lowe if she had the chance? It's stupid, because America makes such gods out of its matinee idols. Years ago it was Valentino, now it's Rob Lowe. Hollywood puts him up in a sexual position. That's the whole focus. That's the publicity. They market him so that little girls will go to the movies, buy his posters, fantasize about fucking Rob Lowe." Suddenly, the Club was besieged by customers wanting to see the "Rob Lowe Room." Rio T shirts, tote bags, boxers, and socks and visors were in demand. Other T-shirts on the club circuit included: "Free Rob Lowe," "I Didn't Sleep with Rob Lowe," and "How Lowe Can You Go."

One of his former girlfriends revealed: "It's not like no one else has ever done this. Lots of movie stars are into this video stuff. It's almost like a boredom thing, doing this for the danger, the recklessness."

Rob himself has said: "I get bored really easily with a lot of things. I like to change things around. I've got a lot of energy." He once even jokingly referred to himself as a porn star named "Raw Blow." After an Off-Broadway performance of "A Shayna Maidel" in 1987, he playfully jammed a can of mousse down his sweats backstage and shook the can until he was "satisfied." The gambit went over so well he asked a friend to videotape him doing it again the next night.

On May 23, members of the Los Angeles Vice Squad along with the FBI raided Rob's home on Mulholland Drive in the hills above Hollywood, a multimillion-dollar bungalow with a pool and a basketball court, decorated in grays, blues and white and furnished with repro deco, California modern and Japanese electro-tech. On the walls is a collection of paintings by obscure artists in a style described as "Jean-Michel Basquiat meets Pee-Wee Herman." In the garage is a gray Porsche 948. The cops were operating under a search warrant instructing them to look for and seize any videotapes that might be used as evidence in the Fulton County investigation and they found a sophisticated setup in his bedroom with hidden video cameras and two-way mirrors.

"Somebody like myself," Rob says, "or other actors-our lives are under the microscope all the time. If people are watching me 365 days a year, 360 days they might be bored to tears. And on the other five days, maybe I would qualify as Satan. Those are the five days everybody wants to read about.

"I felt like I'd been taken. I felt like something I thought was private was now threatening to become public unless I paid an exorbitant amount of money to somebody and that made me angry. I felt betrayed. Half of the anger was at myself, for putting myself in a position where I could get taken advantage of. Then there was, not anger, actually more of a hurt, that people's motives aren't always what they seem.

"Everybody has to live life to the fullest but especially an actor. If you don't experience life to the very fullest, what are you going to draw on? Unfortunately, that means getting into some messes, although I don't think that excuses you. You show me someone in today's world who has seized every opportunity, who's embraced every challenge and I'll show you someone who's probably done some things in their life they're not proud of. And show me someone who has led a perfect life and I'll show you a dullard.

"But I think people should be allowed to do whatever they want in the privacy of their own home or hotel room. When people consent to something, they should be able to do whatever they want.

"I work hard and play hard. When you do a job that demands adult behavior there are times when you want to act your age. I don't have to prove I'm smart and well-mannered and businesslike. Sometimes I want to be silly. I grew up a lot between fourteen and sixteen. Now I must be in remission."

One of the star's personal favorites is his role in John Richardson's film adaptation of John Irving's novel "Hotel New Hampshire," playing a clone of Irving himself: "It has a lot to say about growing up and the development of sexuality and all the consequences of experience. There are no rules there, it doesn't accept categories as defining the world. I want to see more films like that because I think they're truer to life. I don't want my life a bunch of steps leading to some preconceived goal. The characters in that film are faced with ideals and struggles yet they don't let things get them down. That's life right there, you know?"

In 1990, while his close friend and longtime manager Tim Wood lay dying of AIDS, Rob promised he would check himself into a clinic.

Two days later, Wood died and Rob said: "Tim can't get another chance but I can. I know it's not going to be easy but I'm going to do it." Tim had told Rob: "Sex is no longer cheap – it can cost you your life." Rob said: "I know Tim loved me and he wanted me to clean up my life." On May 11, 1990, Rob checked into the Sierra Tucson clinic signing a pledge saying he wouldn't have sex for six months after finishing the month-long $550-a-day rehab program.

When he got out of rehab, Rob spent a good deal of time in New York, hanging out with his pal Jodie Foster and younger brother Chad, who lives on the upper West Side and is working in theater. (When Chad was appearing in the play "Grotesque Lovesongs," the *New Yorker* raved about him: "Chad Lowe gives a beautifully modulated performance." Chad has much of his older brother's sex appeal and a face that was summed up by a character in one of his films, "Nobody's Perfect," in which Chad dressed in drag. Another boy tells Chad: "You got the kind of face that could go both ways.")

When "Bad Influence" was released in 1990, it was not a box office success in theaters but it went to the top of the rental charts when released on video in the fall. In one scene, we were permitted another glimpse of the famous ass and Rob's character had just the right Mephistophelean overtones, as one of the female characters observed: "Sleep with the Devil and sooner or later, you have to fuck."

Rob says: "As an actor, you deal in fantasy, imagination, and concentration. Those are your three weapons. Those are your bullets. It's easy to live in a fantasy world and that's why I refuse to live in an isolated environment. I'm not going to stop talking to people who come up to me in an airport. I'm not going to worry about what may be their ulterior motives. "

It was during the film "Stroke of Midnight," a comedy featuring Rob as an Italian dress designer in Paris, that Rob videotaped the notorious 3-way, and when preview audiences turned a thumbs down on it, it went directly to video with tepid sales. A distributor says that the timing was bad: "It came out when there were many new high visibility titles to buy so nobody bought it." Still in studio vaults is "Helena (A Woman with a Dream)" filmed in New Zealand and another film he made in Israel. During 1991, Rob took a cameo as a sleazy Hollywood talent scout in buddy Judd Nelson's "The Dark Backward." *The Village Voice:* "Nelson and Lowe strain so hard to break their images that we end up sweating as much as they do." Except for "Class," Rob has never been successful at comedy but he keeps trying. A stint as guest host on "Saturday Night Live" convinced the executive producer Lorne Michaels to cast Lowe as a ruthless TV executive in the feature film "Wayne's World," starring the programs awesome dude duo, Mike Meyers and Dana Carvey. Rather than take his usual salary, Rob accepted a share of the profits of the film, which went on to gross $120 million domestic, meaning Rob probably never has to work another day in his life.

Rob says people mostly see him as a "sensitive type. That's kind of what I am, what I look like anyway. I only want to be tough because I admire that in actors. I love Clint Eastwood movies. It would be so much fun to play that once, but not as a career or anything.

"Acting is instinctual for me only because I don't have the training. For me, every character will have something to do with my personality. I can't even imagine fabricating some totally alien personality by immersion into a character-almost like doing an imitation for months. You have to admit that the best performances generally come out of common instincts, normal reactions."

Liz Smith says: "Rob's good looks, uninhibited penchant for shedding his clothes, and off-screen carrying-on have gotten in the way of any assessment of his acting talent."

Rob says he lost his virginity to an older woman. "She was a friend in the neighborhood who was four years older than I was. It was my fifteenth birthday and she cooked me a birthday dinner, and afterward her friends were, like, 'Oh, we'll leave you two alone.' And I was, like, 'Well, why? It's my birthday.' I was a little dense. Then her best friend said, 'Here's my present to you, but open it later.' I opened it later and it was a box of condoms... About that time, the light went on.

"I don't think Hollywood knows what to make of me. I've

been acting since I was eleven; I've been arguably famous since I was fifteen. Since then I've done movies that made a lot of money, I've done movies that were bombs. I've been in and out of favor with the press, and now my life is so quiet – I don't even live in L.A. anymore. My wife and I and our son moved to Santa Barbara.

"I gave up drinking on May 10, 1990. For me the battle was changing the craziness that surrounded the drinking. My wife Sheryl was responsible for that.

"It's best not to have a void to fill. The people who really have it together don't have a void. I, however, do, and I fill it by really going ape on cappuccinos and cigars. I feel like the fucking king of the world when I've got a cappuccino in one hand, a Cuban in the other, I'm in my chair, and the magic words come: 'They're ready for you now.' Nothing could be better. *Kill me now!*

"I was a young lunatic, not unlike any 20-year-old man with the wherewithal and success. I lived my life – some were the greatest memories I'll ever have, some were the worst. As I got older (I realized) that wasn't the life I wanted. That really, truly is it."

In July 1990 Rob showed the world that he had the same kind of concerns and cares as everyone else when he made a surprise and last-minute appearance at the Knebworth Charity Festival where Elton John and Phil Collins were among the artists performing. Offered the chance to take part, Lowe immediately took a plane from France where he was filming and flew to England. It was a lastminute dash that took him five and a half hours to reach Heathrow Airport. Then he had to wait an hour for a taxi, but made it just in time to introduce Phil Collins.

Rob could have stayed in France. He could have complained that they should have asked him earlier. His reason for wanting to go, was because "I had heard it was for charity and I knew Elton John. I worked a lot with AIDS and I felt this would be good. This is the best of both worlds. You get to hear great music and help people."

Rob of the sculptured cheekbones and bright blue eyes concedes his looks have been a problem and lately he's been seen sporting a well-groomed beard. "I mean," he says, "if I was starting out and I wanted to be an actor, I wouldn't have chosen this look, quite honestly. But this is me. I mean, I didn't go out and buy my face, right?"

Rudolf Nureyev

Rudolf Nureyev

"He was an extremely, extremely attractive young man,"
Maria Tallchief once sighed.

In his review of Otis Stuart's 1995 book about Rudolf Nureyev, *Perpetual Motion*, Paul Parish recalls, "...When I saw a lot of Nureyev - in 1969 and 1970 when I went to the ballet in London almost weekly – Nureyev's impact on me was more like John Lennon's than Mick Jagger's. Peace, freedom, love, justice, the holiness of heart's truth is what I remember getting from Nureyev. Lennon made high-mindedness a part of rock music, and Nureyev made mass appeal a part of high art. Both confirmed me in my idealism. There was such striving in him, the image that made him unique was the way he pulled his legs, stretched his lines, lifted his breastbone, opened himself up, hid nothing.

"Stuart is more interested in the Nureyev of the '70s, when from the audience it could be seen he was already fading as a great dancer and was taking desperate measures to hide it from himself: dancing himself into a lather, never taking a break, telling interviewers that he danced best when he was tired. He wasn't telling the press that he was getting laid every 12 hours and needed sex like other people need sleep. But many people had noticed that Nureyev looked exhausted; already in the early '70s, when I saw him in Berkeley, he had lost all his elevation. I'll never forget it: I was beside myself. I thought he was going to die onstage. It was awful; I felt like I'd lost my innocence.

"Nureyev's decline was saddening, and his refusal to acknowledge it was shocking and *he got away with it*, like Liz Taylor and Elvis. Stuart identified so strongly with Nureyev's act of defiance, it's obviously what got him through the day's writing. It led him to cast his net wide for tales of Nureyev's sexual prowess to back up his case that sex between the acts restored his glamour. And he's pulled in quite a haul; it reads like Andrew Holleran in there. I'm glad he did, for nobody else would have, and it is a part of the tale. I feel certain someone else will tell us the rest."

"Rudolf Nureyev, the first male ballet dancer since Nijinsky to become an international superstar, and the first whose saperstardom could be transmitted and preserved by the electronic media, rocketed through this world like a runaway train," Michael Feingold commented. "He lived at such a furious pace. Leaping across so many barriers and smashing so many taboos, that the extraordinary length of his dance career, in retrospect, is a bigger shock than any of the sexual or financial revelations in Stuart's biography. A creature as vehement as Nureyev in his demands on life might have been expected to burn himself out far sooner.

"Stuart's breezy tone is a perfect fit for Nureyev: The man who put animal sexuality back into ballet was never one to be bound by manners, rules, or discretion of any kind. In addition to his many achievements as a dancer and choreographer, Nureyev offered himself enthusiastically as a bridge between the ballet elite and everything from which it has traditionally been sequestered. He offered his electrifying body as material for emerging choreographers to sculpt; he did more than anyone to turn the silent, suspicious truce between ballet and modern dance into a wild garden of cross-ballet dancer in history, he himself made the most reactionary and elitist of art forms into a massmarket money machine, energizing hls nonstop tours by letting his celebrity spill over into talk shows, feature films, documentaries, and – a kind of ultimate – his immortal pas de deux on national television with Miss Piggy.

When Nureyev staged ballets later in his life, "…The man for whom sex was at the core of dancing put new urgency into the seductions, rape attempts, and opium orgies scattered through the old scenarios.

"He revitalized old dancers, too, most famously Britain's pinnacle of ballet refinement, Margot Fonteyn, who when they met in 1962 was 19 years his senior and on the verge of announcing her retirement. Instead, for the next dozen years, she and he became an onstage love match that smashed box-office records worldwide. An offstage one too: More than one of their Royal Ballet colleagues swore to Stuart that the 45-year-old Fonteyn had miscarried Nureyev's child. His sexual pursuits of course, notoriously didn't stop with women: Fonteyn was furious with Rudi, Stuart records, after he was arrested in Melbourne during a performance, for having sex in a public restroom near the theater – in full costume, makeup, and wig.

"Though he never came out publicly, even while dying of AIDS Nureyev's homosexual side was as public a matter as his headline-grabbing defection from the Kirov: another bridge between ballet and the real world, another leap to freedom. Never concealing his male lovers or disguising his presence in gay bars across Europe and America – or in their backrooms – he probably did as much for the cause of sexual freedom as he did for the virility and athleticism of ballet. 'As a dancer,' said the ballerina Violette Verdy, 'he has *both* sexes.'

"Stuart discovered his own HIV-positive status while researching *Perpetual Motion*, and died of AIDS shortly after its official publication date. His first book is also his last, as complete a picture as a life so complex is ever likely to receive."

Stuart explained, "Anyone attempting a biography of Rudolf Nureyev is, of course, volunteering for a stroll through a minefield. Half of the story centers on subjects you're not supposed to talk about in mixed company – sex, money, violence, passions that would make a Bronte blush. The first half of Nureyev's life was spent in a place where secrecy was the norm, the second in a profession that lives to talk, but hushes 'don't quote me.'

"...Nureyev was among the first of another new breed, a star who stayed famous for being famous. In the decades since the Hollywood studio system had taught the world just how to sell a product, the American mass media in particular focused on individual faces. The personality approach was one Americans enjoyed; particularly after the television boom of the 1950s, celebrities could, come right into your own living room."

According to the media scholar Jeremy Tunstall, "The American popular press from its earliest days stressed personality and celebrity. The Associated Press, when it appeared, that were: "bright, innocent, tender, spontaneous, playful, joyful, spiritual, mystical, sensual, and full of reverence, (and) just as easily...dark, dirty, terrifying, mindless, self-indulgent lonely, mad, and hurtful. Nureyev also had, in spades, the rebel sexuality that had been bankrolling major mainstream careers since Elvis first wiggled those hips and James Dean first pouted those lips; by the end of the decade, Nureyev had done for the turtleneck what Lana Turner had once done for mohair. The most popular buttons among the Rudi groupies went right to the point: 'We want Rudi in the nudi.'"

Stuart said, "The combination of rebel, poet, and stallion Nureyev embodied in appearance, in manner, in the context of his own history was right out of McLuhan."

"This was not a safe face," Stuart enthuses about his subject. "The eyes traced the subtlest slant upward. The cheekbones were so expansive *Newsweek* called them cruel. The lips were too full to even approximate inexperience, especially with that faint suggestion of a scar tilting off the upper lip and adding the very lightest suggestion of a threat somewhere in the immediate vicinity. (Tellingly, Nureyev got his scar as a child during an altercation with an angry dog he was trying to feed.) From the beginning, photographers lined up. Within a month of his defection, Nureyev already was posing for Richard Avedon. Nureyev became the most photographed figure in his profession and one of the most photographed men in the world.

"After his defection, Nureyev became the one dancer everyone in the know had to see. He also became the man everyone wanted to know offstage as well, and in the biblical sense if possible. However much Nureyev reveled in the applause of his new Western audience, he took less well to their offstage intrusions. The tradition of the Nureyev "court," the tight inner circle of devoted friends Nureyev learned to keep close by, began within the first six months of his defection as a means of warding off the uninvited personal interest. The inner court remained a feature of Nureyev's personal environment for the rest of his life, only adding to the sense of distance and mystery that surrounded him. The faces in the circle shifted over the years, as Nureyev moved more and more freely through the new worlds of show business, international society, and haute gaydom.

"Nureyev put an end to the male dancer's second-class status. Under his tutelage, men in ballet learned three things: to let go, to step forward, and to fight back. His innovations were the result of his quest for the grail, the public viewing of a lifelong personal struggle, Nureyev's battle to reshape and redefine his recalcitrant body. A ballet dancer, the saying goes, has to be born with two assets: the right body and the right parents. Nureyev lost on both counts. A major contribution his parents had made to Nureyev's success was by default. A mother desperate to give her favorite child a taste of a finer life and a father determined to dictate the future of his only son can generate enough friction to get a real fire burning, and the combination helped to forge the blind determination that characterized Nureyev's life from beginning to end.

"Nureyev was a very competitive dancer from first to last, from top to bottom and vice versa. The number of his sexual adventures perhaps has been exaggerated since the theatrical orgasm of his first celebrity, when a huge photograph of Nureyev nude from the waist up hung in the window of the Royal vauxhall Tavern, a gay bar in South London. 'I know his bed was empty many a night,' one of Nureyev's companion bar-crawlers in Paris remembers. Especially among gay men now of a certain age, if all the people who claim to have slept with Nureyev did, in fact, have sex with Nureyev, he would not have had time for a career. Whatever the legend, Nureyev's sexual career was not simply one more case of anything goes.

"Rumors of a cold heart to the contrary, Nureyev was, for example, capable of deep and lasting love relationships, encounters that changed the lives of his partners forever. However much globe-trotting Nureyev did, he spent most of his life in the west with a significant other somewhere in the not-too-distant background – dancer Erik Bruhn in the sixties, Wallace Potts in the late sixties and early seventies, Robert Tracy through the last decade of his life. Nureyev's relationships with Potts and Tracy demonstrate the contradictory effects he could have on the people closest to him. Nureyev's relationship with Bruhn was of a different order, something large and explosive. Although their union collapsed under the pressure of two considerable careers – and Nureyev's wandering eye – the mutual affection and regard was lifelong. 'Their sexual relationship didn't last very long at all,' a friend of both men recalls. 'Rudi was already into playing around and that was very difficult for Erik. The professional competition proved crippling. Erik was a bitter man by the time I met him in the early seventies. He felt cheated. He was a great, great dancer, but a dancer's dancer. He had a very public career, but nothing like Rudolf's, none of the money, none of the fame. Rudi demoralized him to such an effect that he had to leave to go into a nursing home in Denmark to recover. He never did recover completely. One can date the beginning of the sad decline of this superb dancer from the beginning of his relationship with Nureyev."

According to biographer and Warhol pal Bob Colacello, in the '70s, Wallace Potts, a tall, good-looking easy-going college student from Georgia Tech met Rudi and they became lovers and remained together off-and-on for many years. Rudi met Wallace just after breaking up with Erik Bruhn, the Danish dancer and the great love of his life. Bruhn and Rudi met in August of 1961 and they were lovers through much of the decade.

"The impact of Nureyev's years in Russia has been largely overlooked in the recorded history of Rudolf the Eternal Erection," Stuart says. "The pressure cooker of his formative years, repression as the norm, and the fear of reprisal – they send you to the gulag – were a critical factor in Nureyev's attitude toward his sexuality, right up to the deathbed refusal to acknowledge his AIDS diagnosis. The Russian language does not even have a word for homosexuality.

"Like Marilyn Monroe, Nureyev developed a sexual perspective that, for all its vigor and conflicts, was surprisingly mundane. The earliest stories emphasize a taste for anonymity, distanced but to the point, with a taste for worship. Regular sex became as much a part of his regimen as a good meal at the right time. From most accounts, Nureyev's attitude toward sex was largely matter-of-fact. First bed and then dinner. A pattern was set for life."

Gay investigative reporter Milton Rexford said, "Rudi was once said to be not only generously hung, but very talented in the sack." In an interview two years before his death, Rudi said, "To know what it is to make love as a man and as a woman is special knowledge."

Monique van Vooren, an actress who knew Rudi for over 30 years, agreed: "He was not completely homosexual, at least not in the beginning. Rudolf was tortured, tormented by his sexuality. He was ashamed of being homosexual. And I think he wanted to be degraded. He liked street boys, toughs, the lowest of the low."

Even after he was outed in Dave Kopay's memoir, Rudi did not want to play gay on the screen when he finally got around to taking a stab at movie stardom. That's why we got the heterosexual version of "Valentino," the inept 1977 film by Ken Russell, who Rexford calls "a hetero sissy whose screen flirtations with homosexuality belie a deep-seated homophobia." While Rudi did manage to show his glorious buns in the film the body part most gays were interested in was as hidden as his private life. Rudi, despite what some felt, was as full of contradictions as the rest of us. "Being precise and forthright was a hallmark of Nureyev's life and art," Robert Groskovic says. Looking back from the heights of superstardom, he consistently and plainly recalled his nitty-gritty beginnings in Ufa, just this side of the Urals. As he told it, his commitment to dancing came early, but for an uncommonly long time, his only exposure was to the folk variety practiced by Soviet youth groups. Provincial ballet came next and finally, at the none-too-early age of 17 and a half, he gained acceptance to the renowned Vaganova dance academy in Leningrad. There his long-standing determination to dance, and dance well, was spurred by some ridicule he got from his already advanced peers for his provincial manners and his still primitive technique.

The British journalist Lynn Barber recorded a telling incident in her memorial tribute to Nureyev in *The Independent on Sunday:* "The young Scottish dancer Michael Clark told me that he once went to a dinner at Nureyev's apartment in Paris with his boyfriend and at one point kissed him – Nureyev was furious and practically threw them out."

"Rudolf was a stage animal, theatrical to the bone," New York City Ballet principal dancer Heather Watts explains. "That's why he never worked well on film. His impact was in the flesh." Nadia Nerina of the Royal Ballet agrees: "Nureyev was first and foremost a stage presence, (which) explains his lackluster performances in front of the camera. His film career was a failure because in an arid studio bereft of his sustenance, his audience, his performances were wooden and two-dimensional."

Nureyev and Russell had first met when Russell was considered briefly for the Nijinsky project in 1970. The introduction was unhappy on both sides. Nureyev felt patronized by Russell, and "while I admired his work, I did not like him personally." The "Valentino" experience did little to change Nureyev's opinion. "You know I did one film that I regret having done," Nureyev said when he was approached about a second feature film project a full six years after "Valentino," "and I detested the director."

Stuart explains, "The combination of a nervous, uncertain Nureyev, away from ballet for the first time in twenty years, a director who'd made a career out of Glenda Jackson's bared breasts in 'Women in Love,' and a crew of more than three hundred people wedged between them was an explosive mix. The British actress Felicity Kendal has only glowing memories of working with Nureyev on 'Valentino.' Nureyev was in the initial stages of planning his own danced version of 'Romeo and Juliet' for London Festival Ballet, and the two had endless conversations about the play: "There were a lot of difficult people on the film, and personally I didn't find him one of them. He had absolutely no presumptions to being a great actor. He was himself. He didn't pretend to be the best actor in the world, but he was the best dancer and that was what they wanted him for."

When director James Toback suggested to Nureyev that a little intimacy might charge his on-screen romance with Nastassja Kinski in "Exposed," Nureyev's response was conditional: "Cut her tits off, sew on a dick, and then I'll think about it."

Unable to transfer his stage presence to the silver screen, in later years, Rudi toured in a production of "The King and I" and took up conducting and producing ballets. In October 1992, at his last public appearance for his Paris Opera Ballet production of La Bayadere he got a ten minute standing ovation.

On January 6, 1993, Rudi died from complications from AIDS. He never admitted he had the disease, even to having his obituary made up ahead of time, saying he had a grievous illness, again not wishing to share his private life with anyone, to carry the secret to his grave. "No trespassing," he often told reporters.

After Nureyev's death, Mikhail Baryshnikov came to his friend's defense when many obituaries commented at length on Rudi's insistence on performing, sometimes disastrously, when he was well past his prime. "For people who knew and now know that he was H.I.V.-positive for nine, perhaps ten, years, it was absolutely understandable why he wanted to be onstage. Definitely, for him, it was a death to be offstage. No matter how he was dancing, at least it was killing time because he knew time was killing him."

Baryshnikov tells of the last message he received from Rudi, just after he had been to see him at the hospital. The message demanded the return of a pair of battered pink ballet slippers which Rudi claimed Baryshnikov had stolen from him. "I would never be able to wear them, Mikhail says, because they were too small for me. He was very depressed that I had a bigger foot. But he had just remembered something about the shoes because I used to tease him about them. That was our relationship: we teased each other all the time."

No dancer has ever earned as much money: Rudi's estate was valued at $80 million and, according to Rexford, includes what may be the largest-ever private collection of paintings of men's bare bottoms. "Talk about a bun vivant!"

We don't know about all those hot buns but Rudi's art collection from his Paris apartment brought nearly $10 million when was auctioned in early 1994, with the Ballet Promotion Foundation and the Rudolf Nureyev Foundation, which helps injured or ailing dancers, reaping the benefits.

In sum, it's as Nureyev himself said: "The only critic is a full house."

Keanu Reeves and River Phoenix
in "My Own Private Idaho"

River Phoenix

*"River Phoenix is blond and smooth, and his face, softened
with erotic pleasure and with sleep, is angelically empty. His
Mike is like a dreamy piece of sculpture."*
- Critic David Denby, reviewing "My Own Private Idaho"

There was an alarming eeriness to it. On Halloween eve 1993,
River Phoenix, nearly finished with the film "Dark Blood" and
set to begin work on the film adaptation of "Interview With the
Vampire," playing the Interviewer, a part later to be played by
Christian Slater, collapsed in front of Johnny Depp's club in
West Hollywood, the Viper Room, and died soon after.

All Sunday night and Monday, as reporters ghoulishly
awaited the coroner's autopsy results, they phoned former
co-stars and co-workers, padding River's obituary with terse
quotes about how shocked everyone was to learn he had died.
Early news reports continued to perpetuate the myth that River
was obsessed with his health, disdaining cigarettes, alcohol,
drugs and even dairy products. He was obsessed with his
health, certainly, but, as his closest friends in Gainesville,
Florida, where he lived, know well, River was a typical hippie,
addicted to pot and beer and having a good time. Indeed, one
producer who worked with River said that it was time the
image be revised: "Yes, at one time he was absolutely
anti-drug, but lately he's just gone crazy." Another actor
remembers attending a wedding the year before in Hollywood
where River appeared to be totally out of it. She says, "It was
a formal affair. Even the Red Hot Chili Peppers were wearing
cheesy '70s tuxedos. But River arrived at 9:30 a.m., drinking a
bottle of wine, dressed in sneakers, a pair of shaggy, ripped
shorts, and a dirty T-shirt. People were angry with him."

River was staying at West Holywood's plush Hotel Nikko, in
Room 328, a $350-a-night executive suite. On Halloween eve, he
and his buddies were in the room until 10:30, playing loud
music and ordering up liquor and food. When the room service
brought them steaks and fries at 10 p.m. he said River's eyes
were bloodshot and he was dancing around in circles in the

middle of the room. At 10:30, he called for his car to be brought around to the front of the hotel. As he and his friends walked through the lobby of the hotel, they were yelling and making a scene. Witnesses said River looked as if he was out of his mind. "Only the driver of the car looked sober," said a witness.

They were headed for a jam session at the Viper Room, a cave-like club where the decor is black and lighting dim, where River met up with his "This Thing Called Love" co-star Samantha Mathis and his 19-year-old brother Leaf. Included in the group of jammers was Gibby Haynes of the Butthole Surfers and Flea (Michael Balzary), the bassist for the Red Hot Chili Peppers, a longtime friend of River's. Flea rode in the ambulance that took the star from the club to Cedars-Sinai Medical Center. Ron Davis, a photographer who was stalking the club hoping to record the comings-and-goings of the celebrities who frequent the place, said that Phoenix's friends acted dazed and confused. He saw Mathis and River's brother Leaf arguing with the doorman about the actor's condition as he writhed on the ground. Leaf finally made an anguished call to 911 saying that his brother might have taken Valium. Club owner Depp, a would-be guitarist and a casual acquaintance of River's, rushed outside to find paramedics lifting the actor into an ambulance.

Said Peter Bogdanovich, the director of "This Thing Called Love," in which River played an aspiring songwriter in Nashville: "We were all worried about the crowd he was with. L.A. always bothered him. Something about it triggered all the more difficult parts of his life." A crew member recalls that River was drinking heavily during the filming. "There was one night they couldn't get a performance out of him."

After the autosopy was performed and additional tests made, it was determined that River had a lethal mix of drugs and liquor in his bloodstream. A friend of the actor said: "I saw River using heroin and cocaine on several occasions. He told me, 'Life's too short not to live it up. I don't want to die from old age in a nursing home. I want to be the best looking guy in the morgue. At least he got one of his wishes."

But for his family and his fans, it was a tragic, pathetic end to one of the moviedom's brightest careers. "Upon River's death I had to really re-evaluate all the people in my life that had passed away and what they had meant to me," Michael Stipe of REM said. "And I realised how much more profound his loss was than any other that I had experienced. Possibly just because of my... just because it was so tragic, so incredibly tragic. River's death was just an awful, awful, awful mistake." Sidney Lumet, who directed Phoenix in "Running on Empty," for which the young star was nominated for an Oscar, said: He's one of those people who's so talented I don't know where he's going to go. The world was open to him."

The singer/songwriter Natalie Merchant said, "I didn't know River Phoenix that well, but his death struck me powerfully. I thought, There's someone who was a kindred spirit. Somebody whom I always wanted to spend time with but never got to." Their friendship was mostly by phone. "In the few times we spent together, he inspired me to push out boundaries. He had such a vibrant personality. I felt cheated when he died."

River's mother Arlyn denied her son was not a regular drug user and that his death stemmed from a party scene that was way beyond his usual experience and control."

But Johnny Depp had had enough: "How many times does his little brother have to hear that 911 tape? How many times do we all have to hear it? There has been enough pain already. This very talented young man made a fatal mistake. I hope kids learn from it." Depp was shocked when stories appeared saying that River's death meant that drug use was on the rise. "This epidemic has been going on for years. I just hope kids know...it's very dangerous."

When the Viper Room reopened shortly after Phoenix's death, a dealer, who observers said sold River the fatal dose, was back in action. "At the club's door," Dana Kennedy reported, "he greeted a friend with a knowing look and words that carried a sinister threat: 'Welcome back to the night.'"

Immediately a cult seemed to be building, especially among the gays who, like me, treasured his appearances at 15 in 1986 in "Mosquito Coast" and, that same year, "Stand By Me." Our adoration of the non-conformist River continued all through his career, culminating with his splendid performance as a male hustler in "My Own Private Idaho." A fan wrote a letter to the *Village Voice*, which they headlined: "My Own

Private Icon: It's a good thing Phoenix won't witness what will become of his image. If the Gap does an ad saying 'River Phoenix wore khakis.' I swear I'll move to China! But perhaps more distressing and immediate was Michael Albo's eulogy in last week's *Voice*: 'Together Alone,' in which he tried to 'out' the late actor and make him a gay icon. Why do we gay men feel compelled to justify our sexuality by projecting it onto celebrities like James Dean, who can never respond to our assertions? Are sensitivity and ambiguity necessarily the telltale signs of homosexuality?"

Obviously, the fan hasn't read all the books I have about Dean. The reader was disturbed about how the eulogy was contributing to the cult of Phoenix, which, he asserts, will memorialize the late actor into a frozen, idolized piece of Industry machinery. Albo, the reader says, appreciates Phoenix's image for himself and his gay male friends but doesn't want other generations (and other sexualities?) idolizing the actor. He bemoans having to see Phoenix memorabilia, saying: I liked him before it was cool to.

Paradoxically, the reader says, "although Albo wants to save Phoenix's image from idolatry 'on flat surfaces,' his 'relationship' was grounded in consumption of Phoenix on flat surfaces: film and publicity. While Phoenix didn't exploit the media, he appeared in magazines, but he was a conspicuously low-key actor who stated that he relished how his ambiguity kept audiences guessing his true identity. Albo romanticizes Phoenix and does not distinguish the image from the person, filling in the ambiguous areas with his own fantasies. Ignoring the wretched manner of Phoenix's death, Albo sticks to bittersweet and self-serving thoughts."

Albo began his eulogy by quoting what he had written when he was in the ninth grade: "I am such a gaywad, and I know this is going to sound totally queer but River Phoneix, I think, has the looks, personality, and characteristics that I would want for a roommate or something."

Albo says that a year later he came to terms with being a gaywad and he didn't want River for just a roommate any longer. "I am not some insane stalker of stars, mind you. I never wrote him a crazebag fan letter, or stood outside a premiere waiting to touch his shoe or something. My liking of

River Phoenix was very manageable: a few magazines, the poster for 'My Own Private Idaho,' a dedication to seeing all his movies, good or bad. He seemed as understated and calm about his stardom as I was trying to be about liking him. He shined through the self-hating, homo-psycho, PR-scheming heap of robotic actors who seem to make up Hollywood. He never was named gay but my freiends and I settled for his quiet ambiguity on the screen almost satisfying our small, yet-unfulfilled request for a young, openly gay actor.

"So I guess I'm still gaywadover River Phoenix, and totally queer about being attached to a celebrity I probably never would have met. I imagine the cruel, vital lesson I am suposed to learn at 23 is that I am still a fool for the illusion of Hollywood and stardom."

River had his share of devoted gal fans too. Katherine Diechmann: "A year or two ago, *Rolling Stone* ran a photograph of River Phoenix that caused me to do something I rarely do: cut a picture out of a magazine and tape it to the wall. Like a teenager, really, except the act wasn't one of crushdom. In this photo, River Phoenix was posed against a white building with a red door. (I think it's a church.) He's sort of spiraling sideways in space, fallen angel-style, arms flung wide, head tipped so you can read only his forehead, eyebrows, and nose. His fingertips (so eloquent in 'My Own Private Idaho') are slightly out of focus. I taped this picture because it perfectly recalled the vigor, confusion, and grace of a certain stage of youth; with that little twirl, River Phoenix nailed a particular state of being so palpably, just as he nailed so many complicated emotions in his now bizarrely truncated (let's not call it 'tragic') career. His most powerful moments on screen all had to do with a fluttering possession of melancholy and longing, a fact that seems a little spooky now that there will be no more of them. He shattered masculine taboos and let himself break wide open, often in tears... His work was so sophisticated, so inflected, so extremely generous. His most powerful moments on screen all had to do with a fluttering possession of melancholy and longing, a fact that seems a little spooky now that there will be no more of them.

"Like James Dean, his death was a catastrophic, sudden end to a career that seemed to be really taking off, one that appeared to have so much promise."

"What one got from River Phoenix," Hilton Als said, "was what he gave a nearly luminous, distinctly American kind of film acting. While Americans are generally embarrassed by male beauty and punishing of female beauty, he combined the two so that it always appeared, in his films, he was embarrassed by his talent; exhibiting it was punishment enough."

Als says there are three films of River's which caused his heart to go out to him because he simply asked for it: "I Love You to Death," "My Own Private Idaho" and "Dogfight." In each, the question of who Phoenix was in and out of character became so palpable to his audience that he became a star. One definition of the star: the ability to be collectively imagined. River's death brought to mind my previous stories about him; he was always one of my favorite stars to profile. I remembered how he said he wished to remain far outside the Hollywood nexus of bad influences and superficial values. Sauntering, wild-in-the-streets River's own world is a farm near Gainesville, I wrote at that time. But he didn't hang out with the university students there; mostly musicians, all terrifically polite, just like him. He was in a band, too, Aleka's Attic, and loved it, writing songs, singing songs, playing guitar. Island Records was interested in signing them, but River didn't want people to come see the band just to see him." In fact, when Albo did go to see River playing in the band at his Student Activities Building, he spent the entire night trying to figure out which guy he was on stage, since the band is composed of his siblings and everyone on stage looked like scruffy replicas of each other."

In many interviews, River denied he was into the drug scene: "I just stay away from it. It depresses me. The biggest thing that really gets me are the girls. Because of being used, the way men use women. It really upsets me."

Upsetting to many was the mere thought of River suffering so. Ann Powers said: "I'm thinking of River Phoenix in convulsions on a sidewalk as his brother shouts into 911's tape recorder, making his panic public without meaning to. Just another tragic case of a young man falling apart is so common and varied at this moment in America. Repulsed by the details, bystanders on the electronic highway can't turn away, or don't. We tune in to grief that isn't ours by right. Maybe it's easier, feeling someone else's mortal pain instead of the dull ache that haunts the regular person for a million unsolvable reasons. It's easier to feel one life falling apart than to consider the crumble of states, laws and human decency. We love River Phoenix for unraveling before our very eyes."

Self-serving or not, I did adore River Phoenix. Not for unraveling mind you, but for being willing to test the boundaries. When asked if he was a boy or a man, River replied: "I'm a lad." He wished he'd waited to experiment with sex: "Yeah, I was four. With other kids. But I've blocked it out! I was completely celibate from ten to fourteen. I really haven't had sex with many people - five or six. I've just fallen into relationships that were fulfilling and easily monogamous. You know, that's the way it is: monogamy is monogamy until you screw someone else."

"When River was a young child," John Glatt explains in his biography of River, *Lost in Hollywood*, "his parents were involved in the Children of God, which had husbands and wives and their children participating in orgies and pornography."

"You could do anything in God's name if you did it in love," said one of the ex-members. "That included sharing sexually with other people. We were taught that the ultimate sacrifice that a man could make to God was to share his wife with another man."

Shepherd Wotilla, who has since left the Children of God, now describes it as a "Christian sex cult."

"We built that group with converted hippies and rebellious youth who were already into the whole hippie trip with its promiscuity and sexual freedom.

"During the next few years," Glatt says, "the Phoenixes were rewarded for their loyalty to the cult by rising through the Children of God hierarchy to be given extra responsibilities. As River reached his formative years he accompanied his parents on a never-ending trek from commune to commune, helping them to recruit new members. He was a thoughtful little boy but already seemed guarded and withdrawn, not as animated as his playmates."

At four, in line with cult's teachings, River began to experience sex regularly with the other young people of the group in the nurseries at night. Years later he would acknowledge in an interview with Joe Dolce of *Details* magazine losing his virginity as a young child: "I'm glad I did it when I was young," he said. "But I didn't want those young vaginas and different body parts that were in my face to make me perverse when I'm older, so I blocked it out. I was completely celibate from ten to fourteen. You're just born into that reality and you accept it."

Jonathan Sherman, who grew up with River in two communes, says he too was initiated into sex at four years of age: "Sex was part of our upbringing," he remembers. "It was part of the lifestyle and seemed quite natural as we didn't know anything else. They involved the kids in all aspects of sexual activity from a very young age. I was put together with other young boys and girls and we played around. It was part of that whole post-hippie genre in the early seventies of free love, free sex, free everything. We're all God's children."

Jonathan says the cult also physically beat children to keep them under its tight control: "Children were community property and we were raised to be submissive. We were beaten and put in isolation and seclusion. You can't be rebellious at all. You're brainwashed."

One night, River and his sister Rain gave a show-stopping performance of "You Gotta Be a Baby to Get to Heaven."

"I fell in love with River when I saw him playing guitar at seven and singing," recalled Sky Sworski. "River was definitely somebody who was a grownup at seven. You could have a conversation with him like you could with a thirty- or forty-year-old person."

Sky would become the family's benefactor and was instrumental in eventually getting River before Hollywood casting agents. "The pressures to succeed were immense, and River would soon be carrying the financial burden of his whole family on his very slender shoulders," Glatt said.

"This is a fantasy world," explained Hollywood casting agent Sheila Manning. "We're turning children into little adults, asking them to do an adult job for adult money. But they're kids."

River began by making commercials. The standard day's pay for a commercial in the early 1980s was $317.40, which was huge money to the Phoenixes. Soon he had been established as one of the hottest young stars in the business. "He was the angelic-looking, all-American kid in ads for Mitsubishi, Ocean Spray and even Saks Fifth Avenue, where Arlyn had liked to shop at lunchtime during her days as a Manhattan secretary," Glatt says.

Then, abruptly, River suddenly announced he did not want to have anything more to do with commercials...they were "phony," he didn't believe in the products. His mother's persistence and River's hard work finally paid off with a succession of minor guest appearances on TV shows such as "Hotel," "Family Ties" and "It's Your Move." But his breakthrough came with key roles in two well-received television miniseries. In "Kennedy: The Man and His Times," River played Robert Kennedy as a boy and attracted much attention among Hollywood casting directors. In his next TV movie, "Celebrity," River played the role of a young boy having to come to terms with his father's homosexuality. At the climax of the controversial film River's character surprised his father in bed with another man.

"It was a big dramatic scene," River would characterize it.

During the making of his first film, "Explorers," River became attached to Ethan Hawke, discovering what it was like to be a more-or-less normal kid for the first time in his life. By law the kids could work only four hours a day so there was time to play after they finished their daily studies with their tutor. One day River walked in and found MTV playing on a studio monitor. He was spellbound and sat for hours as though mesmerized by the high-gloss videos.

But River, who had been taught to keep Hollywood at a distance by his father, was determined to keep his feet on the ground and not become a spoiled movie kid. "There are some Hollywood kids who are really brats and it's just hard to deal with them," he would say. "I've been lucky that I haven't been such a brat. I'm trying my best not to be."

Long after making "Stand By Me," the sleeper hit of 1986, River said that there was a lot of himself in Chris Chambers: "I just went on a lot of instinct and my own emotions. I was very young. I was going through puberty and I was hurting real bad. Personally I didn't think my work was up to my own standards. I have a tendency to be super-critical of myself."

River's portrayal of the chain-smoking leader of the gang was singled out as "particularly outstanding" by the trade paper *The Hollywood Reporter*, and the *Washington Post* said that River's performance gave the film its "center of gravity."

People magazine called River "One of the most exciting young actors on the screen," describing his "quiet intensity" as being reminiscent of Steve McQueen and Montgomery Clift.

The success of "Stand By Me" would change the Phoenix family's lives forever, launching River into stardom and giving the family financial security for the first time. It also presented a whole new set of problems as River began trying to cope with being a celebrity in Hollywood.

By the summer of 1986, River had become recognizable wherever he went. His face started to turn up on the covers of teen magazines, and each day brought thousands of requests for fan letters and autographs. It was scary stuff for the shy, introverted fifteen-year-old who was determined not to be sucked into the so-called Hollywood Babylon and let success change him. Further, he was torn by his mother's ambition for the future and his father's wanting to keep his family dream intact by turning his back on worldly success.

Because of his unique upbringing, River had no real friends outside of his brother and sisters and very much wanted to have some companions his own age and outside of the Phoenix clan and he started hanging out with a fast young crowd.

"It was like living in the drug capital of the northern hemisphere," said River several years later. "I know drugs were rampant everywhere in town. I've been so much more exposed than my folks think."

The teen magazines served up trite profiles of Phoenix for their readers, telling them everything they wanted to know about their hero, from his favorite color to his taste in girls. He was quoted in one magazine saying: "I like girls who are so natural because I'm natural in everything that I do." In another: "It's a great feeling to think that I can be a friend to so many people through my movies."

"River hated being on the cover of *Tiger Beat*," said Dirk Drake, who had been hired to tutor the Phoenix children when the family moved to Florida. "Pulling a fancy T-shirt down and exposing a nipple. He was totally ashamed of doing it but he understood that was part of it all. The mission. The purpose. The job. But he also found it ridiculous at the same time. That's heavy pressure when you're a self-conscious lad of sixteen."

Moving to Gainesville allowed Phoenix to live a normal life for the first time ever and he thrived on it: "I was feeling very lonely for a while," he later told Joe Dolce. "I've never had friends before now."

But Gainesville was not a panacea for River's internal troubles. When his girlfriend Martha Plimpton came to stay during the summer of 1988 she was shocked by the disharmony in the family. River was now a serious drinker as well as smoking Gainesville Green, snorting cocaine and tripping out on magic mushrooms. The troubled father and son had also started drinking together, as though trying to build bridges in their crumbling relationship and find a common bond.

Two weeks after River agreed to do "My Own Private Idaho," Gus Van Sant flew to Gainesville to meet his new star for the first time. The thirty-eight-year-old director instantly hit it off with Phoenix and they spent an hour talking before Van Sant asked to photograph him.

"We had been talking very intensely on the phone about the film," remembers the director. "He was the kind of person who was very analytical and he wanted to know everything there was to know about the movie and what we were planning to do."

By the time Van Sant flew back to Portland, Phoenix, uneasily, told friends such as Drake that he thought the director had a crush on him. But River did like Van Sant's quiet intensity and the fact that he played guitar in a Portland rock band called Destroy All Blondes. He was also excited about doing "My Own Private Idaho," which he felt could establish him as a serious actor and finally bury the teenage heartthrob image he so detested. To help him prepare for his role, Van Sant had made videotapes of a former Portland street hustler called Mike Parker, who was the real-life model for his character Mike Waters, talking about his life and his experiences as a male prostitute. Van Sant had been smitten with Mike Parker when he was first introduced to the cherubic-looking blue-eyed boy when he was just sixteen years old. At the time Parker had just come off the street after three years of hustling, and Van Sant was fascinated by his tales of prostitution.

"He's very voyeuristic when it comes to that kind of thing," explained Parker. "My time on the street was really a search for acceptance. My father left when I was very young and I was looking for acceptance. And I was going to get that any way that I could, even if it was a dirty old man that wanted my body. It wasn't a gay thing. It wasn't a straight thing. It was a search."

Van Sant, who came from one of Portland's most affluent and respectable families, courted Parker and adopted him as his young muse. Parker moved into Van Sant's sprawling mansion high up on a hill in the Vista district of Portland. This way the director could observe his life closer.

"I was still streeting," explained Parker. "I wasn't a street person but I still hung out on the street. I knew what was going on. I guess Gus was attracted to that and wanted to know more."

In 1987 Van Sant produced his first full-length feature film, "Mala Noche," about a Portland grocery clerk's infatuation with a street boy less than half his age, incorporating much of what he had learned from Parker. Made with just $20,000 from his own savings account, "Mala Noche" won the Los Angeles Film Critics prize for best Independent/Experimental film in 1987 and brought Van Sant the recognition and financing he needed to make his next film, "Drugstore Cowboy."

In April of 1990 Parker, who had a small part in "Drugstore Cowboy," flew to San Francisco to meet River Phoenix, who was in town to shoot some exterior scenes for "Dogfight." By now River knew about Parker's hustling days from the heart-rending interview videos he had watched back in Gainesville with Drake. With his work on "Dogfight" almost finished, River was slowly easing out of the macho Eddie Birdlace to prepare for his most challenging role. To help him research his new role Phoenix befriended Matt Ebert, a production assistant on "Dogfight," who had been a real-life street hustler and a former heroin addict.

"River started with heroin out of malaise," Ebert told *Esquire* in March of 1994. River brought Ebert with him to work as his assistant on "Private Idaho."

"River had an involvement with a minor member of the [male] cast, so he could be ready for 'Idaho,'" according to Parker. "I think maybe he had feelings that way. Everybody has a level of curiosity. River struck me as real curious. Maybe not because he was gay but because he wanted to understand. I can see him doing something like that, getting into it, figuring the role out and coming to see it from every point of view. River wanted to become Mike Waters." Parker says that he never felt "interviewed" by Phoenix and found it easy to open up to him. On their first day together Parker and Phoenix sat on the grass in a public park, high on a hill with a sweeping view of the entire city.

"We talked the entire day," said Parker. "Even though he had never been in my particular situation I felt he understood me. He knew the pain. He told me about the times as a child when he'd played on street corners in Hollywood without knowing where he was going to sleep that night or where his next meal was coming from. In his own way he had also been there.

"I think River caught the drifting part of it. I felt that even though River had a deep sense of family he had no solid base or anything really to call home."

Later Phoenix would admit just how much he related to Mike Waters' search for his mother and a happy homelife after his own unsettled childhood: "For me there's something so universal in his quest for home," said the actor. "It has the sentiment of so badly wanting that home, that Beaver Cleaver reality that so many kids don't have in this country."

During the summer Phoenix and co-star Keanu Reeves became frequent visitors to Portland's Old Town district and spent nights with the hustlers who cruised a strip outside the gay City Nightclub on Thirteenth and Burnside known as "Vaseline Alley," where boys as young as twelve trick. "Keanu and I made a blood brother pact," River said. "Anyone who has a problem, fuck 'em. That's all I can say. A big capital F and a U-C-K, and then THEM. I get negative shit all the time. I don't care."

Phoenix said he felt like a "guerrilla" hanging out with the hustlers, whom he befriended. "It was very sensational for us," he told *Interview* magazine in November, 1991. "It was all in character. We were just hangin'. If anything, they thought this is another cat who's trying to take my spot on the street. It's a brotherhood on the street, man. You all watch for each other's backs because no one wants to see anyone get stabbed."

"It's our responsibility to go as deep as we can," said Reeves, "and to explore all the directions that might be suggested in a script. Just so we have all our bases covered."

During the next few months Phoenix and Reeves flew in and out of Portland to research their roles. Parker patiently taught Phoenix "all the marketing tricks," showing him how to lure "dates" by adopting a look of wide-eyed innocence while giggling nervously like a little child: "I showed River how to market himself on the street," says Parker. "You have to look really innocent and display. In my experience there are two kinds of hustlers. The ones that are rowdy and look like they haven't taken a bath in a week and the glamorous ones, who don't have a hair out of place. River took the underdog, grunge-type look, which is a definite pick-up on the street."

But even though Phoenix outwardly seemed to feel comfortable in the Portland gay scene he was still very nervous about actually having to play homosexual nude scenes in front of the cameras. A year later River would play down his nude scenes with Reeves and German actor Udo Kier: "Hey, it was just this mass of flesh. And Keanu and I have known each other for a long time."

As River got to know Van Sant better he started quizzing him about his sex life. Van Sant remembers River asking personal questions about his gay relationships: "'What exactly do you do in bed? Which side do you sleep on? Do you ever tell him to shut up? If you're angry at him do you still buy him an expensive birthday present?

"River dropped clues about his sexuality but I never really followed them up," said Van Sant. "River was always doing things like saying, 'I just love you,' and lunging to hug me. I'd freeze, maybe because my father used to grab my knee in a certain way. River didn't like that, so he'd hug me again, and I'd freeze again, and he'd yell at me."

During the making of "Idaho" River became taken with the difference between love and sex, which he felt was the dominant theme of the film. With this in mind he actually wrote the film's pivotal scene, in which Mike Waters declares his love for Scott Favor and kisses him, saying he can make love to a man without being paid for it.

"River wrote that entire scene after a conversation with me about being able to love people, maybe even a man, without getting money for it," says Mike Parker. "It was intense."

"As River came out of 'Idaho' it became painfully obvious to his friends that something had gone wrong with the gifted actor, Glatt insists. "After living and breathing his Mike Waters character for six months, it had, it seemed, become a monkey on his back that he couldn't shake off. He did spend Christmas with his family before flying off to New York to celebrate the new year with friends, but temperamental and moody, he was veering out of control, fueled by the combination of cocaine and alcohol."

On January 2 he walked into the Limelight club after a night's partying. Still dressed in his 'Idaho' street-kid clothes, he sat by himself in a deserted corner of the converted church club resting his head in his hands. After a few drinks he suddenly came to life and started talking about how he was still doing "research" for his part as a male hustler. Then without warning he ripped off his shirt, wrapped it around his head and ran onto the dance floor bare-chested and started dancing. When the club's paparazzi followed him onto the dance floor and started taking photographs he shouted at them to leave him alone.

But River always liked to keep people guessing. Indeed, in one of his last interviews he said, "I try to lie as much as possible when I'm being interviewed. It's reverse psychology. I figure if you lie they'll print the truth, and when I tell the truth, they'll lie. I have lied and changed stories and contradicted myself left and right, so that at the end of the year you could read five different articles and say, 'This guy is schizophrenic.'" But then he added, "The truth is so individual. Unless you act on your truth, all you are doing is aiding and abetting someone else's lie. You're not even lying to yourself. You're lying to everybody around you."

It was no lie, though, that this shy boy could be sexy. But it wasn't until "A Night with Jimmy Reardon," when he was at last having sex, that I decided, quite firmly, that a night with River Phoenix would surely be one of the most joyous of my life. You had to love someone for whom " Fuck 'em" was a normal reaction. He once said: "In society there's this confusion between love and sex. People think they want love and that they'll get it through sex. Very rarely do the two merge cohesively. The character I play is very clear on the difference between love and sex, because he has sex for a living. That's why his line was so important (in the big scene he does with Keanu). 'I love you, and you don't pay me.' I wrote that line. I'm glad I wrote that line. They tell me nobody's ever said that before on screen. I'm so proud. That's great! Cool! We're movin' along. Being that homophobia is like a religion, I don't know that there's going to be that much space in the marketplace for this stuff. This helps it, though, get underway."

Critic Lawrence Frascella said that director Gus Van Sant discovered previously unimagined depth in Phoenix. I doubt there has ever been a screen character who embodies such fragility, helplessness, and defenselessness. A deeply moving experience. You don't need a film degree to appreciate it. Just an open mind. Van Sant had to assure the producers there would be no pickle shots, Hollywood's term for exposing the male sex organ. One executive cried, If he's going to show erect dicks, I don't know what we're going to do! Van Sant says, "Of course, it's only a problem because men get embarrassed when they see dicks on the screen. We needed to get an R-rating, that was in the contract. If I had complete freedom, it might have been different. So we had to make do with the two boys with actor Udo Kier in a three-way which is filmed in a series of tasteful tableaux that change too quickly to tell who's doing what to whom, even when freeze- framing it on the VCR. And then there's the moment when Keanu idly plays with River's tit while taunting police officers who are afraid to do anything to Keanu's character, the mayor's son. Plus, we have River in a g-string." Gay writer Lance Loud described the scene: "Draped semi-nude over a rough-hewn cross, his hairless body drenched in golden light and his loincloth bulging with the help of foam rubber padding, River Phoenix is posing for the cover a magazine called, 'G- String Jesus."

River said that the secret of his performance could be found in the fact that he invested fully in the characters that he played: "That's the only thing that gives me security. Not myself. Myself is a bum! Myself is nothing. I am a peon. I'm an idiot. I'm totally removed. I'm in the closet, out of sight. You can't touch me. My character that I'm living takes me over for a while. I want to be able to believe these characters that I create." At the time of his death, it was suggested that perhaps River invested too heavily in the character of Mike and the counter-culture lowlifes he hung out with during the filming and that may have contributed to his decline.

"He really worked on it and changed a lot of things about it himself," Van Sant says. "He made the character gay. [Mike] calls himself bisexual, but I don't really know what to call that. In the story I wanted the hustlers to be neither straight nor gay, to be asexual. But River made it into, like, I love you and I want to sleep with you. Whereas in the screenplay as it was written, the guy was just bored and he was like wanting to fool around, instead of just beating off, was just wanting to beat off with his friend which I thought was accurate, like what might happen, not really any emotion tied into it, just sort of something to do River made it much more humane.

"I never specifically asked River or Keanu about their sexual experiences because it didn't really matter to me but I think judging by the way we were talking about the characters I don't think they were completely blind to that side of themselves. I just left it up to them to do whatever they wanted and we didn't really know up until that moment what they were going to do. I guess I could have said, KISS, and they probably would have done it. But I wanted them to do it."

Van Sant said that River's character may be gay but you're not really sure because he's not really sure: "The hustlers and johns don't think of themselves as gay. In real life, the clients for these street hustlers tend to be middle class businessmen or construction workers with families."

River agreed: "There are a lot of street hustlers who are 'straight' who, to make money, do whatever they have to do. And then there are people who are part of the street gay life, who enjoy that, and that's their life. Mike, my character, is from the first group. He does it just for money. He's not part of that whole scene, which doesn't change anything, really, it's all the same scene, but that's how their psychology works. That's how they justify what they do." By observing the scene, River says he learned a lot: "I learned the importance of home. What he (the character Mike) doesn't have, I feel very lucky to have. It made me rethink what I have going for me."

"Mike is sort of an embryo," Van Sant said, "and I think River was playing it like that. He was doing things that I didn't even know he was doing. You only get to see Mike having pleasure when he hugs the guy at the end...in that scene where he watches 'The Simpsons.' He was supposed to hug the guy like it was something he lost that he needed very badly. He did it only once, it's true, but it was one of the main ideas behind his hustling, that he needed to be held, and touched. He didn't necessarily need to have sex. But he needed to be close. We didn't really explore that, except in that one little detail, which is really too bad, because it sort of was one of the inspirations for the whole film, the emotional breakdown in the mind of a street hustler. In this particular character, one of the main things he had was his need to be wanted, and he could be wanted by men who wanted him for various reasons, slightly different reasons than he wanted them to want him. He was really after attention and affection. But still what he missed was basically from a man, and not from a woman. He didn't have a father."

When asked if there was any part of his relationship with Keanu on the screen, River said: "No, you'll never see that. That's the fun of what we do. It's a different world out there. I have a lot of chameleon qualities. I get very absorbed in my surroundings."

River was approached by German director Volker Schlondorff, who made "The Tin Drum," and wanted him to star as the tortured young gay poet Arthur Rimbaud in an adaptation of Henry Miller's "Time of the Assassins." "As soon as Phoenix started reading Miller's book he was stunned, as the book about the tragic nineteenth-century artist could easily have been his own life story," Glatt observes.

"That book *is* River," said his friend Nick Richert. "He

totally related to it and became obsessed. Who can know what effect it had on him?"

From then on Phoenix would carry the book around with him, often reading key parts he had marked to his friends. Seeing himself as an artist, River was captivated by the 1946 book about Rimbaud, who saw the civilized world as a jungle and did "not know how to protect himself in it." He also read *The Basketball Diaries* and told the author Jim Carroll he wanted to play him in the film version, later played by Leonardo DiCaprio, who would also essay the role of Rimbaud.

After wrapping "Idaho," River and Keanu were eager to work together again. The project? River wanted to do Shakespeare. Keanu said, "It'd be a hoot. We could do 'Romeo and Juliet.'"

"Yeah," River said, "I'll be Juliet."

Tragedy echoing tragedy, now we shall never see River in what may well have been his greatest role.

John Travolta in top physical form in "Staying Alive"

John Travolta

"Maybe John Travolta should just make a declaration about himself one way or another because everyone else in his life is talking to the tabloids. Now his ex-driver Nassim Tahzid is saying John loves seducing married men and hunky surfer boys. Other revelations: John was much more interested in Olivia Newton-John's husband than her (which makes sense given Matt Lattanzi is cuter than she is). And when Sly Stallone rejected John he said, 'If he doesn't want me, I'll get fat.' And he had a huge crush on Muhammad Ali."
– Outlines, June 1991.

When he was six, John Travolta was following his sister around on a road tour of "Gypsy," absorbing the atmosphere. By the age of 12, he made his own stage debut and at 16 he was starring as Hugo in a touring version of "Bye Bye Birdie." Then he went to Hollywood and four months later, was cast as a numbskull loverboy Vinnie Barbarino on TV's "Welcome Back, Kotter." During the series' summer hiatus in 1977, John starred in "Saturday Night Fever," earning a Oscar nomination. He followed that spectacular success with one equally as gratifying, the starring role in the movie version of the long-running Broadway musical "Grease."

After those films were in release, the interviewer Rex Reed went to see the star. Here's his description: "Travolta stretched his colt legs on top of a glass coffee table to work out the kinks, tugs at his turtleneck sweater, fingers the Kirk Douglas dimple in his Cinemascope chin, and ponders the latest ordeal in what upwardly mobile movie stars have come to expect from life in a fishbowl. At twenty-three, he's the hottest thing to hit teenybopper heaven since space shoes. More over, Elvis."

In his famous interview in *Rolling Stone*, John discussed his sexuality: "You know, of course," the interviewer said, "that your own appeal is androgynous. Why do you think your sexuality appeals to men as well as women?"

"I really don't know," John replied. "My characters have always been very masculine. If I am androgynous, I'd say I lean toward the macho androgynous."

"You also know one of Hollywood's favorite games is to claim that all leading men are secretly gay?"

"Oh, yeah. That's a notorious rumor."

"Then you know that people say that about you, that you're gay?"

"They say that about me, Brando, every male, especially the first year you become a star. It wears off after a while, but I've heard it said of just about everybody."

"Did it bother you the first time you heard it about you?"

"Not really, because the rumors about me were so extraordinary. The gay rumor about male stars is such a classic that it didn't surprise me to hear it about me, because I'd heard it about the others. All I thought was, 'Oh, I see the game now.'"

"Are you gay?"

"No," he replied flatly.

After the early big successes, Travolta's career took a nosedive when he made the bomb "Moment by Moment" with Lily Tomlin. Lily says,"'Moment by Moment' was a terrible shock. None of us expected to be massacred for it. John Travolta was so hot, I'm sure it was devastating to him. Jane (Wagner, her scriptwriter and companion) and I didn't escape either, by any means. I'd seen a sneak of 'Saturday Night Fever' and I loved John. And he came backstage after seeing 'Appearing Nitely.' He owed Robert Stigwood another movie so he told Stigwood he wanted to do it with me and Jane. We thought it would be a good movie. I had a great time with John. Everybody said we were just awful and we didn't have any chemistry at all, so what can I tell you? I spent much more time with Travolta, playing around, being pals, rolling on the sand, than I did with Steve Martin during 'All of Me.' I felt almost maternal towards Steve. "

And speaking of maternal, it was at the time of "Moment by Moment" that John's friend, actress Diana Hyland, 41, died of cancer. Eighteen months later, John's mother died of the same disease.

"After 'Moment by Moment,'" John recalls now, "...that was the first time I heard the words 'Your career is over.'" His career was resurrected for a while with "Urban Cowboy," but then he followed that with the commercially unsuccessful

"Blow Out."

In the spring of 1982, he parted company with his longtime mentor and manager Bob LeMond, who had been managing the lad's career since he was 16.

But the switch in management didn't help his flagging career. In 1983, he starred in the disastrous sequel to "Fever," "Staying Alive," directed by Sylvester Stallone. Bob Satuloff said: "If it has occurred to you that the disco movie movement came and went quite some time ago, stagger down memory lane for a few seconds and check out 'Staying Alive.' Sly, whose aptitude for the realities of the milieu, the Broadway musical theater, in which the film's story is set, was at the height of his 'Rambo' popularity when 'Staying Alive' was made. This seems to be why Paramount gave him carte blanche in terms of budget and production values to bring to throbbing life the story of a not very private dancer whose busy choreographic ideas not only save a Broadway show but make him an overnight sensation. One could compare Travolta's character to the one played by Ruby Keeler in '42nd Street,' but I prefer to think of 'Staying Alive' as a cross-gender version of 'The Debbie Allen Story.'"

It took "Look Who's Talking" in 1989 to put Travolta, at the age of 37, back on Hollywood's hot list. Edmond Grant in *Films in Review* was amazed by the film's success: "It's astounding. It's amazing...that an awful scripted, resolutely dumb gimmick movie could set a new box-office record and then remain number one in ticket sales for more than a month is unthinkable." He had this to say about the star: "A somewhat bloated John Travolta, the hip-for-fifteen-minutes star of the '70s, whose last feature was something called 'The Experts' that was of such dubious merit that it was never given a U.S. theatrical release, plays his character as an older, paunchier Vinnie Barbarino." And the sequel was even worse!

Another bomb starring John was "Perfect," considered by many as one of the worst films of all time. However, John has reason to remember the film because a porn star had a small role, the same porn star, Paul Baressi, that, in 1990, out-ed John in *The National Enquirer*.

But the whispers about John, and tabloid headlines, didn't stop. In September 1991, the *Globe* ran a story about John's wedding to Kelly Preston, 28, and headlined it, "Weirdo Wedding." It seems the couple got married in France, where a couple must be married at a town hall by a mayor. Just a religious ceremony means nothing. Thus, they had to get married all over again in the U.S. Kelly was pregnant with child at the time. She lost that baby but gave birth to their son, Jett, in the fall of 1992, about the time John's film, "Chains of Gold," was released on video. In the film, which went straight-to-video (read "bomb"), John plays a social worker who befriends a 13-year-old (played by teen idol Joey Lawrence) who is involved in a crack-dealing gang.

As his appearnce in "Chains" reminded us, gay or straight, he's quite a package, as he himself says: "I find myself more interesting than traditionally handsome. But I've been told it's not just the handsomeness, anyway, it's the acting ability, the sexuality, the singing and dancing people like, so I take it all as a package."

As far as his personality goes, columnist Mike Greco comments: "I personally observed during the location filming of 'Urban Cowboy' that John is shy or arrogant, generous or selfish, trusting or paranoid, depending on the circumstances. He's a prince around people who massage his fragile ego with flattery and adulation. But with strangers or people who have failed to demonstrate their loyalty, the insecure Travolta erects formidable barriers to protect himself."

Bob Evans, the producer of "Cowboy:" "I don't know what his personal problems are but he is scared to death. Not only of the press but of anything that might make him look ridiculous. He was even afraid of shaving his beard in one scene. That's how unnerved and traumatized he is."

For "Cowboy," though, it was all worth it. Critic John Devere joined many in raving about Travolta's performance: "Disarmingly charming, eyes alive with lust for life, a winning vulnerability tempering his overt sexual charisma with a touch of boyishness, Travolta proves once again that he is both a subtly modulating actor and a screen presence for whom the word 'star' seems to have been invented."

"I think," John says, "people misinterpret my sensitivity or perceptiveness as insecurity and indecisiveness. I'm given less credit for being a strong individual than I deserve. No one could've gotten to the place I am and survived this long without being strong."

When it comes to sex, John says, "I wish now I could talk as freely about sex with white people as I do with blacks. See, I love talking about sex in detail, I like talking about what I like to look at, what I like to feel, what I like to experience, but I find I always edit myself around white people.

"I have a strong sex drive but it needs to be unleashed by someone who likes it. Otherwise, I tend to inhibit it. My priority now is to weed out the baggage in my life so I can enjoy things to the fullest. I want to work and play with people of comparable value, who put as much into a relationship as I do. Equals, in other words, so that I'm not this sympathetic person dealing with unbalanced people, constantly being drawn down with them.

"I don't want to withdraw any more. I just want to choose the right people. But that's hard, because I love people so much that if I find any attractive attribute, I glom onto it. And I think all the other areas of the person's life are as appealing. But then I find out, 'Oh, my God, some things are way out of whack.' I'm learning to take care of myself a little better."

John's participation in the "Fever" album made him a millionaire and it is said that he lives like a billionaire, with two planes, three homes, and all the toys. All he needed was work.

In 1993, Travolta found himself in the enviable position of being part of the hunger for '70s kitsch and an attempt to make "Saturday Night Fever" a "cult film," a Midnight Movie to be adopted by the folks who made "Rocky Horror Picture Show" a monster hit. Peter Rainer in the *Los Angeles Times* says, "Most of it stands up remarkably well - especially John Travolta's performance." And the same might well be said of the star himself.

In 1994, he took a gamble and appeared in "Pulp Fiction." His performance won him a second Academy Award nomination. "If anyone holds this movie together, it isn't Tarantino – it's John Travolta," raved *The New Yorker*. "He strolls through it without a wink of vanity, having long since relinquished the oily posing of 'Saturday Night Fever' in favor of the first law of cool: Don't try to be cool. While Tarantino clamors for our attention, Travolta knows that he has it and isn't going to lose it in a hurry. He can afford to rumple and fatten his character, turning Vince into a slob and a patsy, driving the picture beyond the regulation hipness of 'Reservoir Dogs' into a shabbier territory, where a man is known not just by his suit or his ruthlessness but by his hits of bliss and his flashes of panic, the big mistakes he can make as he tries to correct the little ones. What stays with you after 'Pulp Fiction' has ended (and amazingly little *does* stay with you) is the closeup of Vince's slow, drugged smile as he drives through the darkness to meet Mia, or the rather endearing shots of him sitting on the toilet reading 'Modesty Blaise.' Travolta has the nerve, in the midst of what feels like an action movie, to remind us of the pleasures of inactivity, the deep need to hang out."

As Bob Satuloff noted, "It wasn't long ago that Travolta's career was at such a low ebb, his only screen appearances were in the excruciating 'Look Who's Talking' series, but now everybody's standing in line for a piece of the 'Pulp Fiction' star's action. With Desmond Nakano's 'White Man's Burden' in the can for Miramax, Barry Sonnenfeld's film of Elmore Leornard's 'Get Shorty' in production at MGM, John Woo's 'Broken Arrow' in pre-production at Fox, and 'Lady Takes an Ace,' with Sharon Stone, to follow, Travolta is seemingly booked through the next millenium."

And all night as well. In 1995, Nick at Nite revived the "Welcome Back Kotter" series which first brought John to fame. As Ken Tucker says, "...The chief pleasure of 'Welcome Back Kotter' in the mid-'90s is what made all the girls in the studio audience scream in the mid-'70s: Travolta. Sure, a lot of the goodwill a modern viewer has toward Vinnie Barbarino now is because it's a kick to know what this good-looking, shaggy-haired kid did post-Kotter: became a pop culture fixture...

"Travolta steals every second of 'Kotter.' His Brooklyn accent is more convincing than that of anyone else in the cast, and, alone among his co-stars, he exudes a friendliness and vulnerability that makes the machine-gun pace of the jokes bearable. In his time, Barbarino was Fonzie with a soul; seen now, he's Travolta on a roll."

Jan-Michael Vincent in 1978
(Courtesy Jack Mitchell)

Jan-Michael Vincent

*"I first saw him in 1970 in 'Tribes,' a TV movie with Darren
McGavin, playing a drafted hippie in a Marine boot camp. He
can't be broken and eventually his survival methods are adopted by
his barracks mates to the consternation of the drill instructor.
It was a rebelliousness that appealed to me at the time.
Besides, I didn't think there was a more beautiful creature
on earth than blond, green-eyed Jan."*
– A Fan

Jan-Michael Vincent a *legend*? Wait. Think, who was the *first*
major star to appear completely naked in a major motion
picture, permitting the audience to see his most private parts?
It was 1974 and the film was "Buster and Billie." And, god,
even at the advanced age of 28 he was still cute as can be. The
preeminent gay magazine of the day, *After Dark*, showcased
him in all his splendor with splashy color photographic spreads
and the editor said, "Always testing, Jan-Michael challenges the
camera to catch his essence: vulnerability and strength."

"I don't care that I might be an asshole," he was saying after
he had finished "Billie." He was appealing then, the kind of
kid you'd want to take care of. Granted, he was married and
had a child of his own, but there was still a lot of kid in him.
His key words in those days were surfing and surprise. About
"Billie," he said: "I had already established a much higher
price, so I took less than half of what I ordinarily got, but I
loved the script. I had something in my heart about it." He
wasn't the only one. A couple of years later, Jan had grown a
beard and settled into some success with actioners such as
"White Line Fever" and "Vigilante Force." He'd become a
man you'd want to take care of you.

By 1978 he was saying: "The thing I've figgered out about
myself is that I have nothin' to hide. That I'm a sterling example
of nothin' to feel bad about. Before, I always functioned as if I
had somethin' to hide even if I didn't know what it was, but
I've lived long enough now to realize that I'm a total citizen. I'm
surely not an angel, but there's nothing I do that's wrong. Sure,

I've tried to break all the rules, but now I'm thirty-two years old, I'm just an outlaw, without a law to break!"

Now, don't you just love a guy like that?

And the "outlaw" had divorced his wife. "I'm proud of the fact that I have a woman I've lived with who's been my wife and I'm proud I have a child. We had a hard time livin' together, really hard, because of what I'm stuck up against, how much I have to test people. I mean, I'm sure I tortured her to death, testing her, and she doesn't need that. It's too passionate and hard to live with her, but I'm very proud of the fact that I don't have to consult my lawyer to communicate with her. It goes right back to how deeply I feel. If you have friends, they're going to be your friend no matter what and I'd expect the same from my wife or my woman, my kids, or my parents. If I'm in the hospital, or in jail, or whatever, I'm sure they're going to come and get me out and what's important is that I'd do the same. If I have a friend, I'm committed to that friend. I would be there, no matter what. I like somebody who'll push me. I need to be demanded of. A challenge is important to me. I'm only turned on by challenge."

Jan has said that he spent his childhood trying to "please somebody else, trying to placate other people and being afraid not to be nice." In his youth, he went through a period of rebellion, then went back to his "trying to placate other people" when he began acting. He excelled in playing handsome young men in search of their identity. "Baby Blue Marine," stunningly photographed by the master Laszlo Kovacs, presented the star in the role of Hedge and he gives what is probably his most affecting performance. One reviewer remarked, "He brings to this part a pervasive warmth, gentleness and strength that carries the film."

But, despite good reviews for his performance in "Marine," "Big Wednesday" and other films, by the late '70s, things seemed to fall apart for Jan. He saw it coming early on: "Something that's always in my mind is that, 'You're just an actor, boy, and it's your day like that, but it could be tomorrow with your doin' some other things.' That's one of the reason, maybe, why I try to keep sort of an aloofness from it, because I realize it's a very tentative thing. Comes and goes, no matter who you are. There's no guarantee about anything. Let's put it this way: If I never did another film I'm so thankful I've had this opportunity, because of the education I've gotten, and what I've been able to find out about myself, other people, and what goes on in the world. And I like the fact that it isn't the same job all the time. Every job has an end date on it. If I had stayed in what I was doing when I was younger, and gone into the commercial sign business with my father, I would have dealt with, mostly, the people I dealt with when I was in high school, and my life would have been pretty predictable. Honestly, sometimes I can't believe all this is happening. I always feel there's a hook at the end of that line some place. I'm wary of the hook. I just keep waiting for the hook."

Eventually, the hook grabbed him. The good parts didn't seem to come his way and, with only an occasional juicy role such as in the hit mini-series "Winds of War," the star had to make do with roles in TV series such as "Airwolf" and movie stinkers such as "Raw Nerve," "Hangfire," "Animal Instincts" (second-billed to Maxwell Caulfield!) and "Beyond the Call of Duty," which do well as rentals.

"If ever there was a true-life tale of the seamy underbelly of Hollywood," Mark Ebner says in an interview with the star that appeared in 1995, "surely Jan-Michael Vincent would be its star. Having degenerated from '70s James Dean hopeful to '80s TV star to a life of alcohol, drugs, and lawsuits, Vincent is now the center spoke in an all-too-common wheel of exploitation films, star-fucking women, and residual fame. But at least he knows it."

"I used to drink and do blow and everything," Jan boasts. "Then I went without a beer for two years, and that thing happened with my wife and I was on again." Why? "I got tired of everyone pointing their fingers at me."

Ebner says, "Behind Vincent's dark shades and trace plastic-surgery scars is a world of self-inflected hurt. He shakes so badly he nearly knocks the tape recorder off the table he clutches – all other support systems long gone. But humility somehow prevails as he reflects on his career."

"I guess I've been pumping out films," Jan acknowledges to Ebner with a shrug. "I'm a journeyman actor. This is no way for a grown man to make a living, you know? (He laughs). I'd be a lot better off if I was Jesus, carpenter or a fisherman. That's what I do best. I could've turned 'Airwolf' into something more than I did, but it wasn't what I was used to doing. I was used to working three to six weeks on films...(On TV) you work twenty-six hours a day, and then you go to a different crew and start all over again."

In addition to writing the screenplay for the sequel to "Big Wednesday," Vincent reports he's working on another film called "Guitar Man" and going to Russia to appear in a film for Menachem Golan. Ebner says, "Wherever there's a producer willing to put up another $100,000 for the 'one-take wonder' to stagger in front of the cameras and read his lines, Jan-Michael, it seems, will be there."

But, as Jan-Michael himself said once, "I'm not turned on by an easy ride. That's what I like about the movies. They are a one-hundred-percent gamble. It's funny, because I don't gamble at cards. I don't have the heart, yet I'll gamble on anything. I'll do anything."

MUSIC STARS

With movie stars, it is possible that behind the facade of perfection is a trip to hell but we never really know it. With music stars, we are put more in touch with reality. It seems we find out more about them. They're more forthcoming in interviews. More books are written about them, there are even movies made about them. But the movies, music critic Owen Gleiberman says, "are almost always a sham. They inevitably tone down the seamier sides of the pop life-style: the drugs and alcohol, the orgiastic profusion of sexual adventure, the sheer ego-maniacal craziness that, for better or worse, have all been as integral to the rock mystique as the music, the clothes, and the fame."

For the 1991 Oliver Stone film about Jim Morrison, a boy who grew up a fat and became a sex symbol, critics said Val Kilmer got the star's look exactly right. "Trouble is," former Morrison girlfriend Eve Babitz says, "Kilmer has always been a prince, so he can't have the glow; when you've never been a mudlark it's just not the same." Prince or no prince, Kilmer even used a body double for the big love making scene in the movie. Besides, she says, "People these days, they don't know what it is to suddenly possess the power to fuck every single person you even idly fancied, they don't know the physical glamour of that, back when rock 'n' roll was in flower and movies were hopelessly square. And we were all so young."

No, but it's fun to imagine, imagine that "every single person" might just include you.

Morrison's and Mick Jagger's narcissistic sexuality held a promise that implied that, just possibly, under the right conditions they were available, that they would not be fussy where the adoration came from.

When Christopher Anderson's book "Jagger Unauthorized," was published by Delacorte Press, *Entertainment Weekly* commented that the 50-year-old rocker came across as "a sexually insatiable, miserly brute who's reduced to tears by a bad haircut." They went on to give other more unscrupulous details: He was 13 went he began to think of sex all the time; 27 men and women that Jagger had sex with are mentioned by name; and the word *sex*, or a variation, is used 102 times by the biographer. And, yes, the biographer revealed, Jagger has slept with many men, not just David Bowie. His conquests included the Stones' first rhythm guitarist, Brian Jones, and their manager, Andrew Loog Oldham. Mick also slept with Madonna before she was famous, at the Plaza Hotel in New York City, no less.

Craig Lee says: "After the inevitable burnout of the '60s iconoclasts, a lot of the more threatening and explosive themes in pop culture were watered down. But what Morrison implied often became more explicit: Ray Davies fell in Kinksy love with a he/she named Lola and Lou Reed took his walk on the wild side with transvestites and hustlers.

"Iggy Pop, who publicly stated he had no problems with guys giving him a blowjob ("It's like squirrels grabbing at nuts down there," he wrote), continued the aura of physicality and danger inherited from Morrison before entering a so-called partnership with David Bowie. Elton John's own admission of bisexuality was a great surprise to some, but it was a sign of the times. In the '70s the Ramones sang about hustling, displaying a knowledge that obviously came from personal experience. But with the advent of the '80s, the bisexual subterfuge was no longer needed for the new wave queen performers such as Boy George, Jimmy Sommerville, and Erasure's Andy Bell, who were gay and proud of it.

"The new hard rock rednecks such as Axl Rose and Sebastian Bach are one-dimensional Pans, sexy but deadly homophobic studs, who idolize the Morrisons and the Jaggers but are terrified of acknowledging the all-embracing sexual implications their role models present. Their sexuality is a blunt, reactionary weapon, in keeping with the neoconservative attitudes of today. They often play on their adolescent audience's fear of being an outsider.

"Morrison fueled both straight and gay desire to explore the unconscious underworld of sex, death, resurrection and art. For libertines unafraid to ride that snake, Jim Morrison provided the open door to self discovery."

Today's inheritor to the Bad Boy of Rock (or, in this case, rap) mantle might well be the notorious thug Marky Mark. Will he fizzle or become a legend in his own time? Only time will tell, but the effect he has had on gay men is astounding. Erstwhile photographer (and lustful fan) Stuart Bailey recounted, for *Better Homos and Gardens*, his "opportunity of a lifetime" to accompany his friend Holly, a teen fan magazine writer, to a Marky Mark concert in California: "Most of the audience was your standard gum-chewing wide-eyed-fuck-me-now-Marky teenage-girl-type, but my eagle eye spotted a few boys in the crowd.

"When Marky slammed onto the stage, the crowd went wild. He performed all of his greatest hits and towards the middle of his set, he crooned 'Sugar Cool Mack Daddy.' I couldn't quite make out the lyrics but I'm sure it was something about spotting a hot 30-year-old male photographer in the audience and falling madly in love with him and how they would spend eternity together living off Marky's earnings.

"So I could record this momentous occasion, a friend had loaned me his camera, complete with a huge zoom lens that would put Jeff Stryker to shame. I conserved film wisely at first, knowing Marky would be near naked on stage before the concert was over. Sure enough, during the last few songs, Marky did his trademark strip tease, removing his jacket, his cap, his shirt, and finally pulling his shorts down to reveal the top half of his underoos. My camera was as overactive as my libido. His pecs! Click! That washboard tummy! Click! He flexes his biceps! Click! He shows his armpit! Click! He grabs his cock! Click! Click! Click!

"Backstage, Holly and I were the only VIP's over 20. Marky sauntered over to us, his stud boy torso covered by a 'Censorship is Unamerican' T-shirt. 'Hi, Holly,' he said, recognizing her from previous interviews for her magazine.

Holly introduced me. 'Hi Stuart!' Marky said. 'It's nice to meet you!' Marky offered his hand, giving me one of those funky 3-part handshakes. My hand didn't respond, making a repetitive jerking motion on his hand instead. I couldn't speak. I wanted to tell him how zesty he was. I wanted to ask if it was all steroids. I wanted to offer to lick the sweat off his chest. I wanted to be his backstage sex slave for the rest of the tour.

"Suddenly, Holly had an idea that we should have our picture taken together with our bellies exposed. We both peeled our shirts up. Marky sneered for the camera. My tongue fell out. Click! Marky shook my hand again and we exchanged goodbyes. Somehow, this time I felt his touch was warmer, his eyes friendlier now that our belly buttons had been formally introduced.

"The next day, after waiting 60 breathless minutes at the photo developer, I was told my entire roll of film was overexposed. I hadn't set the flash properly. Outside on the sidewalk, I dissolved into a puddle of tears. Ironically, the only thing that was visible on the roll of negatives was a strip revealing our bellies.

"In the '70s, I cut out David Cassidy photos from *16* and *Tiger Beat* magazines, taping them to my bedroom wall. Each night before sleep, I dutifully kissed my Davids goodnight.

"At college, my dorm room was plastered with a mural of Menudo. Now, Marky adorns my West Hollywood refrigerator. As for the future? Let's just say you can be sure I'll be first in line when Macaulay Culkin records his first record album."

In an interview with Boze Hadleigh, a famous rocker, now in his 40s, summed it up: "What it is, is nobody really cares that much what the opposite sex does, as long as they come across in the end. But everyone gets antsy-like if their own sex don't act like they're supposed ta."

David Bowie in the late sixties

David Bowie

*"The lights finally dim and the alla marcia from the Beethoven
Ninth, played on the Moog as recorded on the 'A Clockwork
Orange' soundtrack, is played on the sound system at Assembly
Hall in London. The footlights, gelled a furious red, come up and
David Bowie and his band, the Spiders from Mars, hurl themselves
onto the stage. David's hair is dyed a brutally bright orange. His
soft-featured, childlike face is painted clown white. He is wearing an
astonishingly multi-colored jump suit and he looks as if he were an
Ariel who had somehow flown to Hell and had come back to tell all
about it. The Spiders, resplendently dressed in gold costumes, begin
to play some palpitating rock 'n' roll. They wheel around the stage
like demented tops. Occasionally David's hand rests on his hip while
he's belting out his tunes. The lights playing on his innocent,
unlined face color him an unearthly green. More unearthly than his
face is his crotch, which seems unusually large, even inhuman.
Mick Ronson, the Spiders from Mars's lead guitarist,
a silver-haired giant who glitters under the intense spotlights that
are flashing on and off above him, then breaks into an intense
electric guitar solo. David disappears in a blaze of throbbing strobe
lights and re-appears in a white satin Elvis costume, complete with
long white scarfs. A balloon floats across the stage and he crushes it
between his thighs. He suddenly grabs Mick's buttocks, then slides
between his legs. He performs fellatio on Ronson's extended guitar.
The audience seems pleased."
- A Fan at Bowie's concert in London, 1972*

I must confess I hadn't given David Bowie much thought
until 1976 when a boy I picked up in a bar in New York took
me to see "The Man Who Fell To Earth," the star's first movie.
Suddenly, I was captivated by a man playing an alien who was
distinguished by a lack of genitalia. The critic Pauline Kael
thought Bowie was playing, of all things, "a leering lesbian
Christ." (I found out later why everyone was so confused. We
in America, land of the free, were permitted to see only a
censored version of the film. The full version runs 138 minutes

and is now on video.)

Bowie became famous for his androgyny and pansexuality. Rock researcher Irwin Stambler says: "For many, Bowie's talent tends to be overshadowed by his private life, particularly his avowed bisexuality." In fact, David was the first major rocker to admit he slept with other guys and make it part of his act, his persona and his music.

It's always been an entertainingly strenuous chore separating the man from the image, and there have been so many versions of the latter of the last decade that his predilection for elaborate reinvention has long since surpassed mere calculation or ritual self-parody. If only by virtue of its crazy-quilt staying power, the "concept" of David Bowie has achieved an integrity all its own. David has brought artifice strikingly close to art.

In the seventies, sex was considered a revolutionary force, like drugs and rock 'n' roll. It wasn't just a marketing slogan. But people these days have blurry notions of what the sexual revolution actually was. According to David Frost, a recent poll showed that most Britons agreed, yes, there had been a sexual revolution in their lifetime but regretted that somehow or other they had missed it.

David Bowie hadn't missed it, but a lot of it was blurry: "That period in my life is none too clear," David says. He suffered through what was essentially the drugs-assisted unraveling of a "hurt, broken mentality; a fractured person," while living in L.A. in the mid-1970s. "That was the wipeout period. I was totally washed up emotionally and psychically, completely screwed up. I was fed up hallucinating twenty-four hours a day. I'd always had the natural instinct to be curious about life in all its forms - the arts, whatever. But I had an increasing tendency not to recognize the future. Everything became more and more just living from day to day."

In 1972, the star's incarnation as Ziggy Stardust was cited by *Esquire* as one of the key events which helped "homosexualize" American pop culture. Their reporter observed, "He adopted the posture of pederast when onstage with his lead guitarist."

In 1976, in an interview in *Playboy* magazine, Bowie stated he and his wife Angela were both bi. "Angela and I knew each other because we were both going out with the same man." Later Angela admitted, "David had scores of men and women when we were married and so did I. Often, there would be three of us in bed, usually another girl..."

Earlier David told Mick Watts in an interview in *Melody Maker*: "I'm gay and always have been..." Watts, who had covered David through many of his transformations, could not take him seriously. "His present image is to come on like a swishing queen, a gorgeously effeminate boy. He's camp as a row of tents with his limp hand and trolling vocabulary."

David says: "I get floored when people ask if I'm straight or gay or whatever. I don't want to recognize those categories. I refuse to. I will not be tied down by those kinds of things. I am drawn to people with whom I have a sexual empathy even though I still do not think that everybody has to go out and say who exactly they're laying and why they're laying them if they did lay them and why they didn't enjoy it if they did.

"I have a lot of friends in Gay Lib. I have no intention of waving a banner for them. People who join together when they're a minority are picked off much more quickly than individuals.

"Sex and risk are the foundation of rock 'n' roll. Life is about sex and risk but that doesn't mean that's all that life is. I think a life of sex and risk can be very satisfying. I've had a lot of it myself. But I would add relationships to that."

In the late '70s, David fled Hollywood to West Germany where, in his words, "this parallel thing happened, where as I came out of that last bad period, I grew more aware of my son's life and the responsibilities I have toward my son." (Zowie Bowie recently graduated from college.)

By the '80s, *Newsweek* found that Bowie was "promoting a new and more conservative style in sync with frightened and reactionary times." Despite what he had said in earlier interviews, he told *Rolling Stone* that he wasn't bi and had never been gay. In 1987, a woman in Dallas charged him with rape and demanded he take an AIDS test. He did, in Switzerland, and it was negative. The case was later thrown out.

David's past came back to haunt him when, in the spring of 1990, Angela told Joan Rivers on nationwide TV that she'd once caught her husband in bed with Mick Jagger. Joan asked what she did and Angela said: "I made breakfast." Free to talk after a 10-year gag order had lapsed, Angela's remembrances made new headlines. Jagger: "I have to confess that I've slept with men. I'm a passionate person. I love living life and being hungry for all kinds of new experiences. I went through a phase where lots of men were attracted to me and I was quite turned on by it all." David had no comment.

Elton John reacted to David's calling him "rock's token queen": "I try not to be bitchy, even though at times we're all bitchy in conversation. Saying it in print is another thing. I didn't retaliate even though he's had a couple of go's since, because I know what's happened to him. I'll always remember going out for dinner with him and Angie when he was Ziggy Stardust. It was a fabulous evening and over dinner he admitted to me that he always wanted to be Judy Garland, and that's the God's honest truth."

Keith Moon, the drummer for The Who: "David's had more images than any other singer. He can be anybody because at heart he's a nobody. Or nobody he'd recognize."

Or it may have been the drugs. Says David: "Cocaine puts physical holes in the brain. I've been tempted to have mine looked at."

And Bono says that Bowie is the nicest fella from Mars he has ever met.

The only image we're really sure of is that of a star. "I definitely like being a star," David says. "It's the only thing that I can do that doesn't bore me. When I'm on stage I give more than any other time of my life and that makes me feel good."

His last major popular recording success, "Let's Dance," was a wink to all of those costumed denizens of the nightworld who have carried forth his prophetic vision of sexual ambiguity, androgyny and dramatic self-caricature onto the dance floors of the '80s. "But he speaks to them," a reviewer stated, "not so much as a fellow traveler, but as a middle-aged survivor who relates the perspective of one who has come through all the distortion into the daylight of identity. Journeying amidst the carnal, opium-scented, red-light districts of 'Criminal World,' Bowie intones avuncular counsel in his groggy tenor; in a criminal world, where 'the boys are like baby-faced girls' (and vice versa), he proposes to 'hold a candle to your high-life disguise,' confiding, knowingly, 'I guess I recognize your destination/I think I see beneath your makeup/What you want is a sort of separation.'"

Rolling Stone named "China Girl" (from the "Let's Dance" LP) to its top 100 music videos list and said: "While Bowie's album, with its slick production and overt dance-pop feel, was the Thin White Duke's first blatant stab at mass acceptance, the videos he made in support of it were quite daring their way. "China Girl" tackles the ambitious topic of Western cultural imperialism, with the relationship between Bowie and the sometimes unadorned, sometimes lavishly made up Chinese woman in the video embodying a whole slew of complex issues. Iggy Pop's mordant lyrics – 'My little China girl,/You shouldn't mess with me/I'll ruin everything you are' – are fleshed out by director David Mallet with a good amount of wit. Too bad most of the attention this video gets is focused on its beach lovemaking scene, in which Bowie's naked buttocks were visible. MTV, of course, excised the offending cheeks for airplay."

Bowie's film career began in 1969 in "The Virgin Soldiers." "Actually, I'm in it for about twenty seconds as an extra. I've never seen the movie so I'm not sure I'm actually even still in it! I know that I was thrown over a bar in it. My true film experience began in a movie called 'The Image' which was 14 minutes long and awful. But 'The Man Who Fell to Earth' was a great movie. I think it's surely taken on other qualities over time and is a most intriguing science fiction movie, especially in relation to a lot of the stuff that's out at the moment. The uncut version is the only one we know in Europe. I was floored to find they had chopped, and I mean that literally, hacked, twenty minutes out of it for America. It brought the film to its knees." The uncut version is finally available in the U.S., on video, and for those who have always wondered what Bowie has had going for him all these years, here's how Aaron Travis, famous for his "Hollywood Hunks in the Raw" series, describes it: "Bowie's enormous uncut dick and lemon-sized balls swing between his legs during the sex scene only in the 138 minute version by Thorn EMI."

David loves making movies: "I work best trying to produce a fantasy life. When my private life is in an entangled state, I just disappear into a role." His disappearing act has been quite successful. In addition to "Man," he has appeared in "The Hunger," with Catherine Deneuve and "Just a Gigolo" with Marlene Dietrich and Kim Novak, arguably his sexiest role.

In 1991, he made "The Linguini Incident," a comedy starring Marlee Matlin, who said (through a lip reader): "David's so much fun. He's so sweet. Just a regular guy."

Sure he is.

David Cassidy's sensuous pose for *Rolling Stone*
magazine made him a gay icon.

David Cassidy in 1993 (with Paul Stanley of KISS),
still displaying his hefty bulge.

David Cassidy

*"When I was a kid, there were few magazines available that showed
naked young men, or nearly naked. That's why the photo of
David became my most prized possession.
You could buy Rolling Stone on any newsstand,
and there he was. He was simply incredible."*
- A gay fan, recalling May, 1972

In September of 1970, the TV sitcom with music, "The
Partridge Family," debuted on ABC; by December, the series
was in the top 10 and the Family's first single, "I Think I Love
You" was No. 1 on the pop charts. In November, 1971,
androgynous "Family" star David Cassidy's only solo, a
remake of "Cherish," hit the charts. His cute mug graced
everything from teen magazines to coloring books to lunch
pails.

One female fan reflected: "They don't make teen idols like
they used to. He was a silky-voiced, sandy-shag-haired, green
speckle-eyed, bell bottomed, thoroughly delicious pop-god. Not
only was he blissfully lovely, but almost all of the songs they
had him sing were about him loving a girl to pieces not being
sure she loved him back."

In May of 1972, David appeared bare-chested on the cover of
Rolling Stone and said, "There'll be a time when all this will be
over." And, by 1974, the show was in the ratings cellar and
pulled off the network.

In 1978, David appeared in a TV series, "Man Undercover,"
which was cancelled after two months because of low ratings.
He turned to the stage, appearing in "Little Johnny Jones" and
"Joseph and the Amazing Technicolor Dreamcoat," and, then
in London in "Time." Of his performance, one reviewer said:
"He looks cute and sings in tune and little more is asked of
him."   David increasingly began to feel he had been robbed of
his career: "I enjoyed playing the blues, playing Clapton and
Hendrix. People had no conception of what my own musical
taste was or of who I really was.

"Now I'm enjoying just being who I am."

Part of that process found him divorcing his second wife and making two movies, "Instant Karma" and "Spirit of '76," co-starring with another former teen idol, Leif Garrett, both of which went directly into video stores without theatrical release.

David also recorded a new album which was released late in the fall of 1991 called, simply, "David Cassidy." Appearing on ABC-TV's top-rated news program "Good Morning America," the star told how the album came about: "On my birthday about 15 months ago a couple of disc jockeys from a hard rock station in L.A. started making remarks about me and wondering what I was doing now...So I said, I've gotta have a go at these guys! Called in, putting on this drunk act, being irreverent about my fame, the whole bit. And they invited me down. I had in fact just finished doing a film and started another one. And I'd been writing songs; I have one on the new album and Cher was going to start recording an album with some of my songs on it. But I had no deal for my own album. I'd given up the idea of a solo album. I took my 8-track demos to the station and they played them on the air and the reaction was amazing. After three hours on the air with them I had three separate offers!

"The perception people had of me was distorted because of the part I played on 'The Partridge Family.'"

After the album was released, the reviews were scathing. *Entertainment Weekly* said: "Imagine the former Keith Partridge as (an) ersatz hard rocker, the forgotten member of Journey. His heavy-metal remake of the '50s classic 'Hi-Steel Sneakers,' with a bit of 'I Think I Love You' electronically sampled within it, is one of the year's high-camp highlights." The *Rolling Stone* reviewer was even more caustic: "Keith Partridge returns as Cher! Whether he'll also be able to turn back time with bubble-gum metal like this is probably a matter of how he looks in a body stocking." And from what we've heard for years about how well David is hung, that may be very fine indeed!

Yes, not only was David adorable as a teen but when he posed for *Rolling Stone* and the word began to spread how long and beautiful his cock was he quickly became a gay icon of the first rank. The Cassidy brothers, David and Shaun, through a wonderful stroke of fate (they both had the same father) are marvelously endowed. David is said to have a beautifully long cock while Shaun possesses one that is astoundingly thick. Celebrity penis researcher Gary Griffin reports that one of his spies met Shaun in the Embers in Portland and eventually went to bed together. The spy says that he had never seen a cock so thick, and he had seen many. He could not encircle it with his hand, and he has large hands. "A good approximation of his size is 8" in circumference and 9 to 9 1/2" in length."

By 1993, David seemed to be enjoying the nostalgia boom, with appearances with "The Partridge Family" traveling show and promoting their "Greatest Hits" album, singing his solo hits, "Cherish" and "Could It Be Forever." Ever gracious, he appeared at several record shops to promote the album, greeting fans warmly and signing autographs.

Ann Powers, writing in the *Village Voice*, explained the Family's appeal: "On one level, it was about 1960s mores being absorbed into conventional, domesticated America. The show certainly tapped that decade's flavor, making reference to hippie chicks, saving the whales, Hell's Angels, Joan Baez, sit-ins, and the Temptations. But in fact it is pure '70s, alive with the anxiety that plagued a time most people viewed as one long, gray morning after. Focusing on teens living through AM radio's watery substitute for rock and roll, the show captured the predicament of the 1970s kids, the first to experience rock's rebellion as a hand-me-down.

"Manager Reuben Kincaid is unstable, a swinger with a dozen girlfriends and no permanent mate. And despite his alleged promiscuity, he comes off as effeminate, always offering 'manly' advice that Keith (Cassidy) turns down with a roll of the eyes.

"Keith and his sister Laurie, as the oldest siblings, possess the latchkey kid's tendency to be more grown-up than the average grown-up. The incest tie of this lovely androgynous couple surfaces in episodes like the one where Keith 'dates' his sis to impress another girl and in the low-rent Nick and Nora patter they're forever trading.

"David Cassidy's performance as Keith oozes with a wiseness beyond his years. It's as if the inexperience that gets Keith into scrapes is simply circumstantial, not a matter of real youth, as if he's just playing at being a normal kid. How could

Keith – or David – really care about making the basketball team when 3000 adolescent girls are writing him love letters every day? Cassidy's cynicism resonated for kids who could feel something wrong with the world beyond their Friday night dates.

"The show's humor relies on misunderstandings recovered through sarcastic commentary, nothing ever resolved without some snide aside. Life's tendency to embarrass often seems the point. 'I think this whole thing taught me a lesson,' Keith says to his mom after a particularly excruciating bout with fate. 'What's that?' she asks. Keith offers up a world-weary sigh. 'I don't know yet. But there must be a lesson in there somewhere, from all this pain.'"

In his autobiography *C'Mon Get Happy*, David says, "I found I had a pretty strong gay following. I kind of liked it. Gay publications ran pictures of me; I was named gay pinup of the year by one. I'd get fan letters from gay guys saying things like, 'I can tell by the look in your eyes that you're one of us.' A gay liberation organization in London wrote to ask me for my support. I never did anything to encourage or discourage anyone's interest. If there were guys who found me attractive and perhaps fantasized about me, I was flattered. I found it mostly amusing how much people were discussing my sexuality like it really mattered if I slept with men, women, snakes, or sheep!

"In my teens I was fortunate to become good friends with Sal Mineo, who had done some television work with my stepfather. Then in his late twenties, this onetime teen star (who'd specialized in playing troubled youths) was being ill-treated by Hollywood as a has-been. A swarthy, handsome, black-haired guy, Sal had found fame in Hollywood quite early – after having been kicked out of school, I might add. (I could relate to that.) He'd been just sixteen when he got an Oscar nomination, for his supporting role in 'Rebel Without a Cause' and another for 'Exodus.' And then opportunities to work suddenly dried up. Sal Mineo – one of the kindest, most honorable people I've known – was tragically abused by the Hollywood star system, rejected by most of Hollywood as old news by the time he reached his mid-twenties. (And believe me, I can relate.) Hollywood has a way of chewing people up and then spitting them back out. In the later years of his career, Sal appeared in mostly minor films. He directed plays also – some with gay-related themes."

"...So much overt sexuality was being directed at me, and I was extremely horny. I never hit on people. I didn't have to do that, fortunately. People said things to me all the time like, 'Hi. Want to fuck?' I always liked that blatantly honest approach. No bullshit, right? Ah, it makes me miss the seventies even now just a little when I think of how wild a time it was. And free; or so we thought. Sex was just sex. It was there. It presented itself to me numerous times during the course of the day, and I could take advantage of it or not. Pick anyone. Who would you like to meet? It gave me a chance to actually be in contact with the real world through the sexuality. Then it was a matter of living up to –after we'd talked a little – their own sexual fantasy.

"Fortunately I've never had sexual problems. I was comfortable with myself sexually. Women began to ask me, after they met me, if the rumor about my dick was true: that I happened to have been rather well endowed, they told me. My penis became sort of legendary, in an underground sort of way. My brothers call me 'Donk.' It's their nickname for me." And no less a star than Gina Lollobrigida referred to David's penis as "the monster."

Says David, "One fellow even published a book on the Hollywood scene that described me as pulling down my pants, and an impressed female fan gasping, 'Oh, man, oh, man. You really have been blessed with a rock-and-roll cock.' Well, I don't know if I had been blessed with a rock-and-roll cock or not. But I decided that if I *had* it, there wasn't any point in just keeping it in the holster all the time. I'd have to let it out. And let it out I did. I also never thought I'd be writing all this private, embarrassing shit about it, either!

"I mean, okay. So I had a serious sexual appetite. When I was in my early twenties to mid-twenties I was really raging. And as the pressures of my career mounted, I felt like, *If I'm not going to be able to go down the street anymore, not going to be able to go to any public places, not going to be able to live life like a normal person – at least I'm going to have sex.*

"And as soon as people started to talk to me, they'd find out

I was not that guy on the TV show. I had much more adult thoughts and sexual fantasies. Part of the game became: I can do anything, I can have anyone I want. I mean, come on, who wouldn't get turned on by that?

"I became fascinated with women who really enjoyed the art of giving oral sex. The dialogue became the aphrodisiac. The fact that they wanted me. I felt sexually aroused by their wanting to please me, wanting to satisfy me, wanting to touch me, wanting to be intimate with me."

In an interview with *Rolling Stone*, David acknowledged he hadn't had a meaningful, committed, long-term relationship with a woman. "Then, after we'd finished all the interviews, *Rolling Stone* requested that I do some photo shoots with Annie Leibovitz. They'd be nude shots but very tasteful, I was assured; maybe they'd show a hint of pubic hair or something, but nothing more graphic. The photos would simply reinforce the idea that in my interviews I'd had nothing to hide. I liked the idea. Annie Leibovitz was the best photographer in that genre. I thought – and still think – that the photographs she took of me were great. Revealing and real.

"Maybe too real for the masses in 1972 America. I hadn't envisioned what the combined impact of the nude photos and the equally revealing interview would be. Nor had I envisioned the tone the writer would take. She wasn't greatly impressed by me.

"The article created tremendous controversy. I'm sure there were plenty of mothers who never actually saw a copy of *Rolling Stone* in their life, who were telling each other over coffee or games of bridge, or at PTA get-togethers, that David Cassidy (scandal of scandals) had exposed himself, posing nude for a notorious *Rolling Stone* article, and had admitted to all kinds of debauchery.

"...I never wanted to be a role model. But even so, I must say I was very much bothered myself by the writer's implication that I smoked pot. I've admitted in this book that I tried *everything* as a teenager, from heroin, cocaine, and LSD on down – but at the time of the *Rolling Stone* article I was not using any illegal drugs. And the writer *knew* that, but chose to take the low road; she violated my trust. The pot she'd smelled wasn't mine; she knew that.

"I would hardly have thought the article's suggestion that at age twenty-two, I had a sex life would shock anybody. But surprise, surprise, it did. The article was written in such a vague way that different readers drew different inferences about me. The writer Dennis Cooper concluded (and expressed in print) that Cassidy 'as much as came out' as a homosexual *in Rolling Stone*. Of course I'd done nothing of the kind. But I can see how someone could have reached such a conclusion upon reading that I didn't have a meaningful, long-term relationship with any one woman, and that my roommate was sunning himself nude while I was being interviewed."

About his father's bisexuality, David says now, "Though I'd heard some rumors, I never really knew of my father's bisexuality – although apparently a lot of other people did – until after he died. Certainly he never discussed it with me, although he could have been open with me had he chosen to. But I guess, in some ways, he was very private. I can understand that.

"My brothers and I have talked about it. Thinking back upon it, the idea that my dad may have been bisexual makes perfect sense. I mean, even though he never said anything about it, I can see it. It fits with the man I knew.

"I'm not violating any privacy now in discussing my father's sexual interests, inasmuch as others have already made it public.

"Cole Porter, for example, shared with his friend, writer Truman Capote, details of his extended sexual relationship with my father. In Gerald Clarke's best-seller, *Capote. A Biography*, Capote is quoted as saying how Porter described 'his long affair with that actor Jack Cassidy.'

"Of course, my father revered Cole Porter and Cole knew it, which I'm sure made the keep-it-cool psychological power-playing stuff more palatable. Being close to Cole Porter, one of this country's most important writers of Broadway and Hollywood scores – especially when my father was a young, aspiring singer and actor – could only have helped my father's career. My father was definitely guilty of creating himself and of doing whatever it would take to get ahead. So he may have had some opportunistic motives there, in addition to sexual and affectional ones.

"In Boze Hadleigh's book *The Vinyl Closet, Dance Magazine* editor William Como confessed that when Jack Cassidy – in his eyes, I guess, an unapproachable star – made a pass at him, he initially thought it had to be a joke." But it wasn't. David reveals his father "flirted with the whole world."

But sexy David didn't just "flirt," he fucked. He lost his virginity at 13 and he mentions having sex in 31 pages of his autobiography. He also spent five years in analysis.

Lately, David has made a career out of appearing in the musical "Blood Brothers." His half-brother Shaun appeared with him for 10 months when the play was Broadway. Even though it wasn't written for them, could have been. They played brothers who are separated at birth, one to live in luxury, the other poverty. This mirrored, to a degree, the real-life existence of the boys. David's mother was Shirley Jones and after she divorced Jack Cassidy, she married Marty Ingels, a comedian and successful showbiz promoter.

In his heyday as a teen idol (1976-77), Shaun was huge in Germany and known for his incredibly tight white pants. In May of 1995, Shaun, now 36, married for the second time. The bride was an actress, Susan Diol. Shaun is a talented writer who penned the series "American Gothic" and the 1991 USA Network thriller "Strays," about a band of killer kitties.

In commenting about the brothers' appearance in the play, Liz Smith asked, "Where have you boys been hiding those voices? The brothers Cassidy, once more famous for the tight cut of their pants rather than any vocal prowess, are the new siblings of Broadway's 'Blood Brothers,' and while we can't give a rave to the show itself, the former teen idols acquit themselves remarkably well. Both have surprisingly strong, deep voices, and both men do as much with their roles as they possible can. People seem to be crazy about 'Blood Brothers'."

And about the brothers Cassidy.

Menudo in 1984

Menudo

"I love Menudo...
they have some hot tight young humpy bodies of desire...
16 is the magic number, you know.
I have a group that is the female Menudo called Cholita. We'd like
to open for Menudo, that would be hot!"
- Vaginal Creme Davis

Before there were the New Kids on the Block there was Menudo. The group first came together in 1977 and became known as Latin American Music Ambassadors to the world. Their managers decided to replace certain members when they reached sixteen and outgrew the Menudo sound. As a result, they continued to thrill hundreds of thousands of prepubescent girls, to say nothing of gaymales who prefer their partners young, and made the men who formed the group wealthy.

Menudo was the brainchild of Edgardo Diaz, who perfected their wholesome image and demanded that each member retire at the age of sixteen, assisted by his attorney Orlando Lopez (who is also a choreographer with Puerto Rico's Fine Arts Center) and Jose Antonio Jimenez, president of the act's Panama-based holding company.

By 1984, the group was Puerto Rico's leading export. After a dozen albums, two movies, and a Saturday morning TV show, Karen Hardy reported that "Menuditis is approaching epidemic proportions reached by Beatlemania in another generation."

Such wild enthusiasm wasn't really expected when Diaz recruited three sons of a cousin and two sons of a friend to form Menudo, meaning "little change."

The members of the act had to be able to sing and dance (master 46 dances) and be serious about their careers.

Then in May of 1991 came the allegations that the three men who made a fortune packaging their musical commodity were sexually abusing the boys in the band. Reporter Juan Gonzalez of the *New York Daily News* uncovered the "sex, drugs and financial scandal" that ruined the act. According to Gonzalez, the pretty lads were being sexually assaulted and regularly plied with alcohol and drugs by their handlers.

Freelance photographer Bolivar Arellano first made the accusations to a largely disinterested media. It took an appearance on the television show "Controversial" in Puerto Rico to bring public attention to the fact that nine of the band's 28 members (they were regularly rotated when they became 16) were abused "but were too ashamed to admit it publicly." Arellano began his investigation after two of the members were busted for pot in November 1990.

The three handlers are very powerful and have political ties in their native Puerto Rico, but they were unable to squash the story because family members of one of the victims spoke up with sworn affidavits saying they witnessed Diaz in bed on three separate occasions with some of the underaged boys during "drug and sex" parties.

A few of the retired band members have gone on to have other careers. One, Robby (now Rob) Rosa, now with Maggie's Dream, was questioned by the authorities about his activities with Diaz and, through a spokesman for Capitol Records, came the terse statement, "No comment." Likewise unavailable for comment was Ricky Martin, now 21 and starring on the Mexican TV soap opera "To Reach A Star." He does say that he keeps in touch with other members of the act, especially Rob, who has returned to his native New York City, and Sergio Gonzalez, the son of an architect and a special favorite of the fans. Says Ricky, plans to come to Los Angeles in 1994 to study acting, "Most of the guys are students now and some of them are married."

The last newsworthy item we spotted on Menudo appeared in the spring of 1993 when Michael Musto reported that an anonymous source called to tell him that the night before a former member of Menudo was being devoured in the back room of an East Village gay bar by a coven of lusty men. "Alas," Musto said, "I suspect this source probably works for the bar. And the fact-checking back-ups he's offered ("Call the bartenders for verification") might just be in on this as a devious way to promote the place. Besides, few in the public spotlight would behave so indiscreetly, even if it was kind of dark, and they are kind of has-beens."

George Michael, relaxing in Rio.

George Michael

"Maybe George Michael was howling with laughter while the cameraman panned adoringly up his jeans at the opening of 'I Want Your Sex.' But I doubt it. Michael opted out of his last video, leaving a gaggle of supermodels to mouth the words of 'Freedom,' his too-little-too-late renunciation of the fame game. 'Sometimes the clothes do not make the man,' he sings, while his famous black leather jacket burns. But it's impossible to erase our collective image banks. The sex symbol wants us to know he has a mind - and a taste for irony: his subversion of MTV idolatry is the very model of MTV idolatry. Fine, noted; now, let's get back into those tight Levi's."
- Vince Aletti, The Village Voice

Chums as they grew up in North London, Andrew Ridgeley and George Michael (born Georgios Panayiotou – and Yog survives as his nickname), first scored on the pop charts in the U.K. in 1982 with "Young Guns (Go For It)" followed by "Bad Boys." Preening and pouting in scanty shorts at their concerts, they often stuffed badminton shuttlecocks down their shorts and then tossed them into the audience. Billed as Wham!, they scored their big smash in the U.S. in 1984 with "Wake Me Up Before You Go Go," off the album "Make It Big."

And make it big was what George did once he parted with Andrew and recorded "I Want Your Sex" in 1987. The video was incredibly hot and the song went to Number One despite being banned by over thirty percent of U.S. radio stations. Now, with a personal wealth at $130 million, with income of about $130,000 a day, in a world where nothing costs enough, George Michael can relax. But he won't. He must go on.

Andrew, who now lives in Monaco, says: "George is very, very single-minded in his approach. And I think a lot of the things that he has said and done have been misconstrued as arrogant rather than the single-mindedness they really are. People get very put out when someone is as forceful in their views and in their methods as George is."

Dismayed that his partial color blindness and nearsightedness would keep him from becoming a pilot, at the age of seven George set his sights on music. When his parents bought him a tape recorder, he says he "literally never entertained any other thought after that." Then he met Andrew. George was a shy, pudgy boy with eyeglasses and Andrew was the cocky pubescent fashion plate. "There was always a bit of tense air when I went round there," Andrew recalls. "His parents didn't like me for quite a while."

At 15 George was dancing to the latest black dance songs, got into disco early and shunned punk. "It was a matter of sexuality as opposed to individuality," he says. "I had nothing to rebel against, you know, and I was far more interested in going out and strutting my funky stuff, learning the latest steps and having the latest records and seeing how many girls you could pull. That was far more attractive to me than the idea of punk."

About his relationship with Andrew, George says, "In retrospect, I've never seen two people that were so influential on each other's lives and characters. Andrew and I, in a sense, totally changed each other. I suppose we spent all that time aspiring to be different parts of each other. His clothes were always perfect, he was really stylish, all the girls liked him. And that was something that I always wanted to be, because I was such a mess to look at. The whole idea of being physically attractive personally never occurred to me until I met him."

Their relationship fueled rumors about the duo and, because "inquiring minds want to know," *Rolling Stone* popped the question: "Are you gay?" George's reply: "I've never been concerned with who was doing what with who in bed, you know?"

In 1988, when *Paris Match* asked him if he were gay, would he say so, he replied, "I'd be crazy to say so, don't you think? But I won't contradict further because to defend oneself signifies that one's ashamed of that if it's true. I have many bi and gay friends and I believe in free choice in that area."

On TV, George said: "Um, I've never said 'No.' I've never said, 'Yes, no I'm not.' In other words, I don't think it benefits anyone listening to music to know whether or not I was in a bed with a dog or a man or a woman last night."

To *US Magazine* he said: "No, you'll have to find the place where I've denied it. I've never denied it."

In his autobiography, Boy George tells about the night he ran into George and Brooke Shields on a date. Boy whispered in her ear, "He's a poof, he's a poof!" "She didn't know what it was," writes George, "but looked worried."

Poof or not, the simple truth is that George considers all this inquiring into his sex life is an invasion of his privacy. "I've always thought that people ought to get on with what they're doing in their own beds."

A critic covering one of George's concerts for *The Los Angeles Herald-Examiner*: "He dressed in tight-fitting black, stripping down as the evening went on to vest and pants and -no surprise - finally baring his (hairy) chest. Still, one dance routine with a male member of his band does nothing to support rumors that he might be heterosexual."

Perhaps he is straight, at least in his dreams. Remembers the star, "I had a great dream once. It was set in New York and it was all in black and white and it was so funny. I was like, a gigolo, a cross between a gigolo and a chauffeur...And I can't tell you who I was a gigolo for because she's a famous actress and I might meet her one day, and, well, it would be embarrassing.

"I was a gigolo, but I wasn't having sex or anything. I was walking behind her in New York with this trolley that was full of cardboard boxes with my album in them. And the funny thing was, I didn't want her to know who I was, 'cause I liked the idea of being anonymous with her, so I was terrified that she was going to look into one of the boxes. And she kept threatening to look in the boxes. And I then sat down talking to this hobo and I lost her. I was just panicking, running about New York with this trolley looking for this woman, when I got woken up by a phone call. My dreams aren't usually like that. I couldn't find anything vaguely Freudian in it, you know. Though there's probably something perverse in the fact that I probably now think I should be paid for sex."

Paid or not, George was at one time rumored to be obsessed with his ass. *Rolling Stone*, in naming his "Faith" video to its list of the Top 100 of all time, said: "Touching off much humorous speculation that the former man from Wham! was obsessed with his own posterior, this video eventually inspired a now-classic 'Saturday Night Live' sketch in which a leather-clad Michael (Dana Carvey) exhorts Frank Sinatra (Phil Hartman) to 'Look at my butt! Just look at my butt!' While director Andy Morahan accepts responsibility, he points out that the loving close-ups of Michael's buns actually refers back to another, not insignificant rock idol. 'It was our homage to Elvis,' says Morahan. 'We are thinking of his early days on TV, when he could never be shown from the waist down. Our idea was, we'll show George from just the waist down.'"

We have no idea about his buns, although we'd certainly like to inspect them more closely, in person, but at least George has come to terms with his face. "I've grown up in the last two or three years. One of the things that's been most pleasant about growing up is the ability to face things, to accept all kinds of things about yourself. For years, I used to fight with my physical self-image. Having gone from being unattractive, or being made to feel very unattractive as a child, I then went to a situation where I got this sudden confidence. I was suddenly a pop star and I had all these girls screaming at me and wanting to sleep with me. So I slept with a lot of them.

"Then I found myself in a much more uncomfortable position because I felt I was more aware of the way I looked. I was a huge star, but why? In the physical sense, why? I didn't look good enough to be a star. It was all right to say, Yes, I wasn't unattractive. But I knew the difference between me and a male model. I was really uncomfortable with cameras. And now I'm at the stage where I realize it's okay. So I'm not Robert Redford, but I'm fine. I look fine."

Sex, says George, is very important to him. He thinks about it often. Once every fifteen minutes? "Oh, I'm sure it's more often than that. It's easy to get sex in my position, there's no problem. I can't vaguely remember sex when it was anonymous. It would be nice to have anonymous sex. But maybe it would be terribly dull. Maybe if people weren't trying - ha! - it would be terribly dull."

But sex aside, dull or not, it is his music about which he really cares: "I do like being a celebrity – it's good to get into clubs for free and stuff. But genuinely, I am only really passionate about my music."

Passionate and *serious* as a heart attack: "George Michael's entry in the 'I'm a serious artist' sweepstakes" is what *Rolling Stone* called George's "Freedom 90," made in 1990 and named by the magazine as one of the 100 top music videos. "The defining conceit of this video is, let's face it, kind of disgusting: a bevy of supermodels affecting a lifestyle of romanticized poverty whilst lip-syncing lyrics like 'All we have to do now/Is to take these lies/And make them true/Somehow.' But no one ever said you had to be morally upstanding in order to be seductive...the gorgeous clip features not a glimpse of the serious artist himself. Instead it shows the violent destruction of the childish things he has presumably put behind him: The cheesy ROCKER'S REVENGE leather jacket that he wore in the 'Faith' video has gone up in flames, while the Wurlitzer jukebox he leaned against therein blows up real good."

Finally, in mid-1995, Sony Music Entertainment settled a long battle with Michael and agreed to free him from a recording contract. No details were divulged. Michael originally lost his lawsuit to break his $12 million multialbum contract with Sony. He argued that Sony had refused to back his change of direction from sex symbol to serious musician.

The one thing George hasn't put behind him is his facial hair. The cute Beatle, Paul McCartney, sums it up best: "George Michael's a really good writer but he's thought of as a stud. It's the razor he uses, I think."

Jim Morrison

Jim Morrison

"Morrison let his black-leather bulge do the talking."
- Vince Aletti, The Village Voice

Since he was found dead in a bathtub in Paris in 1971 at the age of 27, Jim Morrison has been the subject of intense curiosity and controversy. Even the cause of death is still a mystery. His manager told *Sound* magazine in 1973: "I don't know to this day how the man died and, in fact, I don't know if he's dead. I never saw the body. Nobody ever saw the body. It was a sealed coffin, so who knows?" A heart attack was given as the cause but many believed it was a heroin overdose. He suffered from rheumatic fever in his youth and his heart was not in condition for what he did to it in Paris, the heroin, the booze. Rumors circulated that the death-obsessed star had staged his own death. No autopsy was performed and the doctor who signed the death certificate could never be found for questioning.

Donnie Wahlberg of The New Kids on the Block, somewhat of a young rebel himself, says: "I was born in 1969 and was, of course, too young to really be into the Doors. But I think Morrison was really very wild, but a very great dude. And when someone dies so young, at such a time when they're still creating so much, none of the questions are answered. I think that's what has made him the legend that he is."

And one of those unanswered questions was, did he sleep with guys as well as girls? Jim remains fascinating to gays because he never really came out of the closet. Those who were intimate with him, however, knew the secret. The late Johnnie Ray: "Jim said 'Light My Fire' to a lot of people, so long as they were as handsome as he was. He told me so! They say he named the Doors after Aldous Huxley's book about mescaline. Not true. The name came from a line by William Blake, the gay poet and artist: 'There are things that are known and things that are unknown, in between the doors.'"

Ray believed that Jim would have eventually come out admitting his bisexual tendancies, but only to the European press, as Marlon Brando, David Cassidy, Richard Chamberlain and others did.

Boze Hadleigh calls Jim "polysexual" and that fact "put him on the FBI's and other lists."

Jim's sexuality, whatever the end result might be, made him the sex symbol of the sixties. Then, in 1969, after a concert in Miami, he was arrested for exposing himself during the show. Columnist Alexandra Tacht: "He finally did it. He culminated his career as the sex symbol of the decade by dropping his pants in front of umpteen screaming teens."

But Jim claimed it never happened and that he was being persecuted for his lifestyle. His manager claimed that police had hundreds of photographs of the concert and none showed any exposure.

Music critic Owen Gleiberman says: "No other rock star ever sang like Jim Morrison. He had a deeply sonorous, almost classical baritone, and when accompanied by the other three Doors, a rhapsodic garage ensemble that sounded like the house band for Satan's discotheque, he lent a unique, mesmeric clarity to the primordial yearnings of the late '60s."

"Jim not only sang in tune," says former girlfriend Eve Babitz, "he sang intimately, as the Doors producer Paul Rothchild pointed out, 'Jim was the greatest crooner since Bing Crosby.' He was Bing Crosby from hell."

Gleiberman summarizes Jim's appeal: "He was also the first superstar hippie with an aura of pre-counterculture masculinity. There was nothing remotely smiley or reassuring about Morrison. He was like some dark Hollywood prince of the '40s who'd somehow stumbled into the role of rock demigod. The image of this glamorously disheveled, pornographic Dionysus spoke to the most feverish undercurrents of the counterculture, to the need to push past any and all limits."

In 1991, the Oliver Stone film, "The Doors," was released to tepid reviews. One critic said, "An infantile biography. It's hard to fathom Stone's idolatry for a performer whom the director himself portrays as a self indulgent jerk." Gleiberman comments: "Morrison spends most of the film in such a haze of intoxication and self-love that we feel fenced off from him. It skitters past you, teeming yet distant. Stone presents Morrison, he doesn't try to interpret him."

"The movie," columnist "Libby Gelman-Waxner" in *Premiere* magazine wrote, "is basically 'Jim: The Life of an Alcoholic Moron.' Jim starts out in film school with a befuddled expression and corduroy pants and sideburns; after a few more scenes, he's wearing leather pants and becomes a drunken, abusive star. For the rest of the movie, every scene is identical: Jim looks dazed, swigs from a bottle of whiskey, and mumbles or lip-syncs. If you ask me, Jim's underlying appeal is very simple: he was pretty, he lived in the '60s, and he died."

The film was also a great disappointment to those with gay sensibilities. "It is a terrible film," Craig Lee wrote in *The Advocate*. "The hatchet job equivalent of an Albert Goldman biography. Morrison was an overwhelming moral quandary for Stone; he is so fascinated and repulsed by the excesses that he does everything he can to make them look ridiculous instead of inspired, debauched instead of heroic. It is a shame the film is so lacking because the timing for the rebirth of the satyr Morrison could not be better. The kind of unbridled sensuality that a bare-chested Morrison expressed is very much in keeping with how male physicality is currently projected. Yes, Elvis was first with grinding his hips, but Morrison took his sensuality into unexplored regions of oedipal longing and stream-of-consciousness lust." His sex appeal, Lee says, set a precedent for a deadly, often masochistic sexuality for rockers to come.

In his biopic, Stone completely missed the homoerotic overtones to everything the rocker did. In his Dionysian revels, Lee asserts, "Morrison was aware of the gay subculture and borrowed from it heavily, whether it was lifting the title of John Rechy's 'City of Night' as the refrain for 'L.A. Woman,' or stealing bisexual poet Anais Nin's 'A Spy in the House of Love' for a song title."

Lee calls Morrison an "artistic shoplifter." Gerard Malanga, a longtime associate of Andy Warhol, says that Morrison stole his pouty leather-boy persona. "In the pre-Door Warhol film 'Vinyl,' Malanga is a passive, blank-expressioned Adonis badly reading an interpretation of 'A Clockwork Orange' with a put-on, self-conscious vaguely homoerotic energy that resembles the Morrison to come. The end of 'Vinyl' dissolves into an orgy of amyl nitrite sniffing and sadomasochistic rituals."

Of course, Lee notes, Morrison isn't the only rock star to pirate images from the gay art world. "Warhol supplied the Rolling Stones with a man's blue-jeanned crotch for the cover of their album 'Sticky Fingers.' The cover could be unzipped to find the same crotch covered in briefs underneath." (It is said that it is the crotch of Warhol's sexiest actor, Joe Dallesandro.)

After a remarkable opening-week gross of more than $9 million on only 840 screens, Stone's movie about the Doors faded fast and was a big disappointment in its theatrical release, but it did well on video, the soundtrack sold over a million copies, and it spawned an enormous resurgence of interest in the rocker, calling attention to the many fans for whom Morrison has become an obsession.

Anthony Spurlock in Berkeley, California, for example. A songwriter himself, Spurlock anointed himself minister of The First Church of the Doors in 1984 when he was 26 years old. He publishes a newsletter which is distributed to his 150 acolytes around the world and every July 3, the anniversary of the singer's demise, he holds a day-long Celebration of The Lizard King. "Morrison is a force of nature you can't keep down," he says.

In the '70s, "classic rock" became the vogue so the Doors' music never really left us. The band' song, "The End," turned into the sonic signature of Francis Ford Coppola's 1979 film "Apocalypse Now." In fact, the '80s became the Doors best decade in terms of sales. Through 1990, the group had sold a total of forty-five million records and were averaging 750,000 a year, according to Elektra Records.

Oliver Stone: "At the end, in Miami, Jim yells, 'No limits, no laws.' As soon as he had success, it bored him. He became a failure just to see how it was. He got fat, grew a beard. He was sick of being a rock star. He was bored with the limits of the law – he got busted seven times. But he tried everything."

And to prove that point in spades, in conjunction with the movie's release, more tell-alls about the star were published. Biographies about him have always been popular but the 1980 memoir co-written by Doors associate Danny Sugarman, *No One Here Gets Out of Here Alive,* was the original and it rose to fourth on the paperback best-seller list in 1991 during the publicity surge that accompanied the film's release. As *Riders on the Storm*, a memoir by Doors drummer John Densmore, climbed to number eight on the *New York Times'* nonfiction list, three memoirs by ex-girlfriends of the star were being pitched to publishers but they'd be hard pressed to top the one by super-groupie, Pamela Des Barres, who wrote *I'm With the Band*. Says she: "I had never seen such blatant sexuality on stage. He writhed in horny anguish, demanding that everybody in the sweltering, stormy room light his fire. He was so out of control that it scared people. When he took a dive into the audience without premeditation, without hesitation, we all held him up, snatching up some of his stuff, oh, so briefly.

"One night at the Whiskey-A-Go-Go, right before he crawled over to the stage and climbed on with the Ohio Express, he slapped me hard across the face for no reason. It was like he was trying to feel something. With my cheek throbbing and teary mascara dribbling down my face, I watched as he grabbed the microphone away from the singer, moaned into it and shoved it down his pants. OK, Jim, enough already. It was heart-breaking. When the music's over, turn out the lights."

"Jim was an asshole at the beginning," Danny Fields remembers. "Believe it or not, his character changed for the better! Back then, whenever his record came on the radio, he would turn up the volume so that no one else could talk. Or he'd vomit in people's lobbies to show that he'd been there. Janis Joplin used to refer to him as 'that asshole,' and you always knew who she was talking about. But there were times when he came across as a guy with absolute style and savvy."

Like everyone in the '60s, Jim hated his parents, hated home, hated it all but he had it worse than a lot of kids who grew up in the '50s. He was fat and he had a father who was a naval officer. If he could have gotten away with it, he would have been an orphan. He tried lying, creating his life anew. He lost weight and the frog turned into a prince. "I mean," one associate remembers, "he awoke one morning and was so cute, how could he have parents? At 22, he was so cute that no woman was safe. He had all the freshness and humility of someone who had been fat all his life and was now suddenly a morning glory."

But he never really stopped being a fat kid, Eve Babitz

remembers: "He thought he was ugly. He'd look at himself in the mirror trying on clothes. He hated looking at himself.

"Just so long as he didn't smile and reveal his too-Irish teeth, just so long as he kept his James Dean smolder, just so long as he stood there in the leather pants, the ones lined with turquoise satin, trimmed with snakeskin and lizard, it worked. But it takes a lot of downers to achieve that on a full-time basis. And no fat."

As Val Kilmer, the actor who played Jim in Stone's movie, joked, "It was the leather pants that killed Jim. It's like living in a wet suit. There's no circulation. I'm sure that's what did him in."

Fields feels Morrison's image was cut from a decidedly Sixties male manifesto: "The more I ignore you, the more desirable I become." Jim's reticence with women, according to Fields, wasn't always part of his act. "Jim was oblivious and, at the same time, willing prey. He wanted women to come worship him - and they did. He didn't fight them off, but I never saw him sending them flowers. That would have gone against his image of himself as a first-class prick." He treated all his women badly and almost reveled in the disintegration of his relationships with them.

Patricia Kennealy started an affair with Morrison when he was also seeing a lot of Pamela Courson, who was in Paris with him when he died. By this time, the star had begun falling apart, lost in his own weird orbit of fame and growing fat. Patricia remembers: "I was knocked out by his manners. He stood up and shook my hand as I walked into the hotel room for my interview with him. No rock star had ever done that before. I was staggered by how literate he was. I began an affair with him even though he already had Pamela. He was a pig to her. He had this really vulnerable psyche, this inner self that he genuinely wanted to protect, the way we all do. He threw up screens to protect himself and sometimes he was successful, sometimes not."

How successful he was depending on the drugs he was taking. Dotson Rader recalls the night he went to a party in the SoHo district of New York before it became fashionable. He spent some time talking with Morrison, whose music he liked and whose poetry intrigued him. He describes Morrison as a handsome, tall young man, with long hair and haunted eyes, as deeply gifted as he was troubled. "I had the conviction that night he was as doomed as any man could be. He was given to sexually displaying himself, a lapse in manners that could epitomize as well as anything the sixties' aggressive egotism and solipsism, sex-as-shock-effect. Only nobody was shocked anymore, such behavior by then seeming almost quaintly tame in a city where to give a party meant possessing a thorough knowledge of how to react if your guests went into drug-induced comas.

"At the party, Morrison lay on the floor with his back propped against a wall. He was quite drunk, having a staggering capacity for liquor, not to mention drugs. Dressed in a dark shirt and brown corduroy pants, his fly open, his penis slowly being worked by his hand. Occasionally he lifted a bottle of booze to his mouth; from time to time, someone slipped over and gave him head while I sat on the floor, making conversation as if nothing untoward were taking place. He seemed to be intrigued, almost possessed, by the thought of death, like a bird facing a snake and paralyzed by fascination.

"Later I followed him to the bathroom where we discovered Edie Sedgwick on her knees before another girl. Morrison sat down on the edge of the tub and Edie moved between his crotch and the girl's, pleasuring each of them.

"In those rancid years, on the cusp of the decade, when the Age of Aquarius had finally found its killing ground, that was one of the ways of making the acquaintance of a rock-and-roll star. Or just about anyone else. Sex and/or drugs being a currency that could buy you a place in the center ring."

As a sex object, Morrison lasted about two years. Once he met Pamela, he became a "death object," which some thought was even sexier. "Jim was a backdoor man and Pamela was the door," Babitz says.

But Pamela or no Pamela, in 1970, Jim married Patricia in a Wicca wedding based on "white" witchcraft, since she was a member of the New York coven. At the end of the ceremony, they signed their names in blood, after which Jim passed out cold. Patricia eventually got pregnant. When she had an abortion, Jim didn't send flowers; he didn't even call.

A few weeks before his death, while Pamela was in Paris

apartment hunting, Jim was with Patricia, more or less, in New York. One day, a girlfriend of Patricia's made a successful pass at Jim and Patricia caught them in bed together. Patricia left the apartment. "It was kind of a disengagement," she recalls. "I really knew then that I was never going to see him again. That was that."

The week before he died, Pamela has revealed, Morrison had a different girl in his bed every night but, considering his intake was up to three bottles of scotch a day, it is doubtful he could have managed an erection. After Jim died, Pamela fled Paris for Morocco with an 18-year-old French count, a junkie who also OD'd on her and died. She returned to the US and eventually was to OD and die on her own.

Morrison's grave in Pere Lachaise cemetery, lying near those other cultural notables Chopin and Oscar Wilde, has become a shrine for his fans and the fourth most visited site in the Paris area, after Versailles, the Louvre, and the Eiffel Tower.

As they said about Elvis in 1977, dying can be a good career move. It boils down to: "Live fast, die young, leave a marketable corpse."

Jay McInerney, the writer, says: "I'd hate to see him at 240 pounds, losing his hair and doing revival concerts. You know, opening for Frankie Valli and the Four Seasons and doing Pizza Hut commercials. So maybe it's better to be a legend."

In a publicity still, Prince shows the "hardness"
that has made him legendary to gays.

Prince

"A lot of people have the idea that I'm a wild sexual person. At home in Minneapolis it can be two o'clock in the afternoon and someone will make a really strange request from the call box outside. One girl just kept pressing the buzzer. She kept pressing it, and then she started crying. I had no idea why. I thought she might have fallen down. I started talking to her and she just kept saying, 'I can't believe it's you.'"I said, 'Big deal. I'm no special person. I'm not different than anyone.' She said, 'Will you come out?'
"I said, 'Nope, I don't have much on.'
"And she said, 'That's okay.'"
-Prince Rogers Nelson

"He looks like a dwarf that fell into a vat of pubic hair."
– Boy George on Prince

Prince's early lyrics were boldly bisexual. His classic steamers are "Head," "Soft and Wet," "I Wanna Be Your lover, "A Love Bizarre." He is arguably the "sexiest man in rock today," according to one historian. Boze Hadleigh, writes, "He combined pouty tomboyishness with stylistic effeminacy - the highest men's heels, the laciest collars, the most mascara this side of Picadilly. "

Rolling Stone called Prince a "suburban doofus" with a penchant for eye-liner and high hair: "A short man, mincing around in high heels, he has managed to parlay his lascivious fantasies into a reported $100 business deal. His slight body in silhouette or chiffon can look quite feminine, a fact that he's milked nearly to the point of self-parody (those backless trousers?)." Much more convenient, those backless kind! And in reviewing Prince's "Hits Collection," Ron Givens said: "The man who once was Prince has never made great videos, so you're better off watching this for fashion tips. The clips show how the clothes made this man and the man made do without much clothing – from the barely there 1980 bikini underpants and trenchcoat ensemble of 'Uptown' to a kinky checkerboard-lace combo from 1992's '7.' Unfortunately, some of Prince's most interesting video 'hits' are missing, including the sultry 'When Doves Cry,' in which the performer's best outfit is his skin."

But while "fashion" such as this and androgyny earned him attention as a singer, in his film debut in "Purple Rain," the star comes across as misogynistic and homophobic. Gays were shocked, even saddened but *Playgirl* magazine raved: "Just when you thought rock movies were becoming ponderously inane, in prances Prince with his astonishingly sensual film, R-rated but with more erotic appeal per frame than the whole library of strip-down triple X censor-shockers. Who says you can't be a five foot four-inch semi-recluse from Minneapolis and still be a sex symbol."

"Twin Peaks" star Sherilyn Fenn: "Prince is so special. He's in touch with a femininity within himself that's really great! He's always encouraging me to be happy. He won't tolerate my being sad."

Prince was so "in touch with the femininity within himself" that he announced he was going to change his name to a combination of the male and female symbols. But then he decided he just wanted to be known as *Victor.* He wrote numbers for the Nick Nolte movie "I'll Do Anything," which had disastrous previews. One attendee said she left when Nolte burst into song, warbling Prince's "Be My Mirror." After the screening, it was rumored that producer James L. Brooks, who scored heavily with "Terms of Endearment," took out most of the music so how much of Prince's work remains won't be known until the film opens. Never discouraged, Prince got busy writing a musical of his own based on Homer's "Odyssey."

One of his paramours, Vanity (Denise Matthews) said: "One thing I cannot handle is the macho man. I look for a man to have some feminine qualities. When they can't cry or feel sorry, it's like, Gimme a break, boy! Pow!"

When Prince appeared in the buff on the "Lovesexy" album cover *RPM* magazine said, "His narcissism nauseates and needles less flirtatious men."

Like Michael Jackson, he's soft-spoken to the point of inaudibility, girlish, and loves to dress up (Mozart is an idol) in thong, garters and stockings. And, like Michael, he's a control freak, preferring Minneapolis to Hollywood because it's easier to contain things. But L.A. and New York do have their charms: "LA is a good place to work," he says. "And I liked New York more when I wasn't known, when I wasn't bothered when I went out. You'd be surprised. There are guys who will literally chase you through a disco! I don't mind my picture being taken if it's done in proper fashion. I don't know why people can't be more humane about a lot of things they do. Now when I'm visiting, I like to sneak around and try stuff. I like to sneak to people's gigs and see if I can get away without my picture being taken. That's fun, like cops and robbers.

"I never believe anything in the *Enquirer* but half the things people were writing about me were true. I was an expert at cutting off people in my life and disappearing without a glance back, never to return."

But he's studied and he's learned from his own failures. "I don't regret anything about 'Under the Cherry Moon,'" he says about his second movie, a box-office and critical disaster. "I learned that I can't direct what I didn't write."

What he did direct and write (and most everything else) didn't play much better: "Graffiti Bridge" bombed at the box-office. It is on tour that Prince reigns supreme, his "Lovesexy Tour" perhaps being the paradigm of concerts. "'Lovesexy' was a mind trip like a psychedelic movie," he says. "Either you went with it and had a mind-blowing experience or you didn't. All that album cover was a picture. If you looked at that picture and some swill came out of your mouth, then that's what you are - it's looking right back at you in the mirror." One critic described his Lovesexy tour as "Liberace-on-acid." For the album, Prince got down all the way, with only a delicately lifted thigh covering his privates, causing the album to be banned in many venues, or at least being covered up.

In naming Prince's "Kiss" video to its honor roll of the Top 100, *Rolling Stone* said, "This is the first video to exploit Prince's sense of humor; while he meets his quota of moaning and gyrating – shirtless, yet – he also does a surprising amount of mugging. Pretty refreshing in a medium in which erotic content is usually delivered with a poker face." The video's director Rebecca Blake said the goofing came naturally because former Revolution guitarist Wendy Melvoin was on board and the singing came from the personal interaction between them. While frequent waits between takes can take a toll of the crew, she says it was worth it. "When a great artist is in front of the camera, he or she gives you something you could never imagine when you're planning the piece. With Prince, everybody's hanging out to watch what happens."

Or what he's wearing.

But there's a double standard regarding androgyny, Boy George says: "You see Prince, he's got heels on, he's got see-through polka-dot panties, but he's got the guitar and somehow that makes him macho."

"Like most souls possessed of a charismatic brilliance," *The New Yorker* reported, "the artist formerly known as Prince can't modulate any aspect of his performing self or his tireless, insomniac work habits. His seemingly endless stream of songs, his constant reconfiguring of studio bands and touring bands, his priapic posturing, and the costumes designed to (literally) show off his ass – all of it is meant to be consumed whole, whether you like it or not.

"Unlike Michael Jackson, his only rival, the singer is not 'nice,' nor does he seek acceptance and love on his audience's terms. If he cared about us, why would he change his name to a peculiar, omnisexual symbol, something no one could pronounce?

"Two years ago, in what may have been a moment of pique with Warner Bros. Records, Prince abandoned his world-famous moniker. Not long afterward, he began referring to himself as a 'slave.' Then, perhaps following Malcolm X's lead, he changed his name, driving home the point that, while the name Prince had been bought, his mind and talent would never be indentured."

Attending the Les Venus de la Mode Awards at the Tunnel, Michael Musto said, "Things cooked up as a guard came to see if the place was safe for Formerly Prince. It was, so FP entered with the word *slave* scrawled on his face (perfect, as I had *master* written on mine), along with a dramatic cape and a cane with his famous unpronounceable symbol on top. Was FP safe for us? The purple one held court alone in a booth meant for 10, but allowed girls to sit and talk with him for a few minutes at a time. And what did he gab about? His formerly tour – he cut it short with six months left because he's pooped, and was stopping to schmooze New York models before returning to

Minneapolis. The next evening, Purple Boy came back to the Tunnel, realized it was gay night, spread his purple wings, and flew. As Veronica Webb once said, "I love you, whatever your name is!"

Ann Powers in SPIN says, "It may be tempting these days to feel sorry for Squiggly (or Zoso, or TAFKA – The Artist Formerly Known As...wow, that's nearly Kafka – or whatever you now call His Wetness). After 16 albums, he's no longer considered the future of rock-meets-soul. It's hard to hear his influence on Beck or Boyz ll Men or any of today's chart-toppers. His own albums do just okay. His movie career is kaput. He wrestled with hip hop and lost. He dated Kim Basinger and lost. And he can't even claim the title of Most Eccentric Superstar until Michael Jackson gets himself to a monastery.

"But for all you fans of Nine Inch Nails and Crystal Waters, Ton Amos and techno, Prince has changed your life, whether you like it or not. The most accomplished auteur of the postpunk era, he's pioneered the studio wizardry that has since borne fruit in all kinds of dance music from ambient to industrial, and His Mauveness continues to build a vision of art and life that is central to these multicultural times. Right now, with so much concern about realness in indie, dance, and hip-hop circles, Prince's mix-it-up pop methods isolate him. But when he boldly blended hard rock, funk, punk, pop, and soul to create that patented millennial party sound back in the early '80s, Prince blasted open pop's parameters, and every artist who crosses a genre today does so with a little Prince-dust on his or her shoes.

"Not to mention anybody who crosses a dress. Sexual utopianism reached new levels of creativity in the '80s and '90s, as drag queens and hot dykes redefined rock stardom, and girls and boys both tried on each other's sensual identities for size. And it was His High-Waistedness who crystallized all the magic moments of rock polymorphousness from Little Richard to Jagger and Bowie to Patti Smith within one glorious orgy of gender confusion. And in the '90s, the Purple One continues to innovate sexual expression, showing men how to swing that thing without always dominating, and praising women for jumping into the erotic driver's seat."

The artist now formerly known as Prince has "the attention span of a 10-year-old," according to Alan Leeds, his former handler. Leeds says that the rock star's main problem with Warner Bros. Records is that the star wants to make three albums a year. "He has studio diarrhea," Leeds says.

Indeed, creating controversy is part of his act and, as Prince says, "When I pray to God, I say, 'It's your call. When it's time to go, it's time to go. But as long as you're going to leave me here, then I'm going to cause much ruckus!"

THEY MIGHT HAVE BEEN LEGENDS

Troy, Tab, Tony, Etc.:
They Might Have Been Legends

Few actors become stars, let alone legends. Many dazzlingly handsome young men showed early promise, tantalizing us for a time with their sexy ways and the hint that they might be possible, the prerequisite for gaymale adoration. But, for one reason or another, they didn't survive in our dreams, although we still remember them with a great deal of fondness.

Tab Hunter, it turned out, was more than possible, but most of us had no clue at the time. I must say, however, that his eyes always bothered me, as if perhaps there was some dark secret hidden behind them, which apparently there was: Tab was gay. Later, when he was no longer mattered at the box-office, he admitted it. Born in 1931, handsome, blond Tab was discovered by Henry Willson, the flamboyant agent who also discovered Rock Hudson (first calling him Roc) in 1947, and went on to bring Guy Madison, Rory Calhoun, and Troy Donahue to fame. Tab scored big in a featured role in "Battle Cry," then starred with Bob Fosse's wife Gwen Verdon in "Damn Yankees." But "The Burning Hills," with Natalie Wood, and William Wellman's "Lafayette Escadrille" give us the best glimpses of Tab's manly chest and lean torso.

Eventually, stardom went to Tab's head and his excessive demands to Warner Brothers were not met. After he went on his own, he made one interesting film, "The Pleasure of His Company," with Fred Astaire and Debbie Reynolds for Paramount before fading, slowly, into obscurity, breeding and raising horses, occasionally taking a character role, such as his parts in "Grease 2," "Polyester," "Lust in the Dust."

But Tab says he's happy not being a star, much less a legend. "I'm happiest when I'm shoveling shit," he laughs.

Warners Brothers replaced Tab in its stable of young studs with Troy Donahue, another Henry Willson discovery with blond good looks and a smooth, surfer's body. The studio cast him in "A Summer Place" in 1959 opposite Sandra Dee and then with Connie Stevens in "Susan Slade." His teaming with Suzanne Pleshette in "Rome Adventure," led to the co-stars getting hitched in a ceremony of publicity reminiscent of Rock Hudson's marriage. The union lasted only a few months. Now Troy wishes he'd had earthier roles; he jokes: "After all those years playing Mr. Clean, I was afraid to comb my hair for fear of scratching my halo."

But the real Troy, as opposed to the reel one, certainly had no halo. By 1963, Troy was addicted to drugs and alcohol. What he earned as a character actor in films, most notably in the Oscar-winning "The Godfather, Part II" in 1974, went to support his habit. In recent years he has had small roles in small movies such as "Grandview USA" and horror films, including his latest, "Showdown," a "Mad Max" send-up, released directly on video, written and directed by Leo Fong.

Another Warners' stableboy, Edd Byrnes, a former gymnast, played a character called Kookie on the popular television show "77 Sunset Strip" from 1958, when he was 25, to his departure in 1963. His success lead to a recording contract ("Kookie Kookie Lend Me Your Comb" in 1960, with Connie Stevens, became a teen anthem and a number one hit single) and roles in several low budget westerns. Lacking proper management and no real drive to be a star, much less a legend, he eventually faded into obscurity.

During this period a young actor who was trained on Broadway became extremely popular with gays, not only because of his boyishly sexy appearance but because of the roles he played. Brandon de Wilde was born in 1942, making him my contemporary and upon seeing him in "Blue Denim," he became a fantasy lover. His appearances opposite Warren Beatty in "All Fall Down" and Paul Newman (who was never sexier) in "Hud" cemented my fondness for him.

When the gifted actor died in a car accident in 1972, the historian Leigh Rutledge paid him tribute: "To many he personified the eternal American teenage boy, troubled, aching, and headed for disillusionment and while his characters often at first admired the icons of American manhood (womanizing, hard drinking, indifference) they later discarded them as hollow and phony."

As TV became the favorite mass medium, it spawned actors who turned on many a gaymale. Often they were featured actors, part of family groups, and gay men were enormously attracted to them, watching them grow up into sexy specimens before our very eyes.

One of the leading "wet dreams" of the late '50s was Tony Dow who was cast in the "older brother" role on "Leave it to Beaver" for 234 episodes that started in 1957, when he was 12 and was cancelled six years later.

Larry Duplechan's tribute to Tony appeared in *In Touch* magazine: "How I dreamed of the chest that lay beneath Wally Cleaver's baggy shirts. Many an episode ended with a scene of the boys preparing for bed, usually with the Beav already in jammies and Wally taking forever, I mean, forever, to unbutton his shirt as the brothers engaged in a few minutes of inane juvenile repartee. Somehow, Wally never seemed to get past the second button before the laugh track crescendoed, the theme music entered, the credits rolled, and my hopes were dashed again. I never glimpsed so much as a nipple."

One of my personal favorites was handsome Ricky Nelson, who I watched grow up on his parents' TV show "Ozzie 'N' Harriett." He became a leading recording artist and was to crossover into films with an appearance in a big budget western, "Rio Bravo," with John Wayne.

While Ricky's on-screen time on the series grew, his older brother David appeared in a few modestly budgeted films, including "The Big Circus," in which he appeared as a trapeze artist. "In white tights," Boyd McDonald was to remark in *Cruising the Movies*, "David's body is more starkly erotic than one that is 'stark naked.' The dazzling white of his costume erases all human imperfections and distractions...Even the middle class can regard David's groin and butt, when wrapped tightly in pure white, as being in good taste, and he was, moreover, an authentic athlete. He was potentially one of the most valuable properties in Hollywood, yet scarcely used theatrically."

As more and more of these young actors became popular with teenagers the phenomenon known in some circles as "Muffin Movies" began in the late '70s. In this genre of film, the stars are boyishly androgynous and physically attractive, especially in a minimum of clothes or none at all. Blond or brunette, tall or short, blue-eyed or brown, they're not yet beefcake, just wholesome, delicious treats, a snack more than a meal, and the movies they are in are usually video junk food. Sex is the text or subtext of virtually every muffin movie and the leading ladies are interchangeable, if not superfluous. In most cases, the guys' beauty exceeds their other attributes.

While Christopher Atkins was the premier muffin and went on to legendary status, most of those who made muffin movies drifted into obscurity. Scott Baio held on, mainly due to TV exposure, although he did do a scene in where we got to see his shapely bare buns, in the unfortunate 1987 film "I Love N.Y.," in which he played a hustling Italian photographer who woos a hostile stage actor's polished daughter in New York. Upon seeing the film, a fan wrote: "I nearly flipped. There were many bare-chested scenes and I tell you, this boy has been working out." Truth to tell, Scott has always worked out and kept his body in great shape. His series, "Charles in Charge," was cancelled but he has a new series in development.

Lacking the old-fashioned star-making machine, potential legends these days have to make it on their own and must possess considerable talent as well as sexiness. And, even with all that, there's still that magic ingredient we spoke of earlier, that sixth sense, that freedom to really be. As Marcel Duchamp said, "It is no longer enough to create art. One must now be art."

Typical teen heartthrob pose for Kirk Cameron in 1986
at the age of sixteen.
(Courtesy Blake Little)

Kirk Cameron

"My fantasy is to get fucked by Kirk Cameron."
- Young male performer in "After Dark," a gay porn video

"I'm flattered that people enjoy my work," Kirk Cameron said. "I feel a sense of responsibility to set a good example, so I say the right stuff: I'm against smoking and drugs. I don't go to a lot of parties. I don't date much. I don't look at myself as the hot teen idol. I hope if I ever do, people will kick me in the butt."

In Kirk's heyday, *kicking* him in the butt isn't exactly what many gays would have wanted to do, but there are many other things we can think of to do to a butt as cute as that one. And then there's the kid in "After Dark," an amateur video released by Image Video, who when asked about his favorite TV star, replies: "Oh, Kirk Cameron. My fantasy is getting fucked by Kirk Cameron."

So here you have a former teen idol who appeals to both the tops and bottoms. Indeed, we could take Kirk any way he wanted it, but, alas, he doesn't want it, at least not now. After many years of starring on " Growing Pains," the cute, cuddly actor hasn't connected with any major projects.

He did, however, connect with Chelsea Noble, whom he married in 1991. Chelsea was 26, Kirk 21. They met on the set of "Growing Pains" and she saw her role expanded as their love blossomed. Chelsea co-starred on Kirk's made-for-TV movie, "A Little Piece of Heaven," wherein he utters the immortal line, "My name's Will and I'm your guardian angel." We should all be so lucky!

"Dream Guy" Kirk was born in 1970 and began acting at the age of nine, doing a Super Sugar Crisp television commercial. He was only sixteen when he landed the plum role of Mike Seaver on "Growing Pains" and quickly became the hottest teen idol in the country. Even before the show began, the teen fan magazines began running articles about him and putting his picture on the cover, with headlines such as, "Look Out Michael J. Fox, Here Comes Kirk Cameron." He was receiving ten thousand letters a week at the height of his popularity. Kirk's parents started his fan club themselves, mailing out autographed photos and membership cards. Sold separately was the Kirk Cameron T-shirt and pillowcase with photo printed on one side. In only a few months, there were seven thousand club members around the world.

But unlike Fox, who lucked into the "Back to the Future" series, Cameron has not been able to transfer his TV popularity to motion pictures. He appeared with Kurt Russell and Robin Williams in "The Best of Times," as a son torn by his parents' failing marriage, but the film, which seemed sure-fire, mis-fired badly.

Kirk was then starred with Dudley Moore in the role-reversal comedy "Like Father, Like Son" and it was one of the few films of 1987 to earn Leonard Maltin's coveted "BOMB" rating.

Kirk's 1989 film, "Listen to Me," about a small college debating team, was another disaster, memorable only in that Christopher Atkins had a minor role and Kirk had what Maltin called, "a shifting Oklahoma accent."

Boywatchers remember Kirk's appearance in 1983 in the series "Two Marriages" largely because of C. Thomas Howell, who was, at that point, at what one fan termed, "the peak of perfection," having also made "The Outsiders" that year.

In 1993, Kirk was set to try his hand at performing in a Broadway revival of "Grease" but producers didn't want his wife as his leading lady. "It was terribly embarrassing," one source revealed. "The producers didn't feel Chelsea was talented enough for Broadway, but there is no easy way to tell a guy you want him and not his wife." (And here we thought we'd been telling him that for years!)

When all is said and done, we know many things about adorable little Kirk: he has light brown hair and hazel eyes, is 5'8" tall, and weighs in at 130 pounds (if he sticks to his Pritikin diet), but what is he really like?

"I'm just a regular guy," he says. And perhaps therein lies the rub. Guys that are so "regular" can begin to bore after a while. Had he had been blessed with more than just a bit of Michael J. Fox's acting ability, and good management, he may well have become a legend.

Joe Dallesandro as he appears today.
(Inset: Rolling Stones album cover.)

Joe Dallesandro

*"All I knew of him is what I saw of him in the movies –
just like everyone else. The truth is he kind of scared me.
But he did have a great body and this lush, pimply ass."*
    - Holly Woodlawn, his co-star in "Trash"

*"Little Joe never once gave it away / Everybody
    had to pay and pay."*
    – From famous poem

"The principal factors in my life are honesty and beauty,"
Joe Dallesandro says now. "In the '60s, when people used to
ask me about my sexual persuasion, I'd say, 'Well, I wouldn't
throw Mick Jagger out of bed.' But now I wouldn't fuck him
because he's so fucking ugly."

It is said to be Joe's crotch with the admirable bulge that
Andy Warhol photographed for the cover of the Rolling Stones'
album, "Sticky Fingers."

Many a gaymale has gotten sticky fingers over Joe's
"performances" in the Andy Warhol films of the '60s, including
"Heat," "Trash", "Flesh," "Lonesome Cowboys," and
"Frankenstein." "Heat," a 1972 parody of "Sunset
Boulevard," is by far the best of the bunch, featuring Sylvia
Miles as a faded actress and Joe as an unemployed actor. It is
in this film that we get, according to Aaron Travis: "the
ultimate ass shot of Joe, while he's getting a blow-job."

"Flesh" is also must-see because of a great shot of "Joe's
famous early morning erection." The 1976 gay porn flick "Hot
House," made by Jack Deveau, contains black and white 8mm
footage of a sex scene featuring an actor long believed to be Joe
because of the unmistakable tattoo.

"Dallesandro's public image was," Doug Brantley says, "the
lone macho archetype in a sea of drag queens, slumming
socialites, speed freaks and other mid-'60s oddities. From the
start the actor was tagged with an unshakable image of a street-
smart hustler, a tough straight guy waffling between
simultaneous urges: to fuck or just to beat someone up. His

trademark tattoo, mane of chestnut-colored hair, pursed lips, nickel-size nipples, chiseled ass cheeks, and rigid cock provided fantasy fodder for an entire generation of gay men."

As Brantley says, Joe has seemingly overcome the limitations of the sexy hustler persona created for him both on- and off-screen. He appeared in supporting roles in "The Cotton Club," "Cry-Baby," "Black Moon," and "Sunset." He most recently appeared with Drew Barrymore in a remake of the 1949 melodrama "Guncrazy."

Born in Pensacola, Florida, in 1948, Joe, along with his brother, was brought up in a foster home. "I learned prejudice early on," he says, "and that what people say and what they do are two very different things. My foster parents would say, 'We treat everyone in our family equally,' while they ate at the dinner table with their two kids and my brother and I ate from a little side table. I built up at lot of anger behind that and eventually took my frustration to the streets."

Joe moved in with director Paul Morrissey when he made the Warhol films. "Paul was my mentor, not Andy," Joe says today. "He really worked with me, not just on my acting but on my anger as well. He would say things to trigger me off. And I'd get so angry, I'd crash through a door, then another, and by the third door I'd start to understand how unproductive it was. I mean, I was the one who would have to fix the doors I busted." It was obvious to everyone where Paul's sentiments lay: Jackie Curtis demanded that Andy take over the camera during the filming of "Women in Revolt" because "Paul only makes Joe look good."

Morrissey himself says Joe went through a lot of strain and emotional turmoil in those years. "Most of it he generated for himself. As with the majority of people who present a certain image to the public, he was not as simple as the image he portrayed."

Author Dotson Rader, a biographer of Tennessee Williams, recalls: "I spent an evening at the house of Joe Dallesandro, one of Warhol's superstars. Joe and Paul Morrissey shared the house and with them I watched a replay of a show about Andy Warhol I had hosted for public television.

"After the show, the telephone rang and it was Tennessee asking us to meet him at Max's Kansas City, which was uptown from the East village, where Joe lived. He was very insistent that I drag Dallesandro along, since he was more than a little sexually intrigued by Joe.

"Joe was nothing if not physically beautiful, with a handsome Italian face, a well-proportioned body, well-endowed. He more than a little resembled the late Frank Merlo and perhaps that was the real basis of Tennessee's pining for him. Joe came from a working-class family in New Jersey, like Frank, and he was, if not well-educated certainly street smart. Before Warhol discovered him in the wilds of New Jersey, he had made some blue loops and done some soft-porn. And yet there was to him, uncorrupted, a gentleness and sweetness of disposition that was utterly beguiling. When he wasn't making movies for Warhol, or running errands, you could find him at the Factory, sweeping up the place, taking out the garbage, doing menial chores. He was like a member of Andy's household, and Warhol's relationship with him was like that of an indulgent father and a slightly delinquent son. Of the Warhol superstars, Joe lasted the longest and ended up having a credible, if unprofitable film career."

Dotson tells about the time Tennessee went to the Venice Film Festival on the same plane with Joe, Warhol and Sylvia Miles. Later, at the hotel's bar, Tennessee spotted Joe and his eyes lit up. "My traveling companion," he hollered. Tennessee talked about the beauty of Sicily and Dallesandro listened uncomprehendingly. "I took his silence to be acquiescence," Tennessee said. "I told him how poor my health was, that I hadn't much time and I couldn't be alone. I wanted only his presence until I fell asleep. Well, I rushed upstairs, quickly showered, brushed my teeth, I must have gargled an entire bottle of Listerine! And then I waited and waited in the dim light, a three quarter moon above the balcony. There was a knock on my door. I threw it open. I was only dressed in a silk dressing gown. 'Joe!' I cried, as dramatically as I could, 'Joe! Hold me. I'm dying!' I fell backward in a swoon on the bed. He came over and took my hand. I said, 'Hold me!' He said, 'I *am* holding you.' And that was that."

"Over the years," Dotson says, "Joe maintained Tennessee's affection and interest, and for a while he tried to interest movie producers in casting Joe in the title role of 'One Arm.' It is, I believe, the only completed film script of his that has never been produced, probably because no Hollywood studio is willing to take a chance on a movie about a down-at-the-heels male prostitute who ends up on Death Row. The story on which the script is based was written after the success of 'The Glass Menagerie,' when he fled to Mexico to escape the foul smell of success and lived in Mexico City, where he was happy for a time. "

"Flesh" is described by John R. Burger in *One Handed Histories* as an "ersatz underground gay film, sometimes homoerotic when focusing on always-naked, ever-flaccid hustler Joe Dallesandro interacting with his male johns, drag queen companions, and lesbian wife, but more often than not the narrative extols Dallesandro's search for heterosexual niceties.

"It is interesting to look at the span of Dallesandro's early career for it encompasses many different aspects of the evolution of the homoerotic film, and provides a gauge by which to measure the success of the movement.

"Among Dallesandro's first expenences in the genre were his modeling sessions for physique photographers Bob Mizer and Bruce of Los Angeles. The dates of the sessions are inexact. Art collector Volker Janssen dates the Bruce of Los Angeles sessions circa 1960. Dallesandro appears unchanged in the Mizer photos, dated in Leyland (1982) merely to the 1960s; the model's statistics state he was 19 years of age at the time of the Mizer shoot.

"In 1967, Dallesandro worked on two films with Andy Warhol: 'The Loves of Ondine' and 'Lonesome Cowboys.' In both films, Dallesandro participates in very blatant homoerotic activity; allowing Ondine to nuzzle his crotch in the forrner film, and carnpily alluding to an incipient elopement with Tom Hompertz in the latter. Via his physique modeling and Warhol work, Dallesandro began to achieve a well-established position as a gay cult idol.

"His next movie, 'Flesh,' (1968), was directed by Paul Morrissey and produced by Andy Warhol. Dallesandro becomes less homo-oriented in this film. He prefers women, and has actually fathered a child for which he deeply cares, but will still tum male tricks in order to pay the rent. Dallesandro did not appear in another Warhol/Morrisey film until 1970. In fact, neither Warhol or Morrissey produced a Factory film between 1968 and 1970. By this time, the Stonewall riots had occurred and gay pride and visibility were quickly becoming more predominant. Homoerotic content in underground films was, in the public eye, much less daring, and sexual ambiguity no longer *de rigueur*. Consequently, Dallesandro consistently becomes less gay in his films over the next few years. 'Trash,' made in 1970, merely implies that Dallesandro has tentative connections with the gay subculture through his interaction with drag queen Holly Woodlawn. By 1972, Dallesandro is completely heterosexual in the film 'Heat,' jumping in and out of bed with Pat Ast, Sylvia Miles, and others, and never once appearing fully nude. In fact, he has undergone an almost complete de-eroticization. Dallesandro's heyday as a sexual icon is waning by 1974, when both 'Andy Warhol's Frankenstein' and 'Andy Warhol's Dracula' were produced. The films prior to 1974 all focus on Dallesandro's polysexuality. His sex life gives the films their narrative impetus. 'Frankenstein' and 'Dracula,' however, display Dallesandro as a monster-movie superhero who has sex with women (although in 'Dracula,' by deflowering virgins, he saves them from the vampire's bite), and lolls around in states of undress. But he no longer embodies the homoerotic sexual prowess of his pre-1968 career. As gay men came charging out of the closets, Dallesandro and his queer film persona surreptiously crept back in.

"Concomitant with the dissolution of Dallesandro's (homo)erotic persona is the dissolution of his Amencan film career. In 1975 he went to Europe and appeared in a string of obscure movies, most of which were never released in the United States. Although he has since been cast in small roles in several domestic films, most notably Francis Ford Coppola's 'The Cotton Club' (1985), John Waters' 'Cry Baby' (1990), and Tamra Davis' 'GunCrazy' (1992), Dallesandro has not enjoyed the same level of cult status he achieved in the 1960s as a primarly gay, and secondarily sexual, movie icon.

"An interesting tangential note regarding Dallesandro's work in homoerotic film regards the 1977 gay porn feature 'Hot House' (Hand in Hand), directed by Jack Deveau. Included within the movie is a segment in which several of the characters screen a black and white eight-millimeter gay porn loop. The loop features two men, one of whom appears to be Dallesandro. Rowberry states that the actor in the film-within-a-film is defimitely Little Joe. In an update to that same publication, Rowberry amends his statement: 'While Jack is helping the upstairs neighbor climb in a window, some of his visitors enjoy a black and white hardcore film (in which Joe Dallesandro allegedly appears)' The folowing year, Rowberry states, 'The short film of Dellesandro [sic] has always been a hotly-contested item, but the tattoo on his arm is a dead giveaway.' The eight-millimeter film is of very poor quality, especially after having been filmed again. The actor most definitely appears to be Dallesandro. The haircut is similar to that which he sported in 1967...and the impish smile he beams as he gets fucked by his partner is unmistakable.

"An educated guess puts the date of this underground hardcore stag film at 1965. If this is indeed the case, and if the performer is Joe Dallesandro, it positions Dallesandro as a vital and key player in the late twentieth century evolution of homoerotica and gay hardcore pornography. Beginning with his physique posing sessions, continuing through his illicit stag film appearance and his homo-experirnental ventures with Warhol... It is interesting to note that the end of his heyday coincides with his progressive rejection of his sexuality (whether homo-, bi-, or hetero-)."

In an interview with PeeWee Herman in 1994, published in *Interview* magazine, Joe said, "I had a drug dealer in the same building Andy was shooting [a movie] in. A friend said I should stop in and say hi. I said, 'Who the fuck is Andy Warhol?' I had no idea. Could care less. I walked in and Paul [Morrissey] came over to me and talked to me for a little while. He got me to do a small scene. I was this guy who came in to meet with this couple. The wife wants me to teach her husband how to do some college wrestling – supposedly. So I get down into my underwear and we do this wrestling. He's trying to grab me all over the place. Very silly. That was my first film, 'The Loves of Ondine.' I was seventeen. I had no idea anyone would see it."

He described his early years: "When I was three or four I was put into a Catholic institution to wait for foster care. It was in Harlem. All black children except for me. When a white family walked in, I had first dibs. The prospective foster parents could look through this window where the playroom was, and we were taught to say, 'Will you be my mommy?' The day I started misbehaving I was booted out. Finally, my father decided to take us home. We moved in with him and my grandmother in Queens. But things escalated, and I became the tough guy. I started doing crazier and crazier shit. I started stealing cars and got myself busted. I wound up in a youth camp in upstate New York. We'd go out and chop trees and learn forestry work. I escaped from the youth camp. Stayed in the woods for three days, then hitchhiked to New York. Went to Florida with my dad. Then I came back to New York and got in trouble for robbing a movie theater.

"Later I was in New York doing my hustler routine. Me and a friend took off for California. He was fifteen and I was sixteen. We hitchhiked. Texas, Mexico, Los Angeles.

"We met some strange people by the bus station who got me into photographic muscle work. They oiled me up, put a sailor hat on me, and got me naked for these muscle magazines. That didn't last long.

"Toughest thing I ever did was kick the habit. And I kicked quite a few times. Now I have nine years' sobriety from everything. In my spare time, I'm a computer nerd. I have a never-ending quest for knowledge. Basically, I build computer systems. It's my hobby, when I'm not acting.

"When I was doing movies I met a lot of famous people, like Tennessee Vllilliams. I hung out with him, got to know him.

"I met some royalty when I lived in Europe. I was introduced to Sir Laurence Olivier after a performance of his; he was a fan of my work.

"And Norman Mailer would tease me. He was always trying to get me to be a tough guy with him. He'd punch me in the arm and say, 'Come on, hit me.'

"I look at my life and I have no regrets. I think of everything I've done as an experience leading to another step.

"My hustling days were more about trying to take care of myself. Having met those people kind of calmed me down. They showed me a different part of life. My attitude was that it widened my life experience. When I was young, my desire was always to be with my father. This desire and love was so tremendous. I realized later that I was looking for a father figure and someone to love me."

Had he made "One Arm," with a script by Tennessee Williams from his own short story, Joe Dallesandro might well have been the legend he deserved to be.

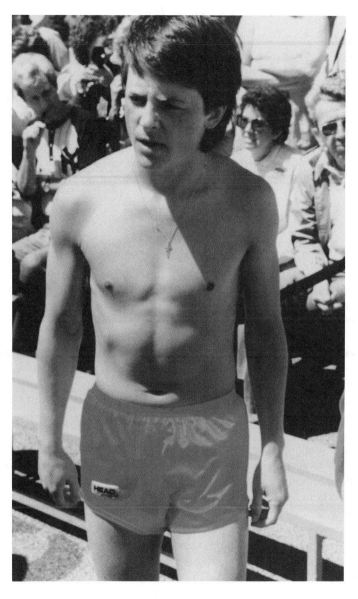

A rare shot of bare-chested Michael J. Fox.

Michael J. Fox

*"I didn't want to go the bodyguard route so we educated ourselves
through a security outfit: what to do, how to recognize a high risk
situation. One time a man comes up to me and says, 'I keep having
a dream about you.' And then I see this man again and again. I
saw him in five different cities. And I thought, how the hell does
this person know where I'm gonna be? And that's when I called the
security person: 'Just so you know...'"*
- Michael J. Fox

Television made Michael J. Fox a household name. His
appearance in the 1985 release "Back to the Future" (and its
sequels) made him a movie star and a "muffin" to be
contended with. Despite the fact that he is diminutive (barely
five-four), the foxy Michael J. managed to nail every aspect of
"Future's" 1985 loser who wins big when time-machined back
to 1955. While undone by the ludicrous script of "Teen Wolf,"
which was made prior to "Future" but was held back for
release to capitalize on the success of the later film, Fox was
charming, hilarious and adorable in both films. He parlayed
these qualities into having two of the best-grossing films of 1985
and has gone on to appear in hit comedy after hit comedy.

His dramatic films such as Brian DePalma's "Casualties of
War," Paul Schrader's "Light of Day," and "Bright Lights, Big
City," have not fared as well, but that's one of the things we
admire about him, he is willing to stretch. "Fox won a measure
of acclaim for his work in these movies," says Peter Alson, "but
some critics have questioned whether he has the inner
resources to bring off more dramatic roles." Director of "The
Hard Way" John Badham says, "Michael has got such basic,
terrific, million-dollar instincts and as he matures he's going to
be able to play lots an lots of roles because he's a very solid
actor. He has the thing that's hardest for anybody to get, which
is likability."

"In person," Alson says, "he's friendly, funny, charming,
open, articulate, accommodating and unpretentious - just the

Fox you'd expect. And, of course, he's still cute: boyish good looks atop a kid's body."

"It's one of those phenomena of physics that Fox looks small even when he's standing by himself," notes writer Rick Telander. "That's a limiting element for playing dramatic roles, but it's not, as those in the industry point out, an insurmountable burden for someone with talent."

For instance, in "Bright Lights, Big City," the set designer made everything to Michael's scale, two inches smaller than normal. Michael is always the first one to acknowledge his shortness, Telander says. When he won his first Emmy, he thanked everyone by saying, "I feel four feet tall." He laughs at his lack of height, just as he laughs at almost everything else that other folks, critics mostly, seem to take so seriously about his performances and life. "You know what the difference between a short actor and a short star is? The short actor stands on an applecart, and the short star has them dig ditches for everybody else."

Gary David Goldberg, creator of "Family Ties," says, "Talent rewrites all the rules. Even if Michael was on stage for just a few moments, it was electric. We'd look around and say, 'Why is the audience leaning forward?' Michael has an ability to let the audience in, to get people to breathe with him."

This foxiest of young actors started his acting career in high school: "I took drama in school because I felt it was a great way to avoid mental work. The drama teacher told me that a TV station was looking for a really bright ten-year-old kid. Since I was a small fifteen-year-old of average intelligence, I figured I could pull it off.

"When I was a kid," Michael remembers, "I was amazingly out of control. It's a testament to my family that they put up with that and encouraged the positive side of it. I don't think I ever knew that acting was what I was going to do. I wanted to be a hockey player, a Mountie, an artist, a writer, everything. Acting was just the first thing I got a check for, and I said, 'Well, this works.' So I just continued. Everyone was so concerned about what I was going to do because I was small and semi-hyper. When I was a kid I was just insane. Luckily, when you grow up, there's a job that fits that particular disorder – it's called acting."

Bitten by the acting bug, Michael left his native Vancouver for Hollywood: "On my eighteenth birthday I packed my bags and ran away. Now, coming all the way to the U.S. may sound sort of brave. In fact, I might say so too, except that I was just too stupid to realize there were any risks involved."

Before he left, he promised his mother he would finish high school. "I'm still holding him to it," his widowed mother, Phyllis, who still lives in Vancouver, says. Michael is now carrying around a preparation book for the GED (general equivalency diploma) in his blue-and-white duffel bag from the Gap. "I don't need a high school diploma right now in the practical sense, but I deserve the right to go to university, and in order to do that, I gotta play the same game everybody else does. Being Michael J. Fox does not get you into university. You gotta have a high school diploma."

Little is known about how little Michael, who must have looked all of 13 at that time, survived those early days in Tinseltown but, happily, he eventually found work, using his TV credits from a Canadian show called 'Leo and Me' at 15 to grab roles on "Lou Grant" and "Family."

Then came the script for "Family Ties" and he became one of TV's hottest young stars. His performance as the conservative Alex Keaton made the show a hit. The fan mail avalanche started. At one time, he had a 10,000 letter backlog and finally had to admit there was no way he was going to answer every letter. However, he does enjoy phoning people, such as a boy in the burn unit who wrote him, and make their day. The other advantage to stardom, he says, is the ability to travel. Vancouver remains his favorite place to live, L.A. his favorite place to work, and New York City his favorite place to party. But lately he's been partying a lot more in Hollywood. It seems that his 1988 marriage to Tracy Pollan is shaky because of his heavy drinking. "Michael likes to goof around and have fun," says a close friend. "He likes to go out with his buddies and be spontaneous, but Tracy is a very strict and structured type of person. It's like oil and water – a bad mix." Although they are technically together, they haven't been to bed together in over a year, the source says.

"In truth," Jess Cagle says, "all movie stars have their scandals. And if they fail to supply one themselves, the public assigns them a rumor. We like to say they're addicted to heroin; we love to say they're gay. The word on Fox has long been that he drinks too much or used to. Fox refuses to talk specifically about such reports."

"So many of these issues are personal," Fox says. "And not just personal like none-of-your-business personal, but personal to the extent where you go, '*I* haven't figured this shit out, you want me to explain it to *you*?' I got married and made a lifestyle change, and that was pretty much the extent of it.

"When I was in my 20s, I had a real good time, and in retrospect I came out of it pretty well. I just kinda grew up. You know, one thing about partying, I mean *hard* partying, not a glass of wine with dinner...but again, I wouldn't want to characterize what I do now, whether I don't drink or whether I do, because frankly, it is truly no one's business until I get behind the wheel of a car.

"When something good happens to you, why do you get really hammered to celebrate? I figured out that it's because, if you really get drunk, then you can – a million times – go, *Yeeeeah!* You know? And at a certain point in my life I just said 'I don't have to run and scream across a room and go, '*Yeeeeah! This is great! Fifth season* 'Family Ties!' *Duuuude!*'"

Michael did clean up his act for a while, friends concede. He tried Alcoholics Anonymous but photographers snapped him as he was leaving the meetings so he went to sessions at private homes. But while making films in Hollywood, away from Tracy and son Sam, who live in Connecticut, Michael gets to partying.

Since the failure of "Life With Mikey," which one critic said had bombed "thermonuclearly," Fox fired his longtime agent Peter Benedek, signed with Mike Ovitz's CAA and established his own production company. "I was feeling this malaise," Fox says. "It kind of unfolded around the time of 'Mikey.' I just got tired of hearing, 'Well, he was good but – ' And so I was just saying, 'What do I do now?' I got a deal to make films. I got a television development deal."

"The deal" includes starring in and *directing* "Thirty Wishes," in which he hopes to "re-position himself as the poster boy of the post-boom Generation X," Cagle says.

"I relate to that group," Fox admits. In the movie, he plays an aimless young man who, upon turning 30, is awarded every birthday wish he ever made, but the character soon becomes disillusioned. struggling to find out what he wants in life. "There's a lot of Michael in this movie," Matt Tolmach, the production chief of Fox's company, Snowback Productions, says. "He's very savvy. I find him much edgier, a much more complex character than I've seen on film."

"He's going to make a great director," Benedek says about his former client. "People who have spent a lot of time in the half-hour television business...tend to make really good directors. They're trying to turn out something funny and moving in 22 minutes."

Recently Michael has chiseled away all extra flesh. "He likes to show off his biceps," Cagle reports, "and eats only 10 grams of fat a day, at the most. The baby fat has fallen from his face, leaving an extraordinary sculpture of planes and angles. Up close, he no longer looks so boyish – more like a perfect, slightly reduced version of a thirtysomething man."

Marky Mark holds his greatest asset

Marky Mark

"I hate to admit it but I went to the Off-white Party at Limelight with about 600 other dedicated party boys. I stayed until Marky Mark was 'depantsed' on stage by three boys with a plan. It was a beautiful sight and night to behold."
— *Gay Columnist R. Couri Hay*

After their parents' divorce, Mark Robert Wahlberg and his eight brothers and sisters remained with their mom, Alma, in Dorchester, Mass. In this predominantly black neighborhood, the boy had to learn some smooth moves just to stay alive. He and older brother Donnie joined break-dance groups and eventually came to the attention of Mary Alford, a music manager on the Boston scene (whose biggest client was Rick James). Her dream was to put together a group of kids along the lines of the Jackson 5 or Menudo. Then one day Mary happened to meet an old friend, Maurice Starr, manager of the New Edition (Bobby Brown, Johnny Gill) and explained what she was doing. He said he was trying to do the same thing; they decided to pool their efforts. The result was a group called New Kids on the Block. Mark was only 13 and Maurice and Mary liked Mark and Donnie and added them to the act.

But after six months, when the group gave their first concert they were booed off the stage. The chemistry was wrong and Marky, who couldn't sing, could only rap, was dropped from the group. It was a tough time for the youngster. Donnie, his best buddy, his brother, was becoming a phenomenal success with the most popular singing group in the world at that time and Marky was stuck at home. Marky went back to the streets, got arrested five or six times. "I was on the verge of ruining my life," he admits. "I used to chill, smoke weed, I quit school." But finally he was able to get it under control. He started spending time at the Dorchester Youth Collaborative, a youth center where kids like me hang out to get away from trouble. "They just tell you, 'You screwed up once. Look at your life.' So what I discovered was that I was into rapping and performing and that's what I truly loved. Hip hop, street rap

---

was close to my soul."

Marky's mom recalls: "One of the family jokes is that when Marky was about three he would get in front of anything where he could see his reflection. It could be the toaster or the oven and he would climb up on top of the counter and sit in front of us and, you know, trying to flex his muscles when all there was was little bones."

One day, in the flush of the New Kids success, Donnie came home and the brothers began rapping together, just like in the old days. Donnie suggested they write some of the stuff down and before long Donnie decided he'd invest some of his New Kids bucks in his little brother. Donnie put together the Funky Bunch, his posse of six dancers and rappers. "They sing dance and act crazy like me," Marky says. On the Kids' 1990-91 tour, Marky's group was the opening act. That did it. Marky was becoming a hit. With a handful of rap demos, Mark approached the record companies and on July 23, 1991, his first album, "Music for the People," was unleashed on the public. Donnie was the producer and co-wrote most of the tracks. MC Spice, a Boston rapper, co-wrote and co-produced a couple of tracks. The album was a smash, helped, without doubt, by the videos on MTV.

"You know man," Marky reflected at the time, "we could've taken a pretty face and made a hardcore kid. But this is me. This is my way to express myself, to tell the whole world how I feel and maybe do some good. Music has that effect on people. I will not do anything to make myself feel uncomfortable. Not put on a cute smile, not get pretty-boyed up. The most important thing to me is that I do it my way, without hiding myself.

"Music is my life. The last job I had, I was a bricklayer's apprentice. And I was happy with that job, too, because it was something that made me feel good. To build a wall for the side of a building felt really good to me."

At the time, many critics felt only a black person can rap but Marky said he was the "real deal. Hip-hop, street rap was close to my soul. I had always done freestyle raps. The first raps I did with Donnie were real down-and-dirty. People who understand rap aren't going to say anything about my being white. Hip-hop was almost whitewashed and turned into

Vanilla Ice." Marky says Vanilla Ice claimed a right to rap because he went to a tough school in Miami. But it turns out he was mostly from an all-white, upper-middle-class suburb in Texas. "Hip-hop isn't black music, it's street music."

The Advocate's Lance Loud called him "Hip-hop's answer to the Venus de Milo." Lance watched him filming a video in L.A., driving the damsels dizzy, and announced that to the world that cute Marky was queer-friendly. Between takes Marky joked with girls and lots of gay guys assembled on the edge of the parking lot. He performed several unscripted crotch grabs, winked at the swooning audience and generally showed himself to be a unisexual cockteaser of major proportions. At one point he grappled the chain-link fence between him and his now-flaccid followers and pretended that it was a – how would you say? – glory hole. Then, with breathtaking aplomb, he proceeded to demonstrate something that looked an awful lot like fellatio on an imaginary member with such zeal, eyewitnesses swear Linda Lovelace would have found it educational."

At an autograph-signing session, girls were screaming, shouting, crying, and asking if they could rub their photos on his chest. He agreed to everything, except when one girl wanted his cap. There was no way he would ever give up his cap. He said he only takes it off when he's in church, but we have seen him in concerts without it. Must have been his hair that day.

The music critic Adam Block said Marky was "an Irish Catholic who threatens to give the church a good name. The buffed pud-boy is getting as famous for flashing his underwear as he is for his endearing musical chops.

"Although he's hetero, he's quick to say he's comfortable around queers and is even flattered that they find him attractive. It's rare," Block asserted, "for a male pop star with teen appeal to be so plainspoken and supportive about queers. It's rarer still in the world of rap, where Mark has at least one foot tapping." Among brown-haired, hazel-eyed Marky's nicknames - I kid you not: "Mizo," "Miz."

"When dissecting Mark's mode, the obvious feature is more substance than style," the author of a biography about the star, Randi Reisfeld, wrote. "He has worked to create an almost perfectly sculpted chest, with bulging biceps and, as one reviewer put it, 'a stomach as rippled as a potato chip.' His close-to-exhibitionistic display of his upper body is a large part of what sets him apart from the other young rappers and performers. He has marketed himself as a hunk, a studly package few can resist. His effect isn't limited to prepubescent princesses. It knows no age boundaries. The older women leave him love notes, with their phone numbers attached to very personal items. They come right out and (even on hand-painted banners) say exactly what it is that Marky does for them (and what they'd like to do for him.)"

With all these fans wanting him, what about this boy's love life? How about a girlfriend? everyone wanted to know. In the video version of "Music for the People," Marky has a rap that goes, "I try to show 'em the joint, so maybe I can get a little bit of juice back at the hotel." But, if you can believe his comments to the press he isn't getting any "back at the hotel" or anywhere else. "Sure," he admitted, "I'd date a fan but mostly I'm in and out of town too quick and nothing comes of anything." (Nothing comes? Come on!) Marky laughed, "I need one bad. Donnie still gets all the girls. I haven't done anything really romantic so far.

"My preference is for females," Marky insists, "but I respect anybody for their sexual preferences. And gay people are probably the most harmless people and would never try to do anything to hurt you, you know what I mean? Which is good. I feel very comfortable around gay people."

Gay publisher Casey Klinger commented, "Take a number. Marky ain't puttin' out for no nellies, but we can dream can't we?" (In his picture book, he at least admits to kissing his brother Donnie.)

To ingratiate himself with the gay community, the star lent his presence to celebrity affairs held to raise money to benefit AIDS research and appeared on the AIDS awareness video, "Red Hot + Dance," dressed completely in black. "I'm glad that gay people are so free with their words," he said, "and they're not hiding. If I were gay, I wouldn't want to have to hide it."

Hiding it certainly is hardly Marky's style but he swears showing it all began as an accident: "It was a funny thing about dropping my pants. I was performing in L.A. and I loosened my top button. The pants were loose anyway and they slipped while I was doing some moves. Rather than stop and pull my pants up, I waited till I finished the move. By then, my pants were around my ankles! The crowd went crazy. Actually, I don't do it in my show any more.

"Although, when I come out for my slow song at the end of the show, I come out with just my boxer shorts and a robe and do this big safe sex thing, just to let people know that if you engage in sexual activity that you are protected and that your partner is as well. There are a lot of people dying over something that is so pleasurable. So we have this big condom thing and this big talk at the end." (It would have to be BIG.) By this time, journalists were saying that Marky had the baddest mouth they'd ever heard. Said one: "He talks constantly, about anything that comes into his head: muscles, food, his rise to fame, his friends, cars, girls, and more girls. And there's not a single sentence that doesn't contain a four-letter word. And when he's not talking, he's making up risque raps."

Some of those raps ended up on Marky's follow-up to his million-selling "Music For the People," "You Gotta Believe," which opened to mixed reviews. One critic said: "Dismiss him as a trouser-dropping bubble gum beefcake if you want but Marky Mark and his brother and producer Donnie Wahlberg make fine pop rap records and here they've toughened things up a bit, more to fine effect." Donnie and Mark teamed for the cut, "Loungin'."

But Marky's honeymoon with the gay boys was not to last. The trouble began with Marky's remark to the English press: "I seen (sic) Madonna in person and before that I thought she was kind of cute but she looked like somebody out of 'Beetlejuice,' man! Seriously!" Those remarks (and please note, we quote Marky exactly as he speaks, as above, without changing his use – or rather, abuse – of the English language) led to what became known as the "M & M War." The end result of this battle had Marky suffering the put-foot-in-mouth fate of Donna Summer as far as many gays were concerned. The "tremendous set-to" between Marky and Madonna reached a climax (of sorts) at a birthday party in Hollywood for

"Truth or Dare" director Alek Keshishian. Marky says he went to the party by himself and was only there ten minutes when Madonna came after him. "I was like, 'What's up?' And she was like, 'Don't fucking say hi to me. You know what the fuck you fucking did. You dished me. You're a fucking asshole, a fucking fake.'" They exchanged more heated words until Madonna said she was going to find someone to "kick" Marky's ass.

Marky tried blowing it off when a Maverick records executive, Guy Oseary, travelling with Madonna, jumped in. At first, they simply sassed each other and left but then Oseary came back and threatened Marky a second time, telling him he'd settle things outside. "I know you don't want to fight me," he said. "I knew you was a pussy."

Marky said, "All right. Whatever."

But soon Marky saw there were two others joining Oseary. That's when he started swinging, landed a punch, and brought Oseary to the floor and they began wrestling. The other two Maverick records people started banging and kicking Marky until other guests broke up the melee. A guest at the party told New York gossip columnist Liz Smith that this incident did not happen the way Madonna says it did. Her version goes like this: "Marky is not a bad kid, but he and Madonna are both dopes and have too much attitude. Marky pinched Madonna when she went by him. She turned on him and said something like, 'Don't try to be friendly, considering your rap lyrics about me.' Marky did NOT make any homophobic remark."

Michael Szymanski, in *Genre*, claimed to have the *true* scoop as well: ". . . The *real* story about Madonna and Marky Mark (and this is from someone who was there) is that the boy-toy rebuffed her persistent advances, and that's why she started the rumor about the anti-gay remark – knowing it would cost him a Donna Summer-like avalanche of hate from his homo fans. Leave it to M to take being evil to a whole new level. Anyway, Marky likes younger, virginal girls whom he wants to touch for the very first time."

Whatever really did happen, the hostess of the party, Angela Janklow Harrington was grateful: "Thank God that happened. It was such a *bad* party!"

At the peak of the hype, Jim Mullen, in *Entertainment Weekly*, said "the whole country was talking about it," and "Madonna vs. Marky Mark. They were really fighting over who has bigger breasts."

Early in 1992, the stud puppy was the first celebrity to be honored with a pullout centerfold in *People* magazine's "Teen Idol" issue. Even the venerable columnist Liz Smith made note of it: "Don't you all just love the issue with its amazing pull-out of bare-chested Marky Mark? I understand that many People staffers were laughed to scorn by their friends from other publications over this little addition. (Just jealous they didn't think of it first!?)" And, for once, Marky's briefs weren't showing. But he was photographed with his hands in the pockets of his jeans, pulling them up so that the crotch is magnificently displayed.

Marky said his pants-dropping began in L.A., at Magic Mountain, right after his first record, "'Good Vibrations," came out: "It was just one of those things, man. I was doing something kinda berserk and I just dropped my pants. And I remember I saw 50 million flashes and I was like 'Oh, shit!' I was like 'This might be something.' Then it started getting a little out of hand. Now my fans tend to demand it."

Because his fans demanded to know, Marky revealed that he lost his virginity over a course of five encounters with the same girl. We mean, this is a stud who takes his sweet time! Heaven! He was 16 and it was the first time for each of them. And just in case you get to meet him and manage to steer him to your bed, be aware his condom of choice is: "Trojans, ribbed, in the gold box." It's good to be prepared.

Celeb watchers called Marky a "hip-hop hunk" and he did admit at the time that he worked out "about two hours every morning. I usually do it in the gym of whatever hotel I'm at. If I don't work out in the morning, I don't feel too good for the rest of the day. Weight lifting is the only time to let my frustrations out. And the cuties love it." Indeed, the "cutie" readers of *Teen* magazine named him "the hottest hunk" in music.

The star got into body-building when he stopped smoking. He began eating like a pig and gained thirty pounds so he started going to the gym. Soon Marky's muscles looked as if they were topped with more muscles. The 5'8", 160 pound stud said, "I enjoy doing push ups." (You can do push-ups over me anytime, honey.) The stud puppy has a 31-inch waist and 16-and-a-quarter-inch biceps. One can only fantasize about the *other* measurements. The heaviest weight he has lifted is 300 pounds. Besides the obvious benefits, Mark said the regimen has made him "feel good."

What gay men were doing at this point was just trying to cope. Steve Saylor said: "God forbid you should turn to MTV, where Marky Mark is eternally stripping down to his jockey shorts and fondling his sweet sensation over and over and over again."

This "sweet sensation" was duly noted by the teen magazine *Sassy*, whose stories are all written in the voice of a teenage girl: "Marky Mark...disrobed, sporting boxers over a pair of those groovy Calvin Klein undershorts," said one piece, "and well, all I can say about what happened next is, I hope Marky respected himself in the morning."

Of course, there were some fans who didn't groove on his sexiness. One said, "Actually, I don't like the way he pulls his pants down and grabs onto...(she laughs). Well, anyway, that's my opinion. What was the question again?"

When asked if he weren't famous, would they still love him, one fan replied, "Be serious. He's cute!" Another: "If I saw him walking down the block, I swear to God I'd go up to him and I'd go, 'Excuse me. What's your name?' Just like any other guy."

But Marky's not just like any other guy. In fact, he's got that rarity, a third nipple. He says: "It's cool, it's unique. Not too many people have them, and it's not hazardous to my health or anything. It's not something to be ashamed about. It's dope. And bitches like to suck it."

And then there's the tattoo on Marky's ankle. "It's Sylvester the cat with Tweety Bird in his mouth. I went to the tattoo store and said, 'Give me that tattoo!' I only picked it because I wanted to cover up what was there before, which was a playing card, a club. I did it on my own. I made the club out of India ink. But it's corny. I regret getting it because it marks up my body for life. And if I ever do anything bad they can identify me by it."

To further assist his fans in identifying him, Marky exposed himself to Lynn Goldsmith's camera to create *Marky Mark*, a $15 photo book liberally spiced with Marky quotes. Quite appropriately, the stud puppy dedicated the book to his *dick*.

Indeed, his dick was supremely exposed by Calvin Klein for about two years, gently tucked into white briefs, of course.

As Steve Gaines reported in his book *Obsession*, when David Geffen bailed out Calvin Klein's company, "before long he couldn't help putting in his two bits. As brilliant a predictor of trends as Calvin was, some of Geffen's suggestions were home runs. It was Geffen's idea that Calvin hire Marky Mark, the muscle-boy rap star, as his next underwear model. The beefy nineteen-year-old rapper from the streets of Boston was already giving Calvin a free ride by wearing his jeans so low on his hips that the waistband of his Calvin Klein underwear showed. Mark was causing a sensation at his personal appearances by dropping his jeans to his ankles to reveal just how well he filled out his shorts. Geffen helped Calvin make a deal with Mark over chops at the Old Stove Pub in Bridgehampton. A $100,000 contract was negotiated with Mark to become Calvin's official poster boy. The ads of Marky Mark were certainly eye-popping...Mark almost burst out of his sixteen-dollar button-fly shorts, twenty-one-dollar cycling shorts, and old-fashioned Y-fronts. In one, he stretches his already tight underpants across his crotch so snugly that the shot had to he airbrushed before it began appearing in magazines and bus shelters in October 1992. Calvin also rushed into production two 30-second TV spots that featured the butch bodybuilder alternately grabbing his crotch or pressing a bare-breasted, teenaged model named Kate Moss into his chest. Mark hit a live nerve with the public, and in just three months, sales shot up 34 percent over the previous year. Within twelve months the men's underwear division was grossing a remarkable $85 million per annum. 'Marky Mark,' said Kal Ruttenstein, vice president of Bloomingdale's, 'is the male equivalent of Brooke Shields.'"

Marky's version of how he became famous is even more tantalizing: "Calvin Klein and David Geffen saw a picture of me on stage. Somebody called me and said, 'Calvin Klein wants you to do this advertisement. They want you to model for them.' I met him the first time at Calvin's house. They were like, 'The only reason we want you is because you were doing your own thing, and that's what we want you to do for us. We think it's cool.' So I was like, 'Cool.' So I went to Calvin's house, and Geffen was just hanging out. We were just talking. They were laughing because my pants were hanging down. I tried on some stuff. And then we talked again. Calvin said he would like Herb Ritts to shoot me."

Soon Marky's assets were not only gracing the pages of almost every magazine in the country, they were also on display on every bus and/or shelter, first in New York, then San Francisco. Indeed, the crotch of Marky Mark must be the most photographed one of recent times. It all started when Bruce Weber shot hundreds of feet of film of it for a spread in *Interview* magazine. As Vince Aletti commented in *The Village Voice*, "Marky Mark crunches up his face, drops his pants and squeezes the bulge in his Calvin Klein briefs."

Marky talked about his relationship with CK: "You know, he's just been so la-arge. I mean, even in the neighborhoods, if you had a pair of Calvin Kleins, you was the man. So I went to his house and I met him, hooked up. We had one set deal. They gave me $100,000 to do the commercials and the photos."

Seeing the first underwear ads, Susan Orlean, writing in *The New Yorker*, said: "Of all the guys who are standing around bus shelters in Manhattan dressed in nothing but their underpants, Marky is the most polite. For instance, even though he is very busy getting ready to go to Japan for a promotional tour, he took the time to call from Los Angeles the other day just to chat about his new role as the Calvin Klein Underpants Boy.

"Underwear has always figured prominently in his performances but it is only in the last weeks (as the CK model) that Marky has ascended to the status of lingerie luminary. He actually was a little late in calling me but said he was at the gym doing some upper-body work. Who could begrudge him that? After all, if photographs of you nearly naked were plastered everywhere, then upper-body work is exactly the sort of thing you would be wise not to neglect. Nonetheless, Marky was apologetic. 'I'm sorry, really sorry,' he said. 'I hope I didn't screw up your day, or anything.'

"In the ads, which were photographed by the master Herb

Ritts, Marky looks like a horny and impudent sixteen-year-old pleased with his pecs, his abs, and his underwear.

"Now, about his *thing*. Since he was a little kid, Marky has favored gigantic pants riding very low on his hips. 'I can't move around in tight pants,' he says. 'I've always been into the baggy thing.' But he has always favored Calvin Klein underwear. 'It's some crazy shit seeing the posters of me in my underwear all over the place,' he says. 'But the pictures are really me, you know? But I've pulled my pants down in front of people millions of times. It's not that big a thing for me.'"

Not a *big* thing? Come now. And those posters became a hot item on the black market, fetching hundreds of dollars apiece on the deprived West Coast. Musto spotted The Underpants Boy on a typical night out in New York: "Marky Mark showed up to discuss his Calvins with David Lee Roth, who boasted of wearing Fruit of the Looms. 'Twas truly a meeting of remarkable behinds. Earlier, at the Palladium, Marky had politely refused to strip for a public access cable show, saying, 'I have to get permission from my label and my manager before I do anything.' You mean the guy has to notify them when every time he drops his drawers? They must comprise the busiest communications center on the entire planet."

When Marky first came upon the New York scene he was much less inhibited. Musto reported he spotted the star at the Ritz in the Big Apple, that quickly turned into something from the gay strip joint Show Palace: "Shedding his jacket and strutting around bare-chested, later dropping his pants to reveal briefs tightly encasing what could only be described as a baseball bat. A waifish urchin no longer, he grabbed his crotch repeatedly and quipped, 'How's everybody in the motherfuckin' house doin' tonight?' Dancing and rapping like a demon, he barely remembered to pull the pants back up before stumbling offstage and hurting his knee. This guy makes Madonna's masturbation shtick look like an Anita Bryant orange juice commercial. The girls in the crowd went berserk, the guys booed."

But it was not just the crotch of Marky that captivated his fans at this point. His glorious chest left everybody breathless. George Wayne, writing in *QW*, recalled Marky's showing up at the "Boathouse Rock" party to aid AmFAR: "Marky Mark (I just want to eat his tits) was there too, but had only leers. Marky didn't like the idea of me shouting, 'Show us your tits!' as he butched it up for the paparazzi."

When promoting the Klein line, Marky sometimes had the clothes designer himself, now much married and drug-free, in tow, beaming delightedly as Marky scrawled his name on anything and everything that had the CK logo.

A spy on the scene in San Francisco at Macy's department store reported the rapper was "flirting outrageously with all of the guys." When someone asked him if he'd ever wear Fruit of the Looms, Marky said, "Well, I ain't gonna say while I'm sitting here next to Calvin Klein." Calvin just smiled. (I mean, if you were Calvin, wouldn't you be smiling?)

At the beefcake boy's San Francisco appearance, kids started lining up at 8 a.m., but it seemed no coincidence, Jim Provenzano reported, that the first in line was an older gay man, Tony Bruno, who had actually seen Marky at a concert at the Warfield Theater. "He's great," Bruno said. "He shows he's non-judgmental, no matter what you are, your race, your sexuality." Bruno confided that he was not going to wear his Marky-autographed briefs, he was going to "frame it." Provenzano said that a small herd of gay men showed up about an hour before Marky's appearance. "We're devoted but not demented," one fan said. Another fan reported that Marky's bus shelter posters were a hot item in S.F. "The one at Castro and Market was broken into twice." Then the fan revealed, "It's an Allen wrench that you need."

In January 1993, Liz Langley reported, Marky showed up at Dwyer High School in West Palm Beach to strut his stuff to help raise money for band uniforms. The director of the band said Marky was "very positive, well-mannered. He did a little bit of that dropping his pants thing but he had three pairs of pants on. He had pants on top of boxers on top of briefs and he didn't drop his pants, they just sort of slid down. He personally made $3,500 that night." A student said, "He was a nice guy. Not at all like 2 Live Crew. He talked about staying in school, how he's sorry he didn't finish school and he's determined to go back." Marky still is insisting he *will* someday get his G.E.D.

At the end of 1993, while *Rolling Stone* was crying, "Pecs ahoy!" and had reduced Marky to a "lite rapper underpants shill," Woody Harrelson was taking Marky's place on Times Square in CK underwear – but not in many big gay hearts.

"In today's world, Peter Pan is a pervert," noted Fenton Bailey. "On the one hand, the idea of the pervy Peter Pan is a very hot concept. Marky Mark, the essential all-American boy, has been milked to sell underwear. Sure, he's old enough to have sex (the kid even dedicated his book to his dick), but the whole concept stinks of teen spirit. His cherubic face toys with the idea of the underage – Lolita with muscles. But we all know that when he grows up, his ability to sell y-fronts will fall off a cliff."

In the 4th edition of the *Movie Buff Checklist*, Campfire Video's bible that lists all the stars and the films in which they expose the most skin. The latest issue sports a wonderful picture of the moment in Marky's video when Donnie Wahlberg pulls the kid's pants down. That butt is as gorgeous as the rest of him.

And then it all went sour. Early on, many gays were troubled by a continuous stream of Marky "outlaw" quotes, such as the ones he supposedly made on a London tabloid show. "They were totally disrespecting me," the stud says now. "The show is known for that. They were going crazy on me. So I was just sitting there in my own world." While he was sitting there, Shabba Ranks was being interviewed separately. When Marky heard Shabba quote the Bible and say that gays should be crucified, Marky said, "Well, wait a second here." And then they wanted Marky to perform with Ranks. Marky didn't want to do it, but pushed him on stage and they did a little rap together before Marky had had enough and said, "Fuck you! Fuck *The Word!* Fuck everybody! I can say whatever the hell I want. Shabba can say whatever he wants. And you can say whatever the hell you want." At that point, Marky walked off and threw the microphone down: "I stole from my mother, stole from my father, stole from my brother, stole from my neighbors. I stole a lot, stealing was hot. I stole from stores, houses, people, stole cars." Perhaps now that he's in the money, he'll return everything? Back up the truck.

Marky often discussed his troubled past, admitting arrests for "shoplifting, drinking in public, assault and battery, fighting, drunken disorder. Stupid stuff," he told George Wayne of *Vanity Fair*, "but no bank robberies."

At the end of 1993, *Vanity Fair* named Marky to its Hall of Fame: "Because he has proved Dorothy Parker right, in demonstrating that brevity is indeed the soul of underwear. Because he can grab his crotch for fashion's brief encounters and make us want to cry, 'Down, boy!' Nothing can stop the upward curve of the bulletheaded rapper with the boxer's physique. Marky Mark can tan while the rest of us burn, and we should bless the day M.M. went starky stark." This accolade irritated some readers: "Hall of Fame deserves much better. Marky Mark is a desperately soulless media fabrication who cannot rap to save his pecs and will undoubtedly go the way of Vanilla Ice, Gerardo, and, uh, the dinosaur?"

But by January, 1994, *The Advocate* was giving Marky "his turn." As a preface to her historic interview with Marky, Judy Wieder said, "After a year long and often rapturous affair with Marky Mark, the gay community ended 1993 feeling spurned by its primary heterosexual object of affection. Charges of homophobia and gay bashing gave credence to rumors that the rap star and supermodel's flirtations with the community were only skin-deep.

"Spurned fans, like spurned lovers, often react impulsively – and melodramatically. On Los Angeles' Sunset Boulevard, an explosion of bloodred paint obliterated Mark's crotch on a 40-foottall billboard, and across the country, billboards of the rapper and waifish model Kate Moss were similarly vandalized. Some showed their displeasure by resorting to even more extreme measures: mailing boxes soiled underwear to Calvin Klein's chic Manhattan office."

In his defense, Marky said he had lots of gay friends. "Now, me and David Geffen are real cool. I talk to him all the time. I call him up for business advice. It's very rare that you will find somebody who will not only give you advice but good advice.

"So when people make accusations without asking me, it affects a lot of gay people close to me. That's why I say if people would listen to me instead of just looking at me, they would understand. Usually when magazines talk to me, they ask senseless things. Hell, if you're not asking anything important, why bother?

"I don't think I really had a beef with the gay community. I think I was a big scandal. I've always known that I had a big gay following, and I was always doing my thing to be as open to them as everybody else. I was out there doing gay shows and all that stuff. Whoever wanted to listen to my music? Cool. *People* was calling me gay for doing It. That's why I can't even begin to figure it out or try to set somebody's head straight. But it goes a lot deeper than people think. It all started with the underwear syndrome, and a lot of the gay community's got a beef with Calvin Klein and not me."

As further evidence to prove he's hardly anti-gay, Marky offered this: "I did an interview for a gay writer who is a friend of mine. Whenever I see him, we always go to a club or something and hang out. He said that he thinks that I'm gay and I just won't come out with it. I think it's just because I am comfortable around him and around the situation." *Entertainment Weekly's* Jim Mullen cracked a joke about it: "Gays won't buy Calvin Klein's underwear until he drops Marky Mark; some straights won't buy it until he drops his prices."

Wieder asked Marky if he had ever had a *relationship* with a man, he said, "Nah." When she asked, "And you don't ever see that happening?" Marky replied, "Uh, not now. But you never know. You *never* know."

In the same interview, Marky revealed his stepfather's brother, who lived with the family for four years, is gay. "He makes the best chocolate-chip cookies ever! He's very much like an uncle. He still spends Christmas with us. He buys us the best Christmas gifts. Fly shirts and sweaters! I'm talking fashion! But I don't feel that I should have to say all this for people to believe me." Marky says he's somewhat of a drifter; he has sneakers "in New Jersey and at my mom's house in Braintree, Mass." which his brother Donnie bought for her.

Advocate readers seemed to be delighted with the interview. One fan from Utah wrote: "I'm tired of the criticism Marky Mark has received. How many of us at 22 didn't say stupid things or could have survived the scrutiny of the media?" Another fan said, "Thank you, *Advocate*, for renewing my faith in (as well as my crush on) Marky Mark." Another said: "Granted Marky did not stand up tall and proud (with Shabba Ranks) and defend gay sexuality, but when we can't even get our own closeted film and TV stars to do it, why should we expect a straight boy to do any better? GLAAD has bigger fish to fry, and maybe it should direct its energies in that direction. Have they ever heard of the pope?"

All was not sweetness and light, however. One reader said, "I cannot believe our community is without interests other than pecs and abs." Another: "You devoted 13 pages and the cover to this fluff!" And yet another: "Bullshit! Marky Mark has played the gay community like a fiddle while laughing all the way to the bank." Our answer to this is, Marky can play with our fiddle any time, as long as we get to play with his!

In the fall of 1993, Marky appeared in his first movie. He was cast, to quote the publicity copy, as "a high school wise-guy with a reputation! He learns a deadly lesson the hard way" in "The Substitute," a made-for-USA-network movie. The lesson was given by a psycho teacher to one of her most playful students, Marky. She ends up shooting him dead half way into the picture. But Wahlberg played himself very well (he's had lots of practice being obnoxious in a classroom, of course) and looked heavenly even with all his clothes on.

Then Marky was signed to play a recruit in Penny Marshall's production of "Renaissance Man," a comedy starring Danny DeVito. Marky was worried about getting the part because the Madonna set-to occurred just before he was to go to his interview with Marshall. "Penny had already heard from Madonna," Marky says. "She asked me, 'What happened?' I had to defend myself. I told her about the press thing, and she told me, 'Yeah, well, Madonna's real sensitive to that stuff.' But it really hurt me too. As much as I try to go out and promote, 'do your own thing,' I can't believe people would listen to that. You'd think people who know me would know I wasn't a gay basher." The film fizzled at the boxoffice but by then Marky was playing oposite Leonardo DiCaprio in "Basketaball Diaries." That film was generally well-received by critics, who praised Marky's acting, but it died at the boxoffice. While music may be Marky's first love, it was clear there were more acting jobs, not records, in Marky's future.

"When we think of Marky Mark," *Tutti* was saying, "all we can say is 'WOW!' This dude has gone from a shy, skinny, chain-smoking kid to a massively muscular, outgoing, intelligent, talented rapper/model/actor in just a couple of short years. Way back when big bro Donnie decided it was time to take some of the spotlight and produced his 'Good Vibrations' (*the* record of 1991) and Marky was suddenly in demand."

According to *Playgirl*, Marky is *still* in demand as a bed partner and they said that Marky has such a stash of CK undies left over from his heyday that he's giving them to his paramours after a nice roll in the hay.

And, making the understatement of the decade, Marky said, "People really seemed to enjoy it when I was in my underwear and nothing else. People still expect me to come into a room with my pants hanging down." But, the stud puppy says, "you gotta move on."

Patrick Swayze

Patrick Swayze

"The only thing I ever let (my fans) see
was when I took my clothes off and
you saw my rear in 'Road House.'
I'm not interested in sex for the sake of sex."
– Patrick Swayze

When he was only 20, living in sinful Manhattan and a struggling ballet dancer, Patrick Swayze posed, scantily clad in briefs and makeup, for an ad for a men's boutique. When the photo resurfaced again in 1990, a prominent New York gay said: "Gay men swap these kinds of pictures and this is one of the more popular ones."

All the publicity fueled new rumors that Patrick was gay. Truth is, the press reported, he's been happily married for 14 years to blonde Lisa Niemi, whom he met at his mother's dance studio when she was 16 and he was 21. "Patrick," a close friend said, "is about as far away from being gay as you can get. He's the picture of an all-American, red-blooded regular guy."

But wait, he's a guy with demons! Consider what he told *US* magazine: "I don't care what image I have! Take any image you want of me, I'm going to change it, because we are chameleons. We have the crazy person, the shy person, the angry person, the intellectual person, the ignorant person, the gay person, we have the little boy in us, the little girl in us...Oh! Heaven *forbid* we have a feminine side! I've now ceased to worry about image, because I don't care what people think of me anymore. Because I've had such a battle with what I think of me and with trying to find a way to like myself.

"My demons are plaguing me *every* second. I had a lot of rage growing up, and I tried to deny it, lie about it and therapy the rage out, but I realized that that intensity is going to be with me forever, so I've stopped lying about it and trying to blame things – life or people – and just accept that it's a part of me. But I love these demons. I don't fear them anymore. I've embraced them. I nurture them. I've found if I fight them, they'll kill me. If I lie about them or deny them, they'll kill me. *(Laughs)* I've been in *everything*. I tried this therapist and that therapist, but I've discovered that so many times 98 percent of the people you find out there just read it out of a book. (They didn't live it.)"

We'll probably have to wait for his autobiography to find out what those demons were. Meantime, we'll remember the good times we've had at the movies with Patrick. Especially the sight of that gorgeoius ass in "Road House." Although the movie was indeed what one reviewer called "sexist, homophobic and cliched," it nonetheless is a must-see for Swayze fans and any gay who prizes beautiful buns. Lovingly photographed by Dean Cundey, who received an Oscar nomination for "Who Framed Roger Rabbit," Patrick is offered up like a prized bull, the camera examining him for size, shape, and texture. In one scene, actress Kathleen Wilhoite visits his bedroom and gapes in awe at the sight of the star's bare, ballet-dancer-tight buns.

With his ruggedly handsome looks and boyish sincerity, Patrick appears on screen to be a decade younger than his 38 years, which lent credibility to his role in "Point Break," playing an enigmatic surfer named Bodhi opposite Keanu Reeves who played, of all things, an undercover FBI agent. Patrick dyed his hair blond for his role and does his own stunts: "I'm an adrenaline junkie," he says. "I love danger and putting myself in situations where, if I don't do it, I'll die."

In 1993, only die-hard Swayze fans could sit through "Father Hood," what critic George Mayer called "as misguided a movie as you'll find this season. Nobody found it. The movie was unceremoniously dumped by Disney into only 20 markets after it tested poorly. One Disney executive called the film "a dog," and it should have gone directly to video.

Celebrity watcher Anne Thompson says Swayze has been fighting his true persona - as a ladies man - in order to pursue macho roles and increase his acting range because Holywood's male executives don't appreciate his sex appeal. But producer Sean Daniel understands: "He should be in steamy romances. This is a shirt-open kind of guy."

Either than or dress him in Chanel. In "To Wong Foo, Thanks for Everything, Julie Newmar" he starred as a drag queen named Vida. Explains Patrick, "I did Vida to honor a lot of friends in my life, from real drag queens, who were some of the closest friends I ever had, to beautiful beings stuck in a redneck body – like my dad."

Hey Patrick, baby, you go on talking like that and you may become a legend after all!

THEY MIGHT BE LEGENDS

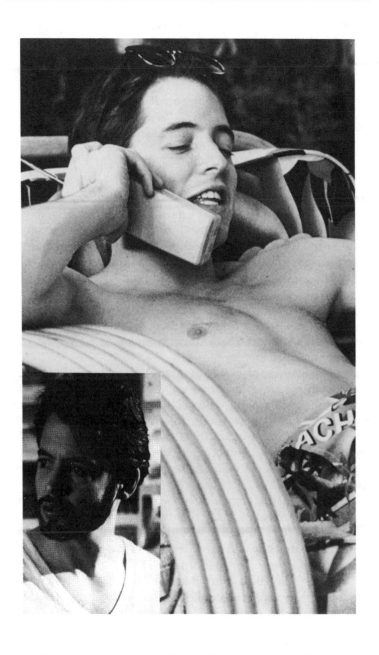

Matthew Broderick in "Ferris Bueller's Day Off" and
(inset) "The Night We Never Met"

Matthew Broderick

"On stage or off-screen, Matthew has the comic timing of an 87-year-old Vaudevillian in the muffin face and body of a teenager."
- William Spencer, Stallion magazine, 1986

Among the more delectable teen stars to emerge as a young actor of major talent is Matthew Broderick. As far as gays were concerned, Matthew reached perfection by accepting the role as Harvey Fierstein's lover in the 1988 film version of landmark play "Torch Song Trilogy." Matthew had played the role of the gay teenager in the original production when it was off-Broadway and agreed to do the film because of his respect for Fierstein.

Matthew delighted audiences with his appearances on Broadway in Neil Simon's mega-hits "Brighton Beach Memoirs" and "Biloxi Blues," and went on to make the film version of "Biloxi."

William Spencer says that in "Max Dugan Returns" Matthew was qualified as a "muffin-ette." But by "WarGames," the hackman-fever film whose domestic box-office was $74 million back in 1983, Matthew was a full-fledged muffin and really became a muffin supreme in "Ladyhawke," top-billed as the knight-hero's sly and unwilling squire, although Leonard Maltin says, "his manner and dialogue seem better suited to a Woody Allen movie."

Matthew's distinguished career was greatly enhanced by his marvelous performance as the leader of the black man's regiment in 1989's superb film "Glory," which also featured the stunningly attractive and sexy Denzel Washington, who won a supporting Oscar for his performance.

The only scandal to touch Matthew occurred several years ago when he was dating Jennifer Grey and was on a holiday in Ireland. An automobile accident resulted in the death of two people.

When the case came to court, the star didn't attend, leaving his lawyers to make a dramatic plea to the jury. "It is a tragic situation and no one will ever know exactly what happened. I am instructed to indicate that Broderick will always feel extremely upset." Broderick had even written a letter expressing his sympathy to the victims' family.

The charge was reduced to one of careless driving and Broderick was fined £100. There was fury from John Gallagher, whose wife and mother-in-law were the fatal crash victims. "Justlce has not been done," he complained. "The whole thing has been a travesty. Although nothing will bring back Anna or my mother-in-law, or even ease the heartache caused by their deaths I owe it to their memory to publicize our family's feelings at the outcome of the case. It's really incredible that in the circumstances the more serious charge was withdrawn. In my view, the facts of the accident would have justified upholding the more serious charge originally brought against Matthew Broderick."

At the coroner's inquest, verdicts of death from multiple injuries were returned. A police officer who was at the scene of the crash said, "Mrs. Gallagher was travelling on her own side when struck by a vehicle coming from the opposite direction on her side of the road."

Matthew did not attend the inquest. But it was, he said, "a terrible, terrible accident. And it's something I'll remember for the rest of my life. I was badly messed up."

Lately, Matthew's been cast in several comedies not worthy of his enormous talents, although about his performance in "Out on a Limb," Michael H. Price of the *Fort Worth Star-Telegram* said: "Broderick has never been more dashingly silly. Broderick's gift for reactive comedy gets a workout here." We also got the treat of seeing Matthew forced to strip and we have a swell shot of his naked butt. In 'The Night We Never Met," made for $4 million in New York City, Broderick plays a Dean & Deluca buyer who couldn't afford decent housing. He ends up sharing an apartment with two roommates who never actually meet but get to know each other by the clues and belongings they leave in the apartment. He agreed to make the film for scale and may see some profit from it as a video release. To make him appear older, he grew a beard for the role and he's quite sexy with it.

These days, Matthew seems to be getting more press for his love life than his movies. In July of 1992, Robin Adams Sloan broke the news: Sarah Jessica Parker, who was involved with "sexiest man alive" John F. Kennedy, Jr. (before Daryl Hannah – John's attracted to actresses) and was Robert ("Less Than Zero") Downey Jr.'s love-in for seven years, was now dating Matthew, whom Sloan called "the *cutest* man alive." Sarah said all her male friends, except Matthew, are gay and that she likes gay men because they understand her.

She said she had been with Downey for all that time but still isn't sure about him because he "loves to play cat and mouse. His life is such a surprise to me that if he told me tomorrow that he had had a gay experience, I wouldn't be shocked. I'd probably say, 'You know what? That's probably why I love you so much, because you are willing to be whoever and whatever you feel like.' I'll say this, if Robert is gay, he should be open about it."

For his part, Downey says, "I was dishonest with her a lot."

Parker said she was attracted to Matthew because he was: "immediately likable, funny, wonderful and sort of available. It's so nice to date somebody who rides the subway." And he didn't have a "complex" life (such as Kennedy) that would make having a relationship difficult. "Matthew lives in New York where I live, he loves the theater that I love, he loves Broadway musicals. I mean, no one I've gone out with loves Broadway musicals!

"And he's not gay. He would like me to say that once and for all. He asked me who I was doing this for and when I told him he said, 'They out me every other issue.' I said, 'The first thing I'll tell them is that you're not gay.'

"I'm trying to convince him to marry me. All my friends from high school are married. He asks me, 'Does that make you feel bad?' and I say, 'Kinda.' And he says. 'We'll talk about it later.' It makes him nervous when I talk about it. And kids. We talk about kids all the time. I said, 'Can we have children?' And he said, 'Yes.' And I said, 'When can we have them?' And he said, 'In two years.' "

Parker says she doesn't know what makes a good penis except that it's good "if it feels good." Size isn't important to her, "unless it's really small. I would hate to think someone is going to suffer because they have a small penis. What if they are a really great lover and they just have a really tiny penis?

But, in all honesty, I don't want a toothpick. But I'm not interested in a pornographically large penis either. It would be painful. For me, it's really not a prerequisite that the penis be perfect. Let's just say that I'm very happy currently. Let's say I'm satisfied.

"Oh, let's just say Matthew's great! Let's just say that Matthew knows how to treat a woman. And America should know that! He's mine – and he's straight."

Okay already.

Matthew won the Tony award in 1995 as best actor in a musical for his role in the revival of "How to Succeed in Business Without Really Trying," the 1962 Pulitzer Prize-winning Frank Loesser musical on Broadway. "What Matthew does he does better than anybody," says Broderick's girlfriend, actress Sarah Jessica Parker. (She is referring to his acting.) "It's hard to make someone who's a bulldozer seem charming," she explains. The bulldozer in question is J. Pierrepont Finch – the role made famous by Robert Morse.

"How to Succeed" marked Broderick's first stage work in more than seven years, as well as his first musical effort ever. "I didn't want to die never having tried one," says the grizzled 33-year-old veteran. Meanwhile, he was wrapping up production on "Infinity," an independent film of which he is both star and director. Written by Broderick's mother, Patricia, it's a love story based on the marriage of the late physicist Richard Feynman and his first wife, Arlene. Was it difficult working with his mother? "I've always discussed everything with her," Broderick says. Parker insists it's no act: "If Matthew ran one of those shell games on the street, and you lost 40 bucks at it, you'd walk away laughing."

Corey Haim

Corey Haim and his "best pal," Brooke.

Corey Haim

"He is this beautiful little kid, this actor kid, and then he got into drugs, and it's so weird to see in the magazine photographs of what happened to him in just a few months."
- The New York-based photographer Larry Clark

Over the years, I've become obsessed with little 113 pound, blond, blue-eyed bundle of fun named Corey Haim. And I'm not alone. J.R. from Ohio wrote our offices, "Tell John Patrick he's not the only one who'd crawl across several deserts to get to Corey Haim."

The diminutive star has become, if you'll pardon me, a *mini-legend* among gay men who appreciate such adorable packages.

I first fell head over heels in lust for the tyke in 1986's "Lucas," which has as one of its many delights a realistic shower sequence in a high school gym. Then came the stylish vampire comedy "Lost Boys," in which the cutie takes a very sexy bath. By 1989 he was getting rave reviews for his fine thesping. About "Dream a Little Dream," one reviewer raved: "Goofy Corey Haim lends his light and silly charm to provide the few laughs in this film."

And, by then, Corey had became a darling of the teenybopper set. What the fan magazines were heralding as "Haimster-mania" set in. There was even a calendar featuring scenes of the adorable lad in scenes from the horrible horror movie "The Watchers."

But suddenly it seemed Corey was overcome by it all; he started hanging out in Hollywood's infamous fast lane. The reports were discouraging. Like me, Larry Clark, photographer and creator of the best-selling books "Tulsa" and "Teenage Lust," had become enamored of the sexy little star and fretted about his survival.

Said Larry: "But then he came back and got a 900 number. I was curious so I called and he went into this incredible rap about how he was all fucked up on cocaine. He was saying things like 'You just wouldn't believe how everyone in L.A. does cocaine and I was doing so much cocaine I got down to about ninety pounds and my mother put me in rehab.' He must have just got out because he sounded like a reformed drunk: 'I'd rather cut off my arm and throw it out on the expressway than ever do coke again.' He was freaking out. And then I read some articles about it. Now he's probably trying to forget he ever said those things, trying to rehabilitate his image."

During 1990, Corey's sometime-pal and co-star Corey Feldman was arrested on drug charges. The story was that when Feldman found out his girl friend was also screwing both Charlie Sheen and Haim, he "tried heroin to forget." Later Feldman said: "Haim turned his back on me all during the drug problems."

In 1991, Corey appeared in his own video, "Me, Myself and I." His publicist was saying the star wanted to clear the air, to counter rumors that had been flying about him: "We did it to let people know what's really happening in my life. I just wanted people not to still have the wrong impression of me after everything that went down. Things are back to normal now." The 45-minute video includes Corey talking about his life, what it was like before he became an actor, scenes of him playing hockey and baseball (and the one we loved, floating on a raft in a swimming pool), driving his new sports car and his thoughts on the perfect date. Corey's sage advice: "Take the hurdles in life that come to you. Everybody has lots of obstacles to overcome. Just go through them, be patient and everything will happen." I sent a friend of mine a copy of this wonderful video and he called me several days later to say that I had shattered his illusion, that Corey was a "brat." "Exactly the point," I said, "can't you just imagine the scenario when you got him alone? Can't you just see what would happen if you tied him to the bed?" My friend, possessing an imagination every bit as wild as my own, quickly saw my point.

Tying Corey down, or being tied down by Haim, was not only my wish but that of many a young girl, even during Corey's extended rehab period. So great was Corey's popularity he was voted "Male Movie Star of the Year" by *Teen Beat* readers while still incarcerated. When he got out of rehab he appeared in *Teen Beat's* first video format magazine, talking about the movies and taking questions from an audience of screaming young girls. He handled it well, although he appeared to be more "out-of-it" than "with-it."

It was reported that he was back in the fast lane again, hanging out with other stud puppies such as Josh Evans, the handsome young son of producer Robert Evans, and Balthazar Getty, at Hollywood's fashionable Sunset Social Club, presumably drinking Perrier.

In 1991, in 20-year-old Corey's "comeback" film, CineTel Films' "Fast Getaway," he played the 16-year-old son of a bank robber. After testing poorly with preview audiences, the film went directly to video stores, where his gay fans could rent it and enjoy his scenes in tight jeans and drag in the privacy of their own homes.

Then came "Dream Machine," which also went directly to video. *Entertainment Weekly* commented: "Reformed party animal Haim plays a clean-up piano tuner who inherits a Porsche with a corpse in the trunk and is pursued by a killer. If this is meant to be a teen action comedy, just where are the laughs?"

Next Corey was on rollerskates for "Prayer of the Rollerboys," still billed over-the-title and co-starring with Patricia Arquette. This bomb also went directly to video. Now if it'd only have been called "Prayer of the Gayboys..."

Early in 1993, Corey was shooting at targets with his BB gun in the backyard of the home he and his mother share with his manager, Michael Bass. When Corey threatened Bass, he phoned police and had Corey arrested. The charge was reduced to a misdemeanor.

When he isn't in trouble with his handlers, Corey is making movies at a rapid rate. In "Oh! What A Night!" Corey plays a 17-year-old who falls in lust for an older, much married woman. Their tryst in a hayloft could have been a spectacular fuck, but it is filmed in deep blue and Corey appears to have worn his boxer shorts through the whole thing.

Entertainment Weekly duly noted: "The post-Lucas Haim has aged nicely."

Our patience waiting for Haim to become "an adult" on screen was rewarded with the 1993 release of "Blown Away," first telecast on HBO and then released on video. Here Corey bares all at last; well, practically all: his ass is as wonderful as we assumed all along it just had to be.

Corey also appeared in "Just One of the Girls," a dopey made-for-TV movie in which he cross-dresses to avoid a high-school bully, only to have the bully fall in love with him. The bully, a handsome young stud, takes Corey, as a girl, home and kisses him passionately on the lips. Aghast, Corey bolts from the car and runs into the house, dashes upstairs and washes his mouth out with Listerine. Of course, then they cut to another scene and we didn't see what Corey did about his erection. To be truthful, Chad Lowe was much more fetching as a girl in a similar movie, "Nobody's Perfect," but Corey was at least a bit more convincing here than in "Fast Getaway."

"Abbot & Costello, Martin & Lewis...Haim & Feldman? Why not?" Chris Nashawaty asked in *Entertainment Weekly*. "Ever since the two actors dubbed by teenybopper fan mags as 'The Coreys' joined forces as a comedy team back in the '80s, they've been virtually joined at the hip – both on screen and in the irony-soaked minds of their Gen X fans.

"While the duo has been out of the cineplex limelight for years, they've been a fixture in video stores, churning out B movies such as 'Dream A Little Dream 2.' In this lame straight-to-tape sequel, the two play pals drifting apart – that is, until two pairs of psychically enhanced sunglasses arrive in the mail, prompting the appearance of a gorgeous killer and a bungling mobster. As they weakly riff off each other while on the lam, the Coreys look like an unsightly 'after' photo of the bubblegum pinups they were when they first teamed up – hilariously – as paranoid suburban vampire hunters in the otherwise run-of-the-mill 'The Lost Boys.'"

"A year later the Coreys shared the marquee for another suburbia-set romp, 'License to Drive.' Compared with such '80s teen-lust comedies as 'Porky's' and 'Risky Business,' 'License' is pure vanilla. But as a high school loser, Haim taps into some real adolescent neuroses when he fails his driver's test but nonetheless takes his grandfather's Cadillac out for a hot date with a girl named Mercedes when he's egged on by his horny buddy (Feldman).

"Unfortunately, the pair felt the need to grapple with more existential material in 'Dream A Little Dream,' a warmed-over comedy-drama about a high school outcast (Feldman) whose body is taken over by a curmudgeon (Jason Robards). Haim is certainly winning as his punked-out pal, but Feldman fails in his bid to become a serious actor.

"No doubt fearing typecasting, the Coreys stopped working together for four years. In the interim, Feldman pled no contest to cocaine- and heroin-possession charges and Haim starred in 'Prayer of the Rollerboys.' When they reunited for the surprisingly sharp thriller 'Blown Away,' out went the boyish pranks, and in came the slo-mo sex scenes. If this detour seemed too good to be true, it was. Their next gig, the scuba-school farce 'National Lampoon's Last Resort,' is grisly. Haim's dazed Bill & Ted imitation to Feldman's sharp-dressed greasiness, it's clear that if the Coreys plan to keep popping up in the New Releases section, they need a serious makeover, and fast."

Christina Kelly of *Premiere* visited the set of "Last Resort:" "Feldman is very sweet and chatty but is doing all the talking. So when I ask the fourth question – Why do you guys like to work together? –I turn inclusively toward Haim. He has disappeared.

"I faced Feldman again. 'It's our chemistry, our timing,' he says. 'We're really tight together. Nobody works like we work with each other. We started off working together as an accident. They just cast me for 'The Lost Boys' and they cast him for 'The Lost Boys.' I said 'Great.' We started hanging out. And then 'License to Drive' was also a coincidence and it was somewhere after that that people started saying. 'It's the Coreys this' and 'It's the Coreys that.' We kind of rolled with that for a little bit and we did 'Dream a Little Dream' and we said 'That's enough of this because everyone calls us the Coreys and we're like this team and our individual persons are getting lost.' After five years of doing our own thing, we figured people have a good idea of who we are for ourselves now so it's okay to get back into it because obviously...

"I am craning my neck and wondering, Where is Corey Haim?"

"After a few more minutes Feldman is called back to work, and the very nice publicist from Trimark comes over to me. 'Corey Haim feels you're ignoring him,' he says."

At their peak in 1988 Haim, then sixteen, and Feldman, then seventeen, were more notorious than any other young actors.

Their celebrity stemmed not just from the movies they starred in, but from their regular appearances in teen pinup magazines.

Randi Reisfeld, editorial director of 16, says the magazine began covering Feldman when he was eight years old and starring in the "Bad News Bears" TV series. She honed in on Haim on the set of Firstborn in 1984. "I knew then that he had the look of a teen idol: cute, unthreatening, almost feminine," she says. "He was very bubbly and outgoing. Feldman wasn't covered quite as much."

When Kelly asked about their prospects for a comeback, Reisfeld is not optimistic. "Comeback from what?" she asks.

"Feldman owns a modest house on a treacherously winding road in Encino. On the wall of his office is a framed 1986 citation from the Commonwealth of Massachusetts. There's a photo of a younger Feldman and his old friend Michael Jackson on the desk. And, like fellow childhood-stardom survivor Jackson, Feldman keeps lots of toys in his house.

"Feldman was legally emancipated from his parents at the age of fifteen, after discovering (he's said) that most of his money was gone. (Feldman's parents could not be reached for comment.) His drug abuse, though, was his own doing."

Still, in Feldman's mind, his career didn't go downhill until later. "It was basically when I got into heroin, which was right when I was doing 'Teenage Mutant Ninja Turtles,' actually. That was my last film to have a big theatrical release. I don't think I even knew what I was doing by that point," he says. "I was doing some Christian Slater kind of thing in the movie. I thought I was being really interesting. And I watch the movie now and I think the character really sucked."

Feldman was arrested in 1990 for possession of heroin and cocaine. "When I went into rehab I had lost so much of my life that the career was not even one of the priorities in my mind," he says. "I had lost my home and my car and my wife [he married Vanessa Marcil two months after meeting her in 1989], and I was $180,000 in debt. I had lost everything that had meant anything to me. I was spiritually bankrupt. I made a deal with God. And my deal was: He says, 'Okay, I'll give you your life back, you gotta do something for me. You gotta stay sober and you gotta help others achieve that.' I honestly believe that the sole purpose for my being is to express my art and to create. Some people might go, 'He's out of his mind.' But I'm not out of my mind."

"Clearly, Feldman has become extremely sincere and twelve-step now, and though he was always the darker of the two Coreys, they're very different these days. 'Corey and I are like brothers,' he says. 'You'll find from talking to Corey that there's no match of spirituality or intellect in that sense. I mean, Corey's intelligent, but he doesn't put it toward figuring out the ways of the world. He puts it toward having a good time. I really don't think he gives himself enough credit. So I guess my job in the relationship is to keep him inspired and to keep him motivated into going forward.'"

Kelly was finally granted an interview with Haim. "At least half an hour early he calls my hotel room, catches me in the shower, and asks if I can come downstairs and do the interview immediately so he can go to the beach. 'Of course,' I say, in the warmest voice I can muster. I don't want him to feel slighted and leave.

"Haim is sitting with his assistant at a poolside table; he is talking on a cellular phone to his sister. He has the new bleached-blond, shaved, faux-dreadlocked hair, which he has gotten especially for 'Double Switch,' the Sega Genesis video game he is about to start shooting.

"His Caesar salad is delivered with a flourish by a waiter, who douses it with pepper. 'I feel quite lucky at this very second,' says Haim. 'Plus the Caesar salad is very good.' He doesn't seem concerned about whether 'Last Resort' will get a theatrical release, although he does indicate that he is happy with the movie. 'It was so funny,' he says.

"Like Feldman, Haim followed his sister into acting. He was ten years old. 'We applied to become clients at an agency called Faces & Places,' he says, laughing. 'This was in Toronto. Originally it was just gonna be her. I was, like, 'Take me, take me.' Mom took me. Snap, snap. Stanley Jaffe and Sherry Lansing happened to be in my agency one day. They put me in a lineup with 39 other kids. It was between me and one other kid and they flew us both to New York. I met Teri Garr, and she liked me, and I got the part (in 'Firstborn').

"He pauses. 'This happens to be the worst Caesar salad I've ever eaten,' he says, looking upset. 'So I'm going to smoke a cig, if you don't mind.'

"On his relationship with Feldman, he is totally positive at first. 'Oh man, Corey's the coolest. I've known Corey since I was fourteen. Plus he's clean now, so he's even cooler. When we were younger we didn't know about life. And our childhood was weird because of our parents and their problems and being pulled into the business. I mean, Corey started much younger than me. I think I passed him, though, moviewise. We always compare movies.'

"I ask about their hiatus. 'We both didn't want to keep doing movie after movie with each other. It got a little boring – too much 'the two Coreys' thing, you know? So we both had our slump kind of thing and fortunately we're back and we're healthy and we're together again. It just all worked out again. Thank God.'

"When I ask Haim about fame, he says, 'Did you ask Corey that question?' I had. 'What did he say? He's-God's-messenger kind of thing?' I nod.

"Haim sighs. 'I love him and all, it just gets too deep for me sometimes. We did 'Entertainment Tonight' and he said, 'I'm God's messenger through song and dance and vocal something-or-other,' and I blushed, you know? I was embarrassed. I understand, like, I feel I'm God's messenger too, in a certain way, but not as far as holding the Ten Commandments. Which is why we're such good friends, because we're so the same but different."

In *Hollywood Raw*, Joseph Bauer talked to a regular on the Hollywood party circuit, David Faustino, from "Married With Children," who said, "One of the most surprising things, I guess, would be…uh…when Corey Haim was a big star.

"One time, Corey and this big guy…this is a really popular guy, but a man! He's like thirty. He's really fat, big, ugly…rosy cheeks, always wears pink ties. And one time, you know, he always hangs out around Alfie's because he used to be Alfie's boyfriend. Alfie goes both ways. But they don't like each other anymore. They got in a fight. So Haim and this big guy started hanging out together. And one night there they got in a big fight, and Haim spit in his face, screaming at him, 'I've had better lovers than you!' Right in front of everybody. And we all knew right there that Corey was…you know…like…"

Brad Pitt, photographed by Jeffrey Thurnher

Brad Pitt

"*About Brad Pitt, I could write a country song,*
'He May Have Stolen Thelma & Louise's Money,
But He Only Walked Off With My Heart.'"
- Gay Columnist Michael Musto

Handsome stud puppy Brad Pitt, he of the bad-boy grin, the pretty blue eyes and the washboard abs was voted *People Magazine's* Sexiest Man Alive in 1995. And "Most Desirable Male" at the 1995 MTV Movie Awards. We, of course, saw it coming.

Whatever he does, Brad comes off sexy. When Brad was in "Kalifornia," starring as a scraggly, homicidal drifter, *Entertainment Weekly* said: "The idea of being trapped in a car with a psycho is more appealing than it sounds - if the psycho is Brad Pitt." Indeed, *Movieline* magazine said Pitt could "cover himself with cow dung and he'd still be ravishing."

Characteristically, Pitt said he took the unappealing part of ex-con murderer Early Grayce in "Kalifornia" because he didn't want his fans to become so besotted with his beauty and sensitivity that they would sell him short.

Selling Pitt short is about the last thing gay men would ever do; *buying* his body is more like it, or at least as much of him as one would be able to lay one's hands on.

In "Kalifornia" Brad takes a cross-country jaunt with his girlfriend (one time real-life bedmate Juliette Lewis) to visit famous murder sites. His character swigs Lucky Lager, talks in a Southern-fried drawl and blithely picks his toenails at the table. At least he appears with his shirt off. Before filming began, Brad said, "My smile's too perfect. I'm going to have one of these teeth ground away." Conveniently, he chipped a tooth before shooting started, on a bottle of Mountain Dew. At least now we know what to serve him to drink when he stops by the house.

Brad drew mixed reviews for his performance. Michael H. Price, writing in the *Fort Worth Star-Telegram*: "Recalling such fine extreme performances as Dennis Hopper in 'I Died a Thousand Times' (1955) and Martin Sheen in 'Badlands' (1973), Pitt unveils Early by degrees as a figure of brooding wit and escalating menace."

"Pitt is outstanding," raved *Rolling Stone,* "all boyish charm and then a snort that exudes pure menace."

"One of the most harrowing and convincing performances I've ever seen," said Roger Ebert.

But Ty Burr said, "There's nothing to experience in 'Kalifornia' besides a mountain of ostentatious bad acting. Pitt and Lewis are straining for downscale Method seriousness, but with their strenuous 'Hee Haw' accents, both of these gifted young actors come off as embarrassingly mannered. Pitt's performance is straight from the look-how-many-days-I-skipped-washing-my-hair school of grunge integrity – I'm afraid we have the founder, Mickey Rourke, to blame – and two hours of Lewis' precious waif-like stammer is enough to drive anyone crazy."

The New Yorker: "Pitt's snorting, mumbling performance never quite makes it out of his furry beard."

In addition to "Kalifornia," Brad lit up the screen as part of the cast of "True Romance," which stars Christian Slater and Patricia Arquette as a couple on the run from the mob. Joining Brad are Gary Oldman, Dennis Hopper and Val Kilmer. Slater takes plenty of showers in this but, alas, Brad does not.

But all Brad really has to do is just *smile.* Personally, my eyes misted over every time he smiled that "perfect smile" in "A River Runs Through It." *Premiere* magazine nominated Brad's face in the movie as "Most Cinematic Body Part." But with Brad, it's hard to choose which body part is most cinematic, they are all so luscious.

Indeed, Brad Pitt is so comfortable about his looks and sexuality that he doesn't seem at all bothered by all the fuss about his beauty.

"Why would that bother me?" he asks. But he has a harder time defining what is sexy.

"You can't define it," he argues. "And if you do define it, you're going to be wrong. And if you try and play someone who's sexy, you're not going to get it because you're coming from the outside. I can't explain it. But that's why you get scenes that are meant to be sexy but don't work; they are trying too hard."

After seeing "A River Runs Through It," a straight friend asked me, "Who is that kid who played the younger brother?"

"That was Brad Pitt, the cowboy in 'Thelma and Louise.'"

"Oh really?"

Really. Brad first came to the national consciousness in "Thelma and Louise," sticking it to Geena Davis in a Texas motel room. His pivotal screen time was about 14 minutes but they were *big* moments.

Playing the drifter J.D., he became the stuff of both female and gaymale fantasy: polite, devilishly cute, mildly dangerous, and sexually skillful to a fare-thee-well. And then there was his butt; as Thelma purred, "I love to watch him go."

Commented *New York* magazine's David Denby: "A slender young drifter who presents himself as 'a student,' he is sly and exquisitely polite, demure even, though he prances like a show horse. He's obviously no student, but Thelma, goosey as a teenager, finds him irresistible. What follows is one of the rare sex scenes that manage to be funny and truly erotic at the same time. There's one glamorized shot of Brad Pitt's torso that suggests a commercial for sex..."

Yes, seeing Brad's glorious body nude girls began dishing: "Oh, oh," said one, "this is that cute, outlaw, hitchhiker seducer-boy from 'Thelma and Louise.' If he hadn't stolen all their money he'd be perfect." Actress Tina Louise: "Not only is he beautiful, but he's really good. He works organically." (He could work organically for me anytime.)

A fashion critic summed up Brad's appeal in "Thelma and Louise:" "That incredibly cute, totally sexy, to-die-for guy who brought a whole new definition to jeans and cowboy hats."

Critic Holly Millea says she's "mad for Brad: Lean, all legs and lips and liquid movement."

Lean, luscious William Bradley Pitt was born on December 18, 1963, in Shawnee, Oklahoma, but soon thereafter his family moved to Springfield, Missouri, where Brad grew up and went to Kickapoo High School. He studied journalism at the University of Missouri and had completed four years of college but still hadn't graduated. He decided enough was enough and, having always wanted to act, took off for Hollywood. He told his parents he was going west to study at an art school. Brad's father gave him this sage advice for his trip: "Always keep a spare roll of toilet paper in your car." He still does.

"I had a lot of odd jobs...very odd," Brad says about his early years in Tinseltown. "When I first came to L.A., I was just doing whatever people told me to do. I was new and I was just going with the flow." Brad soon found out that in Hollywood, when you look like he does, "Things open up for you," as he put it.

The talent agent that finally took him on determined that Brad was the "pretty boy next door," but the star didn't feel comfortable with that: "There was too much emphasis on the glamour, the teen stuff."

But Brad didn't have much choice, he goes with the flow you'll recall. In 1987, he appeared on the TV sitcom "Growing Pains" with Kirk Cameron. Movies followed, beginning with "Happy Together" starring Patrick Dempsey, with Brad playing a nerd in college. Next came a slasher comedy flick "Cutting Class," with Brad playing a high school student, co-starring with Roddy McDowall. Brad didn't care for either of those but he did like his work in the 1988 film "Dark Side of the Sun" and got to spend three months in Yugoslavia filming it. An experimental film about a boy with a skin disease, it had very limited showings in this country.

Then Brad landed a role on the primetime soap opera "Dallas," near the end of its run, but all they wanted him to do was "stand there and look cute" as Charlie Wade's boyfriend. He wanted more. He did more guests shots until landing a lead role in a series, "Glory Days," about four high school friends, but it was quickly cancelled.

In 1990, Brad got good notices playing a white trash character in the TV movie "Too Young to Die." It was on the set of this production that he met Juliette Lewis, 15 years old at the time.

Next Brad made "Across the Tracks," playing Ricky Schroder's younger brother. A reasonably compelling teen drama, it is notable for the delicious sight of Brad in running shorts. Meanwhile, the Pitt/Lewis romance continued, but things didn't develop too quickly because the lovers soon had to separate, Juliette to film "Cape Fear" in Florida, Brad to do "Thelma and Louise" in Canada. (Brad got the part when Billy

Baldwin backed out to appear in "Backdraft.")

Upon seeing Brad in "Thelma and Louise," Melina Gerosa wrote: "Pitt's washboard stomach, smoldering stare, and all-around boyish allure have the hype-types predictably touting him as the next James Dean."

But Brad's heard enough of the comparison: "There's this thing about every young new guy getting compared to James Dean. I've read it a million times, even about Michael J. Fox."

In 1993, *Premiere* magazine's columnist "Libby Gelman Waxner," after seeing "A River Runs Through It," declared a moment of silent orgasm in honor of Brad. She said, "His smile can actually cause the onset of puberty."

Speaking of orgasms, it seems it really is as columnist Michael Musto said, "The whole world wants to get into Brad Pitt's pants these days."

And some have gotten at least to his lips. When it was announced that Brad would be playing with Tom Cruise in "Interview With a Vampire," Karina Lombard, who was in "The Firm" with Cruise and "Legends of the Fall" with Brad said, "They're both great kissers, but since I get along a lot more with Brad, it would have to be him. We're kissing a lot longer. There's a lot more heat, and I really *respect* him." (In the morning especially, we presume.)

Director Lou DiGiaimo put it best: "There are stars that aren't great actors. But when I met Brad, I thought, 'He's going to be a star and he can act.' His career is going to be capital B-I-G."

Stardom has changed Brad. As he explains, "What has changed is that you can no longer surprise people. It's more that now they expecting it.

"Everyone wants to say you're the new James Dean and later they want to say you're gay." Pitt shakes his head in confusion. "People just amaze me that they want to get you classified. I don't know what to make of all this – the whole movie star thing confuses me."

Pitt's so hot he's got a cool $7 million for "Seven," a thriller in which he co-stars with Morgan Freeman as cops. And, as producer Arnold Kopelson boldly puts it, Brad's "beyond hot". Kopelson, who worked with Harrison Ford on "The Fugitive" and Michael Douglas on "Falling Down," knows a thing or two about charisma. "I knew Pitt was going to be a star but nobody knew he was going to be the star of the magnitude that he is today," he gushes. "He is the grandest movie star of his age group I have seen in 30 years. He's a throwback to the 1940s – we don't see stars like him today and I think he'll go the distance. Brad is a phenomenon."

Anne Rice says, "He is cute. But I have to confess, when he was declared the sexiest man in the world, I nearly fell over dead, because he does look to me like the Barbie Doll. Young and cute. He looks like he's about 14."

Pitt, who doesn't work much with his shirt on, turns down most articles and cover stories because he worries about overexposure. He doesn't talk much; an open shirt signifies enough.

When Pitt isn't making movies - or hanging out at his newly purchased (from gothic scream-queen Elvira), expensively furnished (all antiques and Tiffany lamps) Hollywood Hills home, with his menagerie of snakes, pigs and chameleons he's satisfying three non-sexual loves, usually at the same time: travel, music and architecture.

"I love to get away and I love music," he says. "I think music is the greatest invention in the world. Getting away for me can be just drifting anywhere for a weekend, popping up a tent, making a fire, playing some good tunes.

"I love Europe, too. I went on a publicity tour for 'Thelma' and stopped in Amsterdam for two days, and I saw this sign that said 'Apartments for rent'. I walked in and it was so easy. I gave them the money, they gave me the keys. I stayed for two *months*."

Keanu Reeves, as photographed by Greg Gorman for
Detour magazine in 1993

Keanu Reeves

"Despite his almost legendary inarticulateness and uninspiring gait, he is what the Pre-Raphaelites in the mid-1800s called a 'stunner.'" – Female fan in Cambridge, MA

"I'm not heterosexual and I'm not homosexual. I'm just sexual." – Keanu Reeves

"Keanu," Bruce Hainley wrote in the *Village Voice*. "I will now have to take a deep breath. I'm spent just mentioning him.

"What I love about Keanu is: Keanu. Pluralized he would be *Keanus*, and while I like the unimaginable, two of him wandering around, him twinned, I like even more that as a word, as a concept, it dreamily dissolves into *key-anus*, as if it were the hidden axis certain worlds spin on. To think about Keanu, to consider Keanu, you need no theory except Keanu; no psychoanalysis except your thoughts trying to get around his structures. If you were to write an ode to him, you would need to formulate a new poetics, a poetics of Keanu to do so.

"What would such a poetics encourage? What would such a poem look like? Could you recognize 'poem' anymore, or would you be too dazed and mistake it for something else? What would that something else be? Such a poetics would turn its back carefully away from imaginary categorical separations of porn and poetry, poetry and prose, prose and philosophy, the philosophical and the erotic, etc. What about Keanu's scar, his skin, his empty speech, what about the fact that everything interesting eludes language, and yet language is the best method of approach? If you, pioneer, were to start your poetics at that place where language started to break down, stutter, babble, gush, where thinking became unthinkable, where you were learning to be ignorant, who knows where it or you would begin or end? Since he came to light/ a massive invasion/ of awe filled my life,/ taking more of my love/ than a boyfriend.'"

In an interview with Keanu Reeves for *Interview*, Dennis Cooper pinpointed Keanu's sublimity and provided an index to much of what motivates Cooper's poetics "That daze is one of the things I really love about what you do. You're always kind of talking around what you actually want to say. Most actors just manufacture emotion and expect audiences to match it. With your characters, it's their inability to produce that's the key. They're often, if not perpetually, distressed, spooked, weirdedout by the world. They're always fighting with their contexts." Which is why, even without having seen it, I'm sure the finest Hamlet in the past 50 years or so was Keanu's at the Manitoba Theatre Centre and why presences "like" Keanu (Matt Dillon, Brad Pitt) enthrall: what is seen is not acting but someone in the process of questioning being.

Michael Shnayerson, writing for *Vanity Fair*, met with the star in Minneapolis where he was filming "Feeling Minnesota."

"For months now, Keanu Reeves has been homeless. There's a story attached, but the details are vague. 'It's just something that happened,' Reeves says. So the star of Hollywood screen and Winnipeg stage lives in hotels, moving as the work demands. His latest abode, as he puts it with that odd formality of his –part earnest gentleman, part grown-up Valley dude – is a businessman's hotel in downtown Minneapolis.

"I know to expect that subtly Asian beauty – the dark, intense eyes, the prominent cheekbones, the golden skin. The surprise is Keanu's lanky six-foot frame. On this gray spring afternoon he bears little resemblance to the actor who appeared in 'Speed,' his surprise hit of 1995. The buzz cut has grown out. The strong jaw sports three days' stubble. He's let the action-hero muscles go, too, and, as casually as he seemed to come by it, the chance to be his generation's Schwarzenegger or Stallone."

Inside Keanu appeared in two films during the summer of 1995: the sci-fi thriller "Johnny Mnemonic" and "A Walk in the Clouds," his first full-blown romance.

The writer found Keanu almost painfully shy. "Asked about himself, he squirms like a schoolboy or lapses into silence. He pulls at tufts of his silky black hair and smacks his forehead with his palm. His long arms windmill the air. If the gods of speech respond to none of these appeals, he falls back in his seat with a resigned 'whatever.' Gradually he relaxes, until the moment is right and the question hits a chord. Then out comes an extended riff, clever and original. But not everyone waits around that long.

"In a strange way, Keanu's good manners hurt him, too: he's so decorous he almost seems dim. Asked about his latest films, he says, 'Oh, thank you for asking.' Surprised or distressed, he comes out with 'Oh my gosh!' You can hear the Canadian in that rousing expletive, and certainly his upbringing north of the border explains a lot about him: they're *nicer* up there. But for a hockey goalie turned actor who guards his privacy zone like a scoring box, etiquette is also a perfect defense. Some assume there's nothing behind it; others think he has secrets to hide."

Shnayerson suggests that perhaps in that first flash of national exposure, playing Keanu-as-Ted, the Valley boy in those two "Bill and Ted" movies-offscreen was a smart way to keep the world at bay.

"No," Keanu says, somewhat offended. "I've never played stupid to keep someone distant. I don't play stupid. Either it's been a failure on my part to articulate, or my naivete, or ingenuousness, or sometimes it's the nature of the form.... And you know, I find myself more able to give an explanation of a project five years later than in the middle of it. It's so present-tense! I can tell you how I feel, but its context is harder to explain.... Sometimes when I'm interviewed I'm not ready to do that. So you say *excellent!* And you know what, man? It's O.K."

Keanu radiates a visceral, emotional intelligence found only in the best natural actors. He has character – an old-fashioned moral imperative that shines through in every role – wrapped around a core of reserve, of feelings withheld. Above all, he's a risktaker, gamely plunging into wildly different roles without a thought for the exigencies of image. "He's a brave, resilient actor who takes the knocks and plaudits with equal grace," says Kenneth Branagh. "As a result, he just gets better and better."

The writer found that Keanu asks a lot of questions. Perhaps because he never went to college, perhaps out of innate curiosity. "Shy as he is, he's also learned that asking questions is easier than answering them."

No matter who interviews him, Keanu keeps insisting what

roles he takes have nothing to do with the money.

"The one thing that's constant," Keanu says, "is the acting. That's what it's for."

Nowadays he stays constantly busy. His existence has been described as hermit-like, cloistered, monastic. "Those are too strong," Keanu says. Long silence. "But they're close."

From hotel to hotel, he brings a single suitcase. "I've got it pretty pared down," he says. A couple of pairs of pants, a few T-shirts, socks, underwear, one suit, a sport jacket, a pair of shoes. He has only three possessions of any consequence. A bass guitar, so he can play with his folk-rock band, Dogstar, and two Norton motorcycles, British-made in the 1970s. Which raises the obvious question of what he does with all that money.

"Ah, what do I do?" He thinks about it. "It affords one a certain amount of freedom and travel, and I can buy older Bordeaux. I can afford my two Nortons, which is akin to sending a child to a middle-expensive university in the U.S. But the travel is great."

In between movies, Keanu appeared in "Hamlet" in Winnipeg. He went alone with his suitcase and found a city giddy with anticipation. One local paper announced a daily Keanu watch. For the play's sold-out run, hotel rooms were booked by Keanuphiles, mostly women, from all over the world; one woman flew all the way from Australia to sit through eight performances. "The thing that impressed me on the first day," recalls Stephen Russell, a veteran of 17 Stratford Festivals, who played Claudius in the production, "was how much *work* he had done. This was not going to be a star turn or walk in the park. And what I realized, too, was how his principles are etched in stone. He carries a lot of weight extremely well."

With international press in attendance for opening night, the weight of expectation felt suddenly crushing. Even now, Keanu groans at the memory. "One of the most horrific nights of my life, oh my gosh! I was surviving, not performing." The critics agreed. Keanu, they wrote, seemed overwhelmed by the soliloquies; one declared he simply lacked the equipment to handle Hamlet's melancholy, and came alive only in the fight scenes. "But," Keanu says, "it got better."

So wrote Roger Lewis in *The Sunday Times* of London. Lewis stuck around to see Keanu's confidence seep back in later performances, and declared his Hamlet terrific. "He quite embodied the innocence, the splendid fury, the animal grace of the leaps and bounds, the emotional violence, that form the Prince of Denmark," he reported. "He is one of the top three Hamlets I have seen, for a simple reason: he is Hamlet."

It was while he was in Winnipeg, Keanu says, that he first heard the rumor that had originated in Italian and Spanish newspapers, then spread to all of L.A. and New York: not only was he gay but he had even entered into a secret marriage with producer David Geffen. Keanu swears he's never even met Geffen. He first heard the rumor when he was in Winnipeg and Claire, a friend, called him and left a message, "I hear you got married. Congratulations."

"I've never laid eyes on him," Geffen confirms, by now more than a little exasperated by the question. "It's a phenomenon: people make this stuff up. I even had a friend say that his trainer said he was at the wedding! You think I could keep something like that *secret?* And then people said I bought Keanu $15,000 worth of clothes at Barneys. I mean, come on. Sure, I'd buy him some clothes, but he doesn't need that. It's just an ugly, mean-spirited rumor meant to hurt him because he's a movie star."

Speculation about Keanu's sexuality goes back at least five years, when Dennis Cooper interviewed him and asked him directly if he was gay. Keanu denied it, adding, rather sweetly, "But ya never know." And of course, Keanu has never had an high profile romances with women; he took his sister to the Oscars. I mean, honey, what's a girl to think?

For his part, Keanu says, "Well, I mean, there's nothing wrong with being gay, so to deny it is to make a judgment. And why make a big deal of it? If someone doesn't want to hire me because they think I'm gay, well, then I have to deal with it, I guess. Or if people were picketing a theater. But otherwise, it's just gossip, isn't it?" But he did joke to his manager, "I guess I should return the clothes."

Another interesting fact is that Keanu's first starring role in his first professional stage play was "Wolfboy," a production with homoerotic overtones. He was cast as a young innocent placed in a psychiatric hospital, only to be set upon by a deranged boy who believes he's a werewolf.

"I didn't want professional actors," recalls director John Palmer. "So I advertised in the personals. I got totally fucked--up hustlers" – and Keanu, who arrived in torn jeans but looked great. For the play's largely gay audience, Palmer persuaded Keanu to appear in a workout scene doing push-ups in white shorts. "You get this innocent kid, one of the most gorgeous kids anyone's seen, in white shorts – and we *oiled* them.... What do you want for 10 bucks?"

Every Sunday, Keanu went to a community theater school called Leah Posluns. One of his close friends there was Alan Powell, with whom he starred in a workshop production. "We'd play off each other; the chemistry was dynamic," Powell says. Keanu, he adds,"was the friend I'd never had as a child. But he was a secretive guy about his life. You could be hanging with the guy for three years; suddenly he'd introduce you to someone who turned out to be a friend of his all that time. You could never get close to the guy."

In the summer of 1995, Keanu appeared on the cover of OUT magazine, with the headline: "Keanu Sets the Record Straight." Ha! Tim Allis began his story by saying, "Keanu Reeves is a '80s twist on poetry in motion. He's got the soulful, 'hey, whatever man' languor of the nameless generation." Keanu told Allis, "I really don't want to talk about my private life." When Allis reminded Reeves that gay men found him sexy, he said, "That's cool."

The interviewer went with Keanu to a bar in Minneapolis. "His presence sends ripples through the after-work crowd, and soon an autograph seeker moves in, followed by another. He takes the intrusions with good humor, even bantering as he signs the proffered scraps." Robert Kamen says that during the shooting of "A Walk in the Clouds" Keanu was stopped like this all the time. "How do you do it?" Kamen asked at last. Keanu shrugged and said, "I'm Mickey [Mouse]. They don't know who's inside the suit." Kamen remembers telling Reeves, "But you're a movie star." Keanu laughed, "So's Mickey."

Now Keanu would like to tour with his band, Dogstar. "We're getting pretty good," he says. "It's folky, but not Joan Baez folky." The group, he thinks, is almost ready to record an album. "But we have to write better songs."

Even with no album out, the band drew sellout crowds on its first club gigs. "He doesn't understand the fuss," says Ken Funk, who started managing the group three years ago strictly out of friendship for Keanu. (He was actually a hockey buddy.) "We were having dinner at a restaurant one night and the hostess, who was gorgeous, kept looking at him adoringly. I said to Keanu, 'I wish I could be you for five minutes, just go up and talk to that girl the way you could.' 'I couldn't do that,' he said. And he was serious. He said to me once, 'I'm from the earth, too.' I'm still figuring that one out."

In 1995, the band embarked on a 25 city Dog Days of Summer tour. Reeves it seems speaks the universal language. "In Japan, if Keanu scratched his head, they screamed," says drummer Robert Mailhouse. "If he went to tie a shoelace, people fainted."

Entertainment Weekly said, "Observers place Dogstar's sound somewhere between alterna-stalwarts Green Day and Dinosaur Jr, with gold stars awarded more for the band's enthusiasm than proficiency. But Reeves knows most fans give more attention to his pecs than his chops – 'that's basically our whole audience,' he admits."

"Mysterious as he may be," Shnayerson says, "even to his closest friends, Keanu is, on another level, as simple as he says: a happy man, doing what he wants to do, only what he wants to do, and getting paid to do it."

Christian Slater

Christian Slater

"Christian Slater has 'Do Not Underestimate' written all over him. He might be having a great career if Hollywood weren't in a severe creative slump. After all, he's charismatic and a natural actor who seems to respect his own limits."
– Critic Rebecca Morris

Limited is the best way to describe the career of Hollywood's favorite bad boy so far. But his popularity with his fans is apparently unlimited. Christian Slater's been the darling of the teenyboppers longer than anybody we can think of but, like Matt Dillon, he has never had what would be considered a major hit movie. "Mobsters" was supposed to be, but it was, as critic Rebecca Morris points out, too-high concept with no feet on the ground. "Slater didn't help," she says, "he proved as misdirectable here as he has been directable elsewhere." He did appear in "Robin Hood," but his part was a supporting one and mysteriously abbreviated."

Speaking of being supported, could the answer to Christian's being a teen idol for far longer than any other star be that perhaps girls instinctively know what's been rumored for a long time, that Christian has what it takes to be a very satisfying fuck?

Indeed, Slater's equipment might well fall – or hang, as it were – in the legendary class. Michael Musto started the rumor that Holly Woodlawn's memoir, "A Low life in High Heels," would be made into a movie by Harvey ("Torch Song Trilogy") Fierstein, with Johnny Depp and Christian as Holly and Jackie Curtis. "If it were true," said Musto, "some serious banana tucking is in order." This was in a Musto column devoted almost exclusively to dish about Roddy McDowall's having one of Hollywood's largest bananas since King Dong fell off the Empire State Building."

Tucking big bananas aside, one thing we know for sure about Christian: he does have a beautiful ass and every time we want to salivate over it again we have only to slip "The Name of the Rose" back into the VCR. In the film, a teenaged Christian plays Adso, a novice monk in a 13th century monastery who is seduced by a peasant girl. The film's director wanted to achieve a realistic love scene so he asked the two actors to rehearse as much as possible and word got around when it was actually filmed there was very little "pretending" going on. Christian remembers, "Here I was, sixteen and naked while this crew of Italians, French and Germans covered that fucking scene from every angle!"

And, in what might be the understatement of all time, Slater adds, "Yeah, I've done some pretty ballsy shit, man!"

His stripping for the movies began at age 12; he broke down crying on the set of "The Invisible Boy" because the script called for him to take off his clothes. But by age 14, when he was told to pull down his pants for the film "Twisted," a film that was never released, he did it. The following year he had to wear a dress and lipstick and a wig in "The Legend of Billie Jean." But, finally, he called a halt when a scene in "Heathers" called for him to show off some of his body, he said, "No, no, no, I'm not showing off any of my things. None of that. I've already put myself on the line. I didn't have to do it again."

But when he made "Robin Hood," with Kevin Costner, Chris was happy because the wardrobe department gave him what he described as "an incredibly large codpiece to wear. They attached it to my costume and I was very honored. But when people see that movie, they won't be watching me, they'll be looking at that codpiece."

Speaking of putting it on the line, ever since Christian landed in Hollywood he has had a reputation as "wild." This has led to speculation about his sexual tastes, but he says: "Anybody who knows me personally pretty much knows that I'm very into women. I do love women. I mean, who knows, maybe I'll get struck on the head with lightning and find that I really like guys, but I really, really doubt it."

And here we thought he looked so fey at times, what with his hair so blond in "The Legend of Billie Jean," playing a character named Binx whose sister was played by Helen Slater (no relation), so he had to dye his locks. And later, he got even cuter in "Gleaning the Cube," with a funky streaked blond hairdo, playing a kid who solves a murder while chasing bad guys on his skateboard.

But whatever the color of his hair, Christian's roots as a stage performer shine in his consistently fine performances. He has the presence that comes with experience. As a youngster, he appeared on the Broadway stage. In 1978, he appeared in a revival of "The Music Man" with Dick Van Dyke. His co-star Meg Bussert, recalls: "He was just adorable! He was so lovely! Of course, he was only nine."

His next show was "Copperfield," which was a swift flop, as was his follow-up, "Macbeth." His next musical, "Merlin," also bombed. Christian fled to television, where he appeared on "All My Children," then "Ryan's Hope," before getting into films.

The movie "Heathers" was Christian's big breakthrough. The role permitted the actor to use his patented Jack Nicholson imitation to the fullest and his characterization of a cool, quiet kid who turns out to be a killer, made him a star in Hollywood. Says Michael Kaplan: "He is an uncommonly talented, intense performer who with the waggle of an eyebrow or a twitch of his upper lip can quickly turn menace into a majestic goof."

The term "majestic" sometimes applies to the star's sex life as well. After practicing for years with a pillow, Christian began actively pursuing his co-stars. During the filming of "Heathers," Christian got very close to co-star Kim Walker. When he was on the daytime soap, "Ryan's Hope," he chased Yasmine Bleeth but she wouldn't give him the time of day, involved as she was with Grant Show, before she went on to date another co-star on the show, Luke Perry.

Christian's career has always been in jeopardy, however, but not because of his romantic escapades, rather his drunk driving arrests. Once, his black Saab got "close and personal" with a couple of telephone poles. But after having his license suspended he retired from drinking and began going to A.A. meetings. He had to learn to get a grip on who he was: "I realized I can't escape this body. So I can either be my own best friend or my own worst enemy, and I choose to be my own best friend." Speaking of friends, when asked once which he thought made better friends, men or women, Christian answered: "Transvestites, because you get a little of both."

Yet the hazel-eyed, nearly six-foot tall actor still does things "to extreme." "I just do it without risking anybody's life, particularly my own. Everybody thinks life is over when you stop (being wild) but I still have a lot of fun." (We'll bet.) His mother says, "He's not an intellectual by any means but he's a good person."

Lately, a more conscientious Christian has been involved with the Pediatric AIDS Foundation. He directed a fund-raiser, a play called "The Laughter Epidemic."

"It was about a mean old guy," Christian says, "Dr. Needle who takes control of this small town. He takes power over the people, and teaches them all that to be whiny, miserable, and pitiful, is really the way to be. He gives prescriptions to make your cold worse and worse - that kind of thing. Then, there's one little boy who remembers that smiling is really the key to life. It's cute. We raised a lot of money, surprisingly enough to me.

"I enjoyed directing the play. I really had a good time. The people that were hired were friends of the family, so that made it a little bit easier for me. The only thing I tried to do was to keep things in perspective; this wasn't going to be a career-making opportunity for anyone. It was purely something to do to give back, to raise money for AIDS, to help out, and just to have fun."

On a personal level regarding the Plague, Christian says: "I'd been an idiot many times and I'm not proud of it. AIDS was the last thing on my mind. I did everything I could to avoid thinking about it. It's a nightmare. It really is. In a way, it has forced me to really deal with some things, maybe even grow up even faster, and maybe even take relationships very seriously. I don't want to say AIDS is the only reason I'm in a relationship now, that's not the reason at all. When you're in love with somebody, you're in love with somebody, that's it. But, it definitely has changed my outlook. All of the people I idolized growing up were all wild, care-free kooks, who I used to hear all of these legendary stories about, and it sounded like fun! That's not really the answer to happiness, or life, so in a way, it's helped me to take that part of my life a little more seriously.

"Now I've started signing autographs, 'Safe Sex from Christian Slater.'"

Slater didn't play it safe with his performance in "True Romance," released in the end of 1993. As an amiable loner who works in a comic book store in Detroit, worships Elvis ("in fact, at one point he croons, "I'm no fag, but if my life depended on it, I'd fuck Elvis") and spends his off-hours sitting through kung fu triple features at the local schlock movie house. During the publicity rounds for the picture, Christian was asked, "If you had to fuck a guy – " and responded, "It's just, uh, so not comething that I'm interested in doing, really. There's no guy I can think of. If Elvis *were* I probably would want to fuck him. But I'm just not up that alley, you know. I've said things about Jack Nicholson. I said once I'd lick his eyeballs. I guess it would be best of I picked somebody who was dead, like James Dean. It would suck if I picked somebody who was alive and then saw him aftyer he read the article!"

Christian gave a touching performance in "True Romance." *Rolling Stone* raved: "Slater is terrific, reminding us of the vigorous promise he showed before sinking in the shallows of 'Mobsters' and 'Kuffs.'"

The New Yorker found Slater's performance to be "smirking, unauthentic," but Manohla Dargis liked everybody in the picture, especially the guys: "The performances are creamy. If nothing else, the preponderance of pretty guys makes obvious that the film's real romance isn't between men and women but men and men. Working the same homoerotic turf as 'Reservoir Dogs,' it tests the limits of fear, desire, and masculinity with a razor wit and surprising heart. Clarence may screw his girl but he's saving the innuendo for the boys."

One thing is certain: it's seldom quiet around Slater. In late December of 1994, Slater was stopped at New York City's Kennedy Airport, where authorities found in his carry-on bag a 6.5-mm handgun and a diamond engagement ring. Since he didn't have a permit to carry a gun, he spent a night in jail and was later sentenced to three days of community service. The ring was for Nina Huang, seven years his senior. He gave her the ring, but in April, Huang was suing him. A Slater pal says the actor could no longer tolerate Huang's attempts to control him. Slater's mom said, "He gave her anything she wanted. Nothing was enough."

Christian says: "I think through the course of my life, I've always been a little of a misfit. I've been a little bit confused as to exactly where I want to go, what direction I want my life to take, and the type of person I want to be – I think naturally it just bled over into the types of characters that I'm trained for. But then there's the other side of me that does like calmness and some sense of stability, and that's where I'm getting to now. There's a bit of staying away involved. It's like a drug - when you walk through a press line and they're yelling your name. The feeling for me used to be very exciting, overwhelming, and thrilling, and now, it's a little uncomfortable. It makes me a little uneasy. I try and shy away from it a bit because it can give you a false sense of importance.

"There is a great deal of importance to it, but it can't be the source of my happiness, and the core of who I am. I don't want that to be the core of what I am. And, by me trying to develop those qualities, hopefully I'll be able to play more characters, and just get a little more in touch with who I am."

"He's very youthful looking," casting director Bonnie Timmerman says, "and I think that's hurt him. But I think leading man parts will be coming to him soon. He simply has to grow into it."

Slater says all he wants is never to be in the situation where he might have to take a part just to make the money. "That would bum me out," he says. "I'm in this business because it's fun and it's enjoyable. I just want to do things that I can be proud of, you know?"

BOOK II.

LEGENDARY
PORN STARS

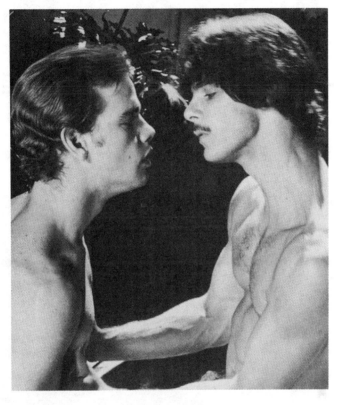

Kip Noll and Jon King,
courtesy of Catalina Video.

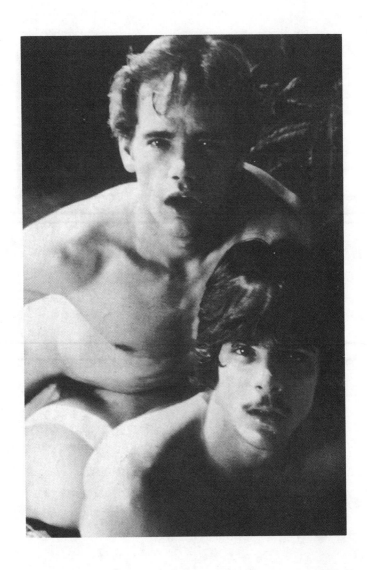

INTRODUCTION:
FRAGILE MEMENTOS

Near the end of Tennessee Williams' play "Camino Real," the character Jacques Casanova stands in the street outside the hotel from which he has been evicted. His suitcase is about to be thrown from the balcony above. Jacques raises his hand, palm upward, as if to stay the fall. As the portmanteau drops from the hand of the hotel manager, Jacques cries out in despair, "Careful, I have fragile mementos."

Occasionally, I'll caress my TV, even kiss it for all the pleasure it's given me. Coupled with my VCR, all I have to do is slip in a cassette, one of my many "fragile mementos," and, as if by magic, there are the boys of my dreams.

Now, to the Feds, I raise my hand, palm upward, as if to stay the fall: I don't want them to seize my "fragile mementos." They've outlawed other forms of adult entertainment, so the forbidding of homoerotic videos would seem to be the next logical step. Such action would put places like my local video rental store and Video Babylon out of business. "Video Babylon is what home entertainment is all about," John Waters says about a visit to *his* favorite video store. "Where else can you expand your film literacy, explore your sexual fantasies, and, if you're lucky, get asked out on a date by a real-life psychopath? "At Video Babylon, porno (excuse me, adult video) costs $3.25 to rent, 50 cents more than regular tapes (guilt tax?). It's located in what appears to have been a sub-basement. The ceiling is so low that if you are six feet tall you literally have no choice but to hang your head in shame as you visually cruise the neatly categorized inventory (gay, bi, straight, chubby-chaser), subdivided by racial preferences - white ("Edward Penishands"), black ("Black Throat"), Hispanic ("Border Buns"). So what if porno is the worst date you could have on a Friday night? So what if it has all the appeal of watching a gallbladder operation? It's safe, isn't it? Maybe people need this stuff to decide what their sexual antasies really are. I never knew that lots of single, straight women rent gay male porno until the clerk told me, did you?"

Well, we did, but we'd rather not think about it. In fact, Jeff Stryker's "Just You and Me" is designed to be enjoyed by both gay men and heterosexual women. He's the master, that stud. And then there was a similar video by handsome Ryan Idol, but it isn't nearly as arousing because it's not as "earthy." Still, it's nice to see these studs doing what they do so well – making love to themselves. Seeing them carry on helps us fantasize about what it would be like to be there with them; it's real, immediate. Indeed, if sex in mainstream movies is the sex we imagine, then sex in adult videos is the sex we see. But the standards must be different. The erudite critic Bob Satuloff in the *New York Native* described this queer, literally, genre of film best: "Are porn movies subject to the same narrative demands as other films? This has been answered with a resounding no. Talking to people about porn, they often say they would enjoy it if it had real plots and characters, with sex scenes that are motivated. Structurally, the parallel would be the musical comedy book, with sex scenes taking the place of the musical numbers. (There are, if you think about it, around the same number of sex scenes in a porn movie as musical numbers in a musical.) The people who are in favor of this approach, however, don't seem to be the genre's core audience. Those who support it seem to prefer one sex scene after another, with as little time spent in between as possible."

What they also expect is hot sex and the men who can deliver on demand, and do so time after time, can build up a following. Questions of personal taste aside, a sexy man is a sexy man, although, as Quentin Crisp says, "Americans prefer cuteness." He recalls: "I was asked to judge the most beautiful men in the world for a magazine called *Blueboy*. On that occasion, there was only one contestant who could be seen to have improved upon his natural measurements and skin tone. He got nowhere. The first prize went to an underfed, blond, blue-eyed boy who smiled a lot. I know Americans do not like beauty; they prefer cuteness.

"I attended a symposia which featured ten strippers. The question of whether the erotic gyrations of the young men assembled would incite audiences to more far-fetched or more pernicious sexual activity than they would otherwise have attempted was not discussed; there was never a mention of sin, without which the word pornography has no meaning. I would have thought that the real objection to pornography in any form was that it tries to sell sex without mentioning the price - the various diseases, the emotion and physical exhaustion, and so on."

But, thankfully, even in an age when headline-hungry dinosaurs like Senator Jesse Helms (R-N.C.) would ban all discussion (even mention of) male sexuality, the porn producers persist. It's not the same as it was back in the golden age of porn, when it was chic and made with great care, but thanks to video, all of it is available to us. The good, the bad, the beautiful, the ugly. Sex is so much trouble these days and porn has become a low-risk variant.

Oh, it's not perfect. As critic Gerri Hershey says, "Orchestrated celebrity sex, however photogenic, can never approach the molten attraction of daily life passionately lived. It's ritual versus the real thing, and it's an apt metaphor for the uses of sex in our culture. Alas, we live in tepid times, and we've got more pandas than monkeys. The passionate are the endangered species. It ain't natural."

No, it ain't, but it'll do, until something better comes along. Like the right man.

By the very nature of the porn industry, there is a better chance of getting into bed with a sex performer than with a movie or rock star. Many have advertised liberally in gay publications. Others have depended on a network of wealthy gays to sustain themselves during lean periods. If you are lucky enough to live in New York, Hollywood, or San Francisco your chances of meeting a porn star are greatly enhanced, but there is always the option of traveling to them or having them visit you.

This phenomenon of the "porn star fuck" is the basis of Dennis Cooper's novel *Frisk.* "Everything I do is based on an urge that I don't understand, though I keep trying to understand it," says the character Dennis, as he flies from LAX to JFK to meet the blank-eyed young hustler/porn star of his current dreams, the one to whom he will explain: "You fascinate me so much that in a perfect world I'd kill you to understand the appeal.

"I can actually imagine myself inside the skins I admire," he confesses. "I'm pretty sure if I tore some guy open I'd know him as well as anyone could, because I'd have what he consists of right there in my hands, mouth, wherever." Dennis refers to his murderous compulsion as "religious," at one point comparing it to an Aztec sacrifice. Later in the book, Dennis concedes that the reality is always less than the fantasy and that resentment causes him to murder his dream dates.

"Desire," writes book critic C. Carr, "at its most extreme is tantamount to murder, a wish to possess or incorporate the love object, thus obliterating it."

Obliterating the objects of my fascination was never my intention when I arranged to meet porn performers over the years. I always approached my time with them as an educational experience and even though most of the time the actual event didn't live up to my exalted expectations, years later, I can still get off watching them on video, remembering my short time with them, editing out what one of my former lovers called all of the "idiosyncratic bullshit."

Yes, thanks to video, reality is enhanced. Thank goodness for Philo Farnsworth, the man who is credited for inventing the television set. His vision has enriched the lives of generations and has kept us informed and illuminated. And day after heartbreaking day, the TV is always there, now coupled with the VCR, ready to spring to life, offering up our idols. We don't even have to leave our bedrooms to enjoy them at their very best. Sex seems most perfect at one remove, unspooling in tape-loops and a VCR remote control is the perfect tool for watching these sexual legends. Ultimately, desire is expressed with the body but it begins in the mind and, in your fantasies, sex can be anything and everything you want it to be.

And those images, Cooper says, "can't lead anyone to a place where he wasn't headed for already. Fantasy becomes an end unto itself."

Peter Berlin, as sketched by
Robert W. Richards

Peter Berlin

"Exhibitionism is a perversion marked by
a tendency to indecent exposure."
- Webster's Dictionary

A man who carried exhibitionism to its fullest meaning was Peter Berlin. After becoming something of a legend in his adopted habitat, the Polk Street section San Francisco, the German emigre somehow got the money together to finance "Nights in Black Leather," an esoteric film featuring intense scenes of exhibitionist and abuse that are bone chilling.

The popularity of "Nights" led to the financing of "That Boy," an almost lyrical study in body worship. Sexy Peter gets off on narcissistically posing and letting admirers suck him off. But like all good fiction, there is an irony here. Peter becomes infatuated by a boy who is blind. The boy can't see the splendidly lean, taut body Peter created, he can only feel it.

And those were his films. Peter Berlin made a career out of appearing in only two, films that were big box office when they were released to theaters and, as videos, remain steady sellers. They are a must for anyone's collection of classic gay porn. Even those who don't care for uncut meat will find these a turn-on, worth returning to again and again.

As Ted Underwood wrote in *Stallion*: "The opening sequence of 'Nights' remains among the most torrid footage ever committed to film. The cassette, like the film, suffers from muddy sound and color variability, but there has never been anyone quite like Peter. His presence alone makes this a landmark film."

Peter became something of fashion legend, too, because he designed all of his clothes himself.

After the success of the films, he divided his time between San Francisco and New York, where we were able to visit with him. He suggested we meet at one of his favorite venues, the baths. He was barefoot and he wore raspberry-colored pants that clung to his body, a cross between sweats and panty hose. His blond hair was streaked with sun and his skin was deeply tanned from a summer on Fire Island. We asked him how the

"Peter Berlin look" came about.

"Very, very sort of natural," he said softly, his voice revealing traces of his German origins. "Before I was Peter Berlin for the public, I was Peter Berlin for myself. When I was seventeen, I started to take in my pants. I felt they didn't show the body like they should. You could buy tight pants but they didn't show the crotch and that was for me, and still is, the nicest part of the male body.

"What I did was to take in the outer seams, straight down. But then I realized I had to redo the entire thing because there was not enough material in certain places to accentuate the crotch, so next I started from scratch and went with the same idea as ballet dancers on stage.

"There are three ways you can wear the cock: left, right, and in the middle. If you wear it in the middle, sort of bundled up, then you might wish to add a cockring, making the whole thing look – um – firm. But if you wear it off to the side, which I think is more sexy, a cockring pushes up the balls in a way that can look funny.

"I find it unfortunate when people say you should leave something to the imagination. Well, most people don't have any so I choose to run around naked-but-not-naked.

"I can get an erection by just looking at myself in the mirror. And I always get dressed for sex rather than undressed. The idea of coming inside your pants by just having pressure or movement is such a different, exciting experience." Reflecting on it, I now consider Peter one of the first true proponents of "safe sex."

"I enjoy sex without ever taking my cock out," he said. "I don't have to penetrate to have completely satisfying sex. I can have sex in the subway, on the street and no one could arrest me for it. I can reach orgasm just by standing on the street corner."

He permitted me to grease his body with oil and then told me, "I am going to dress you for sex." And after adorning me with a sailor suit and cap, he demonstrated just how easily and how quickly I could come in my pants.

Peter also understood that the creation of an image is so much easier for people to deal with than with a real person: "You don't want to have sex with a person with problems, with a mother and father, and this and that. You want an image. And because of those reasons, I think I fit into many people's fantasies. Because it is not a person they deal with, but an image that has been beautifully created."

Casey Donovan's famous pose for the cover of
After Dark magazine.

Casey Donovan

*"'Boys in the Sand' was one of the first X-rated gay male features.
Filmed on Fire Island, this trio of dreamlike sex encounters features
Casey Donovan. In the first duet, Casey rises from the sea to have
sex with bearded sunbather Dick Fisk; in the second, he receives a
magical answer to his sex-matching ad; in the third, a handsome
black telephone installer helps Casey out with his pole."*
- Bijou Video Guide

Wakefield Poole, a former dancer and choreographer and a
former member of the Ballet Russe de Monte Carlo, directed
what is generally thought of as the first gay porn film of real
quality, "Boys in the Sand." It opened in New York on
December 29, 1971 at the 55th St. Playhouse and grossed
$25,000 its first week and continued at that pace for nineteen
consecutive weeks before opening, with equal success, in many
big cities. The film's success made its star Casey Donovan an
instant gay celebrity. And he stole my heart.

The young blond became an obsession with me after a friend
of mine wrote me about the time he met Donovan in New York
City: "I was working in the Chrysler Building and had a
four-to-midnight shift. I would commute on the Long Island
Railroad and got to the City two hours before my shift so I
would have time to hit all the shops and theaters on 42nd
Street. I would also frequent the Regency Baths. I noticed him
immediately, cruising the corridors on the floor where the small
rooms were. His towel was folded in half so his ass cheeks and
head of his cock fell below it. I thought I recognized him from
somewhere and, as I kept walking, it dawned on me. He was
the blond kid in "Boys in the Sand!" When I saw him again,
he was in a room at the end of a corridor and he had his legs
spread so I could see up the towel. I entered the room and he
smiled. He didn't say a thing as I approached him and began to
run my hand up his thigh. Quickly my hand disappeared under
the towel and I fondled his balls. Soon, I was stroking his hard
cock. When he brought his own hand to my cock, I reached

over and shut the door. I dropped my towel, then opened his. He moved over so he could suck me. He gave great head but what struck me more than anything was how beautifully smooth his skin was, stretched over nice tight muscle. I got up on the bed with him and we 69-ed for awhile. Then I pulled his legs up and started eating him out. He kept telling me to go deeper. He had some lube so I used it and started to fuck him. He told me to go easy because I have a big cockhead.

"As I pressed into him, he screamed, 'Oh huge! Huge! I love it! Fuck me hard, deeper, deeper!' Funny how you remember joyous moments like that! I fucked him legs-up for awhile, then we tried it doggie-style. Eventually, he begged me to let him sit on it and was I ever glad he did. I've never had anyone bounce up and down on my cock the way he did! I finished when I put him on his back again, cumming inside of him. We kissed and he told me it was great and that I should come back later.

"I went down to the steam room and was enjoying the rest when someone came in and said a gang-bang was going on upstairs. By the time I got there, six guys were in a queue outside Casey's room. The blond star was bent over the bed taking each guy in turn and by the time I got there, cum was oozing out of his ass. When he noticed who his next assailant was to be he smiled and said he was glad I was back. I jabbed him hard for awhile but it just wasn't the same. Pulling out for the last time, I told him it was fun and that I was late for work. As I left the room, several new faces were lining up outside the door."

I was not to have my own time with him until several years later and I'm afraid ten years after I fell in love with him in "Boys in the Sand," Casey impressed me more as a friend than a sex object. I got so wrapped up in asking questions about his various film escapades, I lost interest in what Casey would be like in bed, but he was, after all, a hustler, and he wanted me to have my money's worth so he quickly got me back in the mood, but I regret I must have been a boring fuck for him. Whenever I see a cock-ring, I always think of Casey. Up to that time, I'd never been in the company of a man who wore one. I'd seen them in movies and assumed men who have to fuck a lot for a living always seem to be equipped with them. Casey told me I was right. "King of the Cock Rings," I called him.

"It helps," he replied.

Casey, born John Calvin Culver in Canandaigua, New York, had a bachelor's degree in education and taught school. During the summer, he would act in summer stock. He was brought into the Poole venture after it had begun filming. The story goes that the boy Poole wanted to use as the star demanded more and more money and the director turned to Casey, who had already filmed one scene, to be in the three other sequences.

"Boys" was not Calvin's first gay porn flick. He earned his name by replacing the star of a film who chickened out at the last minute. The film, for which Calvin got $125 a day for four days' shooting, was titled "Casey" and Calvin became Casey Donovan.

Through friends he met Poole and he was invited to join in the fun as Poole shot what he called a home movie on Fire Island. Casey recalled, "Wake had gone to the Park Miller Theater and was bored out of his skull thinking, 'How come faggots can't do better than this cheesy stuff? How unromantic. How ugly.'" And a legendary film was the result. "People all over the world know me from it," Casey recalled. "It actually made the Variety top fifty in grosses and was reviewed by them. It made me immediately recognizable in New York and as it opened around the country I became a national celebrity. There was nowhere I could go in the cities where it was showing that people didn't do double takes. I loved it, I got off on it, and, looking back, I think I handled it well.

"It made me feel really special. Then I realized that if one movie, an *After Dark* (an entertainment magazine popular at the time) cover and a few stills and a show for Valentino could make people react that way to me, think of what it must be like to be Bette Davis! That thought calmed me down and gave me some perspective. My whole existence is based to this day on that one movie. I've done many others – some obscene, some never seen – but everything is predicated on 'Boys in the Sand,' including my hustling."

He also had a few appearances in straight porn, including the infamous "Ginger" in which he is tied spread-eagled to a bed, seduced and then castrated. In 1973, he appeared in Radley Metzger's "Score," filmed on a resort island and he told me it was one of his most memorable experiences. Meanwhile, as Calvin Culver, he pursued his modelling career and appeared on stage in plays. His most famous role was in a revival of "The Ritz," set in a gay bathhouse, in 1983.

Casey made a remarkable impression in the early '70 soft-core hit, "Score," filmed by Metzger on a pretty little island in the Adriatic off Yugoslavia. That role led to his being cast by Metzger in the straight film "The Opening of Misty Beethoven," the blockbuster hit of 1976 and judged to be one of the best porn flicks of all time. Because of his legendary expertise with the dildo, he was Metzger's technical advisor for the finale of the movie.

Following his success in "Boys," he appeared in "The Back Row" with George Payne and the film remains a vivid, interesting story of how persistence can pay off in cruising.

Joe Gage used Casey's sensitivity and blond good looks to great advantage as a counterpoint to his normal parade of rugged he-men in the third part of his trilogy, "L.A. Tool and Die" and again in his masterpiece, "Heatstroke."

Casey's other notable appearance in the early '80s was in Falcon's "The Other Side of Aspen," where he is featured with Al Parker and Dick Fisk. In this classic adventure, Casey is spread-eagled on a coffee table in a ski lodge and serves as the centerpiece in the gang- bang finale with Parker, Fisk and Jeff Turk taking their turns with him.

Casey recalled the making of the movie: "Al and I had never met until the afternoon we flew from San Francisco to Lake Tahoe. A couple of hours later we were doing our first scene together and he was fist-fucking me! Quite an experience! Al's a marvelous, special man."

Another marvelous, special man is Casey's one-time co-star Scorpio. I asked him once about his favorite screen role: "With Casey in 'Superstars Two.' That's exactly as I am and what I like to do. Even though 'All Tied Up' is my favorite film, because I get to do some fantasy stuff in it. Casey talked me into coming two or three times! Talked me into it!"

When we caught up with him early in 1983, he was appearing in a show in New York, taking time off from his bartending at The Bar on the lower East Side. I was shocked when I saw the show. After Scorpio stripped, he invited two guys to come onto the stage and they commenced to sucking and fucking each other. It was totally unexpected. The normal bill of fare didn't include such goings-on on stage, in front of everybody. He limited the program to two shows a day and that resulted in a lot of dead time during the long wait between the 1:30 and 7:30 shows, time to pick up some extra change in his dressing room or in hotels around town.

His comment: "The guys that come up and do it with me are just as trashy as I am, so it's fun. I like to get down and dirty.

"I love doing the shows because I get off on the audience watching me. When they start jacking off, that's what turns me on. I'll see someone in the audience I want to get up there with me and most of the time they'll come. If they don't, it's because they are afraid someone might see them. It's safer sitting out there in the dark than in the spot on stage!"

I felt my crotch. It was soaked with cum. Talk about safe sex! Here I was prepared to risk everything to get down and dirty with Scorpio, one of the sleaziest men alive, and like Casey had done to him, he had talked *me* into it!

Two years later, visiting the set of "Inevitable Love," we noticed Casey was having a little trouble keeping it up. He joked, "You know, even after I've done eighteen movies, it still takes a lot of concentration." We asked him about how it felt making a movie about safe sex. "I don't think the rules have changed very much about what we can do to each other in bed. Rimming and fisting really aren't done anymore. But the big difference is that a lot of the new films are obviously using condoms and things so people are going to get the idea that these are the precautions to use. But I really hate fucking with rubbers. I mean, I think it's something we all have to get used to."

We had noticed they had not cleared the set for the scene. There were all kinds of people milling about. "Yeah," he said, "I wish they would. You know, it's the most private thing two people can do and it sure is weird to have a dozen strangers standing around. It's not easy, especially when you're brand new. You have a cute kid who has fantasized about doing it and they're all excited and then they discover all these people are looking at them."

Casey went back onto set, got it up, and threw a sizable load.

As he was leaving, several members of the crew converged upon him to get his autograph. I thought at the time, once a superstar, always a superstar.

Casey remarked, "My whole existence is based to this day on that one movie – I've done other films – some obscene, some never seen, but everything since is predicated on 'Boys in the Sand,' including my hustling.

"I'd been selling it off and on for 11 years – first, only occasionally through a madame, but on a serious 9 to 5 basis since December of '77. I'd broken with a lover of five years, a well known actor and famous author who never liked being a public person. He could never handle my being 'Casey Donovan, Porn Star" – it would have been much easier for him if I'd still been a school teacher. I was all at sea; I had no income and no idea of what my next move should be. One day, with lots of time on my hands, a friend told be about a hot ad he'd read in the *Advocate*. I read it, thought about it, and decided to call. I'd never paid for sex before, and I thought I should see what it felt like being on the other side – I'd been *collecting* for years. The boy turned out to be as hot as his ad, and he was the one who convinced me to have a go at hustling. It had always been a fantasy of mine to run an ad in the *Advocate* anyway. Suddenly, I felt like a Park Ave. call girl. I often think that if I was a woman, that's what I would have been. I truly enjoy it *and* them. There have been many instances where I've been able to help clients – so many people are so fucked up sexually – just *so* many!

"I'm often asked how I can have sex with so many kinds of people, some of them seemingly turn-offs. I can always get past their bodies because I'm interested in who they are, what they are, what they think...of themselves...of me. As for age, I've always dated older men, so that's no issue – and about 50% of my clients are between the ages of 29 and 39 anyway. My attitude is to give, if not the *best*, at least the *nicest* sexual experience they've ever had. One strange thing about hustling is that the sex is usually the shortest part of the hour – much of the time is spent in simple conversation. Lots of men work in businesses that allow them no gay outlets, and they just want an hour to be GAY, to let go, to get into what gay men get into. Also, a great many men just need desperately to be *HELD*

– to feel someone's arms around them – to make them feel wanted and important. Sometimes I hold someone, and his entire body just quivers. It's so sweet, so gratifying to fill that need. I hope I can continue doing what I do. I feel I'm contributing an important commodity. I've helped a lot of people. Just last Sunday I saw a man in this neighborhood who is 22 years old – a big, tall, healthy, humpy kid whose first line to me was "Oh wow, you really do exist – maybe you're just what the doctor ordered." I was going to reel off a flip answer, but I decided I'd better listen first. As it turned out, he'd been impotent for the past few months – well...the sexual therapist in me went to work, and we got that boy on the path to sexual fulfillment and happiness. I feel like Dr. Donovan more often that I feel like Casey the Hooker. It's interesting to figure out how to approach a client sexually – do I come on like gang-busters or is it courtship? I love the ones whose clothes I can just tear off and jump into bed with and get down on – but that's often not the case. Some of them are just dynamite – I have a 72-year-old who's great fun in the sack – and some are just the worst sex. I had one yesterday who was so bad I just couldn't believe him – he was on 78 RPM and needed to be turned down to 16 RPM – just too frenetic. I felt sorry for him, he just didn't know how to communicate with his body. It's sad when people aren't sensually developed. I'm a romantic, and my sexuality leans towards the passionate--somebody could be a dog, but I'll tell you, if he can kiss, if he's a hot make out, I'm in heaven--HEAVEN!!! I love heavy petting. I'm just a pushover – kiss me and you've got me!

"I've often thought of writing a manual for johns advising them about how to get the most for their bucks. For instance, if you're hiring a hustler, at least give him the courtesy of having taken a shower, brushing your teeth, using a little mouthwash. If you want me to suck your dick and you haven't bathed in 36 hours, I'm not going to be too excited about getting into it – I'll do it but you won't get the best of me. And if you're into getting fucked – learn about douching! The buyer has as much responsibility as the seller – it's a relationship *between* two people. When I go to a client I'm as squeaky-clean as possible my body is available for anything they want to get into, and every orifice is in top condition. Give me a break...give me a chance to show you a good time – that's what it's about...two people having a good time together."

Thirteen years after the original "Boys," Poole tried again, with a sequel, also starring Casey, and the result was dismal. The magic touch was gone. Still, Bijou Video's editor commented: "Casey Donovan may be forty here but he looks just as good in this as he did in the original." At the time, Casey thought perhaps romance was coming back into films."I think they're going to get lighter and prettier," he said. But it wasn't to happen to him. When he worked, the films were brutally realistic. In 1986, he made his last video, aptly titled "Fucked Up" for Christopher Rage. Here we see the golden boy disintegrate before our eyes. "It leaves a pathetic footnote to a glittering career," *Manshots* said. "Once and for all he shed his healthy boy next-door image and headed pell mell for what turned out to be the end of the line." After the single main title is spelled out in a line of cocaine, Casey's ass appears, being shaved by John Clayton. They appear to be very high indeed and Casey spews out gutter talk that would cause even Jeff Stryker himself to swallow hard. After they have at each other, Casey takes five dildos of various sizes and goes at it on his own.

The star died a year later, on August 10, 1987, in Inverness, Florida, from complications from AIDS.

One of Casey's most endearing qualities was his honesty. He loved New York and rarely went to Los Angeles. He regularly ran an ad in *The Advocate* offering his services and was one of the most popular hustlers of all time. "I only wish I'd done it ten years earlier, at the height of the 'Boys' thing. I could have bought four guest houses in Key West instead of just one." He succeeded because he really cared about his clients. He always liked older men so that part didn't bother him. "My attitude is: to give, if not the best, at least the nicest sexual experience the client has ever had." And he did. He is greatly missed.

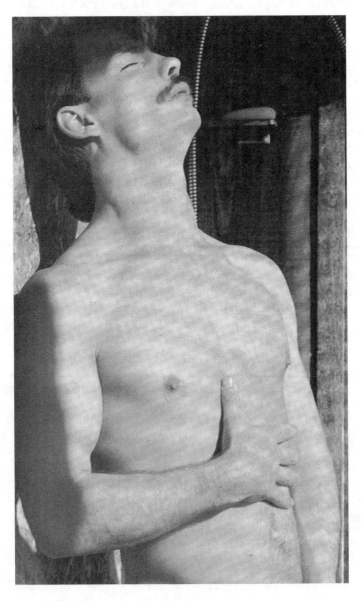

Rick Donovan, photographed by Bo Tate

Rick Donovan

"Some young men who had been invited as companions for other guests at a party I was giving in Fort Lauderdale joined me in my suite for drinks before going to dinner. Rick had been taking a nap in his own bedroom of the suite before taking a shower and getting dressed. The boys and I were in the living room talking when suddenly the star appeared, stark naked, a towel hanging loosely from one hand.
Conversation ceased. All eyes were riveted on the incredibly long appendage that hung lewdly between his legs. It was limp but it was the longest limp I'd ever seen. Addressing me directly, Rick asked, with a sheepish grin, 'Do you want me to wear a tie?'
I don't recall what I replied. I think it was something like, 'I don't think a tie would cover it, Rick. You'd better wear pants.'
'Yeah, sure,' he said with a smile and disappeared into the bedroom wing.
'Is that for real?' asked one of my awed young guests.
I nodded and there seemed to be a collective 'whew' hanging in the air."
- The author, remembering 1985.

We are taught by mass media to admire bigness. The greatest, the grandest, the most beautiful. It makes sense that we should include cocks as an object of our esteem. The downside is that the person with whom you become obsessed can be reduced to a statistic. This was the opinion of Nick Jerrett, whom I chanced to meet after he appeared in "Summer of Scott Noll," wherein he fucked Leo Ford with that incredibly thick, long rod of his.

Nick said, "Psychologically, I don't think anyone minds having a big cock, but along with the benefits come the problems, like people looking at you just for that."

Dr. Charles Silverstein, in his book *Man to Man*, agrees, noting that "in the gay world of today, the penis is revered. The big cock is the prize, adorned and adored, the possessor enormously attractive to the hungry hunter who wants to engulf it or be overpowered by it, with minimal regard for other physical characteristics, and none whatsoever for emotional or social ones." I understood Nick's position completely, that's why I preferred "dates" with the objects of my desire rather than quickie sessions.

While I thought Nick's cock was grand, and he knew how to use it better than almost anyone I've ever met, I was totally bowled over by Rick Donovan's a year later, revealed in a scene lodged in the middle of yet another William Higgins travelogue, this one called "Sailor in the Wild." It was yet another poolside sequence that could have played in almost any other film. Sunbather Leo Ford, Higgins' blond utility bottom, was suddenly coming on to a hunky dude with wide-set eyes, a thick neck and a laconic manner. Once Leo got the man out of his pants, he started hungrily working on the stud's cock and, as if by magic, one of the biggest cocks anybody had ever seen in porn was springing to life. And another porn legend was born.

While the reactions to his endowment amuse him now, in fact, he never realized what he had until he was in his late teens: "Of course, I went through high school having sex with cheerleaders who always said, 'My God, you're SO big!' But my theory was, 'Well, how many cocks has she seen? One? Two? Five tops!' Secondly, girls are taught to think dicks are the size of a thumb, and anybody's is big compared to a thumb. And when I was in the military, there were prostitutes telling me how big I was. But I discounted that, too, because they're paid to tell you how big you are. My first lover was the one that convinced me I was big."

Unlike Roger, another horsehung performer I fancied years earlier who had the biggest basket I'd ever seen, Rick showed nothing - and he loved it. "When I'm soft I don't show a basket," he revealed. "It's the biggest deceiver in the world. It's great because I know people are attracted to me, not my dick because they can't see it." (Can't you hear echoes of the poor little rich girl's lament, "I want a man whose interested in me, not my money?")

Rick played a super-macho role, which was fine with me. That's part of the fantasy in adoring a super-hung stud. Doug Richards of *Manshots* agrees: "The myth perpetuated by the onscreen persona of a mega-endowed star is that a man with a big cock is the quintessential man, and as such, never, assumes what has become known as 'the female role.' The message that a big cock equals control, control means power and power is potency, sexual potency."

So potent is the vision of Rick fucking it is recalled with great joy some ten years later. When L.A. club promoter Billy Limbo began his series of weekly happenings in Beverly Hills, he called it Club 1984. Dirk Festive, writing in *The Advocate*, said: "But we choose to remember 1984 not by breaking out our preppy handbooks, gravity-defying collars, and skinny ties but by bending over a schoolroom desk and taking Rick 'Humongous' Donovan's dick up our ass. The scene in question is the boffo opening from Matt Sterling's 'The Bigger the Better,' and the man facedown in the inkwell was the adorable Matt Ramsey."

Indeed, Rick Donovan was responsible for more "boffo openings" than anybody I can think of. But as he proceeded from one hot video to another, Rick was dogged with the reputation that he couldn't get it up. The truth was, it took a long time for the monster to rise. He joked, "Sure, it does take me ten minutes to get a hard-on, but, Jesus, give me a break. It takes a half-pint of blood to get this thing up!"

He defended himself by reciting a litany of his finest on-screen performances, where he undoubtedly had the biggest hard-on most people had ever seen. He considered Matt Sterling's "The Bigger the Better" his best, and he liked "The Arousers," "The Biggest One I Ever Saw," and his debut film, "Sailor in the Wild." John Rowberry comments on "The Bigger the Better:" "The high-quality production values, mixed with a cast of ever-erect actors, and some ball-churning sex (like Matt Ramsey getting plowed by his student, super-hung Rick Donovan), set the standard for a new generation of gayporn video. The sex never lets up."

Rick's theory was that he had to be a star with his first outing. "The first thing you do sets the standard for good. I lucked out with William Higgins. He's a good filmmaker and he said I could choose who I wanted to work with and they would also want to work with me. And he offered me a lot of money. As it turned out, Leo Ford (his co-star) was a great guy to work with. Everything clicked."

Rick was not to have the same success with every video. In "Boys of Company F" he does a credible job of playing a hard-nosed sergeant but he doesn't have sex until the end and gets lost in the shuffle of the orgy. In the appropriately titled "King Size," Rick is paired with Jesse Koehler. Bijou said, "The sight of Donovan's whang buried deep in Koehler's ass is lusciously lewd, but much of the action fails to rise above mediocrity."

Off-screen, Rick preferred the company of transvestites and lived with Nicole Murray, a regular at the Brass Rail in San Diego, for many years. He made only one video with a TV, however: "She's A He," with a pre-op Lelani.

Dave Kinnick, in his excellent book *Sorry I Asked*, recalls the time he worked with Rick in 1986 on "Stick Shift:" "We were in the little studio in North Hollywood that was next door to The Compound bathhouse. We had a car pulled into the room and the background draped with black cloth. Rick was going to fuck Michael Vincent, but first he had to get that huge thing of his hard. With Rick, it was always a challenge. One can't blame him, not with *that* thing hanging between his legs.

"But we worked Rick that day. First off, you have to know what Rick is into. Rick likes to look at pictures of transsexuals. That's what gets him hard. So, we have these TV mags spread out on the floor in front of him. Michael Vincent waits in the wings drinking Diet Cokes. As Rick gets closer to being hard, stroking for close to an hour, the director signals us into position. My job was running and monitoring the two decks. The two cameramen start to stalk the subject, jockeying into position, trying not to break Rick's concentration.

"It was supposed to be one of those fantasy scenes that directors like to fall back on and it soon came time to bring out the old rented fog-making machine and squirt some white puffy stuff around the set to make it pretty. Of course, these machines work on the principle of very hot oil ejected forcibly out of a nozzle, theoretically making white smoke in the process. One of these production assistants grabbed the machine as instructed and began to make clouds down close to the floor, all around and behind Rick. Just as things started to look promising, a big glob of very hot oil that had failed to turn into smoke shot out of the nozzle and hit Rick around his knees. Rick yelped. The production assistant jumped about a foot in the air. All hell broke loose. Rick's erection ran down the flag. There was a good deal of sadness in the air. It wasn't serious, though; the oil didn't burn and we were back in business a few minutes later. I think some of the oil got on the she-male pictures, however. I don't know if the ink smeared on them or not, but Rick didn't seem to have any more erection problems for the rest of the day."

In "Bi and Beyond II," starring hermaphrodite cult figurehead Delilah, big Rick's a sad sight trying to get an erection with a rubber slipped over his humongous equipment. "The closing orgy is silliness personified," John Rowberry says, "but note that Rick Donovan finally found a condom that fits." Rick manages to get it in and there are a few brief glimpses of him plowing the field, but, again, he's lost in the shuffle.

After that video, Rick retired to teach scuba diving, then bounced back in Jerry Douglas' award-winning "More of a Man," in which he gets it on with Joey Stefano, although he doesn't fuck the infamous ass.

In Falcon's "The Big Ones" Rick demonstrates the reason he's legendary in porn circles. There he is, in 1991, still sporting a macho mustache, looking better than ever, reading lines with aplomb and fucking grandly. He even kisses his bedmate goodbye. It's a short peck on the lips but it's better than nothing. The only thing we found fault with was the fact that there was a noticeable lack of latex in his scene, odd for a star who has appeared in several "safe sex" entries in his lengthy, in more ways than one, career.

In 1994 he returned briefly to the video cameras playing, of all things, a john, who picks up, of all people, Danny Sommers, for some quick sex in "Club Sex-A-Holics" for Fox Studio, directed by William Hunter. "Unfortunately," Hank R. Chief said in *AVN*, "these guys failed to eat their Wheaties, so their huge wienies spend much of the time half-cocked." Especially Donovan, who continues to suffer from an inability to get fully hard, even when tended to by a sexualist as fine as Danny Sommers. (They must not have had any pictures of transvestites around – that's the only thing that sparks Rick's interest.) "Yes," Hank says, "Rick Donovan, otherwise known as the donkey dick of the '80s, displays a temperamental hard-on through all of the oral and anal festivities. I got a good sense of what Hunter was trying to accomplish. In the good old days, having a generous endowment seemed to be a prerequisite for being a top. You don't have to be a size queen to appreciate the hot ass-stretching action. Unfortunately, these performers don't always deliver. Anyway, I hope Hunter doesn't give up trying. Hot video sex can still happen in the '90s. This is one is for those customers who like 'em well hung, even if they stay that way."

Danny saves the scene, however, with his marvelous on-screen charisma and his sweet gesture of giving Rick back his money after he gets off but Rick doesn't.

Rick also was featured in the sequel to the popular "Dynastud," "Dynastud 2: Powerhouse." Kinnick liked it: "Rick Donovan is just one of the all-time best tops and it is a pleasure to watch him work over Tanner Reeves."

John C. Holmes in 1972

John C. Holmes

"A happy gardener is one with dirty fingernails
and a happy cock is a fat cock.
I never get tired of what I do because I'm a sex fiend.
I'm very lusty."
— John C. Holmes

In music, the King was Presley. In the parallel, subterranean world of porn, Holmes existed as a sort of scaled-down (in all respects but one) King. Both came from poor white trash backgrounds and both used a black man's weapons to rise to the top. For Elvis, it was rhythm and blues, for John, a huge cock.

Although he was the top stud in adult films, it never made him a wealthy man and because of his slippery, protean persona, you never knew where you were with him. John Holmes slid down the slope from sex to drugs to murder, aimlessly, without style, typical of a country boy who got in way over his curly head. In the end, he didn't know the truth about anything, much less himself. But he did make sexual intercourse look pleasant to millions of people, he showed care and respect for his partners, and he seemed to be able to laugh at himself. As epitaphs go, that's not bad at all.

Doug Richards in *Manshots* commented: "Holmes had an ordinary face, a thin body and a certain skill, but he became the first male star of heterosexual pornography, strictly on the length of his dick. For many years, his was the standard by which all others were measured."

John came to Hollywood when he was already 27 and quickly made over a thousand 8 mm loops before being discovered by Bob Chinn and Richard Aldrich and cast as "Johnny Wadd," porn's parody of a hard-boiled Sam Spade-type detective. But he was never the swaggering, violent male chauvinist. Rather, he was quiet, gentle, almost artful when he fucked. He let his size do his posturing for him. In every film he made there was that sense of anticipation. We waited impatiently for him to unfurl his cock and let some bimbo try to take it all in one orifice or another. It was said to be a badge of honor in the industry to have taken John anally and lived to tell about it.

How big was it? John joked once, "It's bigger than a pay phone, smaller than a Cadillac." It was billed to be 14" long but some said it was really *only* 12 3/4". One report indicated it was 8 1/2" soft. It had to be that. I was too busy sucking it to measure it, but it was a mouthful. In those days, I could not imagine taking it anally. Today, I would at least try.

Whatever his true measurements, John was made to order for porn back in the early '70s. He came to symbolize the quantity-not-quality aesthetics that had begun to typify America by that time. He was both the bane and the balm for the man who doubted his virility, the perfect "product" for a society of size-queens.

Industry sources have always contended that Holmes was "actively bi," that he would take a trick with a man any time if the price was right. Holmes once said, "I consider myself sexual." He admitted he'd had over 14,000 sex partners, including three governors and a U. S. Senator.

The truth was, his true love could only be bought by the gram. That love got him in trouble in 1981 when, early one morning, four people were brutally bludgeoned to death in a house in the hills above Hollywood. And the case got bizarre as the evidence came in. The house was the headquarters for a drug-and-burglary ring and a fringe member of the group was a drug addict by the name of John Holmes.

Police also knew that Holmes was a favorite of one of the men they believed engineered the killings, a Lebanese gangster named Adel Nasrallah, known in the states as Eddie Nash. Nash was a drug kingpin as well as a nightclub owner and when they raided his house they found cocaine worth $4 million on the street. Police theorized that Nash engineered the killings as revenge for a burglary at his house the week before, an incident some said was planned by John Holmes. To save himself, John led Nash to the burglars and left his palm print above one of the victims. Police arrested him, grilling him for hours, but he refused to give them any information. He fled to Florida and worked at odd jobs but a few months later, he was extradited back to California to stand trial for the murders. The jury acquitted him.

In the aftermath of the trial, he appeared in a couple of trumped-up features but settled into a rut, taking whatever came along to support his cocaine habit. In 1985, one of the things that came along was Fred Halstead and Joey Yale's production of "The Private Pleasures of John Holmes," and even with the very accommodating assholes of porn veterans Joey (who also directed) and Chris Burns around for Holmes to fuck, it is a terrible film made all the more despicable by the sight of an star who was so obviously down on his luck.

Businessman Bill Amerson, his friend for over 25 years, took John under his wing and the star made some comeback films such as "Girls on Fire," "The Return of Johnny Wadd," and "Rockey X." He flew to Rome to make "The Rise and Fall of the Roman Empress" and "The Devil in Mr. Holmes," co-starring Italian parliament member Cicciolina.

Before John flew to Italy to make those last films, he was diagnosed as having AIDS. He consciously engaged in anal sex with Cicciolina as well as Amber Lynn and Tracey Adams, an act that some said was tantamount to murder. "He was chosen to get AIDS because of how he lived, who he was," said his wife Laurie (known in straight porn circles as Misty Dawn). She was divorcing him, repelled by his penchant for low-rent whores. She revealed that he would cruise the boulevards picking up the trashiest people he could find. His coprophilic obsession hinged on the "filthiness" of sex and he practiced it frequently over a period of years.

By October of 1986, the star was in noticeably failing health. He himself spread the word he had cancer. Finally, on March 15, 1988 in Los Angeles, Holmes succumbed to the disease.

When Al Goldstein, publisher of *Screw*, heard that John was dying of AIDS, he wrote this tribute, which appeared on September 7, 1987: "It is the biggest cock in porn. Its eminence looms over the horizon of pornography and casts its mammoth shadow over the landscape of sleaze. Like Paul Bunyan, the cock is mythic, almost cosmic force that has a life of its own. It's a meteor piercing the sky. A rocket tracing fire into the heavens. The cock that defines pornography.

"It is an instrument of pain and pleasure. In itself, a metaphor for life. It is the MX missile of genitalia. As significant as man's landing on the moon, the Wright Brothers' first flight, the invention of the wheel and the discovery of fire.

"It's a bird, it's a plane - no, it's the cock of John Holmes!

"Appearing in thousands of porn films, porking thousands of women, it is the most legendary male member since Adam's fucked Eve. It is bigger than the sum of its parts.

"The cock of John Holmes has obsessed and fascinated me and captured the attention of the porno-goer since 1967.

"In paying our homage to John for being bigger than life, we commend him on his influence and contributions to male and female fantasy. We also take an existential pleasure in realizing that in spite of his gargantuan-sized cock, his life was riddled with drugs, pain, alienation and self-deprecation.

"What this means is that, indeed, the content and substance of life is more important than mere statistical data. The guy with a four-inch cock has no more or no less pleasure than the guy with a 14-inch prod. The number of women he has fucked, the quantity of sexual encounters one has had, have little value in the totality of what makes life significant.

"We salute John for what he is and what he proved to us he was not. We commend him and we take joy that we are not him."

As long as the human penis averages about six inches in length, the memory of Holmes will remain well protected and highly profitable. The best of Holmes can be found in "Insatiable," with Marilyn Chambers, in which he plugs the infamous Ivory Snow girl on a pool table. Critics have always picked "Eruption" (released by Cal Vista), a porn version of the thriller "Double Indemnity," as his best acting job. Filmed in Hawaii, his sex scenes with Leslie Bovee are appropriately volcanic.

Years after Holmes' death the Joey Yale vehicle, "The Private Pleasures of John C. Holmes," is still being heavily promoted to gay size queens. *In Touch* magazine offers it for $24.95 and HIS is peddling it for $19.95, with purchase of another feature. HIS says in their ad: "Rare footage of the legendary John 15 1/2" Holmes in His Only Gay Movie." John would be delighted to think he'd gained five inches in retrospect! "12 B.J.s, 7 anals, lavish sets, willing slaves," the advertising goes on. *In Touch* says: "Watch the master take control of young, hot men as they let go of their forceful spurting loads throughout this 90 minute video of Hot Gay Action. You won't believe your eyes as you watch the Master of Porn enjoying every minute of his secret 'gay' pleasures." They do not even get the title right: they refer to this film simply as "John Holmes: The Man," but, again, John, the master of hyperbole, would be tickled by such advertising copy. Gays will find Falcon Studios has cornered the market on early Holmes solos: The loop "The Biggest of Them All" is on Falcon Pac 16; "Black Velvet" is on Falcon Pac 21; "Pool Party" is on Falcon's Pac 9. While two of the loops are solos, "Pool Party" features John with another man. "Here," *Manshots* noted, "a dozen uninhibited young men are put through their paces in five selected loops originally shot on film. The cinematography is primitive, the editing often clumsy, and the original color has faded with time and in the transfer to videotape.

"Nonetheless, the sparks of sexual heat that characterize later Falcon works were clearly present from the very beginning. Eight of the performers are unidentifiable today: however, four of them – Ray Fuller, Bill Eld, John Holmes, and Dean Chasson – are among the dozen or so early stars of the genre to emerge as distinct, popular icons whose names still resonate today.

"...Purported to be one of only two times that the legendary womanizer John Holmes had sex with a man on film, the fourth loop is set poolside, thus giving the anthology its umbrella title. Holmes truly had a gigantic schlong, and he uses it to great advantage, both orally and anally, with an unidentified blond partner. The anal penetration is prolonged and excruciating, but is finally accomplished both doggie and missionary. This is impersonal, high energy action."

Yes, the man is dead, but the product is immortal.

Ryan Idol, courtesy All Man magazine

Ryan Idol

*"He's one of the best straight, gay for-pay guys. He has a sense of
mischief and fun. The funniest thing about the scene was the
incredible lengths the cameramen went to verify Ryan Idol didn't
need a stunt dick to do his penetrating for him."*
– A fan, upon seeing Idol in "Score 10"

Even on the way to the club in Tampa in 1992 for "the party
of the year," Ryan Idol held center stage. Every inch the
superstar he has been groomed to become, he kidded big-
dicked Kris Lord, who was also stripping that night, that he'd
let him fuck him in the ass for a quarter of a million dollars.
Whether that offer is open to someone with less endowment
than Lord we're not certain, but with Ryan, in true trademeat
fashion, you feel anything is possible. In fact, he asked his
volunteer chauffeur, "You a doctor? You look like a doctor."

"No, but thank you," the chauffeur beamed, checking out
the handsome Ryan in the rearview mirror.

Idol smiled. "Well, you can inspect my ass anytime."

Savoring that prospect, the driver almost ran a stoplight.

Forever the tease, Idol said, "I like girls and I like guys. I like
any place I can put my dick." Talk about trade!

Ryan was a star with his first video, "Idol Eyes," and
shrewd management has created a gay icon who seldom fails
to impress. On stage, magnificently costumed, he's got an act
that provides many highlights, not the least of which is his faux
humping of a member of the audience who has been seated in
a chair on stage. This monkey business is forever preserved on
his video "A Very Personal View," featuring the entire act as
performed at Studio One in L.A.

On the second night of the party, things got off to a bad start
for Ryan when, as the stars were climbing out of the car, one
fan mistook Lex Baldwin for him. Ryan found this inconceivable
considering that at 6'-1" he towered over the others, especially
Lex. Then Ryan had to abort his first performance when he
became dizzy, but he quickly recovered and was soon out
signing autographs promoting his latest video effort, the

appropriately titled, "Trade Off." This video was one of the biggest turn-offs in the history of gay video. Customers who rented this one came back into the store shaking their heads, slamming the video down and asking, "Can I trade this off?" Some renters demanded refunds. Some swear Jesse Helms was behind the production of the video! Some complain the characters are either debased or ashamed of what they are. If this had come from any other producer and starring any other performers than Idol and cute newcomer Axel Garrett it could easily be dismissed, but this was one big disappointment.

Dave Kinnick has called Ryan a "problematic porn star" who was robbed of his best feature, talking dirty, in "Trade Off," since he never opens his mouth. As it is, Kinnick found, he's playing himself: "...a confused young straight man interested in experimentation, but only if it is to be with like-minded, big-dicked muddleheads. We lose interest in this 'to be or not to be' queer analysis."

Just how "problematic?" Well, One fan in San Diego wrote *Urge* magazine: "For shame, for shame. How dare you write such an unabashed puff piece about your 'friend' Ryan Idol and ignore all the harm he's done to the gay community. I've attended three separate nightclub bookings and actually drove 90 miles once to see him and he was arrogant and aloof to those of us who had the courage to try to talk to him after the show. The time I drove up to see him, I was told there would be a question and answer session. He took two questions, and after someone asked him,'Do you consider yourself gay or bisexual?' he got all defensive and said,'Fuck you guys,' and walked off the stage." Well, everybody can have a bad day – but three?

It seems every video Ryan appears in creates controversy. One fan wrote that he fast-forwarded through Idol's "Score 10" except for his final scene and like the fact that special care was taken to show Ryan's dick penetrating the asshole of his partner. The reason for this care, obviously, was the brouhaha caused by rumors that porn veteran David Ashfield had stunt-dicked Idol in his first gaymale feature, "Idol Eyes," directed by Matt Sterling, wherein Ryan was asked to fuck Joey Stefano.

But Ryan insists that he didn't have any trouble with Joey. "I get off if the other person is really into me, really gaga. That's the way Joey was. He's a great kid, and I liked him a lot because he really dug me. We did things when the cameras weren't on; I wish we could have taped them." (Boy, so do we!) Ryan laments the outcome, or lack of same: "It was my first. I was petrified. I'll get better each time."

After seeing "Score 10," Kinnick summed up the Idol phenomenon succinctly: "Idol locks in his screen persona as gay video's favorite beautiful, arrogant and superficial ass wipe." Kinnick objects to these hostile, straight-trade attitude: "Idol is not the cause of this malaise, but merely a symptom of the affliction. At the end of the video, we leave Idol smirking into the camera lens and telling us (and co-star Dcota) that he had 'a good time.' It is the very picture of a man absolutely dedicated to his own desperate specialness."

In an interview given at the time of "Score 10's" release, when asked if he was straight, gay or in-between, the stud replied, "None of the above. I really don't label myself. I feel I could fit in anywhere - no pun intended. There are people who would like me to be straight and people who would like me to be gay. If I say one or the other it ruins their fantasies."

Jerry Douglas agrees and pondered the dichotomy: "Negative responses far outweigh the positive, yet the videos sell and rent like crazy, with swaggering Jeff Stryker remaining the ultimate example of the man we love to hate. If you're going to pay homage to a straight persona, you've gotta hate it. It's a phenomenon deeply rooted in the gay psyche. We hate these guys who seem to slide so easily through life, slipping between the thighs of men and women alike. How can they do this, some ask. Some of us who have been there just like guys more than girls and stick to it, opportunities aside. But with these guys, you never know. And that's the basis of their mystique."

The Idol mystique certainly wows the ladies. Reviewer Pearl Chavez, reviewing the stud's "Letters from the Heart," a straight flick, says: "Idol gets his tired marriage sparked by his exotic teddy-clad wife Leilani. Although he struggles with rigidity at times, Idol is so gorgeous that this is easily forgotten." Well, maybe by her. But gaymale fans said Ryan's limpness in that movie proved he was "more gay than straight."

About "Idol Worship," an aptly named and imaginative AVG release, Sid Mitchell commented: "Ryan's arrogant, almost parodic imitation of Jeff Stryker has never been put to better use than in the opening solo of this pseudo-military tale of life on a submarine patrol in the Indian Ocean. As the sub's commanding officer, Idol's arrogance seems not only believable but even appropriate, and for once, highly erotic. He j.o.'s while commanding his crew to keep their eyes on the radar screens.

"As for the rest of the video, Blade Thompson easily steals the show, first with Domino in the torpedo chute, then with Rick Lee in their bunk." There is plenty of heat in every scene, making up for the absurdity in the connecting footage.

Ryan, who stands 6'1" tall and weighs in at 190 lbs., spends a lot of time at the gym but he doesn't consider himself a bodybuilder. "I'm a body sculptor," he says. "I build everything that should be built to achieve the perfect physique."

Kinnick noted that Ryan has a pair of cherries tattooed above his dick, just inside his bikini tan line. "I wonder," he asked, "where the lemons and oranges are, let alone the jackpot?" The jackpot, it would seem, is Ryan's cock, a perfect cock that's 8 1/2 inches at full strength. Indeed, Ryan's groin, one reviewer commented, "looks as if it were cut by a master gemsmith."

And this is the cock that seems to get a helluva good workout since the star, at one time, boasted he had two lovers, an older one and a younger one: "If the older one can't fill the shoe, the younger one gets to." And poor Ryan, like the rest of us mere mortals, is getting older by the day and, he says, that means less sex. "Two or three times a day, that's it."

As one might expect, the video that shows Ryan off best is "Ryan Idol: A Very Personal View," produced by his onetime agent, Stuart Rosenberg (widely known as the physique photographer Troy Saxon). Although violating the first rule of stardom by introducing us to the man behind the image before creating one, this ego trip is worth the journey for the stud's playfulness during a photo shoot sequence. There are several endearing moments, including early on as Ryan sets the tone by saying he likes to hold off until he can't stand it any more...and that's how you feel waiting for something to happen. Eventually, it does, first at Studio One in L.A. where he shows off for the crowd in a loose black g-string that leaves little to the imagination and then, totally naked, he shakes his pretty appendage and strokes it to the delight of the crowd. At one point, he gets a guy to sit in a chair on stage and proceeds to climb over him, shoving his ass in the guy's face. "I love the power of performing," he tells guest star Steve Hammond, another of Stuart's proteges, before retiring to the mirrored bedroom to talk to the camera as he jacks off.

His dialogue is inspired: "You want some hard cock?" "Just picture it any way you want it." "Goddam that feels good." "I like someone who can bring me to the point and then stop, then bring it back again and again. I know you know what I'm talking about." "You wanna see this big cock come?" "Hey, you want me to come now?" After he shoots he says, "Such a pretty mess, eh?" "Ah, that was so incredible. Hmmm." Got that right, Ryan.

As we found at the Tampa gig, Ryan occasionally fails to impress in his personal appearances. Recalls Michael Musto: "Hundreds fell silent at the Mens' Room when porn star Ryan Idol - who looked as if he was covered in mayo or something – begged us to ask him personal questions as he ground his pelvis into the night. 'Andy Warhol said everyone will be in the spotlight for 15 minutes,' he told us, tauntingly. 'This is your chance.' You mean my big break was going to be in a dank, smoky nightclub interrogating a porn star about his oral/anal preferences? I'd hoped for something just a tad more glamorous, like sucking eyeballs out of fish heads on public access TV."

At the 1992 "party of the year," Ryan looked weird, like something that had landed in Tampa from Planet Hollywood and no way would anyone in their right mind consider taking a ride on his spaceship, but for the 1993 party, there was a fresh new Idol. Tall and fit, he looked sensational in black trousers and a tight white tank top. He sported shorter hair cut in the very latest style and there was a sparkle in his eyes where there was vacancy a year ago. When he smiled slyly at me, baring those perfect white teeth, I wanted to come on the spot. When he shook my hand and we were having our picture taken together, he wrapped his arm around my waist and I never wanted him to remove it. Boy, I thought, I could get used to this, even if it had to cost a grand a night.

Since Esme Russell, the usual master of ceremonies for these "*Affairs Alfredo*," was not to be found, Ryan took over the microphone, showing amazing stage presence. The next night, I understand he wow'ed up at the Parliament House as well.

And amazing is what many called his performance in "Idol Thoughts," wherein he actually sucks dick. Between licks, gobbles, and slaps, he kisses co-star Tom Katt and otherwise goes at it as if he were really enjoying it. Yes, we think this cat's been fooling us all along! Ryan did remark that he "practiced" his technique before filming began. Don't you wonder who was the lucky recipient of all that attention? I can hear the instructions now, "Watch the teeth, Ryan!" "Suck, don't slobber!" "Ohhhhh, God!"

As further evidence of his affection for Tom, Ryan appeared in New York with Chi Chi LaRue and his co-star and when they walked on stage stark naked, with raging hard-ons, they banged them on Chi Chi's thighs. What fun there must have been backstage at that gig! We can only imagine Ryan and Tom walking around with those raging hard-ons looking for places to park them!

Tom was also at the party of the year in Tampa and backstage I complimented him on his performance and told him: "It looked like you were enjoying it."

A big, goofy grin spread across Katt's face and he said, "Oh, yeah!"

As fans will recall, after Ryan gets done savoring Katt's ample appendage, he skewers him with an aplomb that was missing in Ryan's previous entries.

By sucking dick, Ryan was suddenly hotter than ever. He has recently graced the covers of more gaymale magazines than any other porn star and was giving interviews everywhere. Some of his comments raised some eyebrows.

Superhung porn star Tom Steele once told me that he'd swung for a time among the many branches in the tree of the Hollywood Elite, the smart set that includes the superrich (David Geffen) and the just-so-rich (Allan "Grease" Carr) and all the other guys who pay for their play with cash, favors, and assorted knick-knacks. It was while doing his thing with his big thing for these moguls that Steele met Tom Cruise. Steele told me, "Tom likes big dicks." I nodded. I mean, doesn't everybody, especially when they look like Steele's?

In *The Advocate*, Idol was singing this same tune, saying he was swinging with the Hollywood Elite when he was nineteen, and puts Cruise in the company of the "payees" rather than the "payers." His exact statement: "I immediately ran into the producer scene - the Allan Carr scene. I got supposedly taken under their wing but for all the wrong reasons. And it was probably (NOTE: *probably*) about that same time that Tom Cruise was in that scene. So every time I look at Tom Cruise on-screen, I can't help but think that if I had maybe been a little more mature and willing to know and play the L.A. game - that I possibly might be someplace different...I always wanted to be a movie star."

What was Ryan doing anyway? It's rare when a boy will dare to rat on Hollywood's gay rat pack. Joey Stefano found out to his chagrin that to kiss-and-tell on megamogul David Geffen is the kiss of death in show biz. When word got out that Joey was mouthing off suddenly nobody returned his calls.

The same could happen to Idol. First, he announced that he was going to Alabama for a job interview and if he got it, he'd retire. (Alabama? C'mon.) And now the hunk is back in Hollywood and has ambitious plans. In the same interview, Ryan revealed he was going to star in an artsy-fartsy "legitimate" movie project with the porn star everyone grew to hate, Rex Chandler (the top who had his girl friend on the set to "fluff" him "up" between takes!). The plot of the movie sounds like a parody of "My Own Private Idaho," with Ryan playing a hustler and Rex playing a movie star coming to town to act the part of a hustler in a movie and...well, you can guess the rest. But guess is all we'll do because later Ryan announced the whole deal was off. Perhaps it was just another "idle thought."

Although Ryan as yet won't bend over and permit his partner rear entry, there's an incredibly inviting shot of him in "Idol Thoughts" spreading it for the camera. Perhaps a preview of coming attractions?

"Well," Ryan says, "you always leave them wanting more." Still, he says he's definitely a top: "That is what I choose in my sexuality. At this time, it's really not an option. But then, again, in five years - I've come a long way in three - if I decide to choose that route in my sexuality and my personal life, then you might see it." Ryan said he liked being "idolized," but that he wanted people to respect him for more than his ass or his dick: "I want them to respect my mind, my ability, my talent. I'm a Leo...I'm very creative."

Speaking of being creative, he reportedly got $15,000 for sucking Tom Katt's cock in "Idol Thoughts" and munching down on the succulent ass of Steven Marks in "Idol Country," directed by Chi Chi LaRue for HIS. Marks said, "Ryan Idol is a fabulous guy – gorgeous and everything like that – but somebody took Ryan and made him into what he is. If I knew how to do it, I'd do it myself, but I don't."

About Marks, Dave Kinnick revealed: "This 30-year-old blond charmer was, until very recently, gainfully employed as a TV weatherman in metropolitan Chicago! Tribune Broadcasting's CLTV channel 10 if you must know.

"Steven's undoubtedly rosebud-like asshole was selected out of a throng of seasoned industry pro holes. It was then groomed and fussed over and finally bent over and spread wide for the probing lens of cinematographer Bruce Cam.

"Eventually it was subjected to the professional ministrations of Ryan Idol's extremely well-compensated tongue."

It was in the contracts of both performers that mutual acts of rimming, sucking, and open-mouth kissing would take place. "It's funny," Steven told Kinnick, "I haven't even been in the same room with more than a handful of porn stars in my life. But about 2 1/2 years ago I went to the Vortex in Chicago and Ryan was doing a live performance onstage when I got there. I stood and watched. But of course, at that point it didn't occur to me I'd be licking his ass on-camera someday.

"We started off with my rimming him first. It was great. I got turned on to the situation just knowing that this was a big deal to a lot of people for some reason and that a bunch of guys would kill to be the tip of my tongue. And as long as it's clean, I prefer a butt hole to taste like a man's butt. I've rimmed in one other scene so far, and my partner had put a dab of strawberry-something-or-other gook down there before we started. He was simply trying to do me a favor, but it was a favor I couldn't appreciate. Ryan's butt hole, I'm happy to say, just smelled and tasted like a normal male butt hole."

And, Kinnick wanted to know, did notoriously "straight-identified" Ryan ever really connect emotionally with his sex partner? "The best moment for me in the whole movie was in that shot where I was just moments away from coming. I was on my back up on an old, rusty tractor holding on to some sort of smokestack that was about to break off in my hand at any moment. Ryan was standing between my legs, topping me. I was looking at him while he was fucking my ass and fantasizing as hard as I could about his body and the situation – but when I finally looked up, a little to my surprise, his eyes locked with mine and I felt 'connected' to him for real. But then again I guess you could say I was at the time about as connected to him as a guy can be."

Ryan went on to win Adult Video News' Best Actor award for his performance in "Idol Country." Ryan said, "This whole experience is a bit overwhelming. I am very honored." Still there were doubts, especially among potential porn co-stars. Jimi Hendrix said, "I would never work with Ryan Idol, because, first off, I think that Ryan was big at a time, but I think that he is declining. I've met him and I didn't get along with him. And I've heard other people say that they didn't get along with him."

There may be something to that. The summer of '95 was a hot one for Ryan, who was starring in "Matinee Idol," for VCA/HIS. He never finished the video. Mickey Skee reported that first there were four delays with lame excuses – like he got his weenie caught in his zipper. Finally, Idol fell ill, got his stomach pumped after a night of serious partying, called in to say he couldn't get it up for guys any more. Truth be known, he had met a girl from Atlanta who had convinced him the totally-straight life was best. He showed up at a bar in West Hollywood, fish in tow, to croon, "I'm Tired of Being a Sex Thing." Next thing you know, he's flying off to Atlanta with his ladylove. Commented Gino Colbert, director of the aborted video, "He'll be back when he runs out of money."

Jon King

Jon King

"Basically the queens are always the ones who are on the bottom.
Basically, they're just a piece of meat and all I do is use them.
People don't care who they are, people just care about who I am,
what I am doing to them. I don't feel bottoms are as powerful or as
big a star as a top. I don't know how Leo Ford or some of these
other queens ever got to be big stars.
They're always on the bottom. You can hardly see them."
- Porn actor Tim Kramer

Sexy redhead Erich Lange of "Houseboys," "Rites of Winter" and, most notably, in "Convertible Blues" with Damien, was an insatiable bottom. In countless videos he is plowed by the best in the business. "To these people (the producers) my rear is extraordinary," Erich says, "so that makes me a commodity, someone salable. Yeah, I do enjoy my ass...it's a real bubble-butt..and it turns me on to know I'm going to show off my butt and work with a real hot man, a man that's waiting to plow me!" But, said he: "I don't want to go on doing small, nothing parts in film after film and that seems to be what happens to most of the men who are cast as bottoms. They don't make stars out of bottoms." Not usually. Again, there's always the exception.

When porn became available to the masses in the late '70s, Jon King became the first "exception," the first man to become famous bottoming. In a career that spanned the decade of the '80s, Jon was on the receiving end of some of the most fabulous cocks in the world of gayporn: Kip Noll, Lee Ryder, Michael Christopher, the late J.W. King and blond Kristen Bjorn, with whom he carried on an off-screen relationship that was the basis for my best-selling roman a' clef *Billy & David: A Deadly Minuet, A Love Story.*

In Jon's debut film, William Higgins' "Brothers Should Do It!," the young star's wild sex in a scene at the end with his supposed "brother" J. W. was one of the hottest filmed to that time and has endured as a classic example of how hot it can get when two guys really dig each other. Of all his films, this is the one Jon remembers most fondly: "J. W. said I resembled his younger brother. And from that start as a baby brother, it was expected of me to be a bottom. I really don't mind. Shit, somebody has to get fucked! It's never been a big deal to me. Quite frankly, I enjoy everything both on and off screen."

That enthusiasm for sex was obvious to everyone. Producer/director Higgins' memories of Jon and the filming, as revealed to filmmaker Jerry Douglas, are golden: "I wasn't going to let him get away...We went over to our art director's house and shot the scene and in my whole career in pornography up to that point that was the first time, and one of the few times, I just turned the camera on and let it run. I mean, you know, unbelievable. (At one point I said,) 'Okay, guys, you gotta stop now because I have to load the camera,' and I came back and they're still carrying on. It was magic time."

Jon was barely 18 when he made his debut but he had to take eleven months off to go to prison because of a situation in his home state of Florida involving drugs and a car that wasn't his. He has always preferred not to discuss it: "I don't think what I did or what happened is very important. What's important is that I made a very stupid, ridiculous mistake and I've paid for it. Those months in prison were not a big party or a big orgy-they weren't fun. I turned twenty in prison and Christmas and New Year's and Easter...One thing I do know, I'm never going there again! But I was lucky. I could have gotten put away for five years. They were lenient only because it was my first offense and because of my age."

For years, Jon carried his traveling papers with him at all times and had to check in with his probation officer every week. "Contrary to all the rumors being maliciously spread around about me, my arrest didn't involve firearms or drugs. I'm no gun-toting coke freak!"

In the fall of 1985, arriving on the set of "Inevitable Love," having shaved off his moustache, the star looked sixteen. His shoulders were broad and his body still tapered to a tiny waist. He had only one scene in the movie, a frottage sequence. The director, as was his usual custom, filmed the sex first. As a preliminary to filming, Jon played with co-star Bill Kane's cock through his gym shorts. Bill became erect immediately and Jon laughed as he watched his own cock spring to attention. As the camera rolled, Bill laid back and let Jon do all the work. Dropping his shorts, Jon ground himself against Bill's body in a sequence that, to this day, "tops" 'em all. Ever the pro, Jon maneuvered himself into one exotic position after the other without any prompting from the director, exposing all of his best features. The director greased Jon's cock and the scene resumed. As Jon safely fucked him, Bill's hands roamed over the star's body. Suddenly, Jon asked, "Do you want me to cum now?" The director told him any time was fine and Jon shot a heavy stream onto his co-star's flat belly.

"Everybody in this business gets fucked over," Jon said after the filming, matter-of-factly. "What I'm trying to do now is to make my career work for me instead of me working for it. I'm making appearances in a lot of films. (At that time, he was also appearing in a classic from Steve Scott, "Screen Play"). My lover wants me to get out of the business but I figure I've got a few good ones left in me. I'm only twenty-two, you know."

Many of Jon's scenes remain of unusual interest. One done early on and now found on Falcon's Pac 30, features blond darling Kristen Bjorn, who went on to become one of porn's best directors, giving Jon a spanking, an enema and, of course, fucking him royally.

Recently made available on video is Jon's unbelievably hot pairing with superhung Michael Christopher and Bryan Young in the "Surfside Sex" scene in Fox Studios' "Bore 'n' Stroke," released by Sierra Pacific. *Adult Video News'* Sid Mitchell called it "a memorable mini-feature in its own right."

One of Jon's most delicious screwings is found at the tail end of Higgins' "Kip Noll Superstar." For his compilation of Kip's best scenes from the late '70s and early '80s, Higgins enlisted Jon to "interview" the young blond stud who was at that time probably the most famous porn star in the world. Jon, of course, ends up getting far more than an interview from Kip. The twosome's escapades in the Jacuzzi and poolside, although poorly lit at times, remain incredibly hot.

While Jeremy Scott, Kip's frequent co-star and Higgins' live in squeeze for a time, didn't cater to Noll, finding him too "street," Jon delighted in Noll's "professionalism" and that adoration comes across magnificently on screen. Noll, Higgins has said, was "one of those persons that looks incredibly better in photographs than he does in person."

In 1982's "These Bases Are Loaded," Higgins brought Jon and J.W. back together for a romp in a locker room as an orgy goes on around them. They fuck for an incredible 35 minutes straight of screen time. Also in 1982, Higgins' "Members Only" treated us to three variations of Jon's passion at its best. First, in one of Jon's rare top man performances, he lays it into Bill Curry. Then, Giorgio Canali screws Jon in an amazing number of positions. In the last episode, Jon goes all-out, letting Derrick Stanton and Greg Hanson double buttfuck him and Derrick throws one of his patented mega-loads.

If you're feeling nostalgic, try "The Biggest One I Ever Saw," directed by Bill Harrison. Bijou's reviewer says, "The film's centerpiece is a great three-way with King, Lee Ryder and Rick Donovan. King gets in the middle and takes Donovan up the ass and Ryder down the throat. This scene alone is worth the price of the movie!" Later, King joins a pair of sailors (Cole Taylor and Steve Collins) and takes them both. "Collins's orgasm across a tight close-up of King's face makes the scene," Bijou's reviewer said.In his interview with Jerry douglas, John Coletti, who started Fox Studios with his life partner Ken ("Bijou") Harrison, discussed the making of the classic porn movie. Coletti said, "It was a transitional movie, the last one we shot on sixteen millimeter. In 1983, we shot that. Rick Donovan, Jon King, Dave Connors – out of New York – Rod Phillips and his lover at the time, Lee Ryder. We shot a scene that was supposedly shot at a YMCA, looking through the keyhole – that was one of Ken's fantasies. We had to make the keyhole. Jon King was the only person we could put between those two – Rick Donovan and Lee Ryder. Who else could have handled them at all?" Who indeed!

During the early '90s, Jon returned to porn with mixed results. His loop for Falcon, found in "Perfect Summer," is a disappointment. He is pursued into the woods by two guys and he sucks each of them with a great deal of passion, trying valiantly to whip some sizzle to his scene but when he's called on to penetrate Casey Jordan's ass, he just can't work it up. Finally, they are joined by Tom Rucker and they pair off, allowing Jon to bottom for Robert Harris, who finger-fucks the star and then gives him a heavy butt-humping.

Another video made for a San Francisco-based filmmaker, the sleazy "He's Gotta Have It," was sold largely by mail order at a bargain price, and it was sad to see an older, paunchy Jon struggle through with sex scenes with Chris Thompson and Greg Sanchez. It isn't until the end, when he fucks Matt Romero, that he shows any spark of his old self at all.

In a coup, Catalina cast him in "These Bases Are Loaded II." Luckily, his top was the top top at that moment, Zak Spears. The rousing fuck in the locker room that is the finale of the video brings back a flood of memories of Jon's glory days when he was the bottom *everybody* wanted to fuck. Shortly after making the video, Zak retired, saying he'd fucked everybody he wanted to. And considering he'd just fucked the greatest bottom in porn and gotten paid handsomely for it, he wasn't just whistling "Dixie."

"He's baaaack," *Frontiers* cried in their review."Remember Jon King, that hot, dark and humpy boy from early '80s porn? We're not sure what he's been up to all these years, but he still looks hunkeriffic. And he's one of the few pornstuds who is lucky enough to star in his own sequel." The opening titles harken back to the original, with great shots of J.W. King fucking Jon and then a freeze-frame on Jon's well-satisfied face.

"...Our happy little tale begins in the locker room of our imaginary team," *Frontiers* goes on. "We'll name them the West Hollywood Tank Topperettes. All the studs are changing out of their baseball uniforms. They are all wearing jockstraps, but none of them are wearing cups. Coach Jon King swaggers into the locker room and congratulates the guys on a good game. Jon is thrilled to be back in the game. He hasn't played with a team this good in 12 years. He flashes back on the moment he decided to return: Jon is in bed with Dave Logan. He hears a voice telling him to coach. This leads him into a discussion with Dave about whether he should get back into coaching. Dave has an opinion on the subject, but we can't really understand a word he says. It doesn't matter, because soon the studs are kissing, which means they won't be chatting again.

"Dave sucks Jon. They get into some hot 69 action. Then Dave rams his big bat into Jon's dugout which Jon likes a lot.

Dave shoots his load in a cum shot that Reviewer Dave rates as perfect.

"Back in the locker room, Jon recalls a time when his former teammates were so worked up over their game that they had a big post-game jack-off contest. As they hear Jon recount the incident, the guys all brag that they would have won. Jon tells them to put their money where their mouths are. Jon whips out his Louisville Slugger and the fun begins. Pretty much the entire cast is there stroking and licking. Keller Hyde, the blond boy, drops to his knees and sucks everybody. All seven of the guys take turns shooting hitting their own personal pop flies. Suddenly Keller Hyde and Jon King are alone, making out. Zak Spears is watching. Jon explains to Zak that this is part of the training. He invites Zak to join them. Zak sucks on Jon's hoo-hoo while Keller watches. Zak fucks Jon – not just a little bit. Zak goes all nine innings. Keller shoots a big, loud load with Incredible-Hulk intensity. Jon enjoys a big, hot climax and Zak delivers an enormous rocket shot."

The Guide's Michael Lynch says, "Although labeled as a sequel to William Higgins's 1982 hit, this 'Bases' has little to do with that earlier film, except that its star - the ineffable Jon King - stars in both. King, who has been away from porn for almost a decade, looks and performs terrifically. The plot is what you would think: baseball team, locker room stuff, some duos, and a team orgy followed by coach King fucked endlessly by Zak Spears."

"The great success of this comes not only from King's incredible screen presence (and the fact that he takes it up the butt from Dave Logan as well as Spears) but from Taylor Hudson's (Chi Chi LaRue) astute direction. The camera work by Brad Austin is as superior as ever, but Hudson's pacing keeps the film moving along at such a pace that it feels seamless. The team orgy is a protracted set piece that pays off the way that few do – and it is nice to see seven or eight men on screen all slurping and gobbling and yanking at the same time. The final Jon King/Zak Spears fuck is a joy to behold." In this fuck atop a bench in the locker room, blond Keller Hyde stands over them watching, stroking his impressive appendage while Zak plows, and we do mean plows, into Jon. Jon's grimaces during this ordeal would make one believe he was getting it for the first time!

"Jon looks great in his stash/goatee and his little pony tail," Lynch says, "and yes, he has a hard-on that will not go away, but he also has a winning, sexy-romantic look that makes the screen melt, or come in your face, depending on your mood."

Kinnick asked Logan what it was like to work with Jon on "Loaded." "He's really good and very enthusiastic," Logan said. "Normally you shoot the fucking first and then the close-ups and then do some faking [for facial close-ups and long shots]. He seemed quite happy that we carried on fucking even when we didn't technically have to be. Chi Chi was saying near the end after Jon's come shot, like, 'That was for real? You two are *still* doing it?'"

"Although it's been 12 years since 'These Bases are Loaded Part 1' I still remember it with great fondness," Larry Wills says in *AVN*. "In fact, it was one of the first videos I ever owned. So when I saw there was a 'Part 2' I expected a lot. And I wasn't disappointed.

"The vid flows a lot like the original. The scene is a locker room where King is back, coaching a team of horny studs who get to talking after the game and swap hot stories. Unable to hold off, they all start jacking off en masse before the action moves along to an orgy.

"I must admit, King still looks great. His duos with Logan and Spears really lit my fire. And the man still can take a cock up his ass. Dallas Taylor, sans beard, looks good as ever. The orgy falls a little short of its potential, both in heat and length, but not enough to be a real detraction. ...Who says nostalgia is only for songs?"

Chad Knight with Damien, courtesy
Pleasure Prdocutions

Chad Knight

"Chad Knight is God.
"There, I've said it and there's no thunderclap in the distance so
it must be true. Chad Knight is God."
- A video reviewer in 1991
when the ultimate Twinkie began his career.

Chad Knight *is* God, a Sex-God, anyhow.

Just ask Chance Caldwell, the bisexual star of "The Big Switch III:" Chance likes Chad because he likes "someone who's hot and knows it turns me on. I like assertive people, but also someone I can be in charge of. I always thought this guy was very cute. Then I got to work with him and Sharon Kane in the same movie. It was great."

Or ask another "god," versatile Rick Bolton: "Chad is always nice to be with. If you need a visual, I guess as a man, Chad Knight." The two got it on in Bob Jones' "Straight Pick Up II," filmed in Key West. Bolton, a Philadelphia-born master electrician, moved to Washington D.C., started dancing, and got involved with fetish filmmaker Jones. In reviewing "Straight Pick-Up II," Rick & Dave became enchanted with the star: "Rick Bolton is a god. Doo-dah. Doo-dah. It's time for Rick to dance to OMD. He's wearing tiny little cut-offs with black Swiss cheese bike shorts underneath. It is maybe just a little too weird. But then Chad Knight pretends to be a party guest. He tips Rick and then returns to the stage to play with him some more. After the show, Rick and Chad drink beer together (with a cameo by Danny Sommers as the barmaid). You can only imagine what they are saying because Prince is blasting in the background. There's a part where Chad is touching Rick's tattoo. Then there's a part where Rick looks totally wasted and Chad is touching his crotch. We just wish they'd leave the party and go to a private room where we can hear what they are saying.

"It happens. Chad walks Rick to a bedroom. Rick is barely

conscious. But no, that doesn't stop Chad. He strips them both and licks Rick's body and cock. Rick wakes from his stupor and kisses Chad. Neither stud is hard, but we think that's because they are supposed to be drunk and it's method acting. They start 69-ing and finally they get stiff. The scene ends as Chad shoots."

And shooting is what the fans do when Chad appears on screen. Many a *Manshots* reader has said so repeatedly; one sample of the praise: "His perfect body and boyish looks are a real turn-on. I am saving up to buy a new, red Camaro, but if he would spread his legs wide open for me like (he did for Brad Chase in 'Knight Moves'), I'd buy him the car!" Another fan chastised the editors for not showing more of "The Babe who rules my fantasies."

In 1992, Chad's premier performance was in "Don't Kiss Me I'm Straight," directed by John Summers, in which he ends up standing on his head so Tony Raz can fuck him long and hard.

It seems Chad, like all good bottoms, does his best when paired with a hunk who can appreciate him. *Manshots'* reviewer praised the finale of "Buttbusters," a Falcon entry in which Chad is teamed with Matt Gunther, for what is arguably Chad's finest fuck scene overall: "The youthful Knight looks downright tiny next to the gym-built, movie star gorgeous Gunther, who as usual proves himself to be an amazing sexualist, capable of spewing forth some of the hottest, most believable dirty talk to be heard in many a moon. After extensive cock-sucking and rimming, Gunther forcefully rams his hefty cock into the squealing Knight. Ignoring the boyish bottom's pleas for mercy, Gunther screws him animatedly, pinning his blond partner's legs beside his head at one point and proving himself to be a first-rate topman. Before the fade out, both gentlemen provide ample cumshots."

Another dark-haired super-sexualist who ably fucked Knight early on was Jason Ross, in the otherwise absurd "Traffic School," directed by the late Lucky Luc. *Manshots* again: "Perhaps the most exciting performer is Knight, a boy-next-door-type. He and Ross have exciting sex that ends with a rousing missionary screw on the bed – Ross digging and probing with deep, exploratory strokes, followed by quick, staccato, rabid plunges. Knight holds his feet by his hands high above his head, pulling his ass aloft and opening it wide, until his body-wrenching money shot sprays his torso with thick, white cum."

"Knight...devours every cock he sucks," insists critic Troy McKenzie, "hungrily wrapping his mouth around the tubular flesh as if he can never get enough. And whether he is on his hands and knees or flat on his back, he thrusts his ass high in the air, spreading his legs far apart, so that his hole gapes open wide, as if physically begging for the next cock."

Critic Michael Lynch: "Chad's blond hair is a tad too obviously bleached, but he makes a compliant bottom who obviously enjoys what he's doing." Therein lies Chad's secret, and surely the secret of anyone who has made as many videos as he has: he loves his "work." Getting paid for being fucked silly by the likes of Ross, Gunther and Caldwell has got to be one of the best jobs a bottom-minded boy could find.

And, besides, Chad's damn nice; when Scott was asked if there was anyone who "pushed his buttons," he said: "Chad. He's one of the nicest people I've worked with. Most are pleasant, but it's rare that I work with someone who is genuinely nice like him."

Chad also has done some admirable work for Vivid. In "Scoring," directed by Jim Steel, with help from Chi Chi LaRue, the now platinum blond gets it on with Damien in front of a seamless black backdrop, and it's sex the way it was meant to be in these fantasies. Damien gives Chad the rimming of his life and Kinnick describes it: "Damien delivers a rim job like a Ferarri riding the rail through a carwash. He attacks Chad's butt hole with quick jabs of his tongue, tugs with his finger tips, and delivers small drenchings of well-aimed spit. Chad, of course, smiles sweetly.

"When Damien is done, he pops a load right on Chad's upturned butthole. Then, before you can say 'Hoover' he's down on his knees licking up his spunk while Chad shoots on or about his own chin."

In Vivid's "Someone in Mind," a thematic gem about two lovers who stay together out of habit and fantasize about other men while making love, Chad gets to play top as well as bottom. "I'm the top," Arik Travis tells Chad, "and you're the bottom." So Knight fantasizes what it would like to be a top.

His "bottom" is none other than Danny Sommers, and what a fuck Chad throws him, proving a great bottom is also a great top, when called upon.

Jeremy Foxx was another hot top for Chad, in "Beach Blanket Boner," an otherwise odious concoction served up by Garth ("Queen of the Stock Footage") Evans. Rick & Dave: "First Jeremy sucks on the Knightsick. Then Chad goes down on Jeremy. They move on to some ass-eating, dick slurping 69. Then Chad gets it in the end. Jeremy continues to give it to Chad in almost every possible position until they both shoot."

Meanwhile, in "Driving Hard," from Falcon's Mustang division, Chad was playing a groom trying to get to the church on time, only to have the limo driver be Jeff Hammond. One reviewer set the scene: "When Jeff arrives and rings his doorbell, Chad's standing in front of a mirror staring at himself and emoting for all he's worth, in a non- specific sort of emote you're used to seeing from the Chadster. He's clad in basic white Calvins that hug his tight bubble buns just so…Chad says he still has to shower and asks the driver to wait. Jeff is pissed but walks back to the Caddy where he paces impatiently… Finally, when Jeff gives him 10 seconds to get his stuff together, Chad invites the driver up to wait in his apartment." After explaining that the reason he's dilly-dallying is because he's getting married. "This is as much conversation as he's had in his last six productions. This is quite a feat and the Chadster rises to the occasion." Chad says he's not experienced everything life has to offer and Jeff, "ever the accommodating self-employed entrepreneur, offers to help Chad out." The scene shifts to the bedroom where Chad wastes no time, attacking Jeff's titties and pits as he rubs his own crotch. "They go on for a bit before Jeff attacks Chad's butt and rams his ample cock into it with dilly-dallying deference to Chad's alleged cherry condition. Chad moans and cries a lot while he's getting fucked by Jeff." At least Jeff got him to the church on time.

Chad's other exposure for Falcon was in "Someone's Watching," which features him in a hot 3-way with David Grant and Trevor Hansen, with Hansen simultaneously sucking Chad while getting screwed by Grant. Sid Mitchell called it "one of the most imaginative, delightful features of the year," his only complaints being those usually associated with all Falcon productions: that the people responsible behind the camera are never identified and the running time is barely an hour. (They advertise 90 minutes because they tack on interminable previews.) Besides Chad, the film boasts Trevor Hansen as a masculine guy with a pleasantly gay attitude, for a change.

Chad often flip-flops and proves he's just as good at giving it as he is taking it, as evidenced in "Score Ten." In his scene with Blade Thompson, Chad starts by breaking into lockers and sniffing jockstraps. Kinnick raved: "A scene the whole production should strive to live up to...They perform in an extended duo that is perfectly acted by both men. Chad is the locker room tourist who wants to put his dick up a jock's ass just once. In order to obtain his goal, he first gives Blade a nice handjob, resulting in a fist full of come, then bends over and takes Blade's still hard (and rubber sheathed) cock up his butt. Following this, there is some really nice dialogue and a big switch, as Blade softens and plays bottom for the determined boy. After the fourth nice wet shot in the scene, it ends with a really great hug."

Versatile Chad can also perform with a female slut, as evidenced in "Big Switch 3, Bachelor Party," from Catalina, a party to which director La Rue also invited Johnny Rahm, Steve Ryder, and Mark Andrews. By the time of the finale, Chance Caldwell has porked both Sharon Kane and Chad. "Caldwell sucking off Knight as he fucks Kane is what the explicit bisexual film is all about," raved *Manshots*. Kinnick remarked, "The always accommodating and fawn-like Chad Knight's ass takes over for the girl's pussy halfway through each scene."

Chad showed remarkable acting ability in "Spellbound for Action," another Masters production, this time directed by Chet Thomas. As reported by Mickey Skee: "He starts out as a nerd and finds a Love Potion #9 which turns him into a stud with a nine-and-a half inch dick...Chad has a wicked innocence and a killer body with a perky pecker that pokes straight up to his belly button." Thomas said: "So often in my earlier films, I think everyone was wooden. I didn't get a chance to or didn't even have the interest to spend a little more time developing characters until I did 'Spellbound for Action' with Chad

Knight."

Chad seems to make a fan out of everyone he meets, even truckdrivers, as in Thomas' "Loaded," giving head to "truckdriver" Tony Gambino in a public toilet, or what barely passed as a tea-room.

Chad again demonstrated his versatility for Catalina in their big 1992 hit, "Malibu Pool Boys," produced by Masters. Rick & Dave described the scene with poolowner Chad and a pool cleaner (and porn newcomer), musclebound Cody Foster: "Cody happens upon a piece of underwear on the deck and looks up in time to see Chad waving at him from inside. (That's why Chad is always so horny: No one ever lets him out.) Cody abandons his brother to go inside and visit Chad. Chad is rubbing himself through his Calvins as Cody enters. Before you can say 'Blind Man's Bluff,' Chad is reaching for Cody's crotch...Cody sucks and fingers Chad before mounting and riding him like an inflatable pooltoy. Chad shoots his load and then starts plugging Cody (who we hear is straight). Chad finishes off with another impressive cum shot."

Rick & Dave say "Chad is one of our favorite pornstuds because he is always into it and always hard." In their review of the action in All Worlds' big hit "Kiss-Off," they praised Chad's sequence with Michael Brawn: "Chad is lying out in his jock. Michael appears and pulls out his nightstick (not the wood one). Chad's not one to look a gift penis in the mouth, so he sucks and sucks and sucks...Chad sticks a rubber on Michael and takes it up the butt. Chad shoots. Michael shoots."

Rick & Dave also liked the memorable scene in Catalina's "Sexpress:" "In walks bartender Chad. Is he surprised to see Brett Ford getting the finger treatment from Wes Daniels while he sucks on Gino Milano? No. He's 'been there, done that' Chad. Chad sticks his dick in front of Wes' face. Gino pairs up with Brett for some 69 while Wes sucks on Chad, who has finally grown some hair on his balls. (What a man!) Chad sits on Wes while we watch Gino make Brett fuck himself. Chad bones Wes (talk about versatility!) and Gino fucks Brett. The studs all explode. Brett is about to leave when Chad tells him his job isn't over; Chad still isn't satisfied. As Brett drops to his knees once more, Chad calls the office to express his total satisfaction in the 'Sexpress' service."

Troy McKenzie also raved about this scene: "When Knight lowers himself to sit on Daniels' dick, it is exciting to watch them both struggle to pass the sphincter."

Speaking of sphincters, if anyone would be cast as one of Hitler's youth it would have to be blond, blue-eyed Chad and it came to pass in "Mein Kock," from Jeff Lawrence. In this costume epic, the Chadster gets Bret Winters to fuck him. Bret's thick cock and aggressive technique cause Chad to, as Troy McKenzie observed, "bite the knuckle on his own thumb as Bret pounds hard into him, first in a highly arched doggie position and then missionary with legs pulled back and slung over the shoulders."

Chad's had two movies named directly after him, "Knight Moves" and "A Knight Out With The Boys." Of the former, directed by Jim Steel, Kinnick said: "Like an effective snack food, when you see a little of Chad in a video, you want to see him more and more. He is not only a swell-looking specimen of the genus Boy but also a charmer possessing a natural ease with the camera and all of his partners. He's inherently infinitely likable, not unlike one of the better-drawn Disney characters." The video itself was a disaster, with the performers moving "through one weak scene after the other."

This was Jim Steel's first solo effort from Vivid after the breakup of the "Patrick Dennis" team. At the time of the video's release, Sid Mitchell lauded Chad's performance, saying that he gave "undoubtedly the most erotic and most charming performance of his career," saving this otherwise inept video from oblivion with its bad camera work, repetitive music and unfulfilled ideas. Vivid's stable of performers assisted, including Scott Hogan and Grant Fagin, the boy who loves to suck his own dick.

Sizzling too was Chad's stellar turn in John Travis' "A Knight Out With the Boys." The whole point to this video was to "party, party, party," so there is little time for plot or characterization. As Ted Underwood reported: "The orgy itself bounces in helter-skelter fasion from one grouping to another, and perhaps the best way to suggest the feel of the evening's activities is to cite some of the film's most memorable moments: Chad Knight squatting in a suspended cage while Alex Thomas is on the floor beneath him eating his ass as if he hasn't dined out in years." After seeing Damien rim Chad and now Alex sucking Chad's ass makes one want to know just what Chad has back there that's so damned irresistible.

Even more interesting than Chad's antics at the orgy were his wonderful off-stage moments in "Methods and Madness," the documentary Travis made while making "A Knight Out." Here we see Chad with his glasses on, just being himself, the Ultimate Twinkie.

But, of course, even Twinkies can have moments of serious reflection. Columnist D. Q. Callicott spotted Chad looking forlorn at a Matt Sterling party and said he was "probably feeling homesick for his wife and two kids up north." Robert Richards interviewed Chad for *Manshots* and headlined it: "Married Man."

Chad told Richards it all started when a friend of his who, unbeknownst to him, was making videos for Falcon, happened to have Chad's picture drop out of his wallet at just the right time. A producer saw it and asked if Chad would be interested in coming in for an interview.

But before Chad could do it, he needed to talk it over with his wife, who is six years older than he. "Everything goes through her before I agree to do it." He says there were long discussions about his doing films before he started but the money was good and "this is less immoral than other ways of making money." He says his wife has seen a couple of his films (in fact, he's seen only a couple) and although it's difficult for her to watch them, she has critiqued his performance. "She's very grown up," Chad says. Besides, she would rather look at the pictures of him in magazines. She has started a collection. Chad's woman has a tougher time with his doing bisexual videos. "But, she stomachs 'em," he laughs. "The pay's not as good though. The females, we hear, get paid really well but the men are kind of floating. Basically, they can get *anybody* to do them."

Chad denied having had a homosexual experience before he started in porn. "I'd been curious," he said. A *Manshots* reader, after seeing that statement, wrote, "If we're asked to believe that Chad Knight had no gay experiences before entering films, I've got this bridge in New York City..."

Richards did get Chad to admit that he now considered

himself bisexual. But, he said, "I could never be attached emotionally to a man."

His first day on the set he had "butterflies in my stomach all day! Half because of what I was about to do and half because I was going to be in front of a camera – at last. It was quite a day. I remember *everything* about it! " Scott Hogan was his first partner. "He was very nice to me, made everything easier. I haven't heard much from him lately. I guess he's fading out of the business now.

"I was really intrigued with everything that was going on. Besides acting, I've always wanted to be part of the technical side of the business, so I occupied my mind with everything that was happening around me - wiring and all that. And, we were in a beautiful setting out in a little valley in the Bay area. My favorite part was the simple, semi-improvised setup."

Incredible as it may seem now, watching Chad's later videos, on that fateful day, Scott didn't stimulate Chad. The youngster went off the set and got himself up, then returned. As the scene went on, Chad says he eventually was able to relate to Hogan as a sexual partner. He played bottom first, then top. "It was very long and drawn out - they needed a lot of footage. It lasted an hour and a half or more. I'm physically fit, so keeping apace all day long wasn't too bad, but when I got home - whew!" Chad came while Hogan was fucking him, then had to rev himself up again to be able to fuck Hogan."

After seeing "Compulsion - He's Gotta Have It," *Contax* magazine's reviewer was in awe: "I last spotted Chad in 'Someone's Watching' and I suppose at the time I had mistaken that little stud-puppy Jim Montana for God so all I remember about Chad was that he could stand a few extra pounds on those ribs. Strange how these things work. Back then, Montana was god, and now it's Chad Knight. The only way I can possibly make amends to God Chad is to gush about him whenever I mention his name."

In this video, Scott Hogan again gets to lay it into Chad, beginning in a pool. "In a flash he's in Chad's craving love hole (excuse me, I just had to use that one this time.) Scott fucks like a pro, really giving it to Chad who eggs him on with loud moans and sounds to that effect." Noticing neighbor Trevor Hansen watching them, the boys get into numerous positions, the last one being Chad on his hands and knees with a sloped back and his ass high in the air. *Contax* sums up: "Chad deserves sex-kitten status the same as I once conferred on Joey Stefano."

But by the time sex-kitten Knight made "Knight Moves" for Vivid, he'd slipped a notch in *Contax* estimation, from God to Prince: "My but what a difference a few ounces of Clairol can make! Chad didn't go totally weird with his hair so he's still okay in my book. He let it go natural (brown) and got it buzzed on the sides real short. Then with what he left on top he squared it off, flat-top style, and put enough Dippity Doo in it to hold it stiff and spiny in a Force-4 hurricane. But that's okay. He's a twink, and twinks can get away with almost any eccentric type hairdo."

And twinks can get away with a lot of truth-stretching. When Chad says the bottoming on that first day was "more work than anything else," that's hard to believe looking at Chad in action today, especially in the video "Preferred Stock No. 1," wherein he is finally fucked by the stupendously hung Cody James. Wow! He also really gets into it in Garth Evans' "Superstud Fever," with a fuck at the finale that is everything any Chad fan could wish for. Truly sublime! If this is "more work than anything else," at least Chad *loves* his work.

After a year and a half staying home with the wife and kids, "that ever-flexible boyish bombshell with a huge cock is actually returning to the screen," said Dave Kinnick about Chad in 1994. "I guess he really missed all the attention he got from being a porn puppy."

No, we have a hunch he just missed all the sucking and fucking.

Knight showed up in two of David Babbitt's first fuck flicks for All Worlds, "Reflections 2" and "Tales from the Backlot," and in "Hell Knight" for Studio 2000's new director Kevin Aames.

Interestingly, in "Hell Knight" and "Backlot" Chad tops his partners. But in a video made before Chad's "retirement," "Heaven Too Soon," he fucks Nathan Rocco and then gets fucked by Chance Caldwell. His performance, including the smiles on his face, speak volumes about what this boy likes best: he's a born bottom.

Indeed, the fucking of Knight reached its zenith in his other "comeback" video, Club M's low-budget quickie, "Gang Bang Rich Boy." Here Chad fulfilled his long-held ambition to get fucked by a black dude, in this case eight of 'em. The promotion copy (which we have not edited) for this video is stirring: "Chad Knight, the hot ass little rich boy, gets an ass fucking of a lifetime. It all starts innocently enough. Chad's daddy makes him supervise the painting of their mansion. Chad picks up the painters and before long eight of the ugliest; meanest hardened men are up at Chad's mansion. Chad has no respect whatsoever for the working class and it shows in his belligerent attitude as he tells them what is expected. But the rich brat should have been a little more respectful because he's dealing with 8 of the horniest big-dicked painters around who have a combined total of eight feet of long hard cock. And these painters are very worked up over Chad's hot little sweet ass. When Chad changes into his golfing shorts in front of the painters little does he know that he is getting these ass hungry guys so hot that they almost shoot their loads from just seeing his naked tight buns. After practicing with his #9 driver he comes back into the house to check the status of the paint job. When he notices nothing substantial has been achieved he loses his temper on the painters and lashes out at them. He takes one painter into another room and makes him prep the windows. When the painter suddenly grabs Chad's ass, Chad pulls back but is aroused by the big-dicked black man squeezing his ass. Before long Chad has his mouth on the 10-inch black shaft sucking it all the way down holding it in his throat and then pulling back up. The black painter crazed with pleasure moans as his fat cock fucks the hot mouth of this rich boy. The other painters who are now outside taking a break hear what's going on inside the house and sneak up to the window and witness one hell of a mouth fucking by one of their paint buddies. Chad then is pulled inside and forced to kneel on a work table and show off his incredibly smooth round ass for all the horny workers to see. Soon the men strip down Chad and start stroking their dicks as one of the bigger men pumps his swollen cock into Chad's thirsty willing mouth. Chad then submits to the group of ass splitting painters as his tight pink asshole is repeatedly opened up by the group. Fuck after fuck

Chad must satisfy the demanding horny ass-bangers. He is worked over in every fuck position possible."

Whew!

When *Manshots* interviewed Ted Matthews, they asked him about his "Spellbound for Action" co-star Chad Knight. "He has been a very popular performer," Matthews said, "but I never understood why, because I don't find his type particularly attractive at all. I don't really like thin blonds. And he needed to look at *Playboy* to get hard. It was really turning me off. To get hard, he had to look at *Playboy*! And I was closing the magazine, so I could get hard to fuck him, 'cause even seeing that around turned me off. He was a nice guy, but we didn't have any kind of connection. With Jason Ross, he and I really got along very well. In the years since then, I've been together with him and his lover, and I'm friendly with them and I see them around L.A."

"But you don't have tea with Chad and the wife and kids?"

"No, no."

"But as a person, he was all right?"

"Yeah, he was okay. I don't hold that against him, that he's bisexual. But I mean, it didn't turn me on. I'm surprised that he's become as big in the business as he has, because he's not built, he's not defined. I don't think he's particularly good-looking. But I'm surprised by most of the people who are popular in the business."

Of all of his partners, Chad said he liked best working with Danny Sommers: "He's a lot of fun and real easy to be with. I try to forget negative ones." Chad said he has lost count of all the videos he's done. "It's more than fifty, less than a hundred." He's not getting as many offers as he did because, his agent says, the feeling in the industry is that he is on the downside of his career. "Producers don't like to use faces the public has become accustomed to. And I'd like to do more. It's scary."

Chad's planning on going to the Fireman's Academy in California, but would still like to do modeling on the side.

Chad told Richards that he had always been attracted to being in the limelight: "In school, I was always the class clown, always going for attention. I guess this is just a way to get attention. I'm very shy."

Kip Noll

Kip Noll

"I could write a book about why I became obsessed with Kip, why thousands of males like me were similarly obsessed. Kip Noll is a subject that, one way or another, I have always wanted to pursue."
- A Fan in Rochester, NY, founder of Kippers Anonymous

A true superstar draws the audience into the action. Even something you don't like in general can provide specific moments in which you forget everything else in the world around you and concentrate on the action. The action of the star. Kip Noll had that ability. No matter what situation he was in, he reigned supreme. I first saw him dancing with gay abandon at the hottest disco in Southern California, the multi-colored lights swirling across the white jeans that seemed to be glued tight to his sinewy body. He rubbed sweat into his curly blond hair and smacked his lips. He was street trash personified but also glorified. He was adorable. I fell in love. You couldn't take your eyes off of him. He was the chicken hawk's ultimate pet.

After his big score in 1978 in "The Boys of Venice," Kip's appearance began to deteriorate but it was tolerated. In fact, it made the fantasy even more appealing. It seemed he had moved off the street and began to resemble more and more the older hustler you might meet in a sleazy bar, a young man for whom life had been especially harsh, a man you wanted to take under your wing and nurse back to health. You knew he would pay you back, in the only way he could.

Speaking of payback, the fan in Rochester, who founded the Kippers Anonymous Club for others who have become obsessed with the star, says, "My obsession was intense. I first saw him in a magazine called 'Cocky.' It featured not only page after page of full erection but ended with heartstopping shots of Kip with cock in hand, eyes closed, doing it. Unbelievable stuff. One had to imagine the streams of cum, but it wasn't hard. Then, when I saw the magazine, 'Kip Noll Superstar,' I realized there were movies of all of this! Movies where you didn't have to imagine the cum shots! But that magazine had cum shots, too, and pictures of Kip's cock in another guy's mouth and up another guy's ass!

"Finally, I saw 'Roommates' and I was pumping in breathless disbelief at what I was watching. I still think it is the most erotic flick I've ever seen. What made it so intense was its believability - it seemed perfectly reasonable that these two great-looking guys should behave in this sexually playful way, grabbing at each other's crotch and jerking each other off. But when one bent over and actually sucked the other, the earth shifted in its orbit.

"The sucking went on, I came in my jeans, and each time I think of it something in me moans."

Oleg Kamensky in *Gay News*, November 1980: "Kip Noll has freshfaced blond good looks... His photos are bestsellers in gay bookshops all over the world... He has been doing porno since he was 19 - he is now 24 - but he still works as a machinist in San Diego and hopes to complete his apprenticeship. 'It would be something to fall back on; as I'm a pretty good handyman.' On the other hand he'd rather be a fashion model or do television commercials. He has six brothers and sisters and his family all know what he's doing and support it. 'I didn't get on with my parents so well till I started making movies,' he says. 'Then I became happier and more relaxed, and found I got on with them better. One day my mother asked me what I was doing, I told her, and she asked me if I felt I was doing it well. I said yes, and she said in this case she would always support me.' Kip adds that his mother hasn't seen any of his movies. He thinks they might upset her but he intends to show her some of his magazine pictures. 'My girlfriend - I'm bisexual - doesn't know what I'm doing yet, but I'm going to tell her. She won't mind, she always supports whatever I do.'"

One of Kip's first loops demonstrated his considerable gifts for fellatio. Called, appropriately enough, "Try to Take It," it is now available on Falcon's Pac No. 51. Kip and a blond buddy are under a tree and Kip not only sucks his friend's thick cock, he also tongues his boots.

It was under the guidance of William Higgins that Kip became a superstar. "I didn't like him at first," Higgins recalls. "He was a very streetwise boy. And I didn't like that quality in him. But as I got to know him, I think I liked him a lot more. I certainly liked him as much as anybody after we got to know each other. But he is one of those persons that looks incredibly better in photographs than he does in person. The camera loves him. He's got kind of a blotchy skin but it doesn't show on camera. And he wasn't one of those kids that could just snap his finger and get an erection. Sometimes the magic worked, sometimes it didn't. I think it had to do with how much partying he'd done the night before. He said he was straight and he wasn't really straight. So, as far as he was concerned, he could do just as good a job with any male."

After the success of "The Boys of Venice," Higgins rushed Noll into "Kip Noll and the Westside Boys." "It was a very unprofessional job," Higgins recalls, "but for those days it wasn't so bad."

Higgins' follow-up film, "Rear Deliveries," starred another streetwise kid, Lee Marlin. "Now, Kip Noll had his infrequent run-ins with the law," Higgins remembers, "but Lee Marlin, I think he probably knew the inside of the jail as well as he knew the outside of the jail. But he was a very funny, clever person. And, depending on what he'd had to drink the night before, he could perform." Perform he did.

Later, Marlin was to team with Kip in "Roommates," made for Mark Reynolds and released by Trademark at the same time Kip was starring in "Cuming of Age," appearing with his supposed brother Scott and Steve (12") York.

Both these films hold up very well today. Kip's topping of Marlin was so successful it led to their pairing again in "Grease Monkeys," joining with veterans Derrick Stanton and Nick Rodgers to provide one of the most appealing and perhaps the best of the "popular mechanics" movies.

Kip seemed to get turned-on by most of his on-screen paramours but he clearly enjoyed some more than others. Derrick Stanton in "Brothers Should Do It!" was a prime example. They hungrily found each other's mouths during and after sex and walked off into the garden together. Lovers of uncut cocks find great enjoyment in Kip's scenes in "Pacific Coast Highway" and "West Side Boys," proving he could enjoy it with or without.

Indeed, Kip's partner in that first appearance in "The Boys

of Venice," the man Kip called his "Greek god," was uncut and gives Kip his best ass-fucking on film. Kip doesn't seem to enjoy getting fucked in "Class of '84 Part II." His partner is Jeremy Scott and the scenes go on far too long and the sex becomes labored and boring, probably because Scott, Higgins' lover at the time, was on a star trip of his own and found Noll to be far too street for his taste. Judicious editing would have helped immensely.

Higgins left us with the most fitting tribute a porn legend ever had, Kip Noll's own "profile" film, "Kip Noll, Superstar." In addition to the clips from all of his appearances for Higgins, the director was astute enough to tack on footage with Kip and Jon King which makes this film one of the all-time heart-stoppers. Not only is it a joy to get a glimpse of the human side of Kip and see him looking good in his "interview" segments with King, but the fucking and sucking the boys do in the finale is one of the hottest such escapades ever recorded. Their obvious enjoyment of each other's sexuality is infectious. Kip's kamikaze cock reams Jon in an endless number of positions until finally Jon just sits on it and jacks off to orgasm.

Higgins remembers how the movie came about: "Noll called me and said he needed to work. First, he wouldn't do anything more and then he decided he wanted to work. And I thought, well, what can I do real quick?, so I put him and Jon together and it was the only new scene in the movie.

"With Kip you had to do it on his terms. You know, he wouldn't do anything with his hair, which always looked god-awful and so you couldn't touch his hair.

"And now he said he needed to work so we went and set up in that house where we shot 'Westside Boys' and got it done very quickly. When he said that he would do some work, you always had this little window of opportunity. If he said, 'I want to do some work,' and you said to him, 'I'll get back to you in a week,' then forget it because he wasn't in the business anymore.

"Now I understand he's married and living in Wyoming or Utah." In August of 1993, *Manshots* responded to a letter from a reader in England regarding Kip's whereabouts. The reader called Kip his "hetero/idol" and enclosed a greeting card to be forwarded to the performer. The editor responded that he'd recently heard a new rumor that Kip was now living in Minnesota with a male lover. "But, as you know," he said, "one rumor is about as reliable as another."

Late in his career, Kip's legend was able to survive disasters such as "Flashback" with Al Parker, in which the two failed to ignite any sparks and just jacked off, and his own home movie, released as "Kip Noll's Casting Couch." He tried marketing the film himself by mail in 1983 and it was unsuccessful. Later, Boss Video got hold of the video, did some editing, added some glitzy titling, a music score and live sound, and that is the version available today.

In the final analysis, the secret of the Kip's success was that he was not overexposed. Being undependable worked to Kip's advantage; he appeared in only a handful of films. In comparison to today's performers, some of whom rack up thirty or forty appearances in a year, Kip left his fans hungry for more. *Stallion* magazine put it best when they summed up Kip's appeal this way: "He's a gem even in a junk jewelry setting."

Al Parker

Al Parker

*"...Deluxe, a prize, a genuine luxury item. The packaging is
perfect - the smooth golden skin, the pearly teeth, the heavily lashed,
flashing black eyes, the sleekly muscled body, the glossy hair
and that dick of dreams."*
- *Porn Star Interviewer Robert W. Richards*

"Wanted." What a perfect title for a porn film starring Al
Parker. It was to become the quintessential Parker fuckfest.
Directed by Steve Scott, the 1980 Mustang Production was
inspired by the 1957 movie "The Defiant Ones," in which two
convicts, chained together, escape from a road gang. In the case
of the earlier version, it was a black man and a white man. In
"Wanted," one man is straight, the other gay, a perfect set-up
for some spirited hi-jinks and the gifted Scott didn't let us
down. Critic John Rowberry described Al's performance in
"Wanted" as "amazing" and says: "Parker is at his most
humble as the gay con who wants Will Seagers (playing a
homophobic convict) in the worst way but needs to be wanted
back."

Beyond the physical, those who knew him find Al to be an
intensely private person but someone who was gregarious and
intelligent at the same time. Of all the sex icons of the late
seventies, Parker endured the longest. He was able to roll with
the punches, doing more for safe sex and the restoration of
foreskins than any other performer.

But Al simply never understood why he had been one of the
chosen few: "There are lots of better looking people out there
with better bodies and bigger dicks. I couldn't be more
surprised that they've singled me out. I have no idea why."

Born in 1952, Parker was sexually active early on and
demonstrated his ability to do it all when he went to work for
Colt Studios. They assigned him his name and he hated it, but
he was stuck with it. ("It sounded so forgettable to me," he
joked.) Paying him fifty dollars a session, Colt got Al to pose
for their photo layouts first, several of which appeared in the

glossy magazines that were gaining in popularity during the mid-70s. The response to Al was so tremendous that Colt put him on film, caught up in a hot three-way in "Challenger," a loop for Brentwood release. On display here was the legendary jack-hammer style of fucking that has endeared him to fans of the manly type.

In the golden days of porn, when a feature film opened at the 55th Street Playhouse in New York you knew it was going to be an event. "Inches," Al's first full length feature, was not only an event, it became a phenomenon, running for months. From then on, Al could write his own ticket.

Viewed today, however, the fact that this was filmed in the '70s is bothersome. One critic said, "The fashions, the cars, the attitudes, the speech patterns, everything, is from a time some of you may not be old enough to remember. This isn't so weird when watching 'The French Connection,' but when you're watching porno, historical references jump out of the scenery and bite you in the ass." But the critic does concede that the best thing about watching it today is that there is no guilt: "This is a film shot before 'you know what' and although it may have been out there, these participants didn't know it. So what they're doing, in that sense, is perfectly okay."

What this same reviewer didn't find okay was Al's use of cockrings: "Parker is a honey and his pecker looks great poking here and there but I think there's a problem when a guy can't get it up without a cockring strangling his weenie. Parker uses leather cords, leather cockrings – anything – to keep that spongy tissue engorged and his Johnson in an upright position. In the very first scene, Parker ties a double-boline, reverse hitch knot in the leather cord and his pecker starts to point skyward. He splashes on some baby oil and begins to work on himself. He tugs the cord and stretches his balls from here to Montana. Ouch. Some think it's hot. I think it's a crutch."

All his crutches intact, Al followed-up "Inches" with "Wanted," again with his lover Steve Taylor and in it he fucks his man with both his cock and his balls. "It looked great," he recalled.

Sexy stunts helped make Al the legend that he is, as well as adroit couplings with other hot men. The list of incredible Parker teamings seems endless and includes Leo Ford and

Giorgio Canali in "Games," Jack Wrangler in "Wanted" and "Heavy Equipment," Dick Fisk, the Georgia boy who died tragically in an auto wreck, and several others who give Casey Donovan the gang banging of his life in the classic "The Other Side of Aspen" for Falcon Studios, and two hunky jailhouse guards in "Weekend Lock-up" on Falcon's Videopac #4.

Much was anticipated when Al teamed with Kip Noll in his own production, "Flashback," but the chemistry was wrong. The dedicated, hard-working Parker and the unreliable Noll just didn't hit it off and it showed.

Al said later: "I was not impressed with Kip. I never saw him as the boy next door. He was unkempt, ungroomed, arrogant, a street person. But I knew he was a star name, for whatever the reason. I was looking for a Colt type, a Falcon type, not a street type, and I wasn't in a position where I could say, 'Get your hair cut.' Still, I was glad to have him in my movie. Our sex scene was like a Mexican standoff. I am not a bottom and Kip was not a bottom. I think it is well known at this point that I am not fond of getting fucked. It has nothing to do with a head-trip, because I've done it – on film. I look like I'm enjoying it, but I physically don't find it comfortable. So I didn't want to get fucked, and I knew Kip didn't want to get fucked, but I knew there would be tomatoes on the screen if the two of us didn't do something together. So we just jacked off."

Manshots praised the finale: "Noll decides to model for Parker and the film finishes with Noll working on himself – body, cock, eyes – everything that made him a star, is there on full display. Both he and Parker were at the peak of their form in this film."

Al's collaborator, the late Steve Scott, had no patience for the unreliables: "Unless the story calls for it, I don't seek younger models. (Mature men are) easier to work with. They can fill a commitment. Usually when you get into a younger bracket, they're more flighty. You know, they'll get a better offer the night before the filming and they'll never show. They just have a built-in problem: inexperience. I just as soon not work with the problem.

"Al is the easiest person I've ever worked with," Steve said in an interview. "He's totally professional. He knows what the other people on the set are there for. He does not pull the star routine. I've worked with most of the people in the industry but Al's special. And he's got quite a large following. His films are very much in demand. I think *Screw* magazine called him the Cary Grant of gay porn.' He's very hot. And he's sensual. He doesn't come to the set with any preconceived notions - he's never given me constraints like 'I don't work with...' or "I can't do...' You know, it's like whatever I devise, he's more than willing to try to make it into something. He also gets involved in the cutting, music selection, the final mix, the titles. He's not just flesh in front of a camera."

Scott and Parker (and lover Steve) merged their considerable talents as Surge Studios in 1980. Eventually, Scott left the fold before his death and produced some of the best films of the early '80s, including "Screen Play," but the defection did not effect Parker's output. Despite an occasional misstep, such as 1986's overblown, poorly edited "Oversize Load" and "One in a Billion," Al is one of the few stars who can carry a film on his own, as he amply demonstrated in "A Night Alone with Al Parker," which ties all of the loops together with insert shots of the star sticking a dildo and his balls up his ass as he jacks off. Talk about versatile!

Rowberry raved about Parker's work once he was on his own: "Parker is drawn to the sexually extraordinary; he has tempered his personal fetishes in the past only to accommodate the mainstream of gayporn in the marketplace. With projects like 'High Tech' and 'Turbo Charge' he steers the viewer toward the specific, namely his own fascination with cock pumps and pumpers."

"Turbo Charge" documented the real-life affair between Al and Justin Cade. Parker let his hiar grow to the shoulders and sprouted a beard, making him appear as if Christ had gone to Gold's Gym. Cade was a stunning contrast. "His close-cropped hair, his Teutonic features and physique are counterpoint to Parker's tanned and sharply-etched musculature," Rowberry commented. "They are the living homoerotic stereotypes: the Great White Stud and Christ-of-the-Surfboards."

Into the '90s, Al continued to remain active in porn. He even responded to the amateur video craze with "America's Sexiest Home Videos," a technically crude but heated set of four scenes, the best, naturally, featuring Al himself. Playing a construction worker, Al gets into it with Grant Lance and much of the action focuses on Al's restored foreskin. Through Saran Wrap, Parker rims Lance, has Lance slide a rubber on his meat and begins. As *Manshots* observed, "After fingering him a bit, Al fucks him, at first missionary and then in a squat-fuck that detonates Lance all over the star's still enviably defined abs."

Al died on August 17, 1992, in San Francisco of complications from AIDS. He was 40.

Bruno from 1973, courtesy of Colt Studios

The editor with Roger in New Orleans in 1978

Roger (& Bruno)

"There are two things I hate, size queens and small cocks."
– Old Queer Saying

It can take years for a performer to establish himself to such a degree that only one name is needed on the marquee to attract a crowd. You have to be a legend: Elvis, Marilyn, Sinatra, Liza, Judy, and so on.

But by 1977, there were some guys who took short-cuts to and achieved early prominence in porn by using only one name: Scorpio, Bruno, and quite possibly the most photographed of them all, Roger. We first saw Roger on the pages of *Blueboy*, the most popular gay magazine of the day, in a pictorial titled, "The Flasher," photographed by Sodoma, where only his cock was shown. But what a cock! It was a huge, cut, perfectly formed slab of manmeat and it caused an immediate sensation. A layout of Roger as a biker at the beach in filmy pants quickly followed. The sight of that magnificent tool and those impeccable buns were enough to make anyone salivate. But he also had a handsome face and a good body. Later, when Roger got heavy into weights, the body would grow into spectacular. He was short in height but he made up for it with the awesome size of his penis and his constantly expanding biceps.

I admit I have always been a size queen. There's just so much more to see. And I'm not alone in my obsession. As Doug Richards wrote, "Size fixation is certainly not without historical precedence. Phallic worship has existed since the Stone Age and continued unabated throughout the Neolithic Era and the Bronze Age. Phallic stone monuments from this latter epoch stand ten feet tall, direct forerunners of the Washington Monument and Eiffel Tower. Artifacts from ancient Egypt, the Orient, Greece and Rome clearly show a preoccupation with the phallus. Among many awesome examples, the Graeco-Roman deity Priapus, god of fertility, has always been represented with an oversized phallus. So modern day homosexuals are hardly the first to join 'The Cult of the Colossal Cock.'"

As an avowed member of this cult, meeting Roger became a compulsion. I finally struck a deal with the star's agent to have the star make a stopover in New Orleans on his way to Hollywood to make a film. During that long weekend in the spring of 1978, I was to observe the phenomenon of the big basket as I had never experienced it before. No one on the street recognized Roger, but the splendidly skin tight clothes he always wore clung enticingly to his bulging biceps and crotch, attracting the stares of men and women alike even in no-holds-barred New Orleans.

He let me know right off that he didn't get fucked (he saved that for the screen and special occasions) but everything else was okay. I was so in awe of that mighty organ that all I really wanted to do was worship and adore it. It was the first time I had encountered one that large and I quickly discovered one of the problems a man so well endowed might have: it seems the meat rarely hardens to the extent it does with "normal" equipment. This is not much of a problem for these men when they are fucking women. Cunts are designed to accept most anything. But for men with tight assholes, it can be an excruciating experience.

After a few attempts to take Roger anally, I opted just to suck on it. Roger didn't have to but he eagerly got into a 69 position and proved a superb fellatist.

His posing for *Blueboy* pictorials led to a special issue devoted exclusively to the emerging star. And then, inevitably, came films. We first encountered him in a loop from Bullet called "Good Neighbors" (now available as part of Bullet's Pac 7). His first co-star was Bruno. In the loop, Roger needs some help with his geraniums on his patio but gets far more than that from the hugely developed he-man hero of the day. They go down on each other and then Bruno fucks Roger with his usual quick, powerful jabbing.

Roger's second outing was with Chuck Samson in "Garden Party" (Roger always seemed to be near the flowers). Their encounter is very hurried; just Roger licking Chuck's balls and then letting Chuck face-fuck him.

One of Roger's early loops that was used as a layout in Blueboy was Falcon's "The Housepainter," (now available on

Pac 6) in which Roger enters the living room of two lovers and makes them both happy. Another Falcon loop on the same package, "Bigger Than Life," finds Roger playing a model who can't sit still, he has to fuck the artist.

Roger was paired four times with Jack Wrangler, 69-ing and ass-pounding in "Heavy Equipment" in 3-D, "Hot House," "Sex Machine" and "Sex Magic."

Roger was hardly the star of these ventures: The Christy Twins stole "Heavy Equipment" with the hot glory hole scene with Wrangler and while Roger and Mandingo play construction workers in "Sex Magic" and the fuck is good, Wrangler won the spotlight appearing as a window washer who cleans up inside as well as outside.

Although we found the limp humor of "Hot House" a downer, Bijou Video's reviewer says of the star's appearance in the film: "Roger is less tense than usual, making this his best film." Roger proves himself a good foil for Wrangler here, getting into a dandy 69 which ends with Wrangler taking Roger's hefty load. In an earlier scene, Roger interrupts the apartment painter's shower to take a piss and the man goes down on him the moment Roger reels out his meat. The man gets a golden shower first and, after much heated sucking, takes Roger's jism.

Although he oozed sex from every pore, especially when nude, Roger's presence hardly ignited the screen. It was as a stage performer he achieved his legendary status. His manager shrewdly took advantage of the heaps of publicity the boy got through magazines and kept him moving through much of the late '70s from one movie palace to another stripping, wagging that tremendous dong at the throng. And, it goes without saying, performing "private shows" for the more well-heeled customers.

Director Tom DeSimone, who guided Roger through "Heavy Equipment," said: "He wasn't much for giving head. The things he wouldn't do on film: he wouldn't kiss and he wouldn't suck dick. Of course, he was straight. I knew him and his wife."

But I know from personal experience that Roger was good cocksucker when the spirit moved, and I will treasure those hours in New Orleans spent 69-ing with him.

Having been with Roger, I longed to meet the other half of the exquisite "Good Neighbors" pairing. Then I chanced upon a Colt Studio brochure and there he was: his undershirt was pulled up high on his chest, revealing one huge hairy pectoral. The magnificently macho picture was in the obscure lower right-hand corner of the brochure but men like me the world over found it, creating a sensation and a star. Colt said later in a retrospective: "A phenomenon; a quiet, everyday airlines employee who came across in pictures with an overwhelming impact; the studio could not keep up with orders for more! more!; he is what photogenic is all about."

Bruno, as he chose to call himself, was the height of virility in those days. But there was an added dimension to it, a tenderness with the toughness, a gayness that was somehow implicit.

And it wasn't until he started doing films that we became aware of the fact that besides enjoying being worshipped for his masculine charms, Bruno could suck another guy's cock with considerable skill before he fucked him silly.

In the spring of 1980, when I invited Bruno to spend some time with me in my suite at the Barclay in New York, he admitted that, for a while, he was upset about the first film he did for Target Studios, "Bayside."

"I didn't really want to do it," he said in his Spanish-accented English (he was born in Cuba). "Slides and prints are one thing, but it bothered me for a week or two. Now I've done dozens of these things so I guess it doesn't bother me much any more! I've enjoyed doing some of them more than others, I mean, like if you are doing a movie with someone who turns you on, it's great, but sometimes I'm told who I have to work with and I may not be particularly interested in that person. So I have to pretend that I'm not going to be turned on, that I'm doing it just for the money. And I can always do it."

And always quickly get an erection. While we talked, busy Bruno got nude and came over to where I was reclining on the bed. He presented the magnificent uncut cock I had enjoyed so much in photographs. Between licks, nibbles and gobbles, our conversation continued.

He said one film he turned down which might have been a phenomenal sizzler was a gay version of "Grand Hotel," co-starring with Peter Berlin. That would have been the uncut cock lovers' dream come true.

Bruno agreed with me that Roger was a turn-on physically but not intellectually: "He was the one I enjoyed making a movie with the most, but I didn't really care for him as a person. He's nice, but he's not into the gay scene. To him, it was all acting. He has gotten married and settled down to a dull, blue collar existence."

"My reaction to him was similar to yours," I told Bruno as I stroked his cock, which was now fully erect. "He was playing a role. And not all that well, either. I guess he was capable of turning it on when he wanted to, such as the scene with you."

"Ha! I guess, " Bruno chuckled. "But I'd rather get it on with a guy who's gay. A lot of these guys in the business are basically straight, hustling and doing gay porn for the money. It's not a comfortable situation for me."

His pairing with Roger in "Good Neighbors" is available as a Bulletpak (#7) which also features a solo of him oiling up and jacking off. The other definitive Bruno can be found on Falcon's Pak #13, pairing him with Shane in an appropriate "trucker" setting. That particular tape also boasts another mighty man, Gordon Grant, fucking and getting fucked by two beach boys.

"I don't do much modelling any more," Bruno said. "I work for an airline and I really can't spare the time. Anyway, my lover gets very jealous when I go on those assignments. Actually, I don't really like to be bothered by people who call and offer this and that. Ninety percent of them are just taking my time. I've had people offer me the world, but I never believed them. Besides, I have to be with someone I really enjoy. I mean, I'm no virgin. I hustle. I mean, I'm here with you, right? But when it comes to somebody on a day to-day basis, it's got to be someone that turns me on. Otherwise, I'm just wasting myself."

He wasted no time with me, accomplishing what he had been asked to do for me in short order. I greased his splendid cock and took him on doggie-style, the fashion I prefer, watching the assault as reflected in the hotel's gilded mirrors. His jack-hammer style was akin to Al Parker's, which was, for me, very efficient and painful in an ecstatic way. After enduring about five minutes of this ecstasy, I jacked myself to orgasm and Bruno pulled out. I collapsed on the bed.

After washing himself, Bruno pulled on his tight Levis, construction boots and flannel shirt over his gigantic arms and told me he had to rush to another appointment. He was a very popular fuck in those days.

"You have my number," he said, shaking my hand firmly. I guess I did. He certainly had mine.

Joey Stefano

"On numerous trips to New York, I had missed Joey's performances at the Gaiety. I was either too late or too early. Then, on June 10, I finally made it. It was his first show and he showed no rehearsal, no talent, no interest and the audience ignored him completely, not even clapping, which is unusual for the raincoat crowd. I attended the 1 p.m., 3 p.m. and 8 p.m. shows and he was a disaster each time! But, having nothing better to do, I returned for every show on Thursday, Friday and Saturday. Suddenly, he was dancing like a professional, almost like a kid in 'A Chorus Line!' He had good music and his audience watched every move, giving him applause upon his entrance, mid-way through and at the end. On Saturday, he gave the best performance I have ever seen at the Gaiety, and I've been going there since the early '80s! I can't imagine what happened to him! As I left, he was out front and I said, 'I'll be back. Great show!' But he said nothing, as if he hadn't even heard me. Next time I see him, I am going to ask him to autograph my copy of Jock Magazine for January, 1990. It has 25 excellent photos, the best pictures I have seen of him."
— Jimmy, A Stefano Fan from Kentucky

For much of 1991, I pursued Joey Stefano, the boy who had inherited Jon King's throne as the best bottom in the business. I was anxious to do a book about him. After the success of the book about Tim Lowe, *Lowe Down*, I asked Tim to intercede. I had Vince Cobretti, about whom I wrote *A Charmed Life*, carry my case to Joey. I had Jimmy from Louisville, who visited New York frequently, give Joey a packet of information and a letter. Jimmy said, "He told me he'd seen your books but he wasn't interested."

Then I saw an interview in the *Gay Video Guide*, which was new at that time, in which the legendary star was quoted as saying: "I want to write a book by Joey Stefano and you know I'd bet it would sell! It would tell my whole story; the sexual abuse, coming out of the closet, the porno, the drugs, everything. There are a lot of people out there that are still fucked up on drugs and I could show them that it's possible to beat that! I really want to do it. Jack Wrangler did it and his book was really successful. I want to do it, I know I can. My god, with all that I've been through in this business, I'd have a lot to tell."

Obviously, although Stefano saw the value of such a book he wasn't about to go to work on it. I tried to get him interested over the years but to no avail. I saw him at Tampa club manager Alfredo's annual parties over the years and the last time we met, in May of 1993, Joey was looking better than I have ever seen him. He greeted me warmly before the show but still wouldn't commit to a book deal. On stage, he gave another breath-taking performance. The man at the table next to ours summed it all up for the other fans in the audience when he said, "Once in my life, I'd like to fuck that ass."

Joey loved performing live; he said: "I'm giving them what they want. Every jack-off club I did from California to Florida hasn't had as big a draw as me! Every dance club I strip at, I draw more people than even Ryan Idol! When Ryan puts on a show he's just up there on stage performing at the audience. I perform with the audience. The image is pretty hard to live up to. I try so hard and I do too much sometimes. I've done things on stage that I would never do in private life! I've taken two dildos up my ass! And at the 'Black Party' in New York, Jon Vincent couldn't get it up so I told him to beat my ass, finger me, do whatever you want! Afterwards, all heard from every queen around was how I got fisted in New York and how I was this big slut, lots of rude comments. But I'm doing it for other people because that's what they expect from Joey Stefano! I feel that so much has been taken from the real me."

In interviews, Joey attempted to shed his one-time image of the druggie who'd do anything for his next fix. That was true, he said, when he was a teen living in Chester, Pennsylvania, and then when he went to New York, where he'd hustle just to stay high. Everyone who knew him, however, realized because he was making videos like mad and servicing well-heeled executives, Joey could afford to stop turning tricks indiscriminately and get high more often. "I was everywhere," he finally admitted. "I said yes to every movie that was offered to me. Doing everything for everybody. I got caught up with 'Joey' and lost who I was." What Joey was, we fans knew, was a self-proclaimed sex maniac. Jon Vincent, one of his co-stars, said: "Joey is one of the hottest men I've ever worked with. I always talked bad about him and I really feel bad about it because he's a hot kid. He really did the trick for me. Big time. Some other guys didn't do nothin' for me. I need somebody who can match me, like Joey did. Joey'd say, 'Fuck me, fuck me, come in my pussy!' I had to keep pulling my dick out of him, I'd get so hot. He'd just stick that ass up in air and when I was inside of him, I couldn't move or else I'd shoot. He really got me goin'. The best piece of ass I've ever had. He's probably the hottest piece of ass in the world. But he's still mad at me. Won't talk to me. But I guess that's the way it is."

But putting out for anything that breathes can wear a guy down. "I have become very impatient and tired of all the bullshit," Joey said. "Tired of having sex with people I didn't like, stuff like that."

Maybe that's why Joey (born Nicholas Anthony Iacona on New Year's Day 1968), didn't take advantage of all the things the business had to offer. "I didn't want it all. I didn't want to travel around the world doing escort work. I don't want the business to become my entire life. It's too much, doing the movies and escorting. In the beginning, I didn't like doing escorting 'cause it brought back too many bad memories of when I did trick for drugs. But now I'm comfortable with escorting because I can pick and chose who I'm with. I've made some good friendships with my clients and later down the line if I ever get into a bad situation, I know that these people will help me. I have friends that will fly me here and there and it's nice having them for support and not having to constantly work for it."

Joey Stefano's life tragically ended on Novermber 21, 1994. "In late November," Gino Colbert remembers, "before Nick (I never called him 'Joey') got to town, he rang me from New York to let me know he'd be coming in and to touch base for possible film work. He'd always call me with his itinerary. I don't think he ever made a trip to Los Angeles without letting me know. Even if I didn't have any project going at the time, we'd still get together for dinner and a movie. It was routine.

We saw a lot of films together.

"A week later, when I told my boss at Leisure Time/Stallion Video that Nick was coming in, he told me he wanted to meet him and I should invite him to Sunday brunch. My boss was impressed with the fact that Joey Stefano outsold all other gay actors in our mail order catalog. Nick's following was unbelievably strong, keeping him #1 on our sales charts.

"I extended my boss' invitation before Nick got to town. However, Nick wanted to get together beforehand to see a film, so on Wednesday the 16th, we went to see 'Interview With the Vampire' (my second time, but it didn't matter), and afterward we met up with my production manager, Lucas Kazan, for dinner. Lucas was a mega fan of Nick's and had worked with him on one of my sets. At this point, Nick was beginning to warm up to him. Nick was not always personable to everyone; it took him time to get to know someone, but at dinner he and Lucas hit it off, and the entire time Lucas said he regretted not having his tape recorder with him. Nick spoke about his drug addiction during dinner and his boyfriend, a young Cuban he recently was sharing an apartment with in Florida. He said the kid, with whom he was very much in love, moved back in with his mother as the responsibility of a relationship was too much. Nick said he looked forward to getting back to his new apartment and getting back together with the boy. Lucas asked him about drugs, and he admitted he had a problem before he even got into the business. But when he seemed to blame the business for 'feeding' his habit, that's when I went off, telling him he made the wrong turns on the career road. He admitted he remembered my giving him some advice when he was starting, the same advice Vanessa del Rio gave me: save your money, don't get involved in work politicis, and watch the partying. Years later, when he was a big star, he told me he had gone through $100,000 in one year and wished he'd have followed my advice. On this particular night, he confessed he had been smoking crack and finally managed to get off the stuff and felt good about himself. He really seemed to be out of the drug mood, but he was depressed over his breakup. He was looking forward to working.

"That Sunday, Nick called me to cancel brunch, saying he

felt awful and wanted to stay in. Later that night, I spoke to him again to see if he felt better, and he said he felt great and was heading to the gym. On Sunday the 20th, he rang to ask me if I had a copy of his I.D.'s as his wallet and gym bag were left in a taxi. The next day I got a copy from the office and planned to bring it to him, but it was too late. He was already dead.

"My boss was as shocked as I was to learn of Joey's death. He confirmed what I had always felt, that Nick had such striking looks that if he hadn't done porn he could've been a successful print model. He was simply incredible, changing his look every time I saw him (the long hair, the crew cut, the beard, et al), yet he always looked great.

"The last video he did for me was 'Tijuana Toilet Tramps.' He worked with Anthony Gallo in his one scene, and was, as always, a pleasure to work with.

"I first met Nick in 1990, when Tony Davis rang me to tell me about this new model he met in New York, and we later met at the gym. Tony said he was planning on bringing him around to the different companies, but he had just gotten to town and no one had met him yet. I was going to use him, but Chi Chi LaRue asked me not to, saying he had plans to promote him bigtime and would appreciate it if I wouldn't as it would hurt her plans. I discussed this with Nick, and he wanted to give it a shot. Nick was staying at the Saharan Motel on Sunset, and I got him a studio apartment in my building on Whitley, which was his first residence in L.A..

"When I was working as an actor on an InHand shoot, Chi Chi brought Nick on the set to watch how it was done. I sat him down and gave him a little advice, the same, I told him that Vanessa del Rio gave me when I started. It was about saving his money, not getting involved in work politics and partying, and so forth.

"At one point between scenes, I pulled him aside and we practically ate each other. Chi Chi stood by panting, and asked me later if I'd work with him in his first scene since we seemed to have such chemistry. We later did do a scene for her in a military-themed feature, and I was a disaster. I couldn't function worth shit, which didn't help newcomer Nick, who was always as good as his partner! It was embarrassing. Paul

Norman was the cameraman and bragged throughout the shoot how great he was and how he wished he could find someone to shoot his movies as good as himself. Then Chi Chi started screaming across the room who was making what. I really wanted to impress everybody, but it didn't happen. On top of that, when I complained that one of the actors I worked with had a 'cheesy' cock and asked the director to have him wash it off, the director refused, saying he was the director and it wasn't his job. Nick jumped in to fluff the guy, and when he finished he whispered to me, 'He tastes like tacos!' He had an adorable way about him."

Joey was LaRue's first major discovery, and eventually every director wanted to use him. "There's no one, not even Jeff Stryker, who became a sensation as fast as he did," LaRue said. "I was in love with him, and I was jealous because I wanted him all to myself, but the rest of the world fell in love with him, too."

A year after Gino first met Joey, Stefano had become a major star and was signing autographs at Drake's Bookstore on Melrose in Hollywood. "He was on the cover of the Adam Film Guide," Gino recalls, "and signing copies with the editor, the late John Rowberry. I asked Joey to sign my book, and he wrote something to the effect that he'd been through $100,000 in a year and what he didn't understand he did now and he'd never forget the advice I'd given.

"Over the next few years, many times we spoke about saving money and him directing, and I often offered to help him start out. He was interested, then not. He seemed content doing the dance circuit and coming and going as he pleased. During his last year, he made several trips to Los Angeles to do work for me, and he'd ask me not to tell other directors he'd be coming to town. He claimed they'd want to party with him and he really wanted to avoid that scene. He told me many times with great pride how clean and sober he was.

"Then I read in the *Advocate Classifieds* gossip column a tasteless piece about someone phoning in and advising Dave Kinnick to start writing Joey's obituary. This bothered me, so I tracked Joey down. He was dancing at the Gaiety Theatre in Manhattan. He looked great and we chatted several times that week."

Stefano was always welcomed at the Gaiety, the theater where he appeared in photographs with Madonna for the book *Sex*. Stefano liked to tell about the time Madonna walked into the Gaiety to shoot the pictures, looked at him and said, "Well, I'm not the only star around here. Hello, Joey."

Colbert's meeting with Joey in Manhattan led to him coming in to do a couple jobs and Gino's finding out about his use of crack. "He hadn't worked in close to a year at that time," Gino recalled, "living with his sister in Philadelphia. Stefano discovered he was HIV-positive and swore off doing videos."

Later, Sam Abdul would express surprise when he heard about Joey's HIV-positive status, saying that Stefano signed a statement that he was negative. Friends say, however, that Stefano wasn't too distraught about his status and always remained healthy. Stefano insisted he contracted the virus through shared drug needles and not through sex. Not performing, Skee reported, set off a downward spiral of a suicide attempt, two severe overdoses and drug use that included heroin, cocaine and ketamine, known as Special K, the drug thought to have contributed to his death. It's a drug that's injected; used for putting animals to sleep.

"The love of his life, the only woman he said he would ever marry, musician and actress Sharon Kane, helped him through many bouts at drying out. He checked into rehab centers and went to 12-step meetings with his adult industry friends supporting him along the way."

"When he came back out here, his intention was to clean up," sighed Kane. "We talked, and he wanted to go to (Narcotics Anonymous) meetings, but I could see the marks in his arms."

Skee reported that Kane once lived with Stefano and toured Greece with him, but she--like many of his friends--were frustrated to see his constant abuse and distanced themselves from him. "He always got stuck in the same old pattern," she said. "We just couldn't be there for him as much as he wanted us to be."

At the time of his death, he was staying across the street from Kane and LaRue at the house of trans-performer/director Crystal Crawford (aka Brian Maley) and actor/director Christian Murphy.

According to Murphy, Maley recalled, "I had nightmares that I was going to wake up one morning and find Stefano dead in my bathroom!" Stefano apologized and promised to cool his drug use, but he still managed to bump his head on a shower nozzle and give himself a black eye a day before he was shooting a video for LaRue.

"It kept bleeding because the cut was above his eyebrow, but he wouldn't tell us how he did it," said actor Johnny Rey, who also spent time with him the last few days. "He wasn't someone who was very easy to get to know, or figure out."

Stefano stayed out all night before LaRue's shoot for Falcon's Mustang division, and Maley and Murphy tracked him down to a hotel at Hollywood and LaBrea where a drug dealer named Matt was giving him drugs.

"He was dripping with sweat and laying on the bed with his eyes opened," Maley said, clutching the red sweatshirt still wet with sweat only hours after Stefano's death. "Matt wouldn't let us call 911, but we kicked him out and called. They coached us through CPR and I gave him mouth-to-mouth resuscitation until paramedics arrived. I couldn't feel a pulse, but he was warm and they said they might be able to save him."

"I was quite impressed with the way Brian handled the whole thing," Murphy said. "Immediately everyone in the community came together to help."

Crawford called Kane and she joined LaRue and Falcon director John Rutherford at Cedars-Sinai Hospital where doctors refused to tell them his status until Kane feigned being his fiancee. Then, they told him he expired.

"Does that mean he's gone?" asked LaRue. Everyone burst into tears. Later, LaRue reflected how closely this tragedy was linked to Savannah's death earlier this year. "They were both very much in the public eye and they both had a reputation of being very difficult to work with," he said. "They were both very naive and beautiful and both were screwed up long before they got into the adult business.

"This business helped his self esteem, and I'm convinced he wouldn't have lasted this long if it weren't for his family in the business. I was a pseudo mother to him for so long."

"To prove how the show must go on," Skee reported, "the night of Stefano's death, Gender still mustered a brave performance at Atlas Bar & Grill. I joined a group of white-faced dazed friends--LaRue, Rutherford, Kane, Johnny Rey, Maley, Mocha, musician Chris Green and others--as Gender broke into 'Dear Mr. Stefano,' his song to the tune of 'You Made Me Love You.' Maley cried, and we were all stunned.

"The next day Gender said, 'I think it was the last time I could sing this song in that way. It was hard for me to go on that night, but he was always so sweet and child-like, I think he would've liked it.'

"The next day, there were calls to Stefano's friends and family, attempts to raise money for burial arrangements and contacting the police to find the drug dealer who contributed to the superstar's death.

"It doesn't seem like it really happened, I don't want to believe it's true," LaRue told Skee. "The last time I saw him was when he gave me a hug in my bedroom and he told me, 'I love you.'"

"In 1993," Skee says, "Joey appeared in a mainstream short by Robert Ellsworth called 'Reflections.' Contacted in Australia, a stunned Ellsworth said, 'I just finished writing a movie called 'Lifeline' for Joey and it was the role that would have made him crossover into mainstream acting. If anyone could have done it, he could.' The film, in development with New Line, will now be dedicated to Stefano."

Joey's greatest legacy remains his incredible body of sex work; he appeared in more than fifty gay and bi porn videos in five years and played to cheering crowds throughout the U.S. and in Europe. His fans have special favorites among his videos and one of the most rabid fans we know says, "I love all of Joey's work, probably just because it's Joey, but for sheer cuteness I love: "Songs in the Key of Sex", "Total Impact" (including the promo for "Total Impact" that was at the end of "Hidden Instincts"). I also love "Dildo Kings," "Hole In One," "Karen's Bi-Line," "More of a Man," 'Plunge,' 'Raw Footage,' 'Say Goodbye,' 'The Stroke,' 'Man of the Year,' and 'Sharon and Karen.'

"But his sexiest performances are in: 'G-Squad (scene with Sergio Calluchi),' 'Big Bang,' 'Innocence Found,' 'Inside Vladimir

Correa,' 'Obsessive Compulsive,' 'One Man's Poison,' 'Prince Charming,' 'Revenge,' 'The River (with Steve Kennedy),' 'Scoring (scene with Steve Ryder),' 'sex, lies, and videocassettes,' 'Undergear,' 'The Visitor,' and the scene in 'Hard Knocks' with Andrew Michaels.

"I think that the essence of Joey was a cute, light-hearted child-like kind of charm. I think what makes Joey's videos so special is that, for the most part, you see Joey really enjoying himself not just performing."

But it was superstar Joey himself who described his allure most succinctly: "It's not just the money, it's the sex. I'm a sex maniac."

Joey forced Stryker to kiss him in "On the Rocks."

Jeff Stryker

*"While the language is, to say the least, coarse and the sexual
activity brutal, the recipients of Jeff Stryker's masculine
ministrations are always very appreciative;
this is not surprising since the scenes are such overwhelming
incarnations of homoerotic paradox."*
– Brian Pronger in "The Arena of Masculinity"

Ever since Jeff Stryker came to prominence in 1983, there's
been a new challenger to his throne every year. But there's only
one Stryker: The Ultimate Porn Stud. In his solo video, "Just
You and Me," he stands before the mirror and, as he begins to
remove his shirt, he talks into it:

"I've been thinkin' about gettin' home, lookin' at your pretty
ass, running my hands through your hair.

"I want you.

"I want you so fuckin' bad."

Now the beautiful pecs are exposed. "So what do you think?
You like what you see?

"Do you want me as much as I want you?

"Hmmmm, I wanta feel ya.

"Oh, I want you to fuckin' hold me.

"Yeah.

"You like my chest?" He rubs it.

"I want you to grab and fuckin' suck on my tit.

"Hmmm, touch my nipple.

"Take your tongue down my stomach...

"Aaahhhh..."

He reaches into his pants and plays with himself.

"You want my big fuckin' dick, don't ya, eh?

"I'm gonna take this hard body and fuckin' grab ya and fuck
ya with my big ole dick.

"You want me to make love to your sweet ass?

"I want you to feel every inch of my body.

"I want you to love me, every fuckin' inch.

"Feel me. Ooohhhh.

"All day I've been thinkin' of fuckin' you with this big old fuckin' dick.

"C'mon I want you to help me get off.

"Oh, I would make love to you so fuckin' good.

"Oh, I'm so fuckin' horny.

"I want ya, ya know?

"You wanta watch me, don't ya? You wanta watch me, yeah" "Oooh, I want to feel it deep.

"Oh, you make me so fuckin' hot. I want you to make love to me.

"Is that what you want? Oh come on, don't tease me."

He pulls his briefs down pass his asscheeks and turns so he can see his buns in the mirror.

"Look at my fuckin' ass! You like my pretty fuckin' ass, don't ya?

"You wanta watch my ass while I'm fuckin' you, don't ya? "Do ya want me to kiss you?

The stud kisses his own reflection in the mirror. "Oh, I love you, too.

"Do you want me to make love to you with this big fuckin' dick?"

Out comes the cock, half-mast but still formidable. It's one of the most beautiful cocks you've ever laid your eyes on. It's long, thick, cut, perfectly shaped, very pink at the head and halfway back, topped by a small nest of light brown pubic hair. The body that comes with the cock matches it in every way. Perfectly defined, muscular without being absurd. The face looks as if it has been carved out of stone. It's pleasant in a midwestern farm boy kind of way. And when the stud smiles, the face becomes downright handsome. It is a smile that is so inveigling, so thoroughly compromising, as to almost render his partner to silly putty in his hands.

As he continues to stroke his mighty cock he snarls a bit and the contortions of his face add immeasurably to your enjoyment of his performance. Suddenly, the stud is in bed, slathering his body with champagne direct from the bottle. "Oh, lick it off. Oh, yeah, lick it all off!

"Oh, oh, c'mon. Oh yeah!

"Oh, I fuckin' want you. Lick the fuckin' champagne off my cock.

"C'mon, lick it all off my body.

"I wanta lick your body.

"Oh, yeah. Oh, I wanna fuck you.

"Oh, I want you on my fuckin' cock.

"You want it. Yeah, you want it. I'm gonna put this fuckin' hunk a meat inside you.

"Oh, I want you to take it. Oh, spread those pretty legs. Oh, let me in your fuckin' body.

"I want you. I wanna get in your fuckin' body.

"Oh, yeah, take all of my fuckin' cock. Take all of it.

"Oh, look at that hot fuckin' cock! Get on it and ride me! Take it all the way, deep, deep inside of ya."

This raunchy monologue is also featured as a vignette in "On the Rocks" and is quintessential Stryker. In his book *The Arena of Masculinity*, Brian Pronger pays special attention to Jeff Stryker's verbal commentary: "After he has commented on his own masculine force, Stryker will draw attention to the joy of his partner by pointing out the rapture of the same: 'You like that big cock going up your ass don't you? Huh?' 'He likes that, don't he? See, he's got a big ole hard on.'"

Jeff said that in the beginning the directors just let him go crazy. "I wasn't guided," he said, "I wasn't pushed." And Matt Sterling confirmed this, saying the dirty talk was totally unrehearsed, undirected: "It came forth so willingly, so excitingly."

The combination of a boyish face, perfect body, and long, fat, incredibly juicy cock that won't quit coming (he's usually good for two "money shots" per appearance) has sent sales of Stryker videos through the roof since he hit the screen in 1987. The world's best-selling dildo was molded from his magnificent cock by Doc Johnson. Jeff said: "They added nothing in width but they added an inch in length. It insults me that they did that but they said that I wasn't 'fully motivated' when they were making the mold. But it's pretty wild. I always tell people I'm carrying around the master."

Doc Johnson further insulted him by not giving him what he thought was a fair share of the profits, so he sued. And some fans were insulted when Jeff signed a deal to promote a cock enlargement device, then made a video demonstrating its use. "Now look," one fan told me, "if anybody doesn't need such a thing it's Jeff."

Jeff says his cock is between nine and ten inches, "depending," and, in general, he likes to fuck with the lights on so he can watch it in action. But the first time he's with someone, he'll do it in the dark, "just so I don't get any rejection. It is quite intimidating. Gay men are obsessed with it until they have to deal with it, then it's a different story. But even in the dark, they say, 'What is that? Your leg?'"

Appropriately, Jeff's first video was Matt Sterling's "Bigger Than Life" sequel to "Inch by Inch," then he made several punchy flicks under the aegis of John Travis before striking out on his own. It is often said that good friends Travis and Sterling co-developed the Stryker persona, shaping him as well as his career. Stryker came to Hollywood from the Midwest wanting to be a porn star but having no idea how to do it. Going so far as becoming a lover to both Sterling and Travis at various stages of his career, Stryker succeeded because, as Travis put it, "he was in tune with doing this. So many models today have the opportunity but are too busy doing other things. Stryker was dedicated to quality and building himself up." And, Sterling says, Jeff had that special gift great true film stars have: when the camera rolls, they exude charisma. Just hanging out with these pros, he learned from them and he took advantage of the knowledge they freely gave him. The game plan was put into place and Jeff has followed it ever since: don't flood the market with product, keep people hungry, build up a distinct image and take control. In the eight years he's been in the industry, Jeff has made only 14 videos.

Part of the "distinct" Stryker image early on was holding back, not reciprocating. Travis' feeling was that if one lays all of one's cards on the table at once, there is no mystique. "Creating an illusion, creating a fantasy - that's basically what we're selling."

The Stryker mystique, then, was sex as punishment, fulfilling a fantasy, taking to the extreme the idea of the "straight" stud who doesn't mind giving a gay guy a thrill.

Mostly, Stryker gets praise from his bottoms. Erich Lange said: "He's a good fuck, a strong top." And until "Stryker Force," in which he kissed a man twice, he never showed much affection for those willing men he assaulted. Typical of his method is the sequence in "A Portrait of Jeff Stryker," from 1987, which later was incorporated in the first episode of a 1989 Catalina release called "The Look." Herein, Jeff is running a garage and he takes two younger fellows, Ricky Turner and Kevin Wiles (at the time, two of the industry's workhorse bottoms) into his place of business and Jeff disciplines them for breaking a windshield. He makes them suck his cock and then, after he fucks each of them and throws a copious load, he lets the boys overhear a phone conversation. It is then they realize he knew all along they didn't break the windshield and they stand gaping as he hangs up the phone and grins mischievously at them.

If one looks at these bouts as competition, on rare occasions, while letting Stryker think he's always "on top," "punishing" a boy's butthole to the best of his ability, a bottom may actually win the game. Consider the scene in "Stryker Force" with Robert Harris. Stryker offers himself and his huge cock up to the pliant Harris, who, from the looks on his face throughout the sequence, is having a helluva lot more fun than Jeff. And, by taking every inch of that meat, Harris is, in effect "castrating" the stud, bringing him down.

"You know," video pioneer William Higgins has said, "when you're in the business, you're always talking about the one that got away. Jeff Stryker was more or less like this because we always wanted to find somebody perfect to shoot with him. So he sat around waiting for a year and we didn't get nearly as much work done with him as we should."

Higgins told Jerry Douglas that Stryker's creators believe that the only person gays are really interested in viewing is "the quintessential top man who is essentially trade and is insulting to the gays. And you know I can play along with that when I feel like it, but I don't think it's a persona that I find attractive. I think that Stryker, more than any model I've ever known, generates more positive and more extremely negative comments than any other model. And you know, I don't find anything attractive or sexual about his screen persona."

Director Jeff Lawrence agrees: "Stryker is the ultimate effort in the thinking that the heterosexual is the epitome, stationed above us and forever unattainable. It pisses me off. Sex is, after all, sex, and I really do think that regardless of who is participating it brings us all down to a common level."

Manshots traces Stryker's decline to his decision to go it alone: "When Jeff Stryker first exploded across the adult movie screen he made an impact virtually without precedent in the history of film erotica. His gym built physique, masculine good looks, oversized sexual equipment, hypnotically sonorous voice, and amazing gift for raunch rap instantly made his name a household word. Unfortunately, his subsequent career, especially since he formed his own company (Stryker Productions) and took total artistic control of his screen appearances, has failed to live up to his initial promise, and he has been on a slow downward spiral from that day to this."

The first flick produced, directed and edited by Jeff was "Every Which Way," with Nick Elliot ably serving on camera. But it's the little "public service" message about condoms that he tacks on the end that we could have done without. It may be in keeping with his on-screen persona but blowing smoke rings and saying he needs a Glad bag instead of a condom, when added to the fact that one of the girls in the video says, "Take that rubber off and fuck me," is true theater of the absurd.

In his 1991 video "Busted," art imitates life as Jeff comments on his recent troubles with the Feds. (His studios have been busted frequently as part of the government's Project Post Porn.) *Frontiers* said: "Welcome to a world where the innocent pleasures of even way tame adult movies are forbidden by law. Porn producers are investigated, bugged and eventually hauled off by the strong biceps of the law...Jeff is still groggy from a long hard night of whatever it is he does at night (can't be sex; that's his day job) but Gino Collbert manages to give him a toe job, lick his butt and does various and sundry nasty things. Jeff lets him while a surveillance car lurks below his house. A couple of studs show up for an audition and Jeff invites them to join in the action. Basically everybody fucks everybody, except Jeff, of course, who never gets fucked by anybody. Meanwhile, back in the surveillance van, the FBI men start investigating each other. Off come the pants." Proving even FBI men can get turned on if Stryker leads the way. Of all of the Stryker scenes, arguably the best from a gaymale perspective is found in "On the Rocks," directed by John

Travis and featuring a climactic three-way with Joey Stefano and sexy Matt Gunther, who, as Stryker is plugging him, screams, "You're gonna make me come!"

Just when you think you've got ole countrified Jeff figured out, he surprises the hell out of you. He nibbled on Alex Stone's dick in "Powerfull 2" and kissed Joey Stefano on the mouth in "On the Rocks." God, fans were asking, can anal penetration be next? No way. Jeff was surprised by his fan mail after he nibbled on another guy's cock on-screen. "People like that dominant, aggressive image and I'll always keep that."

Yet, as Kinnick says: "More than perhaps any other star in the history of modern gay erotic, Stryker has manufactured and nurtured a screen persona calculated to capture the fancy of gay America. But that is only part of his success; the other part is that he is continually redefining his image, keeping his audience constantly poised for the unexpected, and providing them with surprise after surprise, every time out."

Speaking of surprises, in one interview Jeff revealed that he thought what he was doing was "morally wrong" who knows he's a "sinner" like everyone else but doesn't "choose to hide his sins." Yet, late in 1990, in his interview with *Interview* when asked whether he was happy in porn, he replied: "I don't think there's anything wrong with the movies I do. They're made to entertain people. I'd like to venture out of pornography. Maybe do a couple more videos, then go on to something with a wider audience. And just grow, basically. Because I got into pornography hoping it would be a stepping stone. If Traci Lords can do it, I can too. And I don't even think she can act. If I could get a major motion picture, I'd rely on my acting ability rather than my name. Because I do feel I can act. I've done a pretty good job of it so far, even though I've never taken acting lessons. I've been told that I'm a little like Brando or Dean. I don't know, though. I can't see that when I look in the mirror." One wonders what Jeff Stryker *does* see when he looks in a mirror.

Mostly, it seems, what Jeff can see in the mirror is that fabulous cock. The stud told Michael Musto that his cock has "a mind of its own. It's unisex. I like it and it likes me and we get along fine. It earns its own income. In fact, it supports me. Who's the smart one here?"

Besides that infamous dildo, now available in the "realistic" and the "rotating" models, there's now a complete line of Stryker sex products, including lube, playing cards, the pump and the "How to Enlarge Your Penis" video at $19.95. He also has a nonsexual instructional video, "Strike Back Vol. 1," obviously aimed at gays who are sick of gay-bashing and want to learn about karate self-defense technique.. The muscular stud spends most of the hour-long running time topless so one critic doubted that the viewers of the tape would be practicing what Jeff was preaching. Rather, they would be opting for the "one handed chicken choking hold." In other words, some guys can get off watching good ole boy Jeff doing anything at all.

Director Jim Steel, who has good words to say about just about everybody in the porn biz, calls Jeff "one of the smartest people and, he is the nicest person as well. I first met him a long time ago when he was IT. Before they would release anything, there was just a picture of him month after month. And I could not believe anybody could be so charming. Completely charming. He would give you the shirt off his back, literally! He is square with you and this is the key thing. People who lie, I hate them, I can't deal with it. My deal is but a handshake."

During 1992, with the Feds raiding his offices, Jeff was able to release only "10 PLUS," a compilation of j/o scenes featuring his brother Rick, B. J. Slater, and Chance Caldwell, plus some scenes from previous Stryker productions. The fact that the star saw fit not to include any his own scenes caused critic Dave Babbitt to shout: "Unforgivably, since the famous Stryker name and body is plastered all over the box cover, there's not one new frame of j/o footage of the celebrated Stryker ramrod. Would it have killed Mr. Stryker to jerk his cock for the cameras of his own production? Or does he care not one whit about the ever diminishing legion of fans patiently awaiting a product worthy of his star power? Why would any educated consumer purchase this collection of solos when he could witness enthusiastic sex in dozens of other productions? Don't aficionados of solo flicks deserve better?"

Lately, Jeff's been taking a breather from video and he's become known chiefly for being a party animal. In 1991 he garnered considerable press by attending the Love Ball 2, a surreal evening when over a million was raised for AIDS charities. The Roseland Ballroom in New York was packed with a glamorous eclectic group that included Jeff, David Geffen, Madonna, Calvin Klein and Sandra Bernhard. Musto reported that when club schmoozer Fred Rothbell-Mista told the star, "You know how many times I've slept with you in my dreams?" Jeff had no reply, not even his usual *bon mot*, "Tighten that hole."

The New Yorker explained it all: "From the Kingdom of Sexual Disorientasia/Male Division: Certain members of the press realized that the guy in the bike-shorts-tight leather pants and open to the buckle white shirt was Jeff Stryker and proceeded to follow his every step across the celebrity waiting area, desperate for an interview but too tongue-tied to ask for one."

One who wasn't bashful was *The Advocate's* R. Couri Hay; he had the dubious distinction of getting the last word: "Jeff Stryker's got wrinkles, darlings, and I'm not talking about on his balls. The poor thing looked used, used, used. Well, there are always his early videos to cherish. So, now you know, I'm a bitch. Surprise, surprise. Jeff, wearing leather pants in 80-degree heat and two diamond rings he must have gotten from Liberace, left alone in a cab after telling me that 'love is as strong as your condom.'"

In 1992, he popped up at an AIDS Project Los Angeles benefit showcasing eccentric Parisian designer Thierry Mugler's summer collection at the Century Plaza Ballroom. Stud Stryker strutted his stuff with the likes of Michelle Phillips, Sandra Bernhard and Billy Zane.

Later, across the continent, in a rare strip appearance, Jeff got down and dirty at Webster Hall in New York for promoter Dallas and stayed on in the City to party with his friends, Boy George, Robin Byrd and Susan Barch. He took in Paul Rudnick's off-Broadway comedy, "Jeffrey," and posed with the cast.

In Paris, he was photographed by Pierre et Gilles, who put him in the tightest sequin trousers he could find and gave him satyr's horns, and did the Mugler catwalk in another fashion show. Gay fans went wild. The straights wanted to know who that "funny little man" was. (Jeff is five-eight.) "When the word got out," an observer said, "Jeff's hotel was besieged with men and women with only one thing on their minds."

In London, he appeared at Freak, at a series of themed monthly gay parties. But before leaving for the U.K., Jeff agreed to take Jim McClellan, from the British magazine *The Face*, on a tour of the headquarters of Stryker Productions in Hollywood (he works out of his home): "...an unassuming bungalow on a very swanky street in L.A. As soon as we arrive, Jeff insists on showing us round the warren of guyishly cluttered rooms. The things you might expect to find in a porn star's home – the kind of weird sex toys needed to stimulate a jaded sexual palate, the sad, soiled left-overs of last night's orgy – are nowhere to be seen. Instead there are telephones and TV's everywhere. In one of the bedrooms there's an arcade video game titled *Astron Belt*. In another there's a makeshift video edit suite. Across the hall is a nursery, piled high with toys for Jeff's three-year-old son, Little Joe. Out back, there's a pool and a set of weights (he works out for an hour every day.)

"At the center of the house is the living room, which is packed with kitschy stuff – two wooden horses from a merry-go-round, two mushroom dummies, a glass-topped coffee table whose base is a crouching black panther, some very bad abstract art, a life-size cardboard cut-out of Jeff doing karate (he's done an hour a day for the last eight years), a real zebra skin on the wall, a big-screen TV which plays daytime soaps continually while we're there. The stone wall is covered with flashing fairy lights. I ask Jeff if it's a deliberate design detail. He grins and says that he put them up three Christmases ago and it took so long he couldn't be bothered to take them down.

"Tanned, heavily pumped, sporting tight black jeans, white singlet and cowboy boots, Jeff looks almost too healthy. The boyish looks he had when he first started have mellowed into a kind of soap-opera handsomeness."

When asked what he'd do in his show in London, Jeff said: "I don't know. I usually wear some of the clothes (Thierry) Mugler made for me: cowhide chaps, leather pants, just beautiful stuff." When asked if, at some point in the evening, would he remove his clothes, Jeff said, "Well..."

"Perhaps he'll do his single," the reporter mused. For his visitors, Jeff played his demo tape, "a kind of funked-up twelve-bar over which Jeff delivers a rambling monologue on the subject of his main attraction ("*it's big and it's thick,* "*it'll make you scream,*" etc.)"

Jeff said he wrote the words himself. "It's called 'Wild Buck.' I wanted to call it 'Wild Fuck,' but we had to tone it down a little. I think it'll go over big in dance clubs."

When asked if his gay fans minded his appearances in straight videos, Jeff said: "I'm not sure. I hope not to offend anyone. My objective is that they be satisfied with what they see. I'm hoping to let people see that people are people, and to categorize and stereotype isn't so good."

To McClellan Jeff revealed publicly for the first time how he came to be a father. It seems a few years ago Jeff was pursued by a woman claiming to be an actress who was "desperate" to do a movie with him. He "met" with her for about three days and then she disappeared, only to turn up a few weeks later saying she was pregnant. "At first I said it couldn't be possible. But it was premeditated."

"When Little Joe was born," the reporter said, "Jeff was there with his attorney."

"It was a nightmare," Jeff says. "The mother was trying to get outrageous sums of money from me to visit the child." The paternity was proved and after a court battle that dragged on for over a year, Jeff won custody. The mother is now in a drug rehabilitation center. "He's definitely a terrorist, but I love it," Jeff says of Little Joe. "It's like the ultimate dream – having a child, but not having to deal with that crazy woman."

"Crazy" is what some industryites say Jeff is. Kinnick calls Jeff one of the industry's "biggest spooks." "I've met him only once. It was January of 1990 at the Consumer Electronics Show in Las Vegas. (This was the year the Feds set up a sting to have companies send them product at fake stores in Mississippi and Oklahoma.) Stryker had been in a fist fight the night before and was showing some cuts and bruises on his face and I, like an idiot, swooped down on him with my journalist's note pad and pencil out. Actually, I just wanted to introduce myself and tell him I admired his work in the past. (The present is another story.) When he heard the word "press," he freaked. A very cordial facade became a stormy, muttering, bundle of nerves, and he suddenly spotted someone across the room that he absolutely had to talk to within five seconds. He was off, and

I was left wondering what I had done wrong. The next year, he was at the show again, his face restored to its usual choirboy-gone-antisocial look, wearing a full length black leather trenchcoat. This time I didn't approach him. I say, if a legend wants his privacy, give it to him."

Trey Tempest, star of "Takin' Care of Mike" and "Cool Hand Dick," among others, recalls making "Busted" with Stryker: "I was supposed to top in my scene, but the English guy - Matt Windsor - all of a sudden is telling everyone he can't get fucked. So, I was like, 'Okay, I want my $600 for this so I'll bend over and take it for five minutes, and we'll simulate the rest.' So we finished that scene and they said, 'You'll have an hour or two to rest now, and then we'll have another scene for you to do.' Well, ten hours went by, and they weren't ready to start taping my second scene. It was two o'clock in the morning, and I was really mad because I had been told I'd only be there a total of maybe six hours. I could have gone out and turned three or four tricks in the amount of time I was there. So I walked up to Gino (Colbert, assisting Jeff) and said, 'Look, I've been here for twelve hours. You're going to pay me $150 extra for staying so long and I'm not going to do the second scene.' When Jeff heard what was going on, he was really pissed. He said, 'No one has ever walked out on me before.' So it was like, I made history again."

Also pissed was Joan Rivers, when Stryker rejected a guest spot on "The Joan Rivers Show." His manager said, "Hell, Jeff even turned down Calvin Klein."

Jeff turned everybody down for a couple of years. He was busy taking care of his son Little Joe and making such straight sexvids as "Wild Buck." Then he suddenly decided it was time to tease his gay fans again. His "return" was well-programmed. First he released a compilation tape, "10 Plus (Vol. 2)," which received a lukewarm, at best, reception.

Roger Harding in *Gay Video News*: "Jeff Stryker has his legion of fans, all of them impressed by his good fortune to have been born with a VERY big dick, and good looks. He's also had the astute business sense to assume control of his career, rather than just taking a straight fee for performing in someone else's videos. I just wish he would put more effort into those videos that he releases under his own company banner.

Watching Jeff and company strip and fondle themselves, and eventually jack off is certainly entertaining, but where's the interactive sex that Jeff used to do? Here, we're treated to frequent shots of a guy taking a soapy shower, another guy jerking off on a motorcycle seat, while well-tanned bartender Chris Stone strips on top of a bar. As for Stryker, he seems to think that shots of him slipping seductively out of a blue silk robe, or stroking his enormous endowment underwater while cooing inane 'Yah, yahs' to the camera are alone worth the price of admission. Sorry, Jeff, but I want to see MORE."

Apparently Roger missed the point of the video, that Jeff was offering more – at least on record. He warbled the opening song and provided information on how to order the music. What Jeff didn't tell us is what happened to segments with Steve Regis and Cole Phillips that were credited but both missing from the line-up of studs.

But if viewers wanted still MORE, Jeff wanted to give it – at least from a distance. In January, the star showed up at the Gay Video Guide Awards Show and let it all hang out, netting him incredible coverage in all of the skin magazines and a spot on the video of the ceremonies. Then, concurrent with the release of his new solo video, "Tease," he took his "nasty leather" show on a three-month, 20-city tour. Orchestrated by his pal and porn vet Gino Colbert, Jeff gives more to his fans than he ever has before. At one point during this brief program, he goes behind a back-lit transparent screen, gets it hard, then bursts through the screen to the cheers of the crowd. At Manhattan's Webster Hall, Michael Szymanski reported, he almost caused a riot. The club owner's mother – amazed at his onstage, ah, performance – came backstage afterward insisting she find out if that big ol' thing was flesh or some 12-inch prosthetic device." We're sure ol' Jeff, mother-lover that he is, at the very least allowed her to feel it.

And speaking of prosthetic devices, in "Tease" Jeff finally shows us what he may well be doing at home every night: he fucks himself in the ass with his own patented dildo.

The breathless promotional copy on this one was classic over-sell: "This long-awaited masterpiece stars Jeff Stryker in a one-man show...fucking himself in the ass with first one, then another big dildo. And the whole time he's doing it, he's talking dirty about how much he wishes you were the one doing it to him!

"Jeff has never looked better. His body is in flawless condition, his dick is hard almost all the time, and the videography is excellent. Luscious close-ups of his body, his cock, his ass, and, most compelling of all, dildos being shoved deep inside his flawless, naturally furry ass-hole. Jeff warms up by titillating his own ass with his fingers. It's obvious he's into the anal stimulation because his dick remains rock-hard while he's stroking himself. Then he sucks on a dildo while ramming one up his tight ass. The explicit talk about what he'd like to do if you were there continues, as Jeff shoves in an even larger dildo, almost the size of his own massive endowment, leaving nothing to the imagination. He licks his armpits, then spreads his butt-hole wide open begging you to slide your fingers up his ass and make love to his virgin ass-hole. And while he's stimulating his hole, he's also stroking his impressive dick.

"The entire time he's exciting himself orally and anally, he's fantasizing out loud that it's your big dick going all the way in and driving him crazy with passion! He lies on his side and sucks a dildo while plumbing the depths of his own ass and then sits on it, taking it all the way past his prostate, making his meaty dick even harder. It's a scorching tour de force that very few other adult video stars could carry off successfully."

Nor would many even have the nerve to try. But you got to hand it to ol' Jeff, he certainly surprised us with this one. He cleverly postponed what some say is inevitable: the taking of a *real* dick up that "naturally furry ass." The line forms at the right.

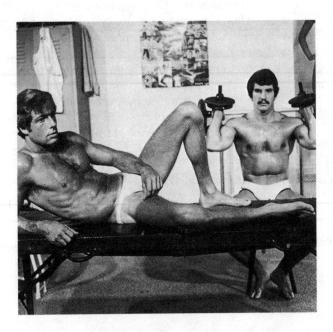

Jack Wrangler, with Roger

Jack Wrangler

*"I wanted big responses from people. I didn't want 'em just
to like me, I wanted 'em to lust after me!"*
-Jack Wrangler

During the early '70s, Jack Wrangler says he "wanted to
create a masculine, all-American gay male image that would
defy the stereotypes." What happened was, everybody wanted
to look like Wrangler: solid pecs, well-worn flannel shirt, often
plaid, and jeans that bulged at the crotch. Suddenly it seemed
Jack looked like everybody else. But while it lasted, more often
than not, it was good.

In those days, productions were churned out to keep fresh
product in the theaters, which usually changed the bill every
week and much of it was as uneven as it is today. We tend to
think of only the classics when we consider this era and it is
upon reflection that we find how much garbage was really
released just to keep up with demand.

"We were experimenting in those days," Jack recalls. "We
didn't know what we were doing, and we were trying every
method of producing erotica we could think of."

Wrangler starred in his share of clinkers, like every other star
of the era, most notably in the dismal "A Married Man" for
what was called the Higgins Brothers (which was only William,
there never was an Edward). In effect, Wrangler was
responsible for Higgins forming what is now the most
successful gay video production company, Catalina. Higgins
recalls that once he made the film he couldn't sell it. "A guy in
New York that owned the Adonis Theater says to me, 'I'd really
be interested in buying this picture except, you know, Jack
Wrangler is a real drag on the market. Why did you use him?
I mean, if you had anybody else as the star, I'd snap it right
up.' At this point, I had no idea Wrangler had saturated the
market. I was from Texas and we're two years behind New
York, he was still a hot ticket there while the rest of America
had gotten over him."

Over Wrangler or not, when the film played the Century Theater in Los Angeles it was a smash and the owner asked Higgins to make another movie. "The Boys of Venice" with street kid Kip Noll followed and success came swiftly for William Higgins.

Having saturated the gay market, Wrangler crossed over to straight porn and, given half a chance, proved he was a splendid comic actor, as well as handily mastering any sexual situation. Ironically, he would have been a natural for the bisexual films that became Catalina's stock-in-trade in the mid-'80s.

Critic John Rowberry rates Jack's performance in 1980's "Wanted" with Al Parker as his best: "As the sadistic chain-gang boss he has never been better, not even in his heterosexual roles where he usually has well-scripted characters."

Other impressive gay Wrangler performances are to be found in "Kansas City Trucking Company," the first of the famous Joe Gage trilogy, in which Jack plays well with co-star Richard Locke, tirelessly fucking and sucking his way through the scenes, and "Boots and Saddles," perhaps the quintessential Wrangler film of the golden age of porn, when it was mostly produced in New York, and it features heavy scenes with such filthy stars as Scorpio and Chip Kingsley.

Jack got an intense workout in "Heavy Equipment," one of my personal favorites. Bijou Video says: "This fantasy portrays Steve Tracy as a young gay bookseller who's given a magical book by an elderly passerby. The book transforms Tracy into muscular, handsome and hung athlete Jack Wrangler. What follows are sexual encounters in his new-found, long-desired body image: a glory-hole suck and fuck with the Christy Twins, 69-ing and ass-pounding with Roger, and a three-way with Al Parker and Chris Adams."

Wrangler has many detractors, especially among his co-stars. The legendary horsehung Roger told me his experiences working with Wrangler in "Heavy Equipment" and "Hot House" were unpleasant ones. By that time, Jack was much into the star trip, very demanding, imperious, and worst of all, used lots of make-up on his face and body which the "natural man" beefcake star found to be obnoxious.

In 1979, Jack made the straight film "Jack 'n' Jill" with Samantha Fox and he was superb, holding up his half of a married couple who try to spice up their sex lives by creative game playing. The film is widely recognized as classy porn director Chuck Vincent's most erotic venture and *Hustler* voted one of Jack and Samantha's sex scenes as the best of the year. Jack did other straight films, such as "China Sisters," but "Jack 'n' Jill" remains his best.

Although his acting was fine in these epics, his heart was really in gay porn. After his first blow job by a woman, done for the camera, Jack was to remark, "Girls don't do it like guys. I found myself going limp."

Jack is the only star who has appeared in a satirical documentary about his early life called, simply, "Jack Wrangler," and wrote (in 1984, with Carl Johns) his own autobiography, *What's A Nice Guy Like You Doing?* The book and the film, in which he dishes about his experiences in porn and dances at the Douglas Dunes Ranch, complement each other and would have made an interesting package had they been released as a boxed set. Jack has also gone on the road with his one-man jack-off show, "Jack Wrangler, Exclamation Point!"

After he retired from films, the star achieved success writing TV scripts and appearing off-Broadway in plays like "Soul Survivor." He has achieved great personal happiness as the long time escort of Margaret Whiting, a songstress who gained considerable fame in the 40's and is still actively appearing at cabarets with Jack billed as writer and director, a major force behind the scenes. They frequently appear at AIDS benefits and at memorial services for friends who have died. It bothers him that gays resent his relationship with the singer. "Why should anyone do that? I should think they would resent me more if I had continued in films and never grown or done anything else with my life. Certainly my affection and attraction for gay men has not changed. My living with Margaret has nothing to do with that."

Even though he says he's gone on to better things, he doesn't regret his past: "Making the films was a very worthwhile experience for me. I did it, I'm glad I did it, and I'd do it again."

THEY MIGHT BE
(OR MIGHT HAVE BEEN)
PORN LEGENDS

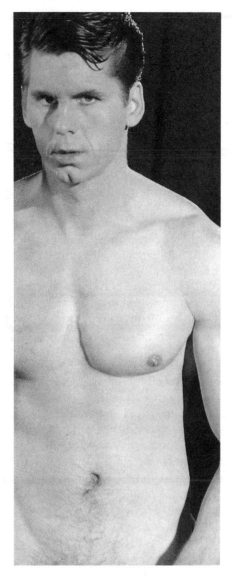

Michael Christopher

Michael Christopher

*"Muscular and well-hung,
Michael made an impression
on all of his co-stars."*
- John Rowberry

"Stud" is a term that's lost its value through over-use, but there is nothing that describes Michael Christopher more aptly. What, really, is a "stud?" Sure, they are male animals kept for breeding, the dictionary tells us that. But in human terms, it means someone who can fuck on demand. That strength was implicit in the Christopher promise. You just knew that when you called on him, he'd perform. It was part of a package that was, simply, irresistible.

In October of 1984, a friend of mine, and owner of a popular escort service in Tampa at that time, Jack Dodge, hosted a pool party and asked me to bring someone who would turn the guests on. Michael was just beginning to emerge as William Higgins' resident stud in "The Best Little Warehouse in L.A." and "Printers' Devils" and I thought he'd be just the ticket. Besides, I had a young blue-eyed blond friend (I'll call him Jimmy) who was dying to meet him.

As it turned out, Jimmy had to wait in line. Jack had so many friends who wanted to spend time with Michael that it wasn't until two days later, the afternoon before the star was to leave, that we all ended up in my suite at the Tampa Hilton.

Anybody else would have been completely exhausted but Michael was, as I said, a stud of the first magnitude. That torso being in perfect condition was part of it, of course. And the natural easiness he had about who he was and the joy and excitement he brought to the sexplay was a big part of it as well.

Jimmy had long admired the perfection of Michael's cock, not only the generous size of it but the shape and massive head and the way it jutted from the powerful body at just the right angle for maximum enjoyment, either when ass-fucking or face-fucking.

Jimmy passionately worshipped the stud's tool that afternoon in my suite. In fact, he was enjoying deep throating it so much, I didn't think he was ever going to get around to having it penetrate his tight little ass, but he did – and it was a glorious sight. He had Michael fuck him in every position he could think of, and Jimmy knew a lot of them.

After Jimmy came, wildly and with much groaning, Michael pulled out and went on to fuck Jack, who was lying on the king-size bed next to Jimmy. Jimmy got up and came over to me where I was reclining on the couch and began blowing me. I didn't want to come, I wanted to do that with Michael up my ass, but Jimmy was such an expert cocksucker I couldn't help myself. Jimmy loved having hot cum spread all over his face and licking it off the cock after the explosion, so watching him do that, coupled with the sight of Jack coming as Michael pumped his cock into his ass, got me hard again.

Michael pulled out of Jack and left him lying on the bed. He came over to the couch where Jimmy was still licking the cum off my now rigid cock. He told Jimmy to prepare the way. Jimmy took orders very well and began tonguing my butthole. Michael stood beside us and Jimmy's hand went up to the generous prick, now extremely well-lubricated. He yanked hard on it, drawing Michael down onto his knees and then guided it into my ass. As Michael entered me, I sighed with the enormous pleasure of having the meat I had so often coveted finally in where it belonged. Michael grabbed my ankles and began pounding my asshole and Jimmy got on his knees on the couch beside me, offering his throbbing prick for me to suck while he jacked me off with his right hand. At that point, Jack had gotten up, gone to the bathroom, and was joining us on the couch, vigorously pumping his beer can-sized cock. I alternately sucked Jimmy and Jack while Michael relentlessly plowed into me. It wasn't long before I came again and Michael pulled out and stood before the three of us. Jimmy started sucking his cock, then Jack and I were invited by Michael to share the prize. We did let Jimmy have the pleasure of taking the gusher of cum all over his face but we all got to lick it off Michael's cock before we had to rush to the airport and put Michael on the plane back to Hollywood.

Some time later, little Jimmy joked, "You know it was a good fuck when you can still feel it two weeks later!"

I laughed. "Hell, I'll feel that one forever."

After that weekend, we all felt that Michael was on his way to becoming a legend. But the problem with Michael's career was his early over-exposure. The stud was everywhere, indiscriminately appearing in flick after flick. Luckily, he was to meet some superb directors: Arthur Bressan Jr., who put him in "Pleasure Beach," Tom DeSimone for "Skin Deep," and Mark Reynolds, who paged him for his classic, "Doing It."

For William Higgins, Michael starred in several exciting videos, including "The Best Little Warehouse in L.A." and "Printer's Devils." "Warehouse" was the best of these, but "Devils" had its moments although it featured, as Ted Underwood points out, too many boyish brunette lookalikes to be able to determine who is doing what to whom in the orgy sequence at the end. Michael tops blond mesomorph Scotty Dixon and sucks Greg Davis' cock.

These videos are Michael's best and they proved he had the right instincts. Although he did not possess much acting ability, Michael was a good reactor. He was natural in front of a camera and, as I learned first hand, he always met the challenge.

He retired, got married and settled down. A loss to the gayporn world. Indeed, had charming Michael Christopher stayed with it, he may well have gone down in porn legend as the "King of the Studs."

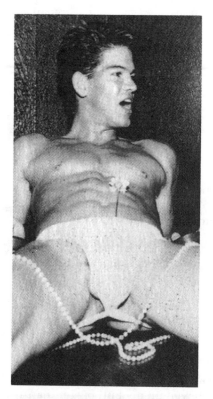

Matt Gunther in performance,
courtesy Marc Geller

Matt Gunther

"How can any guy bulge so much in a bikini?
Matt is just a walking god as far as we are concerned.
This guy has a great face and fantastic chest
(not overdeveloped but manly).
As for his ass, it's just perfect
and those hard-on shots of his
hot cock got us cumming quickly."
- Mark & Bradley, from England,
after seeing Matt in In Touch magazine

Versatility is what many reviewers scream for. Many of Jeff Stryker's detractors loved the day he finally sucked dick on screen and they all gasped when he kissed Joey Stefano in "On the Rocks." And when Ryan Idol sucked Tom Katt's cock and kissed him as if he meant it, there was much happiness in the homes of homos around the world.

But even if Jeff or Ryan never get fucked on screen, at least they have given us a little more than we started with. There are other studs who have romanced the daylights out of their bottoms and even, on occasion, rolled over themselves and the most winning example of this versatility we can think of is Matt Gunther.

"You know who fucked me the hardest – to the point that it was painful – was Matt Gunther," co-star Hunter Scott says. "He fucked me harder than I've ever been fucked by anyone in my life. You can see tears rolling out of my eyes in the video. I've had stuff shoved up my butt bigger than any dick by some of the best top leathermen in the community, but Matt fucked me with a cock ring on, and his dick was big, and he fucked the shit out of me! I couldn't walk for two days, that's how sore I was. People wrote me and said, 'God, that was so good. You looked like you were in so much pain!' I was in pain, and all I could think was that I really wanted to do the job and perform for these people and do a good job. It came out well."

Seeing Matt Gunther in person gives one pause. His sinewy body is even more spectacular than it is on video. His cock is so suckable it is almost obscene. But he is, after all, a performer, and as such, he wears eye makeup, a with-it haircut and clothes that are just so trendy you know he's gay. But the stud obviously loves his work so much you can forgive him anything. Even his sullenness.

That's why the video he did with Jon Vincent, "Inside Jon Vincent," helmed by Chi Chi LaRue, when the tables are decidedly turned, is such a treat. After living through all the scenes in other videos of Matt fucking with such gritty intensity, you can't help but love how Jon must have made him feel with lines like, "On your hands and knees, motherfucker! Get down and suck my cock! I want to pierce that little pink eye of yours."

And then when Matt finally gets Jon off, the raunchy one whips Matt's face with his noble prick. What a way to go!

In this video, versatile Matt, of the tight washboard stomach, protruding nipples, and lush cock that tends to bend tantalizingly to the left, gets his ass eaten spectacularly, then gets his ring-equipped cock blown, then fucks his partner doggie-style, only to roll him over and give him a royal screwing that's icing on the cake. In the next sequence, he's attacking big, dirty-tongued Jon, going down on him with masterful technique as Jon cries, "Let it talk to you baby, let it talk to you." Whatever Jon's cock was saying, Matt must have been listening. Jon says, "Nurse that head baby," and Matt proceeds to do just that, holding Jon back until he can't stand it any more. Matt then goes to Jon's buns, sucking them, slapping them. "I love it," Jon cries, "slap it, baby, slap that ass!" Soon, Jon is so worked up he simply has to plow Matt's slim ass with his big dick, saying "It's tight, baby." Matt: "Loosen it up. Prong that ass." And does he ever.

In another bargain basement production, Stephen Lucas' "Cool Hand Dick," Matt gets blown all the way to his shaved pubes by Sergio Callucci, playing a Spanish warden of a prison in one of our favorite towns, Cornhole, USA. Their opening dialogue is classic:

"What are you in here for, boy?"

"Prostitution, sir."

"And were you good at it?"

"I did what I could, sir."

"You're not like the others here. You've got something more substantial."

And then he proceeds to prove just how substantial Matt is as he blows him, then has him fuck him on top of his desk, sans condom. It's a wow of an opening to an otherwise dreadful video.

He can play bottom, as he does most successfully with Vincent and Stryker, but it's as a true stud Matt stands out, in more ways than one. As one reviewer said, "Tops among the all-knowing tops in Vivid's 'Mentor' is Mr. Sex Machine himself, Matt Gunther. The lad's scarcely Mr. Warmth, but he uses that rock-hard tool where it's needed most."

Matt was "introduced" to porn fans by the team of Patrick Dennis in Vivid's "Hole in One," the third in their "Sports" series. Matt's in the shower in the second sequence and in walks, of all people, Joey Stefano, to take a leak.

One thing leads to another, as these things have a way of doing, and Joey says, "I hear you're pretty good." Matt: "Why don't you find out for yourself?" And he certainly does. And good is putting it mildly. Later, this pair was to reunite to take turns at Stryker's manmeat in the splendid "On the Rocks."

Matt also appeared in Patrick Dennis' "First Mate," a decidedly low-budget effort by Vivid standards. The set was a joke, a 30-foot-long crudely painted seascape set behind some sand transported from Malibu. One reviewer said: "The young men manage to have sex with each other in spite of their bewilderment at being placed on this island by incomprehensible forces. The long and deliberate screwing Matt Gunther gives Nick Leonetti, situated as they are on the ground only inches away from the backdrop, wearing passionless looks on their faces, reinforces the abstraction that we are tools of a machine age capable of creating this 'sea.' Leonetti's limp tool is a symbol of our collective impotence when faced with progress. Industry and science are represented by Gunther's erect member." To say nothing of commerce, since these boys were being paid to do this, but, alas, not nearly enough.

Luck was with Matt, though, because a sequence he did with Buck Tanner ended up in Matt Sterling's "Idol Eyes," introducing Ryan Idol. The *Manshots* reviewer: "Gunther deep throats Tanner and like a cat he spasmodically shakes his head from side to side with his prey in his mouth. Later, he licks Tanner's back while fucking him doggie-style. Meanwhile, Tanner's semi-hard cock flips in the air with every thrust he receives."

And Matt loves a crowd, dancing in a club or the sleazy strip joints in New York or doing a video, especially for Falcon. While threatening to become a permanent resident of Falcon's sperm bank stock company, Matt appeared in two segments of "Man Driven," a duo, inter-cut with another duo going on at the same bathhouse style club, an unusual technique for this producer, and then a four-way at the end. Two doses of Matt participating with his normal lusty abandon in one video is to OD on the stud. This after "Cruisin' II: Men on the Make," the Falcon release preceding it. In "Cruisin'," Brad Mitchell cries, "Give me your cock!" and that kind of pleading always turns manly Matt on. After giving him a wild probing, he gets Dcota and while Dcota is topping Mitchell, he climbs on and jams his meat into Dcota's butthole for the highlight of the video. His scene at the end with Mitchell pales by comparison.

But the crowd never comes to the party in "The Abduction," where there's a secret hideout with cages, dungeons, blindfolds, handcuffs, dildos, hot wax handy in order to assist the commanders in their lusty interrogations. With the requisite atmosphere set early on, Matt and Jason Ross are first up and go at it as if they meant it, then Matt re-appears for a duo but to the video's great discredit, the hoped-for grand finale ala "The Other Side of Aspen (I and II)," the producers' classics of this genre, never materializes.

In Falcon's "Grand Prize," Matt shows us another of his specialties: something nasty. Here's how Rick & Dave described this unforgettable scene (uncensored only in the mail order version, of course): "Troublemaker Matt, who has now graduated to wearing two cockrings, gets sucked by Ray Butler but not for long. Matt gets right into humping Ray. Then he fingers Ray (who is waring a cockring of his own). In the Falcon tradition, Ray takes a huge dildo up his hole. This dildo is really huge. Did we mention this dildo is *huge*? Soon Matt puts on a glove and plunges his whole fist up Ray's butt. That's right. He puts his whole fist up there. Did we mention that Matt put his *whole fist* up there? Just so you know. They take turns jacking off and shooting. The video has ended."

But leave it to Chi Chi LaRue to come up with our favorite Gunther scene, in "Stranded," where he is ravaged by two country studs who pick him up and lay him out in a bar. As Mickey Skee commented, "Matt's spiked short hair and his deep groans are very nice."

Amazingly, Matt can be the fuckee with as much abandon as he is the fucker, as he proved in "Stranded." After lots of kissing, Matt face fucks his partner and comes in his throat. Then he lets the guy fuck him doggie style:

"You like that don't you," Jason Ross asks, "that fat cock up your ass?"

"Yeah, oh, ah, ah."

"Yeah, there we go, boy."

"Oh, yeah."

"Oh, yeah, there we go, boy."

"Oh," Matt cries, jacking off, "oh, baby, ram that home!"

Matt is not only a legendary fuck in porn circles, he is also a legendary "bad boy." *The Advocate* revealed that Matt was spied shopping at a bookstore on Melrose in Hollywood with his occasional roommate, Sharon Kane, when "all of a sudden, a big wet raspberry resonated throughout the room, coming from Matt's backside. As the hateful fumes began to waft throughout the aisles, Matt excused himself, asked one of the clerks for a Kleenex, and went out the door onto the street. According to Sharon, Matt actually wiped his butt on Melrose with no shame whatsoever and then proceeded to take a leak on a nearby palm tree."

Dave Kinnick had better luck shopping with Matt. Dave was there to interview the boy on the day he got his first credit card and Matt even paid for the lunch. While they're shopping, Matt tells Dave about his relationship with Kane: "We're just friends. She's tried many times to... But I'm not bisexual, unlike some of the other boys of gay porn who have been with her. I think some of them are just trying to prove their masculinity or something. She's a very nice person and I love her, so I guess other people feel the same way. Let's hope that's the case. I doubt it, in some cases - like Damien - she's such a queen! The other thing nice about Miss Kane is that we're roughly the same size. We share clothes. This is her tank top I'm wearing. (*A plain white ribbed tank, very, very tight.*) I think it shows off my pecs pretty good." In addition to the tank, Kinnick's shopping companion wore faded and very short Levi 501 cut-offs (with a Calvin Klein jockstrap underneath) and a blue baseball cap turned backwards. Needless to say, Matt Gunther in that outfit turned many a head, both male and female, even on Melrose. The lads went to A Star is Worn, a shop where all the clothes have been worn by big stars. Matt admires a certain dress and Kinnick admires his good taste. "Yes, compared to somebody like Joey Stefano, who has no taste, who probably shops at the tacky little shops off La Brea where you get your sofa and loveseat together for $325 and it's made of fake leather and you think it's perfectly lovely."

Speaking of perfectly lovely, Matt's idea of a wonderful time is just being with someone you love, no matter what you're doing. Kinnick asked him if he'd ever been in love. "I don't know about that. Probably. As close to love as I can get. He was the exact opposite of me. He was blond. He looked like Robert Redford, and he lived in Brentwood. His name was Tom. I met him at the gym. He cruised me for weeks before he said anything to me. I thought it was amusing. I think he was intrigued because I was a porno star. "

The porn star's favorite videos? He has three: "Inside Jon Vincent," which he says was great fun at the time, "but I'm over that now.

"Then there's 'Stranded,' the three way, with guys from Florida that Chi Chi found. And 'Cruising II,' my scene with Brad Mitchell."

Matt says the hardest video to make was his first, for Vivid, "Hole in One." Kinnick told him he liked it because he fucked Stefano so well. "I don't know," Matt said, "I guess. Actually, I think he's kind of sweet in his own way. There's just something about him that bugs me. He reminds me of myself when I was younger, and it's not easy to watch him. It's the attitude."

"Hole in One" was the hardest to make but "First Mate" is the one Matt hates the most: "Hate the box-cover. Hate the backdrop – the scenery. Hate the movie."

Like Dave said, the boy has good taste.

Gunther has "retired" from the scene more times than even Dave Kinnick can count.

"Go East young man! Following his recent retirement from porn and hiring on at *Genre*, word on the boulevard is that Matt Gunther is headin' to Miami," *Spunk* said. "However, his name just popped back into David Forrest's Brad's Buddies ads. Seems Matt is once again available for 'special appearances.' Now, you can retain him for a handsome fee!"

We put little credence in Brad's ads, knowing the agency's penchant for "bait and switch" tactics. But we knew while Matt may well go to Miami (and often – he's big on the dance circuit), he'd never *stay* there. As if to prove the point, when Dave Kinnick originally broke the story that Matt was flying off for good to the Sunshine State, he also told about the 24-year-old call boy well-known in town for placing discreet ads that tout his talents as a fisting bottom and any number of other titles. "It seems," Kinnick reported, "that he received a response to his ad from none other than La Gunther. But our informant didn't realize the considerable notoriety of his would-be customer at the time. The caller described himself only as 'hot, under 30, and hung,' and said in no uncertain terms that he wanted to 'punch some pussy.' Over to our lad's place goes Gunther. He knocks on the door. Our informant goes to answer it. A friend of his happens to be present and seated on the sofa. Said roommate's friend is a veteran of the Boom-Boom Room bar in Laguna Beach a few years back, at a time when a prenatal Matt Gunther frequented the establishment, spreading his then-unimpeachable charms.

"But on this day, Gunther enters the boy's apartment. The man on the sofa grins broadly, spreads his arms wide and with gusto screams 'Princess!' at Matt."

Now *that* kind of thing can only happen in Hollywood! On second thought, maybe that's why Matt wants to leave. Anyhow, the performer continues to pop up in videos to satisfy his many fans. Jim Steel used him to good advantage in "Dreaming In Blue," which starred hairy-breasted Hunter Scott, who awakens from his dreams to find that Matt Gunther is his lover beside him. One wonders how the man ever got to sleep in the first place with Gunther beside him! As Jack Monroe said in *GVG*, "the two perform in a variety of positions as a string combo of angels play the ethereal music."

About "Dreaming," Stan Ward, in *Manshots*, says, "The two memorable sexual scenes are the two extremes, which open and close the video: Matt Gunther's impersonal prison cell exploitation of Randy White, and the intensely intimate bedroom coupling of Gunther and Scott. The first sequence is a dream, tinged with elements of a nightmare, whereas the concluding sequence is a fantasy that promises to merge into reality. Neither Gunther nor White has ever been more sexually compelling on screen, and newcomer Scott holds his own as one of the most enthusiastic bottoms since Jon King. His ass is delicious.

"The second sequence retains the prison setting, but the two men (Scott again, this time with Derrick Baldwin) couple outside of the cell – a step toward freedom with a strong reminder of past imprisonment. Although Baldwin is not as strong a top as Gunther, he is nonetheless effective, especially in his verbal, digital, and phallic appreciation of a genuinely memorable ass."

Jim Steel recalls, "One day I had a scene with Matt Gunther and Danny Bliss, and a second scene was with Rod Tuet and Devyn Foster – and they were both brilliant. Gunther is such an incredible performer, and it's important to put him with somebody who enjoys bottoming. It was a marriage made in heaven yesterday. I was like, on roller-skates trying to keep up. We did not stop. We shot the scene in real time – which is unheard of. There wasn't an 'all right, let's wait for hard-ons.' At one point, he asked me if we could break because he was tired of fucking. That's the ideal way to work."

Let's hope Matt *never* gets tired of fucking.

Danny Sommers, just where you want him,
courtesy Falcon Studios

Danny Sommers

*"Danny Sommers is in everything.
He's like the Michael Caine of studflicks."*
Rick & Dave, reviewing 1992

Danny Sommers wasn't really IN everything in 1992, it just seemed that way. And he still is! And even if what he is in is crap, he is wonderful. You don't get named "Best Butthole, hands down, pun intended," by Dave Kinnick for nothing.

And, in 1992, for "True," Danny earned a Best Actor award from *Adult Video News* for his performance, and got fucked by the incredibly endowed B.J. Slater in the bargain. Nice work if you can get it. "True" was a grand display, down to the boxcover, with a gorgeous shot of Danny's handsome mug on the front. As Michael Lynch reported: "Among the actors, the highest praise must go to Danny Sommers, whose performance approaches perfection. His great characterization combines vulnerability with strength, humor and seriousness, insight with satire. If you don't fall in love with the character he plays, you are made of sterner stuff than I. In addition, his sex scene with B.J. Slater (an anonymous bar pickup who 'dines and dashes') sears the screen, with close-ups of Sommers face that would inspire lust in a dead man. Nor are the other parts of his delightful anatomy neglected – the camera simply makes love to every inch of his lovely flesh. As for Slater, well, his larger-than-usual endowment provides a fine prop for Sommers' virtuoso performance."

In reviewing "True," Sid Mitchell gushed: "When Danny Sommers takes over the spotlight, God's in his heaven and all's right with the world. Here is one of the most engaging, endearing and thoroughly charming performances of recent years."

"Mr. Sommers is a dreamboat!" *Contax's* reviewer raved. "This is quite a comment coming from me because he's just a little more pumped up than I usually allow in my fuck-buddy, fantasy scenarios. But he's blond, can really act and he's just about perfect in all the right places. Yummy! And Danny maintains a hard-on through most of his scenes – no matter what he's doing or what's being done to him. This isn't always the case in porn videos and I have to give credit where credit is due."

In fact, Sommers often proves to be an inspiration to others. Brian Yates had problems keeping it up in other productions but with Sommers in Jim Steel's "Rings" for Vivid, he's hard all the time, when fucking Sommers silly and when getting fucked silly himself by Danny. The finale: "The two guys finish off with a jerk-fest, seated facing one another on the bench. They jizz for days and collapse into a kissy/huggy festival all their own."

Indeed, 1992 was a banner year for Danny's fans. Among the more memorable of Sommers' sizzlers were: Paul Norman's production, ghost directed by Chi Chi LaRue, "Ripped, A Bathroom Fantasy," in which he again demonstrated his impressive fellatio techniques, and Jerry Douglas' "Kiss Off," in which he has a romance of sorts with newcomer Axel Garrett, a blond ex-Marine who expresses his affection with tentative caresses and a concluding kiss. "Douglas should thank his lucky stars for Danny Sommers, whose screen warmth could melt the North Pole," Stan Ward in *Adult Video News* said. "If the final scene works, it is largely due to him."

And Douglas does thank his lucky stars, calling Danny "one of the most appealing stars of our time, a remarkably versatile animal whose ability to focus sexually makes his every performance endlessly alluring, and what's more he is a versatile actor who never stops acting when he moves from the dramatic to the explicit. Almost invariably one believes in the character he creates and sustains from start to finish."

In Catalina's 1992 release "Fan Male," Danny gets off solo and in a sexy scene at the end with exotic-looking Arik Travis. Troy McKenzie commented: "Most of it appears to be by the numbers, but there are exceptions, most notably Danny Sommers...when he impales himself on his supine lover and rides the saddle, his stiff dick, untouched, bounces and waves in the air."

Also for Catalina, in "Night Force," Danny proves to be the "bottom *extraordinaire*," to quote Dave Babbitt, in a barroom scene with Aiden Shaw: "Cute barboy Danny Sommers does what he does best: offering up his buffed bod to the beefy Brit. The ensuing scene ignites the screen. Sommers enhances his reputation as bottom *extraordinaire,* but newcomer Shaw demonstrates starpower as well, with his sexy accent, muscular body, comfortably masculine demeanor, and massive veiny, unclipped horsecock combine to create a riveting screen presence. Most nutbusting shot: Shaw's long, thick meat (reminiscent of Michael Christopher's with a foreskin) slipping out of Sommers' mouth to flex and slap against his own ripped abdomen. The scene culminates with a mean pool-table plowing, and a creamy, limey load all over Sommers' supple buttcheeks."

Danny's buttcheeks were again on display for Falcon in "Man Driven," in the four-way with Matt Gunther, Mark Andrews, and Brad Mitchell. Troy McKenzie described the scene: "Mitchell and Gunther stand cockhead to cockhead, while Andrews and Sommers kneel to suck. The two mouths chow down on both cocks simultaneously, vying for control. Mitchell, usually a bottom, later tops Sommers missionary, while Gunther stands over Sommers' face to have his whole groin eaten. In addition, Gunther leans in to kiss Mitchell, and Andrews dives in to suck Sommers' cock.

"Finally, Gunther fucks Mitchell doggie, Andrews plugs Sommers missionary, and Mitchell and Sommers sixty-nine. The four-way provides an ingenious series of carnal configurations."

Also for Falcon, Danny appeared in "Piece of Cake," from the Falcon's Jocks Division, in a sequence with beautifully built hunk Blake Callahan, who gives him a probing with a dildo that is a special treat. Early in his career, Danny proved he could handle a dildo without peer in "Sailing to Paradise" from AVG; Sid Mitchell commented: "What raises this title a notch above its competition is the solo of Danny Sommers, proving even solo action can be memorable when the right actor is involved. Sommers steals the show hands down, making his dildo into a supporting actor instead of a dead prop."

Indeed, dandy Danny often provides the only reason to watch some low-end videos that are beneath a star of his calibre. Sid Mitchell says: "(He) somehow manages to raise the most predictable of scenarios into the realm of the erotically satisfying." For instance, in Video Resource Group's "Danny's Back," featuring the return of dark-haired, heavily endowed Danny Ozmond, Sommers comes in for the finale to put the rest of the lackluster cast to shame. The "plot" of this trifle has Ozmond returning to town (why he left in the first place is left to your imagination). He starts right off hustling everyone he meets and when he finally gets around to returning to his supposed sweet and only, the lonely boy is being plugged by Sommers. Ozmond walks right in without knocking and shows no emotion whatsoever in catching his lover with his ass in the air. Instead, he starts to strip, still ready for some action after an already very busy afternoon on the streets. Once Sommers catches sight of Ozmond's long, beautifully shaped slab of tubesteak, he's out of the lover and on his knees before Danny, popping the thing in his mouth. Soon the lover is there wanting to share the bounty. Ozmond must have seen a few Danny Sommers flicks because very quickly he wants a piece of that ass. On his knees on the sofa, Sommers takes it all and makes the most of it, although Ozmond fucks as if he's in a trance. Such a slow, steady, uninvolved fucking would be enough to put an ordinary bottom to sleep, but Sommers acts as if he can't get enough and, after Ozmond shoots, Sommers rolls over and has his own heroic orgasm. The video ends with the three boys sitting together on the couch, all smiles. Finally, it seems Ozmond has found somebody worth staying home for.

In "Who's Gonna Get It?" from Mastertape, directed by the late Lucky Luc, Danny was part of an exploration of how sexual favors can bring about advancement at the office. As usual, Danny scored, in more ways than one. Reported Chris Parrish: "Sommers gives extra 'oomph' to the energy of his performance, making it tantalizingly hot. He always seems to get a thrill out of his work. Asslickers will love seeing Storm kneel to doggie rim Sommers, who reaches around to press the dark-haired boy's head to his butt. Other highlights include Sommers missionarily fucking Storm, whose legs are thrown over the blond's shoulders, and the mouth-fucking Sommers later receives."

Of Danny's appearance in VCA/HIS' "Songs in the Key of Sex," McKenzie said: "Sommers seems to be in every video that comes out yet we never tire of him. His acting is always strong and on the mark. He successfully intermingles mind and body into sexual action, making each character he plays uniquely individual. In the finale Randy Mixer and Sommers fuck each other in every position, and play footsie as they climax, masturbating side by side."

Showing to what lengths Danny will go to appear in video – any video - he showed up at a party held over a long weekend in Key West sponsored by Washington, D.C.-based producer of fetish videos Bob Jones. The purpose of the long weekend was to give fans a chance to fuck the stars (for a price) and also see filming done "on location." Danny appears in "Key West Voyeur" as a sexual performer and in "Straight Pick Up II" in a "cameo" as a bartender. Over that same weekend, Danny also appeared for Jones' associate, Steve Johnson, in "Key West Bellhop." For reviewer McKenzie, Danny epitomized the traveler's fantasy of a compliant bellhop: "Whether he is resting his entire body weight on his neck while getting fucked missionary, sucking a guest's dick, getting fucked and sucked simultaneously, or rimming an asshole, he radiates the joy that promises an eventual, climatic, body-wracked orgasm."

Speaking of body-wracking, Danny's co-star Jon Vincent says: "I like him a lot. I was fuckin' him for like three hours on the set and he was hurtin'! I was rockhard the whole time and everybody on the set kept gettin' off on it. It was a rough scene. My dick got purple, like the biggest it's ever been. It turned out to be a great scene with Danny. He bared me."

Danny's favorite scene was with Randy White in "Sailing to Paradise." After showing off with his dildo for a handyman played by White, Danny gets it on with the visitor: "I just really enjoyed myself with him. We got going and just couldn't stop. At one point we were going at it and the crew started shouting, 'Cut! Cut! Stop!' and we didn't even hear them."

Danny's perfect guy? "He's very big. He's muscular and probably tall, and maybe stupid-looking. He's probably in his thirties. He's got a big dick, but it doesn't get rock-hard when he's fucking. When they're not real hard, I can go at it forever."

Going at it forever is exactly what Marc Saber would have liked to have done when he was paired with Danny in "On the Lookout." It was college boy Marc's first video and Danny proves his versatility by fucking Marc. Marc, who went on to take three big dicks – B. J. Slater, Cody James, and Craig Hoffman in "Big As They Come," now calls Danny "a sweet, sweet boy."

Danny again tops in Bruce Savage's "The Producer." Danny brings Valentino Reyes to meet David Griffin, a talent agent, and they get it on together. Troy McKenzie describes the scene: "While Griffin and Sommers kiss, Reyes kneels and jams both cocks into his mouth at once, sucking as though he never wants to let go. On his haunches, he blows Griffin while Sommers plows his upturned, spread-eagled ass. It is not until the very end of the scene that we finally see his own formidable piece of meat. Sommers, as usual, delivers his all. He never fails to be exciting."

Some guys just can't be satisfied, however. Danny's virtuoso turns haven't been appreciated by a porn fan in Pennsylvania, who wrote *Manshots*: "When Danny first appeared, he was interesting: a regular if somewhat vacuous face; a nice, gym-toned body; satisfactory, if not spectacular, equipment; versatile. But this guy has appeared in everything from cheap, one-day wonders to quality products...I've seen every inch of this guy's body, every orifice; in fact, I think I've seen every hair on his body, one by one. I've seen him come every which way...give us a break, man, retire from gay videos."

This letter sparked a storm of protest. Most porn fans agreed that this guy must be retired and spend all day and night watching porn so our advice to him would be to volunteer, get out of the house, be a pal to some kid that needs one. And give Danny a break, he's just turning tricks (on video sets) to put himself through pharmacy school. That's what he told Joan Rivers when he appeared on her show with Chi Chi LaRue. And he's also having a lot of fun doing what he's doing, proving a job doesn't need to be just a job. "For my money," one fan wrote, "Danny can go on making videos until he no longer has any need for tuition funds, or until such time as he does not find pleasure in doing his best to bring pleasure to men everywhere."

That includes Donnie Russo, Danny's co-star in the Bijou release, "Find This Man," who appears to love fucking. Russo, who first appeared for Bijou as "Beat Cop" in 1991, went on to pair with Sommers for one of Bob Jones' fetish frolics. In "Find This Man," Russo's picture on a flyer inspires Danny to leave his small town and come to New York City to search for the well-built dude. Naturally, he finds him, but not without first sampling the joys of peep show sex and one of the strangest three-ways in history, with Jamie Wingo and Steve London inviting Danny up to their office to watch them fuck. Danny sits in a chair, off to the side, with his shirt unbuttoned and watches as the two go at it, at one point even sitting on a two-dick dildo, held on Danny's lap. The finale of the scene is memorable with the two studs simultaneously unloading all over Danny's chest. The Russo/Sommers pairing again demonstrates why Danny is a favorite of fans. Critic Michael E. O'Connor said: "This tangle is more romantic than the others and we close with the two guys back out on the streets of Greenwich Village, arm in arm, strolling off into what we expect will be a more pleasant life for both of them."

And, thanks to Danny's continued presence in gay video, a more pleasant life for us as well.

In 1995, Danny was still being top-billed, with newcomers Steve Marks and Chad Connors in Falcon's Mustang release, "Face Down." And Danny was running The Exchange in Studio City, which he termed a "foreplay" club, mixing coffeehouse, adult video and bookstore, game room, mail room and meeting place. Danny said it was designed as "an alternative to a sex club, and a safe neutral place to meet someone you may later want to connect with." As for me, I'd go just to see Danny!

Hope to see you soon
Love
Tom Steele

Tom Steele

Kris Lord, as photographed by Bo Tate

Matt Powers, courtesy Catalina Video

Tom Steele, Kris Lord, Matt Powers, And Other Guys With Legendary Cocks

"Matt Powers' cock is of legendary construction:
a fat six-inch dick with two somewhat narrower extra inches stuck
on at the end at a rakish angle. When erect, it looks like a Concorde
jet with its forward fuselage lowered for landing. He seems amiable
and kind of shy but performs like a house on fire."
– Dave Kinnick

When a cock is built like Matt Powers', cut or uncut, it becomes legendary, joining the members of several guys who, had they stayed in the business, could have been legendary for more than just their magnificent tools.

Twenty-seven year old Matt's strategy was to make a couple of videos a year while he went to school and he did that, for a time, but then dropped out of the business altogether when studies took up too much of his time. He left us a legacy of only a few memorable opportunities to watch that superb dick in action. The best of his jabbings are of Vic Summers in "Main Attraction" and Ted Cox in "Lifeguard: On Duty."

Matt truly makes love to Vic at the finale of the superior production, Scott Masters' "Main Attraction." If a romantic fuck is what you want, this one is hard to beat. As John Rowberry put it: "...the *piece de resistance* is Matt Powers' romantic tryst with Vic Summers...clearly written from the heart and delivered with both passion and sincerity. I always like it when something romantic happens, and this looks like where the video was headed all along."

In "Lifeguard: On Duty," Matt gets a chance to act a bit and he shows great promise. But when it comes to the fucking, Matt shines like few others. With little Ted hunched over the sofa, Matt rises splendidly to the occasion, causing Ted to come luxuriantly. For the pay-off, practiced Matt lifts Ted up so that the boy is standing up and can explode for the camera, then Matt lets go himself with a gusher across Ted's incredibly cute ass. It's a scene so delightful, director Scott Masters has to play it twice in the same video.

Matt is also one of the participants in Catalina's megahit, "Lunch Hour," one of the better orgy flicks ever made. Matt plays the foreman in a machine shop faced with stiff production quotas and an unsympathetic management; he soon leads a worker's uprising, "filling the front office's orifices instead of their quotas," as Rowberry put it. "No Marxist rhetoric here, just a big, brash gang-rape that occupies the first hour. It's capped off with a romantic and sweet duet between Matt and Josh Taylor."

The phenomenon of Matt Powers recalls another beautifully-equipped performer, Bill Eld, who made loops for Falcon in the early days but eventually dropped out of sight. Bill's cut cock was truly magnificent and became something of a legend during his short stay in the business. His best work can be seen on Falcon's Pac #11 in the loop "Workman's Compensation," in which he royally stuffs it into a room service waiter. *Manshots* praised this loop as being of the sort that made Falcon's reputation: "(Eld) fucks with great vigor and enthusiasm. The camerawork is very good, catching expressions on faces as well as the old in-out. Finally, Eld shoots a very healthy, multi-spurt shot of creamy cum all over the waiter's face and into his mouth."

Another of the beautifully hung performers who made few appearances but their equipment remains legendary is Bill Harrison, star of "Bijou," from 1977, memorable for its hour-long orgy as well as the star's incredible shower sequence at the beginning. Bill went on to direct a couple of videos, including "The Biggest One I Ever Saw," but it is his cock that remains legendary.

Kris Lord was another porn performer whose name was kept alive by the reputation earned by his cock. He first exposed it to the world in *Playgirl* magazine in April of 1992, then went on to make a few videos for Falcon's Mustang label, including "Down Home," "Driving Hard," and "Take Me Home." Falcon's astute management liked the cock so much they had Doc Johnson (famous for the Stryker replica) mold one for them to sell via mail order for $59.95 at the same time their big-budget, "Shadows in the Night," in which Kris starred, was released. At first, Falcon was saying Kris possessed a cock measuring 13" x 9" and; then, apparently after they made the cast, they changed that to 11" x 8", which seems more reasonable.

We know one thing for sure: it's *plenty* big enough. Just ask Danny Sommers, who told Dave Kinnick that the most challenging thing he has ever done in porn was taking on Kris' dick: "I got fucked by him in 'Down Home' for Falcon. He's a straight boy with a dick this big around (gesturing to his upper arm). He's the biggest one I've ever worked with. It's not that his dick is extremely long – it's just so fat! It's not really round either. It's kind of big and flat. I had to turn my mouth sideways to get any of it in. It looks like somebody ran over it with a car."

Being run over by a car might have been preferable to what actually did happen to Kris after he became popular. We had the pleasure of meeting him early on, in May of 1992 when he appeared in Tampa at one of the then-called Carousel Club's anniversary parties. At that time, we went so far as to say "charisma should be Kris Lord's middle name. Even better looking in person than on screen, this performer was the night's dazzling crowd-pleaser. With a body that won't quit, male equipment that is majestic, and a winning smile that never seems to fade, Boston-bred Kris basked in the glow of all of the adulation. He's destined to become a major adult performer.

"Coming on stage in a tight black leather outfit that bulged obscenely at the crotch, Kris quickly got down to business, foregoing any real on-stage performance to circulate through the crowd. The eager horde surged forward to sneak a peek and perhaps a feel for a dollar. By the time the drag queen master of ceremonies, Esme Russell, pleaded to the boy to get back on the stage, he had two fistfuls of cash. In future performances, we suggest he have a slave to push a wheelbarrow around behind to him to put all that tribute in. Later, Lord ingratiated himself further with the throng by chatting with his fans and posing for pictures. But he politely declined to give us an interview, saying his agent frowns on him making any statements to the press; so the story of his life has to wait."

During those first months of his fame, he took every dancing job he could find and popped up in "Grapplin'," a wrestling video released by Winners Media Group. They showed him in a lovely pose, smiling benignly, yet called him an "awesome, arrogant stud machine." And Kris made some low-budget quickies for Bob Jones, the Washington, D.C.-based fetish and bondage king. One video, "Bondage Memories," features the star, aided by Phil Bradley, stripping and humiliating two pledges, including forcing them to suck their dicks. (They had to be straight kids. It's beyond reason Kris would ever have to force any gaymale to suck that dick.) Anyhow, here's how Bob Jones describes what comes next: "Finally, bored with this scene, Kris and Phil tie the boys to a weight bench and call out for pizza. (Only in gay video!)

"Derrick Daniels, the pizza boy, arrives with the delivery only to be grabbed and forced to be part of the college hazing. The pledges and Derrick are ordered to have a circle jerk. No one is allowed to leave until everyone comes."

In "Straight Pick Up," Kris dominates the second scene. The plot had his car has breaking down on a lonely stretch of road (shades of the cult classic "Rocky Horror Picture Show"). True to form, he's rescued by a friendly guy who, as Bob Jones puts it, "desperately wants to worship that gorgeous body."

Jones' follow-up video, "Straight Pick Up II," was filmed "on location" during a weekend in Key West. It's interesting mainly to see the stud Kris dancing and prancing at the Lighthouse Court where, unlike Tampa, he gets to remove everything. Earlier in the video, Jones stages a scene at a gym with Kris and Kyle Brandon and Randy Storm. L. A. critics Rick & Dave describe it: "...It's Kyle's turn to spot but Kris is so distracting. No one can get anything done when he's around. Kris asks Kyle to spot him for some curls. While Kris is lifting, Randy (accidentally, you understand) grabs Kris' crotch. Kris does not react positively. But then Kris and Randy go back to the bench press where Randy reaches for the bar and (accidentally) reaches up Kris' shorts. Then he (accidentally) pulls down Kris' shorts and (accidentally) sticks Kris' penis in his mouth. Kris invites Kyle to join them. Kyle agrees, proving that he is in fact a very bright young lad. Kris suggests they go someplace a little more private.

"Cut to some bedroom where all three guys strip and fall onto the bed where Kris gets worked on by his two new buds.

Randy and Kyle lick Kris everywhere. Let us just say that Kris' tool is mammoth and Randy really knows how to take it all the way down his throat. The scene ends with nicely done cum shots by all three studs."

As nice as it was to watch Kris adored and glorified, Jones retained his amateur ranking with these videos because there is no continuity between scenes; the good scenes end abruptly and the bad ones seem to go on forever. Plus, there was too much emphasis on shaving and weight lifting and not enough sex.

Kris didn't have to fuck anyone in the Jones videos, thus avoiding a recurrent problem he shares with most big dicked performers: keeping it hard. His limpness spoils one of our potentially favorite Lord scenes in Mustang's "Driving Hard." In this feature, Jeff Hammond plays a limo driver and one of his hires is Lord. At one point Kris spots a twinkie (Randy Brooks) jumping on and off the curb onto the sidewalk. Kris rolls down the window and asks, "Playing hop-scotch little boy?" Whatever it was he really was doing, Randy stops then and there and jumps in the limo. I mean, who wouldn't? Kris has Jeff pull into an underground garage and Randy plays with Lord's crotch before fishing out the monster and sucking on it. As one critic said: "Lord decides it's too confining in the back seat and they exit. Pretty soon thereafter Kris is pounding the kid's asshole with his monster meat. We are always pleasantly surprised when a porno star with a big dick can get it up, keep it up and fuck while it's hard. Suffice to say, Kris didn't fit into this category. Whenever he's fucking the kid real hard you don't get to see any penetration and indeed we suspect there wasn't any. "When you do get to see penetration you also get to see both of Kris' hands guiding the monster cock in and keeping it there, semi-hard as it is. Thirteen by nine sounds nice, but I just don't think there's enough blood in the average male to power a body and a monstrously engorged penis. Kris also grins and giggles during this scene. Not good. With or without a fully functional hooter, Kris Lord is very handsome. He's certainly worth a considerable time investment if that's what it takes to get his weenie interested in the job at hand."

Well, "interested" is what "the weenie" of Lord seemed to be in Falcon's "Down Home." Dave Babbitt raved: "Falcon has the good sense to pair pro Danny Sommers with spectacularly hung, tradey newcomer Lord. The sexual positions in this poolside pairing are standard fare: it's Lord's beercan dick and Sommers' efforts to swallow it that give the scene its thrust. (By the way, the prolific bottom has better luck aft than fore.) Sommers is up to his usual performance, yet the viewer's eyes remain riveted on the massive endowment of his butch partner. It is a fat sausage that makes all other dicks resemble bread sticks. Lord also possesses a great body and roughhewn handsomeness, yet his function here is primarily to be 'done,' though he does kiss a bit." In the final segment of "Down Home," Kris arrives as a threeway is in progress and shows the others how to finish off an ass, in this case Adam Archer's puckering hole.

Later in the year, Falcon again showcased Lord, this time in "Shadows in the Night," co-starring veteran Bill Marlowe who, when asked by Dave Kinnick about how he managed to take all of Kris' mighty meat down his throat, said: "I just unhinged the jaw and inhaled it."

Speaking of becoming unhinged, by 1993 things started to do just that for Kris. In the spring, he was invited by *Advocate Men* to match dicks with the legendary Rick "Humongous" Donovan, star of, among many, "Sailor in the Wild" and "The Bigger the Better." The results of this measure-up were to be published in the magazine. Kris agreed. "It was a simple concept," the magazine told its readers when the results were in, "which both guys were advised of when booked for the shoot: Put one cock on top of the other while standing facing each other." The stills reproduced in the magazine showed the sequence of events when it came time to "put up and shut up," as they succinctly put it. What is missing here is a time clock. As we know from personal experience, Rick can take an hour to get it fully hard. He's turned on to transsexuals, so having one around would have helped, or at least pictures of one. Kris, we also know, is "straight." Consequently, he may have been better served by having a gal around to "fluff" him, as Rex Chandler always did when he had to make gay porn flicks. At any rate, after a while, Kris began to take exception to the poses. "Suddenly," the magazine says, "he had questions about exactly what we wanted to do. He refused to get into the position requested by our director of photography. Eventually Kris walked off the set without giving us the clear, hard-on comparison that had been the whole point of the session. Actually, we think it's pretty obvious who has the bigger dick and maybe the biggest dick in porn: Rick Donovan. Since these photographs were taken, Kris has refused all offers for sexually explicit photography or nude photography with hard-ons. He is pursuing a 'legitimate' career in modeling. If he succeeds, he'll be a kind of male Traci Lords. We wish him well." What was obvious from the side by side, and what we knew all along, was that Rick's longer but Kris is thicker. (Later, in their 900 service ad, the magazine was stating that Rick was 11" *long* and Kris was 10" *thick*. Will it ever end?) We know from experience that each of these guys is normally easy to deal with. But one is a legend and one is, well, to be kind, just in it for the money, and, at some point, enough is enough.

The nadir may have been reached in the fall of 1993 when Kris, after dancing in London to crowds that included, his handlers said, Joan Collins and Elton John, journeyed to Florida to appear at a series of clubs lined up by a seemingly unscrupulous producer. The promoters booked Kris into three different Tampa Bay bars on consecutive nights over what turned out to be a long weekend of gossip. The first night, only 100 people showed up at the first bar to pay the $8 cover charge. The following night, at another bar crosstown, only 30 people arrived and Kris refused to perform. Then the management wanted their $3,000 non-appearance bond paid. The angry producer refused; kindly Kris wrote out a check for the money but it was reported the barman tore it up and threw it back into his face saying something to the effect that, "If you had that much money in the bank, you wouldn't be here." The following night, at a bar on the Gulf, the crowd swelled to 80 paying guests, and Kris performed, giving them their money's worth, and the management of Zippers (formerly the Carousel Club) announced they had hired Kris to come back in a few weeks to rekindle the memories of Kris' debut in that venue.

Then rumors began circulating that Lord was "working" San Francisco, having dozens of partners a day and not praticing safe sex. Over the past year, there have been no rumors about him at all, just fond memories of what might have been.

A superstud who has a perfectly splendid long penis, fucks like a house on fire, but who is perfectly happy being gay (and thus could have been a legend) is Tom Steele. He was off the screen for a couple of years but came back in 1992 in "All the Way In" and "One Night Stands" (with his singing dubbed by David Burrill, who has a nonsexual - what else? - role in the video), both for Filmco, and both co-starring with his youthful boyfriend and fellow Texan Scott Jordan, as well as being featured as one of the revellers in "Powertool 2" for Catalina.

First glimpsed in "Powerline," heavy-lidded, petulant-lipped Tom jacks himself off in fine form early on in that video but when he is surprised by two other guys, he unconvincingly tells them he's straight and what follows is a lackluster 3-way during which Tom has considerable trouble keeping it up. Hapless Tom watches as one actor goes down on the other. When he is finally semi-erect, Steele enters the scene and the actor starts to suck him. Steele lowers his head and begins sucking the erect nipple of the third guy, but the scene quickly dissolves to a three-way jack off, then more action from the other two, leaving Steele out in the cold. Finally, he sits on the face of the passive guy while he is being fucked and has him lick his balls while Tom jacks off. That's the extent of Steele's appearance, with only minor oral action and no fuck, a terrible waste!

Equally odious was Tom's second outing, "Soldiers," directed by Vincent DePaul and distributed by InHand. Steele got top billing with Neil Thomas in this absurdity which squanders a good plot premise and some decent production values. For the finale, which comes as a blessing after all the limp action which precedes it, Steele and Neil meet each other in the field and Tom "forces" Thomas back to his tent, where Neil tries valiantly to get a rise out of Tom but it's a losing battle. Failing to sustain an erection, Steele drops to his knees in a decidedly un-Stryker pose, to suck Neil's rock-hard dick. Director de Paul must have told Tom he had to fuck somebody so abruptly the scene shifts to that action, the camera showing Steele already in Neil, doggie-style on an army cot, so we are robbed of a view of the entry. The way Neil is cringing, it is obvious Steele's prick is still semi-hard. "Please, make it quick," he groans at one point. Tom told me that he never actually fucked Neil but he did manage to splatter a small dose of juice on Neil's backside. Then it's little trouper Neil's turn to shine as he rolls over on his back and shoots an impressive load. Then, as the final kiss-off, Steele faces the audience, raises a gun, points it into the camera and, smirking, implores us to want him.

Fortunately, his manager was to save Tom and he appeared in a string of good pairings which secured his position. His best partners have included Joey Stefano in "Say Goodbye," Cal Jensen in Matt Sterling's superlative "Heat in the Night," Tim Lowe and Butch Taylor, separately, in Paul Norman's bi-sexual thriller "Offering," Ryan Edwards (aka Beau Beaumont) and Mark Reardon in "Pledgemasters," and Cal again in "Two Handfuls II" (in a locker room fuck and, later, with Dany Brown), and in a solo, his hard-to-beat jackoff sequence in "Sailor in the Wild II" from Catalina, dressed in cop drag. The best of all remains his pairing with Doug Niles in "Undercover."

Inches magazine readers voted him "Model of the Year" in 1988 and his personal appearances were sell-outs.

For a while Tom owned his own bar in Galveston, Texas, and when he had a night off he'd go to Houston to party. One night in 1990, he saw a cute young blond playing pool and grabbed his ass several times. Finally, the kid walked up to him and said, "Look, what's your fuckin' problem? Leave my ass alone. If there's somethin' you want, tell me."

Tom proceeded to tell him.

The kid blushed and said, "Well, if you'll let me finish this game, we'll go take care of it."

And they did. The romance between Tom Steele, porn star, and Todd Fuller, future porn performer, began. Todd, who at this point had no idea who Tom was, having only seen one porn video in his entire life, told the rest of the story to William Spencer: "We went to a friend's house and had, to be honest, great sex. It was the best I'd had in a long time. And I believe that was like only the fifth time I'd ever been fucked. And up to that point it was the biggest dick.

(Todd would later make "Rimshot" and get fucked by Craig Hoffman: "I've been told I can take a bus, and, honey, if that was a bus, I'd hate to see what a train feels like.")

"But that night with Tom was very enjoyable, wonderful. After we got done, we went back to the bar and closed it down. He asked me if I'd like to go home with him, and I said, 'Sure where do you live?' and he told me Galveston. 'No, no way.'

"Eventually, I found out he was a porn star and I couldn't believe it because he didn't come across as being egotistical and I thought all porn stars were egotistical assholes. Since I've been in the business, I've gotten a firsthand view of how they act and, well, I'm not that way. Believe it or not, Tom turned out to be an egotistical asshole himself. I wound up dating him off and on, while he was living in Galveston, for about three months. But he would never come up to Houston to visit me, I always had to go down there. I got tired of it and I finally said, 'Look, you wanna see me, you bring your happy ass up to Houston.' Well, for about three weeks there was no sign of him and then one afternoon I got a phone call, conveniently just after my mother had moved back to Mississippi. So when Tom asked if there was room at my place for two, I said, 'Sure, you wantin' to move in?' And he goes, 'Well, if we're going to make this work, we gotta be together.' So I said, 'Fine, move in.' I was fairly settled in my lifestyle at the time, so he moved in and we lived together for six months. Now, if anybody ever dates Tom Steele, don't accept anything real expensive from him, because after he buys you something like that, he's gone. He bought me a diamond ring one week and turned around and left the next. I'd been forewarned by his friends, who he'd introduced me to. Actually his manager thought I was the cutest thing and he wanted to put me in the movie business. Well, we had pictures taken and Tom began getting jealous. He did not want the pictures goin' out to California. He did not want the competition, but the pictures got sent out to everybody anyway and Tom got very pissed off. After we split up, I was on my way to California to make my first movie, "The Rolls," for DA Productions. (As "Ricky Skater.")

"At one point, I liked Tom. At this point, I don't like him."

Like him or not, size queen that I am, it was inevitable I would meet Steele. I preferred to do it on my own turf, not in Texas. I found him to be a likable person. On the way to my beach house from the airport, he said he was gay and proud of it. As accustomed as I am to porn stars and hustlers declaring their "straightness," it was refreshing to find someone so into what they were doing. Still, he had stipulations when it came to sex off-screen. With clients, he said, he preferred to play the trade role.

"I love trade," I said.

When I asked what type of man turned him on, he said it seemed the older he got, the more attracted to younger guys he became.

"Join the club," I joked.

He was excited about the prospect my writing a book about him, which I had planned to call *Hard as Steele*, a project that was never to come to pass because, at first, his agent wanted full control.

First thing upon entering my house, Tom wanted to take a shower. I fixed myself a stiff drink.

Coming out of the bathroom naked, was nonchalantly drying his balls with a towel and said, "I love to get sucked."

I know a cue when I hear one but I simply stared at it. I couldn't help it. Tom is not tall and that makes the limp member hanging between his legs appear to be even more enormous than it is. As he crossed the room, I dropped to my knees then and there and nibbled, licked, sucked and otherwise made a terrible fool of myself over that gorgeous appendage.

I was delighted in the quality and quantity of what Tom offered up to my hungry mouth. My excitement was yoked to a clarity of purpose, a desire so thirsting to be quenched and incisive that his cock seemed to leap out at me. His beautiful dick was like pure steel, hard and shining, not quite human. It quivered with an erotic fervor before my eyes. I sucked it with a passion I thought I was incapable of. He held my head and began fucking my throat with it until, finally, the cum that came gushing from it could have choked me had he not released me to watch the violent eruption.

The next morning, I attempted to keep my hands off of him while I interviewed him. He seemed uncomfortable answering questions about his professional life. I tried to get him to be explicit, accurate, to the point, with no bullshit. But he knew that once he said something, he really couldn't say he didn't say it. "No retractions here, please." I kidded.

As he recounted sketchy details of his career to that point, I began to tick off the possibilities. I recalled his appearance with Joey Stefano and how they extended their romance beyond the screen for several days. And how marvelously he fucked Tim Lowe in "Offering" while Tim was fucking the woman. I remembered when I was working with Tim on the book "Lowe Down," he told me that for the entire day before the shoot, Tom would walk by and shake his long dick at him, taunting him, "I'm gonna get ya." But Tim denied that Tom had actually fucked him. Watching the scene over and over, I am still convinced that Tom indeed fucked Tim Lowe royally and that perhaps that was the reason Tim was never fucked again on screen.

Yes, I found Steele to be likable, a stud to be open with. "Hey, man," he seemed to be saying, "all I do is open some doors for you; walk through any door that suits you. I'll get it up for you."

And he proceeded to do just that. The enormity of his cock delighted me. But it was beyond big; it's beauty exceeded all others in current porndom. Having had it once, I knew I would have to have it again. Lowering my mouth over the hugeness of it, words failed me, as they always do when I have a big dick in my mouth. I finally had been delivered from the limits I'd always felt in admiring another man's penis.

Now Tom wanted me to watch as he masturbated and I recalled what a reviewer in *Manshots* magazine had said, that Tom was "ever-hard, and one of the best jerk-off artists in gay video," and the scene from "Sailor in the Wild 2" unfolded before me, minus the motorcycle. As he came again, I gasped at the puddle on his belly and I played with it while I jacked myself off. As I brought my lips to his satiated prick and kissed it lovingly, I longed to have this intimacy endure. But, in a sozzled deadpan, I said, "Let's do lunch."

Returning to the house after lunch, I discovered he shared my fondness for the films of Cadinot and I slipped a tape in the VCR while Tom got naked and made himself comfortable on the bed.

I undressed and joined him, lying across him, returning his magnificent cock to my mouth.

"Ah, there's nothin' better than a good blow job," he said.

I could think of only one thing better and while he watched the glorious gang-banging of his former fuckee Dany Brown, I got the grease and prepared myself. When Steele's cock was fully hard, I slipped a condom on it and then got on my knees facing the TV. As he mounted me, he ran his hands up and down my back. Slowly he introduced the head of it into me, then shoved. I sighed, so good it felt. Soon he was rapidly plowing into me. I had barely adjusted to the size of it before, as the boys in the movie were finishing, so was I. The pain after orgasm was excruciating so I begged him to stop. He did.

As he pulled his fabulous cock from my stretched and swollen asshole, he chuckled and said, with that unmistakable Texas twang, "Yeah, I like bein' a top. I love to fuck."

And, if you think about it, how could you ask for more than that from a porn star, legend or no legend?

OTHER LEGENDARY FUCKS:
THE TOY KING
AND OTHER FANTASY LOVERS

Everybody has a favorite fantasy lover. Or, one would hope, several. If we have neglected yours, we apologize. To become a legend, or to even aspire to such heights, requires a special set of circumstances.

There are some, however, who indeed beg to be mentioned for they have become legendary for their specialties or, if nothing else, their notoriety.

It's hard to put a label on the Sarge, Sgt. Glenn Swann, who was the first to cash in on the "safe sex" craze. Indeed, he came on the scene as "Mr. Safe Sex" and his personal appearances, billed as "seminars" on erotic masturbation techniques, are legendary.

Glenn splattered, literally, onto the screen in "Sgt. Swann's Private Files" and "Discharged," which didn't exactly suit his "safety at all costs" image. The films showed that a man who insists he's a top man privately can enjoy playing bottom if the price is right. But whatever he is, the Sarge's ability to turn an audience on is undeniable.

"I've always been an exhibitionist," Glenn said. "I've traveled a lot, in the Marines and in my private life, and learning about different cultures has taught me how to respect people and appreciate them.

"What's important is that you have to learn to love yourself before you can love someone else. You gotta know how to treat your body and excite yourself before you can do it for another person.

"What I do for a living involves the most private thing that people do. So I have to have a great deal of concentration and a ton of self-confidence. I don't look at myself as a big star. I do play a role, though, because most of the people who attend my shows are very shy. I'll play up my military role and, in a stern, drill instructor's voice, order them to jack off with me. I tell them, 'If you guys wanna see any more, then you'd better join me.' Of course, they always do want to see more!

"Before I go on stage, I get worked up so that I can walk out into the audience stroking my hard meat and get the crowd to join me by telling them it's an audience participation show. I try to keep a hard-on for the whole fifteen to thirty minutes of the show. After five or six minutes, I start playing to the crowd, getting them involved. In the last three minutes, I fall down on the mat because, just before I cum, I like to have sweat pouring down my face and have my muscles all tense. I like to let the people feel the energy.

"After I've come, it seems I really have their attention. In a lot of shows, the performer doesn't come, he just jacks off and then walks off stage. Sometimes I shoot all over the place and other times it comes out thick and slow, dripping out. I always get a big round of applause. Recently, I started splattering into a black pan so that everybody could see it.

"After I've gotten off, I've really got their attention so I go into my little lecture. I tell them to take time to play with themselves, to get into different positions, twirl around on the floor, get their blood flowing throughout their whole body, so that when they do come, their whole body is into it. Now, that's a great orgasm! I tell them that when they are with another man they should take their time and create some tension. To tease. And if they are going to fuck, to put on a rubber."

Swann claims to be sexually only interested in women, saying that men do not turn him on. But having good sex of any stripe does turn him on. In "Private Files," however, he certainly appears to be enjoying the fuck being thrown at him by Scott O'Hara in a hot tent in the desert. Glenn remembers: "The first time I got fucked in the movie, I was all psyched up to take that big dick up my ass. So, for the sake of the movie, I was acting like I really enjoyed it. The only reason I could figure out why some gay men like that kind of anal stimulation so much was because they were thinking about some big cock in their ass fucking them animalistically. In and out, in and out. When I first came out, I used a lot of poppers, which helped me fantasize that I was a woman, or whatever."

Or whatever.

Before his death in 1995, Chris Burns joined the Sarge as an icon of the safe sex movement. Dave Kinnick calls this sleaziest of performers a "porn legend" and in these days when one is forced to be creative, we must pay The Toy King his due. Even in 1993, after years in the business, Chris was still at it, shooting his first video in three years, for the Gay Cable Network, and it is so wild that it can only be shown in Europe.

"When last seen," Kinnick recalls, "our favorite satchel butt was popping rubber goods up his rear at an astonishing rate in All Worlds' 'The Size of His Toys.'"

Just prior to making "Toys," Chris was in In-Hand Video's "Shacking Up," having his first sex in years that involved no toys or rubber appliances. David Kinnick said Chris was presumably in this video because "no one but a real pro could take Michael Brandon's cock and remain good natured." The scene is significant because Brandon manages, with Chris' masterful assistance, a double orgasm.

In more usual terrain, Chris graced Christopher Rage's filthy "Three Little Pigs," as one of the three guys who challenged the elasticity of their sphincter muscles while Jake Corbin (as the wolf) shoves it to them, growling all the while.

"The ultimate bottom" is what director Jeff Lawrence calls Burns, but Chris says, "I'm just the boy next door. But I can tell you everything and anything you could possibly want to know about sex!

"I've had the heaviest tops in the country work on me," he went on, "and they may think they're in charge, but even though I might be tied down, I'm in control at all times. That's where my martial arts training comes in. I can turn on or turn off. I can ignore my flesh. It becomes a total mind trip. It goes through your body, but it ends in your mind. Granted, it hurts, but it tests your capacity to deal with it.

"I enjoy that kind of pain, because to me it isn't pain. You see, a lot of people are into that kind of scene because they think they have to be disciplined, because their father beat them or something. It's guilt. Sometimes they feel that being gay is wrong to begin with, so they think the way to make everything right is to allow themselves to be punished. I don't believe in guilt trips. I'm guilty about absolutely nothing. I don't believe in having your will overcome by another individual. For me, the bottom is the one who's in control.

"You should never let somebody tie you down that you don't know. In fact, you're a fool if you ever let somebody tie you down period, unless, like me, you know you can get out of it. But people do it because they know there's a risk involved. They like the mysteriousness, the challenge.

"There are a lot of heavy tops but I've never found a bottom as heavy as I am. And if a top isn't willing to be a bottom as well, I won't do it with him. I've always believed the best bottoms make the best tops. I'm a very, very good bottom, so I make a very good top. I know exactly what's going on in that person's mind. I know all the symptoms, because it is a reflection of myself. I will never allow a top to work on me if he's never experienced being a bottom. And I'm amazed at how many big macho bodybuilders I've met can only take a little dickie up their booty. And I don't do drugs any more. I've had my experiences with them, wanting to know how I'd react, but now that I know, I don't want them. You don't need drugs to have a good time.

"But I like an arm or a toy. An ordinary-sized cock just doesn't turn me on. I think having an arm up someone's ass is the most erotic thing you could possibly do. I'd like to shove *both* my arms up Jerry Falwell's ass – ungreased!

"And I like groups. I like when everybody is doing something to me. My film 'Rawhide' was good because it was a gang-rape fantasy that I was allowed to show on film. I believe people should fulfill their fantasies. Aside from the legalities, I think rape is beautiful. I don't mean you should go out and find someone walking down the street and just rape them, but it's a great fantasy.

"But nobody would dare rape me! Because of my martial arts training, I can get out of anything. I've been tied down and chained up. I can get out of it. I've gone through some heavy things in my life. I've got scars on my ass from a scene I did in real life. You see, the films are just the tip of the iceberg!

"The one unfulfilled fantasy I have is to be fucked by a horse. The preparations are being made!"

Speaking of horse dicks, he said of John C. Holmes, with whom he co-starred in "The Private Pleasures," for Joey Yale: "Oh, I met somebody bigger than he is! This guy was literally fourteen inches and as thick as a Coke can! I haven't been in films with him and that's all I can say about him. Like I said, ordinary-sized cocks don't turn me on."

"The Size of His Toys" was, in effect, Chris' signature film. He is featured as host and narrator. A compilation of old Seabag scenes, the highlights of the feature belong to Burns. He begins by telling his audience that "toys are fun, safe and will never let you down."

Speaking of never letting you down, you've got to hand it to the true entrepreneurs in gayporn, those who used their screen fame to further their escort careers, becoming, really, more legendary for their success with clients than as performers. And not just for a few months; these guys plowed the field for years, sharing their sexual secrets as none before them. Like Casey Donovan, most of these ambitious guys made sure you had a good time in their company. It was important to them. It was, after all, their business. To me, this is taking advantage of your assets in the best possible way. How many porn stars who hustle on the side blow all the money up their nose? Too many to count I fear. But not these studs.

Ambitious Ron Pearson got tired of taking orders; he wanted to give them, so he set up his own production company and started making porn flicks. He paid for it by giving men like me a good time. When I met him, in the summer of 1982, he was taking a working vacation, turning tricks in Fort Lauderdale, working for my friend Jack, who had moved there from Tampa. En route, Ron made a stop at my place on the Gulf of Mexico.

I was surprised to find him not only a driven, determined hustler, but also a surprisingly sensitive boy. Too sensitive, I felt at the time, to achieve real success as both a star and producer/director in gayporn.

Ron's appearances in J. Brian's "Flashbacks" and "Style" had endeared him to me; I longed to fuck that perfect ass and suck on the perfect cock.

Ron's best effort as an independent filmmaker, with some assistance from Tim Kramer, was "Pegasus," which could have been truly outstanding had more attention been paid to the editing and the end product. The cassette I bought didn't even have any titling. Critic Ted Underwood said, "Derrick Garrison and Ron Pearson try unsuccessfully to fuck face-to-face (in footage that should have been cut) but finally succeed with Pearson sitting on Garrison's cock, as though he were indeed in the saddle and his own cock the saddle horn. Now and then, under the omnipresent roar of the surf, can be heard the subliminal sounds of a horse neighing. 'Pegasus' is filled with fascinating visions of human stallions in heat but the metaphor is never fully realized. The sexplay generally sizzles but all too often the viewer is distracted by the overall pinkish tint of the film, by garbled sound, by illogical editing, and surprisingly enough, by the actors looking into the camera as if in response to a director's commands. (In sum) an ambitious home movie."

Our favorite scene in the film has co-producer Tim Kramer, never looking better, hosing Ron down in what appears to be a stable yard. Kramer is shortly giving Ron one of the hottest rim jobs ever filmed, after which he fucks him royally, with Ron shooting a copious load all over his own mouth and face. After they hose each other off again, the film stops. It doesn't end, it just stops.

"The best thing about Pearson films is the star himself," *Manshots* said. In fact, in the sequel, "Pegasus II, Hot to Trot," they said the best scene in it is Ron jacking off with a dildo up his ass. *Manshots:* "He makes the viewer share his feelings. His body works in tandem with his mind, and the two are never out of sync. His humping the bed is a special delight. Also not to be missed is the unusual moment when he comes - and we are not talking about the amount of cum either. No fan of Pearson's should pass this up."

And no gayporn fan should pass up the moment Ron was back before the Falcon cameras for "Perfect Summer," during which he gives himself an enema and then gets that beautiful ass fucked on a bathhouse's locker room bench.

In 1990, Ron showed up in the AVG release of a TCS/Elite production, Mark Reynolds' uncompleted 1986 video, "Winners." Reynolds had an obsession with willing bottom Danny Parks of the Higgins stable and in this video he re-named him Mark Jennings. Featured in the first scene, a glorious five-way, is Pearson. Dave Kinnick raved: "Ron Pearson shoots multiple loads of come like nobody's business."

That was Ron in spades. Of all the boys I have been with sexually, nobody liked to come more than he did. Nor came as often. Even though when you are fucking a hustler you are keenly aware of the many that have gone (and come) before you, you can, in the hands of a skilled manipulator such as Pearson, savor the moment because they make you feel as if, for that time, you are all that matters. Ron wanted me to have a good time, perhaps to earn a bigger tip. And for me, that means the object of my affection also getting off. This is where Ron shone above most of the boys; he just could never get enough.

Tim Kramer not only invested in Pearson's film projects, he also owned a health food business. Dave Kinnick remembers Tim with considerable fondness: "He was the first true superstar of the industry that I interviewed. It was November of 1988, and I made an appointment with his secretary at the office of the nutritional products buyers' club that he owned and operated...Frankly, I was terrified of him. Tim was one of the very first porn stars that I had jacked off to back home...I used to be so ashamed of my sexual desires that I would steal copies of *Numbers* and *Blueboy*...They were the only things I've ever stolen in my life, but the urge to have those naked men under my mattress was just too great for me to resist...Tim, with his Nordic features, golden blond hair, and huge, dangling dick, looked like an exotic wild animal in the pictures. His layout was the gem of my collection. And still is.

"Looking back on my interview with him six or seven years later, I realize that he wasn't as bright or articulate as I would have liked in my fantasies. But he was something to be in awe of nevertheless. He didn't seem the least bit proud of his work in adult movies, and that bothered me. Didn't he know that I had practically worshipped him throughout my senior year of high school and much of my years at UCLA?

"He told me, 'I didn't really want to do films at all. It wasn't my cup of tea, really. (But) I was constantly asked to do it all the time when I was eighteen and living in Ft. Lauderdale. I didn't want to go with some rinky-dink company that would shoot me in a hotel room or something like that.'"

Tim got his wish, working for Falcon and other major studios of the day. Kinnick says, "He also told me that, at the peak of his film and escort work, he was making 'anywhere from seventy to eight thousand dollars a year tax-free.' "

Upon reading that statement, I remembered why I had never been to bed with Tim Kramer. I remembered that in the video "Trick Time" he told everybody they can't afford him. And he wasn't kidding. "The minute he opens his mouth, he's in trouble," a former client of his told me. "Ambition is one thing, but money-grubbing is another. He has no respect for the people he makes the money from."

His films, including "Style," "Men of the Midway," and over a dozen others, were really just advertisements for himself, getting him more escort jobs than he could possibly take. Tim could be selective and go with the highest bidder. In those days, to me, it had to be worth it. It still does.

"I don't do drugs or liquor or anything like that," Tim said, "so I used the films to build up my name so I could charge more money on the side in my escort service. I only made between $1,000 and $1,500 a day doing movies. That's not much when you only do one or two a year.

"I made most of my money by doing between three and five people a day," Kramer said. And he retired from the business when he became financially secure in his health food business. "I cannot possibly hustle and I cannot possibly have different sex partners and I cannot do unsafe sex in front of a camera because that would be telling people it's okay. Who knows what totally safe sex is? Kissing? Or sucking? I can't promote that type of industry because it's totally unsafe. Safe sex is monogamy."

Tim Kramer passed away from AIDS complications in 1993.

Other guys who have became more legendary for their hustling than their performing before a camera have included, at one time or another, Marc Radcliffe, David Ashfield, Vince Cobretti and Dave Connors.

Radcliffe is another of Dave Kinnick's "favorite" interviews. Dave describes the scene when Marc came to call in 1990: "He marches into my living room wearing white sweats with the name of a surfboard line down the right leg in big letters. His hair is shoulder length and dark blond. From a distance, he could pass for any Sunset Boulevard hard rocker, but up close, we see the hair is silky and well groomed. The bulge in his pants is considerable, especially when compared to his five-foot-eight-inch height. He's aware of this charm as well.

"Marc's business acumen is a contradiction to his laid-back image. He has escort ads in several national papers and maintains phone numbers and services in four cities: New York, Beverly Hills, San Diego, and his home near Laguna Beach. Call any one and you get a machine that gives a complete itinerary as to when he'll be in the area. Even his current business card, a tribute to co-op advertising, blows a horn for his latest movie."

I remember being in Las Vegas in 1991 when Marc was running an ad offering his services there. Out of curiosity, I called the number and left my number at the Hilton. Marc called me back, saying something had come up and he had to cancel Vegas. A while later, he advertised saying he would be in Fort Lauderdale and I called again. Again, something came up. The best laid plans...

There's something about a guy who advertises he's "bi" that has never set well with me. Is the fact that he can fuck a woman supposed to appeal to me? He told Kinnick, "A lot of the bisexual people hang toward the straight and they're not really prejudiced against two guys having sex, but they're sort of prejudiced against homosexuals. I don't know if that makes sense or not." Not to me, when I'm paying those enormous fees. Anyway, he goes on: "It's like being bisexual is OK, but you've got to like women. It's a requirement. They're married, usually." At the time, Marc was dating two couples. One couple knew about his film work and was cool about it: "They like anything - we've already gotten into gang bangs and shit like that. It can be pretty wild. A lot of the porn stars do this stuff. A lot of them like women, and they're into swinging and shit like that, too - go out and get some broad and fuck her brains out - they like doing that. Eric Manchester liked the idea and was turned on by it but didn't really have the balls to go through with it. Nick Cougar does. Derek Jensen does... But I'm still undecided. It's bad. It can sometimes be a problem. Everyone quickly tries to put me in a category. No matter what I tell them, they're going to put me on one side or the other. How do they know? How do they know what I really want?"

An older man who met him when he was seventeen put him to work on Polk Street for thirty bucks a trick. Marc was quick to wise up when the affair ended. He started to advertise and was getting sixty dollars for his time in 1984. "It pays to advertise" has been his motto ever since. In 1988, he started doing videos for Peter Hunter with "Swim Meat II" and he's been steadily busy. But now, he told Kinnick, he considers making videos and escorting "work," although he did admit sometimes he has fun with the people he meets. "The best way to travel is to be a companion and make money while you're in that city. And I do take people off with me on occasion - I mean, I can entertain them for days. I've got free breakfasts and I've got free dinners, so I'm doing pretty well."

In 1990, Marc told Kinnick he was leaving the business. As I write this, in late 1993, Marc's still at it. Like he said, he's often undecided.

In "Bi Mistake," Radcliffe was fucked for the first time in front of a girl and David Ashfield did the deed. After all, David's dependable as they come. First David was billed as Bob Holloway in "One Size Fits All" and Billy Joe Evans in "Locker Room Fever," but otherwise he's been able to stick with one name, a name that never gets top billing but the performer is guaranteed to produce the desired result.

When not before the cameras, he was busy producing great results on stages all over the country - and in bedrooms and hotel rooms as well. We caught up with him in New York, between shows at the Show Palace. He was happy to spend an hour in my suite at the Waldorf but warned me right off: "I do five shows a day and I have to pop for every one of them. I owe it to them, the audience."

I told him it didn't matter to me. I could catch one of the shows to see his "pop."

"But I'm a horny dog," he gleefully confessed. "Always have been. I did my experimenting at ten and eleven with other boys and their sisters. But I learned the female of the species is no fun. They like to play their games, they like to be bitches and that wasn't for me. I could tell. Already.

"Then I ran away from home (Tucson) when I was seventeen. I became a street ragamuffin without a pot to piss in or a window to throw it out of - hardly a good meal once a week.

"That's how I ended up hustling. I met a couple of hustlers

and they told me what they did. It intrigued me. I thought, 'Gee, that'd be kinda neat, getting paid to go to bed with these older guys.' So they fed me to a few men, taught me what to do, what to charge, and before I knew it, I had a job – one I could pick my hours at. I was in Houston by this time and I met a kid who was from L.A. and he convinced me to go with him. He said there were hundred dollar tricks everywhere there. My eyes lit up.

"We arrived in LA in August and it wasn't until January, when I was in a hustlers' bar, that I met these guys who asked me if I wanted to do a movie. When I pulled my pants down they said I had to do a movie! And I did. And I haven't stopped. I got an agent, Daniel Holt, and he keeps getting me parts.

"They know they can count on me to be on time and be up on time. I guess I'm a nasty boy with a big hard cock. That's the most important thing, being able to produce a good hard-on. Who wants to see a limp-dicked boy?"

I told him about my meetings with other boys in the business and how down on it they were, how pissed-off they were at being exploited.

"They're pussies! If you put Brooke Shields in a dirty movie, she'd be exploited. But if you put me in a dirty movie, that's not exploitation, that's giving me just what I want, and you'll see me up there with a big smile on my face."

And it was a big smile on my face as he lowered his shorts. His equipment looked even larger in person than it did on film. And he just stretched his hand along the length of it and it rose, magically, to full attention. Confidently, he brought his heavy hand to the back of my head and pushed me toward his crotch. Still smiling, I opened my mouth very wide and closed my eyes. It's a wonder I didn't choke to death.

Dave Kinnick remembers working with David on "Men on Site:" "David and Randy Cochran were topping a blondish guy and the director said, 'Go ahead and do what you feel like.' David felt like fucking the kid at the same time as Randy. Or in the terminology of the biz, they performed a DP (double penetration). Now, most performers would throw a small fit at the suggestion of performing such a specialty act like that. At the very least, they'd probably take the director aside and ask for more money. Not David. He just said, 'Go ahead and stick yours in him, Randy, and I'll be right behind you.' David's dick never lost its stiffness during the taping of the scene that afternoon - not even during the breaks for soda and cigarettes. He was and is one of the natural wonders of the industry."

David's ability at DP was again demonstrated in one of my favorite scenes of all time, the hot fuck on the lawn in "Below the Belt."

But, ironically, it was Toby Ross, he of the no-name star policy, who gave David his greatest role, in 1986 in "Classmates." David was still featured after the title, not above the title, but it is the lead role, undeniably the "star spot." The first full sex episode in the film, Toby's first film under an arrangement with Bijou in Chicago, is one of the best teacher /student fantasies ever recorded. I would have liked to have seen a more sustained fuck at the end of it (the entry, etc.), but the doggie-style nature of the sex and the obvious pleasure on the teacher's face as David bangs away is lots of fun. In addition to the sexual action, "Classmates" is packed with attractive facial close ups, views of David in the nude and in tight jeans, and wrestling in a jockstrap. The randy hillbilly never looked better, before or since. When it comes to true, down and dirty trash, who could ask for more?

Holt, recognized early on that performers in porn need management, so he became an agent as well as an actor. He kept names like David Ashfield busy. Perhaps too busy. I find all this business somewhat dismaying, feeling that if a young man wants to be a "star" he should limit his appearances. But Daniel treated his boys as he did himself, tirelessly, relentlessly, pursuing every role he can get.

"All producers use agents," he explained. "It is a reliable way of getting the talent to show up when they are supposed to and in a condition to perform. For this service, the agent takes from 10 to 30 percent of the performer's fee. The cut from the escort work can be appreciably higher, but the assistance provided the model is worth it. The agent can field all the calls, process credit card charges, run advertising, and coordinate transportation."

The job of getting the best for his clients, and for himself, was getting more difficult every day when I talked with him a few years ago. "At the moment, I'm very upset with this business," Daniel said. "Too much crap is being put out by too many people who don't know what they're doing. There are too many bad directors and too many sleazy producers who get a little money together and grind out a movie. Their product makes people look unattractive and gives pornography a cheap name. There are a lot of talented people who are trying to do things of quality in this field. This is a legitimate form of entertainment – a necessary form of entertainment – and our audience deserves the best we can give them.

"The market for films changed a couple of years ago with the arrival of video. Suddenly, all of these people had invested in expensive machines and bought five or six films. They got a lot of garbage. These people weren't the 42nd Street Raincoat Crowd. We had the opportunity to give them something good, but they got something of very low quality and now they feel burned. They won't come back because the are afraid of getting burned again. The market is closing once more and it is a shame.

"This is a necessary entertainment because there are a lot of men who are at an age where they have to pay for sex and they can't afford it, so films are as close as they can get to that pretty guy they've seen at a bar waiting for an offer. I'm glad there is something for them. I think it's a shame they can't get good material."

Holt got into the business of being an agent because the thrill of filmmaking had gone. "Sometimes it can be quite horrible. I pretend I'm having a good time. It's important when I'm going to work with someone not to sit around chatting for hours before the shoot begins. The idea of his being a stranger – a total stranger – adds greatly to my excitement. With me it's like a switch I turn on and off. I have this reputation for being able to come on cue. They tell me they're ready to shoot it and I'm ready to shoot it and I do. It's harder for me to kiss someone and look like I'm enjoying it than to have sex with them."

In picking boys to represent, Holt looked for charismatic eyes. "They're most important," he said, "and I'd like to see more exotic types on the screen. It's too easy to cast someone with the All-American look. There are many types of people who are appealing. There aren't enough ethnic types in movies.

I think producers are afraid to use them because someone in the Deep South might be turned off. You hardly ever see an Oriental and they have beautiful bodies. I don't think they should concentrate so much on the size of the cocks. That seems to be all the people who do the hiring care about. It's good to have a big cock, it's helped me, but when people work with me they realize I have a brain.

"The directors I've worked with more than once know they can count on me for more than just a sexual performance. When I first started, I made a film in which I did a lot of odd things and I got a reputation for being into those sexual things. That made people uninterested in using me. I looked like I had been dragged from the basement of the Mineshaft to the set. But I like the things I've done recently. I'm happier with my appearance now."

Holt first appeared in "Sleaze," with Casey Donovan. "Casey made it very comfortable for me," Daniel said. "It was a nice experience. I was in New York doing sex shows at the Show Palace with Scorpio. He introduced me to Christopher Rage and we were on our way."

Speaking of "nice experiences," in 1983, I took a sweet young friend to New York City and was showing him the sights, which for me always includes a stop at Rounds. While my friend was taking a leak, a boyish-looking blond engaged me in conversation. I wanted him in the worst way and made arrangements to meet him a couple of weeks later when I was returning to the city.

When he arrived at my suite at the Waldorf, the blond asked me if I recognized him when I first met him. "Recognize you?" I asked, bewilderingly. "No, I can't say I did."

"Well, I thought you might have. You said you were a porn fan and I've made a couple."

Suddenly it struck me. "You look like..." I gasped. "You are!" I had seen "The Summer of Scott Noll" and admired the tool on the lithe blond who fucks Leo Ford. I couldn't recall his name. "But your ah, professional, name escapes me."

"Nick. I go by Nick Jerrett in the movies."

"Well, hi, Nick," I laughed. "Well, this is a surprise!"

Even more surprising was that I actually waited until after we saw Tommy Tune and Twiggy in the show "My One and Only" and had dinner to sample the monster between Nick's legs. But I had arranged to spend the weekend with him so there was no sense rushing it. Once in bed, Nick demonstrated why he was in such demand as a hustler. He was so incredibly versatile that it became somewhat of a problem to decide just what to do with him, not wanting to stop doing what you were doing but knowing you wanted to savor it all in every position. It was a sweet dilemma indeed.

In Atlantic City, after seeing Shirley Bassey's early show at Resorts Casino, Nick and I toured the bars. Somehow, at one point I lost my little charge, only to have him re-appear a half an hour later slightly richer from turning a trick in the john. He bought the drinks for the rest of the night. Once a hustler, always a...

Nick's filmography is a short one, only three films, all for Studio TCS, and the releases were far apart, due to circumstances beyond his control. It took Mark Reynolds over a year to finish editing "Fantasize," but the wait was worth it for Nick's scene with Mark Rebel in the tearoom alone. It is incendiary. And Steve Scott used him sparingly but to good effect in "Gold Rush Boys." To get even more mileage out of its investment, TCS took all of his scenes and put them into the "Hot Numbers" Series. In Volume 1, Nick fucks Randy Paige's ass in a sequence from "Fantasize." (Randy got fucked by Mark Rebel in the same film and that scene is in Volume 3.) In Volume 2, Nick's three way from "Gold Rush Boys" is reprised. In Volume 3, Nick's doggie-style fuck of Kurt Williams from "Gold Rush Boys" is included, and the hot Jerrett/Rebel pairing is reprised in Volume 4. All are worth the rental.

Another boy who became better known as a hustler than as a video performer was Vince Cobretti. Vince was known mainly as a "boxcover" star because, although his screen time in "Lust Boys" and "Houseboys" was minimal, he was the central figure on the boxes.

After meeting him a few times during his frequent stops in Florida, I decided he'd be a natural subject for a book about how a kid gets started in porn and what can happen to him. The book, *A Charmed Life*, was published in 1991, but by that time, Vince had pretty much disappeared. Nearly a year later, I got a phone call from one of my associates saying that Vince was "looking for me." He'd lost my phone number (again). I knew he was back making videos again because I had seen "Hard Moves," a cheap production sold mostly by mail order in which the once ever-hard Vince can't even keep it up to fuck Joey Stefano. We decided his renewed interest in me stemmed from his having seen one of the ads promoting the book. I discovered later that he had told a club owner he found out about it because his sister had walked into a bookstore in Los Angeles and seen it, saying what a coincidence it was there was someone named Vince Cobretti that looked so much like him. I had heard another version of this "Vince's greatest fears" story before, in connection with his porn video career, which was a more plausible scenario since the star has made bisexual videos and his sister could conceivably venture into a video store to rent a tape and there he would be. But it strains credibility to think she'd even find the bookstores and just by chance spy the book stacked somewhere in the back of the store, most likely in the "Sex" section.

The manner by which the star finally realized, after a year, the book was published didn't really matter. What did matter was his demand to my associate that "it's about time" he start "making some money out of this thing."

When he finally called me, I was out of town and he was forced to leave his number on the machine. Arriving home, I was told that he was coming to Florida and would be dancing at a club in Tampa. I juggled schedules to attend.

Normally, three "porn stars" constitute the entertainment fare on Thursday nights but the boys were being held over for a special appearance on Saturday in honor of transvestite Esme Russell's 30th birthday. There were three "stars" on the bill and because of Vince's last-minute plea to his friend, the club owner Alfredo, one of them had to go, but not entirely, as it turned out. Vince told Al he "usually" got $800 to dance but when the owner balked they ended up agreeing on $100 per show.

When my Tampan friends and I arrived at the club a little after ten, the word was "Vinnie" was coming by limo from Orlando and had left at 9:45. This meant he would miss the first show. This permitted the original threesome to go on as scheduled. The motley crew consisted of Lance, not the uncut blond star of early porn but a true dancer who Esme nonetheless introduced as a "porn star." The dark haired little trooper knew how to work a crowd and stayed on after the show to work it some more to cadge enough cash to make up for being booted from the second show.

Next up was Alexander Jackson, a short, horse-hung Latin who Esme introduced simply as "Alexander," saying he had appeared in "Manhattan Latins," a bunch of solo spots featuring kids fresh off the streets, and "Latin Fever," scenes from "Boys Behind the Bars," badly re-edited. Hardly the stuff of porn heaven, prompting me to wisecrack to one of my associates, "Old porn performers never die, they just go dancing." Hapless Alexander knew from nothing about dancing and even less about crowd-working, but it hardly mattered; most in the audience were content just to stare in awe at the almost gross appendage barely concealed by a black fabric G-string.

The only true "star" in the firmanent that night turned out to be Cal Thomas of Falcon's "Mission Accomplished." This slim, incredibly hung cutie came on stage in purple, skin-tight sequined leotards and a matching cape, both of which he quickly shed, revealing a black fabric G-string similar to the one Alexander favored, apparently de rigeur wear for horse-hung dancers. Periodically through his dance he exposed the full spectcle of his manhood to Esme, who was standing off to the side studying her lines scrawled on a piece of yellow legal paper, and continued the practice as he pranced about in the audience.

At show's end, he mounted the tiny platform at the back of the stage and slyly exposed himself completely, which certainly would have got him busted in the backwater, Bible-thumping venue of Tampa. Cal stayed behind to tell Esme about making his first video, Vivid's "Texas Tales," in which he co-starred with Alexander Jackson. "We were all dancing at a club and somebody said we should do a video and so we went out and did it." As such spontaneous things often do, the end product looks it. Noted critic John Rowberry wrote: "Four dull scenes and the slowest circle jerk in recorded history, all set outdoors." As part of the gala birthday celebration, Cal called Alexander back on stage and they proceeded to drive Esme wild before our eyes, the Latin crouched at her crotch and Cal lifting her black lace cover-up then working her into a transvestite tizzy from behind.

Before exiting the stage, Esme promised Vince Cobretti was coming. As the dj reigned, Al came by with the kind of look only a disgusted hot-blooded Italian could have, complaining that Vince had indeed arrived, in the promised white stretch limo, but accompanied by five others. The star demanded his guests be admitted compliments of the house. Staring the loss of $17.50 in the face, Al flew into a rage, and rather than see Vince lose his chance to pick up some much-needed cash, the group agreed to pay the cover and were admitted, after which Vince proceeded to the dressing room, which at this club is located across the parking lot, making for messy entrances when it rains.

As Esme came back to the stage, the crew Vince brought with him almost shouted her off the stage with cries of "Vinnie!" But, before long, the jets under the platform on stage were spewing smoke and the dj had Vince's personal track on the system. At last, to the strains of the James Bond theme done as an overture and then "Goldfinger," the star appeared. With his wild black hair clamped into a pony tail and his cheeks even more sunken than before, he barely resembled the young beauty that adorned the boxcover of "Lust Boys," used on the cover of *A Charmed Life*. But as soon as his black cloak was tossed aside and he began his patented acrobatic dancing, I saw the splendid, virtually hairless torso I knew so well had not suffered a bit since the last time I ran my hands over every flawless inch of it.

"He still looks good," my friend shouted over the din. I nodded, suddenly to find the star off the stage and gyrating in front of me, his backside wriggling between my legs. But he didn't linger long, slipping from one set of hands to the next and then back on the stage. He lay on his back on the platform and started to slip off the black pants, cueing a great audience participation gimmick, but Vince knows how to seed the crowd and one of his companions rushed to the stage to remove the garment and his boots. Then, clad only in a black satiny

G-string, the star continued his acrobatics and I suddenly found him between my thighs again. I slipped my dollar in the strap just above his crack and he was off without a word. As he danced about the room collecting his tips, it struck me that, unlike some of the other dancers to work this venue, he seldom made eye contact with anyone. It was as if a zombie was high on coke, spinning like a top through the smoky barroom in search of a reason to put himself through this madness and finding it each time someone shoved a bill next to his sweaty skin. Then suddenly it was over. True trooper that he is, Vince had left his audience begging for more. Alexander was back on stage, his weaponry now ensconced in a green pouch that left nothing to the imagination.

Vince, dressed all in black, re-appeared, not to work the crowd but to chat with his companions. "I think," I ventured to one of my associates, "it's time for me to make a graceful exit."

"Aren't you going to talk to him?" he asked incredulously.

"He doesn't have anything to say to me I haven't heard before."

As I eased my car out of the parking lot, the white stretch limo was pulling up at the front door to ferry Vince and his friends into the night. And, at that moment, I remembered Vince, like all sexualists, alchemizes by moonlight, and sometime, perhaps sooner than later, when the full moon rolled out again and the waves were lapping against the shore just yards from the house, I would be in bed thinking about my lips touching his cock during the ritual of sex and the whispered entreaties that begged for an embrace. And I'd be glad for the precious moments when Vince Cobretti was fucking my face.

Neither Nick nor Vince ever hired an agent and that is probably why their video careers were short-lived. "I'd advise anybody who wanted to get into this fuckin' business to get an agent – a fair agent – someone who'll work to get them a fair price and not let them be over-exposed." That advice came from Dave Connors, a gentle man who was among the many whose career was abruptly, savagely cut short by the tragic complications from AIDS.

I saw Dave late in 1984 in New York. He visited my suite at the Waldorf shortly after finishing the film which would eventually be called "The Biggest One I Ever Saw" and "One in a Billion" for Al Parker. Dave had high hopes for both of the films and spoke fondly of his "Biggest" co-star, Lee Ryder: "I think he is building a good image. He and I are very good friends and I wouldn't mind going round two with him – anytime. I also liked making 'One in a Billion' because I got a chance to work with Brad Mason, the taller of the two guys in the scene in bathroom with the two TV repairmen. He has a great, sexy face, a nice body, and a big fat endowment."

Endowment was something Dave knew plenty about, having been blessed with one of the monster dicks in porn. He asked me what I wanted to do in bed and I told him I would love to play greek passive but I was leery of big "endowments," as he called them.

"They don't get hard enough," I told him, settling onto the bed on my back.

"Well, we'll see about that," he said as he lifted my legs straight up and began lubricating me.

When he felt I was ready, he stepped off the bed and unzipped his jeans. Even after 39 years, easygoing Dave seemed in awe of the truncheon leaped from the cloth. He pulled off his shirt and exposed the huge tattoo of Jesus on his upper arm. The scene at that point struck me terribly funny and I began laughing. Dave laughed too as he tugged off his jeans and climbed back on the bed.

"Just keep laughin'," he said with a smile. "It'll hurt less that way!" He slipped a condom over the perfectly shaped purplish head of his cock and unrolled it down the long, thin shaft. He gripped my ass with his huge hands and, as he entered me, he said, "Relax, relax. Trust me...trust me."

"Oh god, I want to!" I murmured, biting my lip.

"You can, you can. Hell, I'm the most trustworthy guy in New York."

Before I knew it, it was all the way in.

It was a slow, driving invasion, with Dave jerking me off expertly. "Oh, yeah," he said, plowing into me for the last jolt. "It's great not to have to pull out."

Feeling the intensity of his orgasm wafting throughout my body, I couldn't help agreeing with him. After all, he said his job was one of helping to keep men's fantasies alive, and he certainly was keeping mine alive.

"You've got to know what you've got and how to use it," he said.

"Well, you certainly know how to use it," I laughed.

I admired his recognition of the facts of life, even if it was a bit late. I remembered his trouble down in Florida, a mess with some drugs, and the time he had to do because of it. "It's something I'd never wish on anyone. I want to stay as far away from that point in my life as possible," he told me. He came to New York at 38 to start over again...and, in his words, become "one of the top ten men in the porn industry."

It was not to be. Dave Connors passed away less than a year later.

AFTERWORD

"Can I be as I believe myself or as others believe me to be?
Here is where these lines become a confession in the presence
of my unknown and unknowable me, unknown and unknowable for
myself. Here is where I create the legend
wherein I must bury myself."
— Miguel de Unamuno

Even The Plague has not deterred those possessed of celebrity fever. Indeed, it seems for some gays the risk of death is part of the romance. The fact that through the late '80s and into the early '90s, many porn actors were still fucking sans condom, giving us the indelible impression that they were literally "giving their all for their art."

Since death is the most intimate act in which a stranger can involve us, it is, seen from a certain angle, the ultimate imposition. "There is nothing," Richard Schickel observes, "an artist can do more definitively diminishes the distancing effect his necessarily complex art can have upon us. Death then comes to seem, sometimes, as if it is the final revision, the last brilliant retouching one can perform on the collected works, a brilliantly clarifying final stroke, guaranteeing the integrity of his effort and rendering its largest meaning unmistakable and permanently poignant."

When we hear that Dick Fisk, Tommy Wilde (my dear coverboy on "Angel") or Leo Ford perished in accidents, we feel shock, dismay. But when we hear of the death of boys such as Casey Donovan, Al Parker, Lee Ryder, Dave Connors and others from AIDS, to return to his movies, watching him practicing unsafe sex, we react in horror.

We cannot help but think that perhaps as we are watching an assignation, that was the time the disease was transmitted.

Jerry Douglas, the publisher of *Manshots* and a successful producer of videos in his own right, has been criticized in some circles for running obits in every issue.

Well, the inquiring mind wants to know, yet we don't. It is

dark, supremely discomforting ground.

Yet these stars have left us with a legacy that has brought pleasure to me and thousands of others. In my vignettes of each of these stars, I have delineated the videos that I and many critics agree are their best works, so that you might experience them and share with us the grandeur of "the world's sexiest men."

"If I'm reincarnated, I want to come back as Matt Dillon's underwear."
– Boy George

Rob Lowe, at his best in "Masquerade,"
Courtesy MGM

THE LEGENDARY
PERFORMANCES

All eyes are on the crotch of Alain Delon in "3
Murderesses"

Denzel Washington

WHAT BECOMES
A LEGEND MOST?

What becomes a legend most? Adaptability. "Take the example of Faust," Douglas Langworthy says, "one of the most resilient of the superlegends with an uncanny knack for reinventing himself to suit the changing times."

The Faust tradition has spread across a broad range of genres and nowhere is it more evident than in the entertainment industry.

Entertainment Weekly ran a "To Be - And Not To Be" column a while back citing who had survived the '80s. "For some stars," Bruce Fretts said, "the '80s were the best of times. For others, they were the only good times they would ever have. But for every celeb the decade chewed up and spit out, there's a corresponding success story."

For "the sexiest men in the world," there were no surprises of course. They wouldn't be in this book if they were casualties, after all. But it was interesting to note that Fretts cited Menudo as a casualty; as we noted, they were a casualty of their managers fondling them, not of a change in public taste. Boys will always be boys, after all, especially pretty ones who can sing and dance.

Fretts' list of casualties included Eric Roberts, Rick Springfield, Andrew McCarthy, Richard Grieco, Anthony Michael Hall, and David Lee Roth, all sexy men to be sure but perhaps not quite sexy enough.

Those survivors on Fretts' list whom we have included here were: Michael J. Fox, George Michael, and Patrick Swayze. He included some sexy men we ignored, such as John Stamos, Johnny Depp, who may well go on to greater things, and Denzel Washington, an incredible actor who is currently our favorite black heartthrob.

Another of Fretts' choices, Robert Downey Jr., we mentioned only in passing, as Sarah Jessica Parker's live-in, but his wonderful portrayals as whacked-out gays in "Less Than Zero" and "Too Much Sun" have endeared him to us. He is, in his own peculiar way, sexy indeed.

Interestingly, Fretts put Madonna on both the casualty and

survivor lists.

Of course, many of the "sexiest men in the world" have survived not only the '80s but the '70s as well. Some, such as Clift, Dean, and Cooper, are immortal in the hearts of their fans. Indeed, the legacy of these legends is available to us as never before, thanks to the VCR.

Over the past five years, U.S. VCR households have increased 33 percent; video rental spending is up 40 percent. In revenue, video was barely leading the recording industry at $6.7 billion in 1988; it just five years, video was leading $11.8 to $9 billion. Meanwhile, box-office has hovered at $5 billion.

Video is now big business and many of the stars in this book have become "video stars." They don't have the box-office clout any longer to sustain a film in theaters but, in films released directly on video, they shine.

Some of my personal favorite fantasy lovers, Corey Haim, Christopher Atkins, Jan-Michael Vincent and, to a certain extent even Rob Lowe, have found new careers in video, providing us with even more opportunities to view them, albeit in decline.

Yes, thanks to the VCR, we can enjoy our favorite performers in private, to savor them over and over at their very best, and most exposed.

It is appropriate here to note Ian Young of *Torso*, in his review of the first edition of this book, called attention to actors who were omitted. One of his favorites that deserves mention is the fine actor Matthew Modine, recently seen in HBO's "And the Band Played On." Matthew has an admirable penchant for exposing himself to his audience; *Movie Buff Checklist* mentions four such instances: "Streamers," from 1982, being the most interesting because he's caught in the shower with the steam obscuring very little of his cock. He exposes his buns in "Private School," "Birdy," and "Vision Quest." Again, thanks to the VCR, these performances are not lost and, if Matthew keeps on like this he could well become legendary for his "exposures" alone.

What follows is a short list of some of the more legendary performances by our favorite sex icons. What we see from their many appearances over the years is their great adaptability while maintaining their ever-zesty phallic energy.

Christopher Atkins today

Movie Stars
(In Alphabetical Order)

Atkins, Christopher
Appears nude in "The Blue Lagoon" and "A Night in Heaven." He is also quite adorable in "The Pirate Movie" and his beautiful buns are on display (along with a loving shot of his crotch bunched in Spandex) in "Wet and Wild Summer," released only on video. In "Dracula Rising" (1992), also released straight-to-video, we have very brief glimpses of his ass while swimming underwater. At the height of his fame, he appeared nude in *Playboy's* November 1980 Sex in Cinema feature and in a 1980 *Playgirl* pictorial.

Beatty, Warren
Warren's sexiest performances are in "Splendor in the Grass," his first film in 1961, and "The Roman Spring of Mrs. Stone," with Vivien Leigh. There is a glimpse of part of his ass in "Shampoo," and he is darling in the scene wherein Julie Christie gives him head under the table at an eatery. This film was immortalized in a *Playboy* feature in November, 1975. Judging by his many conquests, this stud's greatest performances were off-screen.

Bowie, David
The rocker is nude in "The Man Who Fell to Earth," from 1976 and he is sexiest in "The Hunger," from 1983.

Brando, Marlon
Brief buns are shown in "Last Tango in Paris" (1972). Sexioest in "A Streetcar Named Desire" (1951).

Broderick, Matthew
Matthew, called "the cutest boy alive," is also one of the best young actors around. The screen lights up when he's on it. He gives a magnificent kiss in "Torch Song Trilogy," and otherwise is just delectable in that film. A must. Also, nice bare buns in "Out on a Limb" (1992) but it is an awful mess of a movie. One reviewer said she could detect an almost invisible g-string. In "The Road to Wellville," he bares his buns as well as a newly-buffed body. His finest acting, outside of "Trilogy," has to be in "Glory." Most fun: "The Freshman."

Connery, Sean
"Bond...the name is Bond, James Bond." "Goldfinger" is a must. And he made a wonderful Robin Hood in

"Robin and Marian," and exposes his posterior as his costume flips up. His buns can also be seen in "Zadoz" and "The Man Who Would Be King."

Cruise, Tom
There is much to savor in Tom's early career: "The Outsiders," with all the others, including Rob Lowe, the nude scene in "All the Right Moves" and his dancing in "Risky Business," both in 1983. We get a very brief view of his buns in "Taps" (1981) and "Born on the Fourth of July" (1989) as well as the upper half of his buns in "Far And Away" (in 1992).

Delon, Alain
It is hard to imagine a more beautiful man. He is fully on display playing a playboy seducing three women in "3 Murderesses," from 1959, and a year later in "Purple Noon." And the period bathing suit cannot hide his abundant charms in "The Yellow Rolls Royce" (1965). The film "Shock," from 1973, contains his only full frontal scene.

Depp, Johnny
We have to go back to 1985 for a view of his buns in "Private Resort." If he took his sex symbol status seriously, we'd get more. He's gorgeous in "Don Juan deMarco." More

to come from this future superstar.

Dillon, Matt
He's never had a blockbuster hit but his career has been dotted with wonderful stuff for boywatchers: "Over the Edge," "Tex," "Little Darlings," wherein he spends much time in just his briefs, "Rumble Fish," "The Outsiders," and "Flamingo Kid." He finally lets us see his beautiful buns in "A Kiss Before Dying," in 1990. His greatest acting so far: "Drugstore Cowboy."

Fox, Michael J.
The foxy little one's best acting is in the "Back to the Future" movies, but he's sexiest in "The Secret of My Success," from 1987, in which he gives, to quote Leonard Maltin, "an energetic, appealing performance." He finally bares his buns in 1994's "Greedy."

Gere, Richard
Fearlessly appearing nude made his reputation, as did taking stage roles such as "Bent." For gays, his signature works on film remain "American Gigolo," from 1980, Paul Schrader's sleek, stylish thriller that so ably captures the coke-addled, chicer-than-thou sensibility of L.A. at the time, with John Bailey's glossy cinematography a major asset, and

"Breathless," from 1983. There are also views of his buns in "Looking for Mr. Goodbar" "Beyond the Limit," and "Final Analysis."

Haim, Corey
This little charmer's never been better than in "Lucas," from 1986, playing a precocious 14-year-old which features a nice shower scene. Leonard Maltin raved: "A real sleeper." Corey takes a bath in "Lost Boys" (1987) about a pack of vampires. Later, the cutie finally bares all for "Blown Away," from 1993, originally made for HBO, released on video cassette and available in an unrated version.

Hudson, Rock
Perfection in "Giant," for which he was nominated for an Academy Award.

Johnson, Don
He's bare in "Harrad Experiment," from 1973, and in "Magic Garden of Stanley Sweetheart," from 1970. I n 1990, Don proved he still has what it takes in "Hot Spot." Leonard Maltin: "There's so much ornery sex you're compelled to keep watching."

Lowe, Rob
Oh, let me count the ways...this boy is the stuff dreams are made of: "The Outsiders," (1983) with just a towel; in drag in "Class"

(1983), never cuter than in "Hotel New Hampshire," fucking an older woman, natch, (1984), glimpses of skin in "About Last Night..." (1986), in a jockstrap in "Youngblood" (1986), cuts off his own penis in "Square Dance" (1987) and has two magnificent fuck scenes in "Masquerade" (1988), including great shots of his buns. But nothing tops his own home video of his three-way in Paris. God, what drug was he on? Talk about insatiable!

Perkins, Anthony
"The Lonely Man" features a scene in which Jack Palance lassos and hog-ties Tony. "Has to be seen to be believed," says Raymond Murray. Sex-wise, it's "Phaedra," from 1962, playing Melina Mercouri's stepson and lover.

Pitt, Brad
Oh, yes, let me count the ways...again! The Rob Lowe of the nineties! This kid is so cute it hurts. Bares much in "Thelma and Louise" (1991) as he humps Geena Davis; bares his teeth in that incomparable smile in "A River Runs Through It" (1992); is incredibly lovely in "Legends of the Fall."

Prince
The sexiest man in rock has

only made four films: "Purple Rain" (1984), "Under the Cherry Moon" (1986), "Sign O' the Times" (1987), and "Graffiti Bridge" (1990), and he got progressively dismal. "Cherry" could have been the one that made him a real movie star but it was, as Leonard Maltin says: "a supremely silly vanity film with Prince self-cast as American gigolo/entertainer in the south of France who has a devastating effect on women (yes, it's a science-fiction story)... a triumph of self-adoration, and an overall embarrassment."

Reeves, Keanu
Just one look at "My Own Private Idaho" (1991) and he's the one. You can see his buns in his scene with his woman. Exotic, erotic Keanu! I went to see River get a blowjob and came out in love with Reeves. He's at his loveliest in "Dangerous Liaisons" (1988).

Slater, Christian
Although "Heathers" made him a star, the real must-sees include his bare bottom in "The Name of the Rose" (1986) and with sexy blond hair in the skateboard movie "Gleaming the Cube," (1989) retitled "A Brother's Justice" when shown on TV. His performance was great in "Pump Up the Volume" (1990) (Leonard Maltin: "Slater

is terrific as Hard Harry...") and in "True Romance" (we see partial buns while he is fucking (unrated version only).

Swayze, Patrick
Famous for "Dirty Dancing" (1987), his incredible body shows up best in "Road House" (1989), although it is violent nonsense. The stud's at his youthful best in "The Outsiders" (1983).

Travolta, John
Oddly, his worst early film (and biggest bomb) is the one he is sexiest in: "Moment by Moment" (1980) "romancing" Lily Tomlin. They had fun making this, but somehow it doesn't show up on screen. Still, we get a lot of John in bathing suit. Leonard Maltin: "A role-reversal romance with Travolta as the sex object and Tomlin as a bored Malibu housewife that gives new meaning to the word 'dreary.'" John's also perfect in "Saturday Night Fever" (1978) and "Grease" (1979). His best-acting: "Urban Cowboy" (1982) and "Pulp Fiction" (1994), which earned his second Oscar nomination. In "Staying Alive" (1983), his shaved, buffed bod is truly superb.

Vincent, Jan-Michael
He was the first major star to let us see his cock: "Buster & Billie" (1974). This secne was

immortalized in *Playboy* in 1974. His best performance: as a long-haired hippie in the TV movie "Tribes," from 1970. The script won an Emmy and Jan-Michael won my heart. He exposes his buns in "Going Home" and "Hard Country."

Other Notable Nudes

Robby Benson

The adorable one from "Ode to Billy Joe" (1976) can be seen nude in 1990's "Modern Love" and in 1992 in "Invasion of Privacy," with brief shots of his succulent buns.

Mel Gibson

Before he went homophobic, we loved Mel, especially in all that black leather in "Road Warrior" and especially when he bared his buns in "Lethal Weapon."

Danny Russo and Donny Summers make a perfect couple in
"Find This Man," courtesy Bijou Video

Porn Stars
(In Alphabetical Order)

Berlin, Peter
There were only two films, but more than enough to make him a legend: "Nights in Black Leather" and "That Boy." Raw sexuality at its sizzling best.

Donovan, Casey (Cal Culver)
To understand what made him a legend, we need only see these: "The Back Row," "Boys in the Sand, "Other Side of Aspen." He is a superb fuck in the hetero/bisexual "Score." (An excellent interview with Casey can be seen in Bijou's "Men & Films.")

Donovan, Rick
Rick's personal favorites are "The Bigger the Better," "The Arousers," "The Biggest One I Ever Saw," and his debut film, "Sailor in the Wild."

Also of special note is his "comeback" video, "The Big Ones," wherein he kisses his bedmate when it's all over. "Sgt. Swann's Private Files," is technically Rick's first video, but released after "Sailor in the Wild." Herein, Rick fucks a heavily tattooed sailor, Ed Jerome, who *Manshots* said,

turns out to be "a most accommodating bottom." Weren't they all? Has a terrible time getting it up.

Gunther, Matt
The star himself picks 'em: "Inside Jon Vincent," which he says was great fun at the time, "but I'm over that now. Then there's 'Stranded,' the three way, with guys from Florida that Chi Chi found. And 'Cruising II,' my scene with Brad Mitchell." Matt says the hardest video to make was his first, for Vivid, "Hole in One." Dave Kinnick told him he liked it because he fucked Stefano so well. For my money, it's hard to beat Matt's role as the ring-master in "Buttbusters" from Falcon and his spiriting fucking of Chad Knight, also in that great video.

Holmes, John C.
John's solo performances can be found on "The Biggest of Them All (Falcon 16)," "Black Velvet (Falcon 21), and he does fuck a guy in "Pool Party (Falcon 9). His lone strictly "gay" feature was at the hands of Joey Yale: "The Private Pleasures of John C.

Holmes," a hoot which has him being serviced by several youths.

Idol, Ryan
"A Very Personal View" is a must for every Idol-worshipper, and his latest foray into receprecation, "Idol Country," has him being ravished by two guys and its glorious. Of all the current crop of porn stars, he is perhaps best appreciated in person.

King, Jon
Insatiable Jon had so many great fucks but his legendary ones were from: Kip Noll in "Kip Noll Superstar," Michael Christopher in "Bore 'n' Stroke (Surfside Sex)," "brother" J. W. King in "Brothers Should Do It," and one-time lover Kris Bjorn in a loop on Falcon Pac 30. Came back for a rousing fuck by Zak Spears in "These Bases Are Loaded II" for Catalina.

Knight, Chad
He of the "perfect body and boyish good looks" has rarely given a bad performance in his "over 50 less than 100" videos. Stand-outs include the Matt Gunther fuck in "Buttbusters," the Damien rim job and fuck in "Scoring," the massive Cody James assault on his anus in "Preferred Stock No. 1," and the hot Michael Brawn fuck in

"Kiss Off." In "Don't Kiss Me I'm Straight," Chad ends up standing on his head in a wild fuck from Tony Raz. Pretty good for a "straight" boy, who now admits he's "bi," but only for films. The lovely Knightstick also can be put to good use, as proven by his superb fuck of the sure to be legendary Danny Sommers in "Someone in Mind."

Noll, Kip
The Ultimate Kip is "Kip Noll Superstar," a compilation of all of the best of the William Higgins era, including his getting fucked by his "Greek god" in "Boys of Venice." Also noteworthy is the last scene in "Al Parker's Flashback." Manshots praised the finale: "Noll decides to model for Parker and the film finishes with Noll working on himself – body, cock, eyes – everything that made him a star, is there on full display. Both he and Parker were at the peak of their form in this film."
Other legendary moments include: the three-way with "brother" Scott Noll and Steve York in "Cuming of Age," and kissing boots in his first video, "Try and Take It," now on a Falcon Pac.

Parker, Al
Al was good in everything he did but "Dangerous" is his best on his own and "Inches"

and "Wanted," his very best performances. Always hot, kinky sex.

Roger (& Bruno)

These two are together in "Good Neighbors," now a Bullet Pac 7 from Colt. Roger gets fucked. Bijou Video chooses "Hot House" as Roger's best, although we found the limp humor a downer. Falcon's Pac 6 has "The Housepainter," wherein Roger fucks two guys. Like Ryan, he was at his best in his personal appearances.

Stefano, Joey

When the late, great Joey was into his co-star (or, to put it more correctly, when Joey's co-star was into him, figuratively and literally, and Joey's turned on) sparks flew. We heartily recommend: "Billboard," notable for the wild three-way at the end, which features Lon Flexx, who, as John Rowberry points out, "has been with Joey before and knows his way around;" "Hole In One," where he gets a hot fuck from Matt Gunther, "Man of the Year," in which he takes two cocks up that luscious ass, but the screen time is minimal, and, for his very best overall, in the starring role in Jerry Douglas' "More of a Man," which features the sensational barroom fuck with Chris McKenzie and, again, Lon

Flexx. Chris feels Lon's the best sex around and when the two of them gang up on Joey, in front of a crowd at a bar: zow-ee! Joey was also outstanding in his personal appearances, dancing up a storm on stage before an adoring crowd. Pity Kevin Glover cut most of his fabulous dance at the 1993 Gay Erotic Video Awards show from the commemorative tape.

Stryker, Jeff

Must-sees are "Powerfull II," in which big Jeff nibbles on Alex Stone's cock, and "Powertool," winner of *Adult Video News'* Best Video and Best Director awards for John Travis. Plus "On the Rocks," where Jeff gets it on with Joey Stefano and Matt Gunther. For a little mix 'n' match, "The Switch Is On," his best bi-sexual entry containing his superb shower scene. John Rowberry calls this one a cross between "Shane" and "Old Yeller." Whatever it is, it boasts Jeff's finest acting. He is acting, isn't he? Perhaps it's like Spencer Tracy's advice after all, "Never let 'em catch you acting."

Sommers, Danny

On our short list of two of Danny's best fucks overall are "Rimshot," from 1991, the star first gets it on in a locker room with dark-haired beauty Damien, who obviously is enjoying every second of it, first standing and then taking Sommers missionary with Danny sprawled on a bench; the second sequence puts Danny atop a pool mattress getting it from hairy, beefy Glenn Steers, with lots of good penetration shots. Steers' tool is big and thick and hard enough to really be effectively photographed as he's plugging Danny missionary. In 1992, one of his top screwings came at the hands of beefy Brit Aiden Shaw in a barroom setting in "Night Force," culminating in what *Manshots* called a mean pool-table plowing. It's hard to beat the chemistry in "Find This Man." Made in 1992 but not released until late in 1993. Donny sees Russo's picture on a flyer and he goes all the way to New York to find him. There's a knockout shot when Donny, reclining on a couch, stands up and lets his dark bathrobe fall open, revealing his upstanding hard-on, a thick exclamation point on his gleaming, well-packed bod. Mickey Skee was delighted with the pairing, saying, "There's lots of real kissing, boot-licking and intense sparkle between Donny and Danny." Dave Kinnick remarked, "For those of you who haven't encountered Russo yet, he's sort of a Chad Douglas for the '90s. He isn't as horse-hung as Chad, but

what he lacks in mere largeness, he makes up for in attitude and style. The man has an incredible presence, and his tattoo arm band is just one of the traits that make him very much a star for the modern era. Russo and Sommers make as classic a couple as Douglas and Kevin Williams did in 'In Your Wildest Dreams.' This new scene is a lot more romantic than the rowing machine debauch in that classic video."

Wrangler, Jack
Jack Deveau's "Hot House," from 1977, is a must-see. Not only is Wrangler at his best but in the party sequence we are treated to the black and white vintage film of Joe Dallesandro. Bijou's new release is a complete master print. Also, "Kansas City Trucking Co.," the first of the Joe Gage series, is another landmark film featuring Jack's talents, one of the few gays ever to cross-over to straight porn and make it big. Enough said. (Jack can also be seen in a non-sexual role, graciously accepting his "Fall of Fame Award" from Sabin's magazine Gay Video News in the "Gay Erotic Video Awards" tape produced by Kevin Glover.)

Johnny Depp as Don Juan

THE LUST LIST

"John Travolta looks like a combination of
Rudolph Valentino, with that vaselined hair,
Kirk Douglas with that dimple in his chin, and a street hustler."
– Gerard Depardieu

"If there's one thing that unites all 100 years of cinema, it is sexuality," says *Empire* magazine. "As the silver screen has developed from gasp-inducing sideshow to the Technicolor, multiplex dream we know and love today, there has been but one true constant, one ever-chugging motor. Not industrial light and magic. Not great acting. Not spectacle. *Sex.* Sex, sex, S-E-X. Better – and safer – than that, sex symbols. From Rudolph Valentino to Linda Fiorentino, the ability to smoulder, to slink, to suggest, to steam off the screen and into an audience's lap, has been paramount to the star system, to box office, to Hollywood's survival. It started with a kiss, i.e. Thomas Edison's "The Kiss" (1896), in which John Rice and May Irwin just . . . kissed. It races ever onwards with Tom Cruise and Brad Pitt gargling each other's blood. As far as film stars and fantasy-fulfilment go, nobody does it better.

"Unless you wish to be filed under 'C' for Character Actor, you've got to be a sex symbol; if you want to put bums on seats, you've got to put yours in front of a camera; as the old adage goes, he who opens his shirt, opens a film . . .

"However, it's not all pencil moustaches, rippling biceps, silicon mounds and blue eyes. It's *mainly* those things, obviously, but screen-sexiness is a tricky trait to, ahem, pin down."

The magazine's editors did *try*, however, and the results were suprising in many ways, obvious in others.

In the year 1995, *Empire* ranked the screen legends in our book thusly:

1. Johnny Depp. In a word: Enigmatic. Sexiest Role: Don Juan, super-lover, "Don Juan deMarco," 1995. "Before he tops himself, our errant, tousle-haired and possibly mad Casanova tries it out one last time in a hotel restaurant. He picks up a

lone female diner and entices her to bed with the hand-kissing technique he claims has worked for 1,502. Hands up anyone who wouldn't mind becoming 1,504." Also, Sexiest Legs. (It is truly amazing that the star judged Nummero Uno by *Empire* has never had a hit movie.)

7. Sean Connery. In a word: Rugged. Sexiest Role: James Bond, Dr. No (1962).

14. Marlon Brando. In a word: Beefy. Sexiest Role: "A Streetcar Named Desire" (1951).

17. Keanu Reeves. In a word: Adorable. Sexiest Role: "Speed" (1994). "Never has one man made a dirty T-shirt look quite so attractive."

22. Cary Grant. In a word: Suave. Sexiest Role: "Notorious" (1946).

23. Brad Pitt. In a word: Leonine. Sexiest Role: "Thelma and Louise" (1991).

28. Rock Hudson. In a word: Tall. Sexiest Role: "Magnificent Obsession" (1954).

29. Montgomery Clift. In a word: Tortured. Sexiest Role: "A Place in the Sun" (1951).

30. Tom Cruise. In a word: Wholesome. Sexiest Role: "Top Gun" (1986).

42. James Dean. In a word: Anguished. Sexiest Role: "Rebel Without a Cause" (1955).

79. Christian Slater. In a word: Playful. Sesxiest Role: "Heathers" ((1989).

The other stars in this book were not listed by Empire.

ILLUSTRATIONS

When the first edition of this book was published, one reviewer was critical of the photography chosen. We acknowledge that it was an oversight not to include a photograph of each star profiled and we have corrected that in this issue.

We also acknowledge that some of the photographs are not of the best quality. This is understandable since the material available to us is very limited. The reviewer was critical that in some cases what he termed "unflattering" poses were chosen. From the material available, we attempt to chose the photograph that captures the sensuality of the star, not just another publicity still. For instance, the famous Herb Ritts photo of Tom Cruise in the water, taken for a photo spread in *Rolling Stone*, epitomizes the star's appeal. Likewise the splendid shot of Brad Pitt for the same magazine.

We searched, sometimes in vain, to find a star as naked as possible. For instance, it is nearly impossible to find a photograph of George Michael in swim trunks, but we wanted to show him as nearly nude as we could get him (he is notoriously camera-shy). In the previous edition, we used a famous still of Prince in the shower taken for *Rolling Stone*. Because he had his bikini on in the shower, the reviewer thought it "tacky." Indeed, that was the point, and also the fact that the tip of his private part was visible. But, so as not to appear "tacky," we chose a different photograph for this edition, this one clearly showing how Prince gets turned-on by performing before an audience.

The reviewer's criticism that the photos were not in color is valid; we wish we could publish in color as well. However, the cost to do so would make the retail price of a limited edition directed to a specialized audience such as this extremely prohibitive.

Covers: Joey Stefano, courtesy of Rockshots; Chad Knight, courtesy of Falcon Studios; Rob Lowe, courtesy MGM.

Most text illustrations from Mr. Patrick's archives unless otherwise noted on pages with illustration:

Warren Beatty in "Splendor in the Grass" (Courtesy Warner Bros.).

Tom Cruise, photographed by Herb Ritts for *Rolling Stone* magazine.

Rob Lowe and Keanu Reeves illustrations courtesy of Greg Gorman.

Nureyev illustration courtesy Jack Vartoogian.

Jim Morrison, photographed by Joel Brodsky.

George Michael, lounging poolside at the Copacabana Palace in Rio de Janeiro, photographed by Kevin Mazur, for *Rolling Stone*.

Joe Dallesandro photographed by Dean Brierly for *The Advocate*.

David Cassidy illustrations, John C. Holmes at his peak in 1972, Kirk Cameron by Blake Little, Brad Pitt by Jeffrey Thurnher, and Christian Slater by Deborah Feingold are all provided courtesy of *Rolling Stone*.

Matt Powers, Kip Noll and Jon King, courtesy Catalina Video.

Peter Berlin courtesy Robert W. Richards.

Rick Donovan and Kris Lord courtesy of Bo Tate.

Ryan Idol courtesy *All Man* magazine.

Joey Stefano courtesy *Gay Video Guide*.

Matt Gunther courtesy of Marc Geller.

Kip Noll and Jon King, courtesy Catalina Video.

Danny Sommers, courtesy Falcon Studios. Danny and Donnie Russo courtesy of Bijou Video.

Alain Delon in "Three Murderesses" (Courtesy 20th Century Fox)

Special Acknowledgements

The editor wishes to acknowledge the courtesy of MGM and Greg Gorman for providing the portraits of Rob Lowe and Falcon Studios for providing the portrait of Chad Knight and others. Also, the cover portrait of Joey Stefano was supplied courtesy of Rockshots. Rockshots cards are available from STARbooks Press.

The editor also thanks the publishers of *Encounter* magazine for occasionally excerpting of parts of this book as well as providing the photography of the editor with Joey Stefano.

The editor also acknowledges the tireless editing and proofing, to say nothing of the moral support, of John from Atlanta, Philip in New York, and young gay author and artist Peter Reardon, "for services rendered."

And, of course, very special thanks to the many readers of my books who have so generously shared their passions with me over the years and whose comments I have used in this book and the *Superstars* series.

INDEX

Coming in January: THE BEST OF THE SUPERSTARS 1996
The latest and greatest of the perennial guidebooks to the
hottest stars. At fine booksellers worldwide or buy mail from
STARbooks Press, P. O. Box 2737, Sarasota FL 34230.
(Photo of coverboy Lukas Ridgeston courtesy Bel-Ami Video).

About the Editor

The editor in 1993 with porn legend Joey Stefano.

John Patrick is a prolific, prize-winning author of fiction and non-fiction. One of his short stories, "The Well," was honored by PEN American Center as one of the best of 1987. The author's acclaimed romans a´ clef, including "Angel: The Complete Quintet" and "Billy & David: A Deadly Minuet," have now been collected into a single volume. His novels as well as his non-fiction works, including "Tarnished Angels," "The Best of the Superstars" series, continue to gain him new fans every day. Mr. Patrick is currently at work on several new anthologies of erotic tales.

A divorced father of two, the author is a longtime member of the American Booksellers Association, the Florida Publishers' Association, American Civil Liberties Union, and the Adult Video Association. He resides in Florida.